Shared Responsibility,
Shared Risk

Shared Responsibility, Shared Risk

GOVERNMENT, MARKETS, AND SOCIAL POLICY IN THE TWENTY-FIRST CENTURY

EDITED BY JACOB S. HACKER

and

ANN O'LEARY

OXFORD
UNIVERSITY PRESS

Oxford University Press, Inc., publishes works that further
Oxford University's objective of excellence
in research, scholarship, and education.

Oxford   New York
Auckland   Cape Town   Dar es Salaam   Hong Kong   Karachi
Kuala Lumpur   Madrid   Melbourne   Mexico City   Nairobi
New Delhi   Shanghai   Taipei   Toronto

With offices in
Argentina   Austria   Brazil   Chile   Czech Republic   France   Greece
Guatemala   Hungary   Italy   Japan Poland   Portugal   Singapore
South Korea   Switzerland   Thailand   Turkey   Ukraine   Vietnam

Published by Oxford University Press, Inc.
198 Madison Avenue, New York, New York 10016

www.oup.com

Oxford is a registered trademark of Oxford University Press

Library of Congress Cataloging-in-Publication Data
Shared responsibility, shared risk : government, markets and social policy in the twenty-first century / edited by
Jacob S. Hacker and Ann O'Leary.
    p.   cm.
Includes index.
ISBN 978-0-19-978191-1 (hardcover)—ISBN 978-0-19-978192-8 (pbk.) 1. United States—Social policy—1993-
2. United States—Economic policy—2009-3. Economic security—United States. 4. Public welfare—United States.
I. Hacker, Jacob S. II. O'Leary, Ann.
HN65.S47   2011
330.973—dc22   2011013984

9 8 7 6 5 4 3 2 1

Printed in the United States of America
on acid-free paper

Contents

Part Three   IMPROVING ECONOMIC SECURITY FOR FAMILIES

Part Four   INCREASING HEALTH AND RETIREMENT SECURITY

Part Five   CONCLUSIONS

Foreword

Shared Responsibility

CRAIG CALHOUN

The financial crisis of 2008 drew attention to the extent to which some private actors could create enormous public risks. Banks engaged in proprietary trading (that is, for their own and not their customer's benefit), hedge fund managers traded credit default swaps, finance companies issued dubious mortgages then bundled them into securities that ostensibly more prudent investors not only bought but used as collateral for leveraged purchases. Ironically, much of this explosion in financial activity was actually done in the name of risk management. Instruments were created for trading risk and for trading on market fluctuations. The marketization of risk actually enhanced vulnerability in certain ways, however, notably by making actors in the financial system highly interdependent, reducing the transparency of trades and asset values, and scaling up demands for liquidity. When this highly leveraged and minimally transparent financial system crashed, governments stepped in, using public funds to shore up the markets and those institutions deemed "too big to fail."

There has been a great deal of attention to how ordinary taxpayers bore the consequences of risk-taking by large firms and wealthy individuals. But it is not only as taxpayers that individual citizens and families are vulnerable to economic upheavals, risks created by highly volatile markets or new technologies, or indeed the frauds of big investors who break the rules. They also bear the consequences through unemployment, lost health care, lost pensions, mortgage foreclosures, and escalating university costs. And, indeed, they are more vulnerable because during the same recent decades when the scale and influence of the finance industry was expanding dramatically and neoliberal governments were reducing regulations, long-standing systems of shared responsibility, mutual support, and social security were being undermined.

Privatization of risk thus has two faces. On the one hand, deregulation and concentrated control over private wealth allow some private actors to create risks that affect their many fellow citizens and also the government, as custodian of the public good. On the other hand, sharp cuts in programs to help ordinary citizens mean that more and more face risks privately, as individuals and families without adequate social support. And of course, the risks they face are not limited to those created by speculators in financial markets. They range from vulnerability to natural disasters to the risks associated with new technologies to the many more or less routine risks of everyday life: traffic accidents, occupational injuries, diseases.

Though not only government programs have been cut, government programs have special significance both because they reach all citizens and because they embody a recognition of shared citizenship. Nonetheless, government programs have been cut, and cut severely around the world. Some of this is part of austerity programs launched in response to fiscal crises associated with the post-2008 financial meltdown. But the rollback of the welfare state started in the 1970s. Under the generals who seized power in Chile, Chicago-trained economists experimented with privatizing government institutions and reducing spending on social welfare (which not surprisingly had increased under the previous socialist government). These experiments informed state policy first in Britain and then the United States as Margaret Thatcher and Ronald Reagan sought to weaken unions, social welfare programs, and government regulation of private capitalism. Such policies, often labeled neoliberal, spread widely through the late twentieth century. They did not always cut total government expenditures, partly because of high military budgets. And they did not always cut deficits, partly because neoliberalism also favored tax cuts, especially for the wealthiest citizens. But they cut deeply into the social safety net that protected ordinary people from risks. In the wake of the financial crisis, cuts have deepened. Citizens are thus deprived of social support precisely at a time when risks have proliferated.

The development of more effective institutions to share the burdens of these risks is among the great achievements of the modern era, especially the twentieth century. The institutions come mostly through private insurance programs that pool risks and government programs that either offer insurance or offer direct support to those in need. These provide both security, so that people may approach the future with more confidence and less worry, and direct material benefits when hazards become harms. In addition, of course, there are efforts to reduce risks—ranging from regulating financial speculation to monitoring the safety of food products. But risks are never eliminated, and so compensating for the fact that only some of those potentially harmed actually are harmed becomes an important social issue.

Responding to risks is in fact one of the basic reasons for the development of social institutions in general, not just government. Through most of history, individuals and families bore the risks of earthquake, fire, flood, famine, plague, and pestilence without effective state action. Providing assistance to neighbors was basic to traditional notions of community, family, and collective responsibility. Members of medieval craft guilds created funds to sustain each other in the face of market crises. Religious charities aided the victims of misfortune.

Yet state action is still at least as ancient as Joseph's advice to Pharaoh to set aside grain against a coming dearth—a wise policy that saved people throughout the region.

Modern governments have gone well beyond opening their storehouses in times of extreme need. They have built public institutions to promote the prosperity of whole nations and to ensure that all citizens share the benefits. Public schools, for example, have been seen not just as charity for poor children or training programs for private industry but as investments in the future of the country. Like health care, clean water supplies, transport networks, rural electrification, and safe food, education has been seen as a shared responsibility— partly on ethical grounds of shared obligation but largely on more instrumental bases of shared benefits. Yet the enormous achievements made by building institutions to provide public goods are not merely threatened; they are being reversed. The privatization of risk, moreover, involves not only reductions in programs explicitly designed to share risk, but also a result of weakness in the provision of other public goods. Higher education is a ready example. In recent years, there has been a growing tendency to treat university education not as a public good to be shared widely, but as a private good available to those with money to pay for it.

Moreover, cuts in state "safety nets" are not being matched by more effective private or civil society action. On the contrary, pensions and health care benefits have been curtailed or eliminated in a host of private firms; some corporations have used bankruptcy provisions to avoid providing health care and other benefits to retirees who previously thought such support was guaranteed. Indeed, employment itself has become increasingly precarious. Even large corporations have become commodities to be bought and sold, with reductions in employee benefits usually part of the deals. Many of the stable organizations within which employees once made relatively secure careers have vanished.

This is an issue not only in the developed world but also in many rapidly developing countries. There are many new opportunities in China, for example, and the society is getting richer (though also more unequal). But with high rates of labor migration and a host of new employers, older institutions that provided securely for members' basic needs—notably the *danwei* or work unit—no longer function in the same way. Families still provide support to their members, but the development of new larger-scale institutions is lagging behind need. In China, as in many other developing countries, some employers provide health care and other benefits to workers, often in factory towns. As during the nineteenth-century industrial revolution in Europe and America, some do this more generously and more effectively than others. But these are extensions of employment compensation, available only to some, not to all citizens, and often part of a disciplinary as well as a charitable regime.

Charities do important work in many settings, providing safety nets and sometimes helping to create new institutions for the longer term. But they are not able to expand their services to meet the new needs. There is also a loss of dignity for workers and citizens to feel they are dependent on charitable gifts—rather than on protections rightly available to them.

Risks come, of course, not just from financial upheavals, nor indeed from "normal" market processes that do include ups and downs in different industries and shifts in the balance of trade among different countries. They come also from technological innovation—which produces technological obsolescence in competing sectors and which creates new risks even while it may also offer enhanced productivity or direct consumer benefits. Overall, the spread of electronic communications brings benefits, but it also concentrates losses, for example costing postal workers their jobs. Programs like unemployment insurance serve to smooth such processes, sustaining workers who through no fault of their own find themselves out of work due to changes that may in the larger picture bring progress. But technological innovation also brings other risks, as for example new drugs bring unanticipated side effects. The issue is not just determining whether benefits outweigh costs. It is that benefits are often spread widely among consumers and concentrated somewhat among those with property rights, while costs are concentrated severely among those unlucky enough to suffer the side effects in the form of illness, injury, or death.

Frank Knight's distinction between "known unknowns" and "unknown unknowns" has become famous as investors have realized that some risks bring opportunities for trading and profit. Looking at a population, or a period of time, or a pool of transactions, some risks are calculable: death rates from cancer, mortgage defaults, or bankruptcies. This is the basis for most insurance—and for a host of derivative investments based on estimating chances where at least many relevant variables are known. Of course, it is also possible to buy insurance for less calculable losses—the remote possibility that lightning will strike while one is playing golf, for example, or that a ship will be sunk in an as yet undeclared war. But there are also dangerous events that should not really be considered risk in this sense because there is no basis at all for calculation. The insight that some risks are predictable makes it possible to price insurance (though not perfectly) and to plan social responses.

But from the point of view of individuals, the risks that may be calculable in the aggregate become very concrete, particular, and personal suffering. A 10 percent unemployment rate is complete unemployment for some individuals. A 0.2 percent cancer rate is death for some individuals and very specific suffering for their children. A hailstorm destroys some crops completely and exposes some farmers to bankruptcy and loss of their land.

Issues of risk, disease, and disasters should be central concerns for social science. So should the availability and viability of social institutions to minimize risk where possible, to share costs, and mitigate harm. And not least of all, social science should address inequalities in how well people are served by such institutions, whether they are government funded and operated or independent. The question is not simply public versus private. Indeed, as the public importance of nominally private pension funds reveals, the two are inextricably intertwined. The issue is what makes institutions effective, and what makes them responsive to public needs. Social science should be part of the answer.

To live up to its full potential, social science cannot be merely a source of technical expertise, or advice to those with power. Social science must also inform public communication, bringing not only capacity to manage but also understanding and insight to inform public choices. Public understanding, like public policy, needs to be informed by serious, empirically grounded, social science analyses. This is a pressing concern not only with regard to natural disasters and "homeland security" but also with regard to pensions and social security, the availability of health insurance and health care, and the stability of financial institutions and markets.

To investigate these issues and to provide information to inform public debate and public policy, the Social Science Research Council (SSRC) launched a project on the privatization of risk in 2006. This project began with working group discussions and a forum of essays posted on our web site. A grant from the John D. and Catherine T. MacArthur Foundation enabled us to expand the inquiry, and we are grateful to a very helpful program officer, Michael Stedman. We were fortunate to recruit Jacob Hacker to play a leading role. Jacob's voice has been central to bringing a concern for the issue of privatization of risk—and the need for shared responsibility—to public discussion. In addition to undertaking his own research, he helped to build a network of colleagues with related interests. Crucially, this brought together academic researchers, policy analysts, and policymakers. A series of six shorter books reflect this interdisciplinary engagement as they address different dimensions of the issue.[1] Jacob also recruited Ann O'Leary as an important collaborator in organizing two major conferences, one directly linked to the preparation of this book. I am pleased that the SSRC has been able to play a role in this important work.

In this book Hacker and O'Leary have brought together an impressive range of scholars. They take up enduring issues that have been made urgent in the current context. Immediate economic crisis is entwined with enduring structural changes. Governments face macroeconomic challenges at the same time that citizens doubt their capacity to deliver public goods efficiently. Broad ideological changes dovetail with concrete transformations of policy. Yet the concrete implications of different policy proposals are often poorly understood. Creativity in finding new approaches to basic needs is stifled by debates stuck in old oppositions.

This book brings clarity to the often confused and ideological debates. It brings research-based knowledge to analysis of the choices before us. It makes a crucial contribution both to understanding and to addressing an issue that is urgent in the United States and around the world.

Notes

1.   Jacob Hacker, ed., *Health at Risk: America's Ailing Health System—and How to Heal It* (New York: Columbia University Press, 2008); Andrew Lakoff, ed., *Disaster and the Politics of Intervention* (New York: Columbia University Press, 2009); Donald Light, ed., *The Risks of Prescription Drugs* (New York: Columbia University Press, 2009); Katherine Newman, ed., *Laid Off, Laid Low: Political and Economic Consequences of Employment Insecurity* (New York: Columbia University Press, 2008); Mitchell Orenstein, ed., *Pensions, Social Security, and the Privatization of Risk* (New York: Columbia University Press, 2009); Robert E. Wright, ed., *Bailouts: Public Money, Private Property* (New York: Columbia University Press, 2009).

Acknowledgments

This volume was made possible by a grant from the John D. and Catherine T. MacArthur Foundation to the Social Science Research Council (SSRC) for SSRC's Privatization of Risk project. Craig Calhoun, President of the Social Science Research Council, asked the Berkeley Center on Health, Economic & Family Security at UC Berkeley School of Law (Berkeley CHEFS), of which Jacob Hacker is a founding faculty co-director and Ann O'Leary is the Executive Director, to spearhead a culminating project to develop concrete ideas and solutions to the problem of the increased privatization of risk. We thank the MacArthur Foundation and the Social Science Research Council for their support and particularly Craig Calhoun for his leadership and vision on this project. We also thank Paul Price, the editorial director at SSRC, for helping us launch this project, and Siovahn Walker, who was then a program officer at SSRC, for guiding this project throughout.

Thank you whole heartedly to the authors who agreed to participate in this project and contribute their innovative thinking, good ideas and precious time to this volume: Heather Boushey, Craig Calhoun, Mariano-Florentino Cuéllar, Neil Gilbert, Amy Helburn, Amanda Lehning, Martha Minow, David Moss, Alicia H. Munnell, Katherine Porter, Connor Raso, Andrew Scharlach, Stephen Sugarman, Tara Twomey, and Christian Weller.

In May 2009, we brought together these authors in Berkeley, California to present their working ideas to a peer group of academics and policy practitioners in order to receive feedback. Authors then revised their work and made final presentations in October 2009 to a larger audience of policy thinkers and practitioners in Washington, DC. We thank all those who provided invaluable feedback at these conferences, including: Maeve Elise Brown, Karen Davenport, Will Dow, Maurice Emsellem, Michael Ettlinger, Netsy Firestein, Mark Greenberg, Lief Haase, Alexander Hertel-Fernandez, Ken Jacobs, David Kirp, Gillian Lester, Goodwin Liu, Mary Ann Mason, Paul Nathanson, Mark Paul, John Quigley, Robert Reich, Eric Stein, Jamie Studley, Anne Stuhldreher, Siovahn Walker, Sarah Rosen Wartell, and Micah Weinberg. We thank the Center for American Progress, particularly Sarah Rosen Wartell and Michael Ettlinger, for providing a platform to present this work in Washington and Luke Reidenbach at CAP for his administrative assistance.

The entire operation at Berkeley CHEFS made this project possible. We thank Christopher Edley, Jr., Dean of Berkeley Law, for his vision in founding Berkeley CHEFS and for his leadership and encouragement in this project and in all that we do. We thank our team of top-notch law students who have worked at Berkeley CHEFS throughout this project, but especially Joanna Parnes and Zoe Savitsky, who both provided invaluable editing and research assistance throughout this project. And we thank our administrative team Phyliss Martinez-Haarz, Fredda Olivares, and Rachel Pepper, who made our conferences shine and who aided us through this entire project. We also thank the design team of Tia Stoller and Dionne Anciano for their assistance in preparing the manuscript for publication.

Finally, we thank David McBride of Oxford University Press for guiding this edited volume from the beginning to the end. His input on how to improve the volume made it immeasurably better. We also thank him for his patience and good graces as we worked to complete this volume.

Contributors

Heather Boushey
Senior Economist, Center for American Progress

Craig Calhoun
President, Social Science Research Council

Mariano-Florentino Cuéllar
Professor of Law and Deane F. Johnson Faculty Scholar, Stanford
University

Neil Gilbert
Chernin Professor of Social Welfare, UC Berkeley School of Social
Welfare

Jacob S. Hacker
Stanley B. Resor Professor, Yale University

Amy Helburn
Doctoral Candidate, University of Massachusetts, Boston

Amanda Lehning
Postdoctoral Fellow, University of Michigan School of Social Work

Martha L. Minow
Jeremiah Smith, Jr. Professor of Law and Dean of the Faculty of Law,
Harvard Law School

David A. Moss
John G. McLean Professor of Business Administration Harvard University Business School

Alicia H. Munnell
Peter F. Drucker Chair in Management Sciences-Finance
  Department, Boston College Carroll School of Management
  Director, Center for Retirement Research at Boston College

Ann O'Leary
Lecturer in Residence and Executive Director, Berkeley Center on
  Health, Economic & Family Security, UC Berkeley School of Law

Katherine M. Porter
Professor of Law, UC Irvine School of Law

Connor Raso
Law Clerk, United States Court of Appeals for Second Circuit
Doctoral Candidate, Stanford University

Andrew Scharlach
Associate Dean and Eugene and Rose Kleiner Professor of Aging, UC
  Berkeley School of Social Welfare

Stephen D. Sugarman
Roger J. Traynor Professor of Law, UC Berkeley School of Law

Tara Twomey
Of Counsel to the National Consumer Law Center
Advocacy Director, National Consumer Bankruptcy Rights Center

Christian E. Weller
Associate Professor of Public Policy, University of Massachusetts,
  Boston, and Senior Fellow, Center for American Progress

Shared Responsibility,
Shared Risk

Part One

INSPIRATIONS AND CHALLENGES FOR SHARED RESPONSIBILITY, SHARED RISK

1

Sharing Risk and Responsibility in a New Economic Era

The roughly twenty months between President Barack Obama's inauguration in January 2009 and the midterm elections of 2010 witnessed the passage of a number of reforms designed to improve economic security. The biggest by far was the Patient Protection and Affordable Care Act, passed in March 2010—a landmark health care bill with a federal price tag of roughly $1 trillion over ten years that is predicted to newly insure more than 30 million Americans by 2019.[1] But the health care bill was only one of several major steps taken to improve economic security amid the deepest economic downturn since the Great Depression. In addition, Congress passed a financial reform bill that will provide greater consumer protections for home buyers and borrowers; enacted (as part of the health care bill) a new long-term care insurance program and a substantial expansion of direct government student lending; and passed an economic stimulus package that included a major modernization of unemployment insurance.[2]

The chapters to come will examine these measures, their foci, and their effects. This initial chapter provides the broader context. The policy battles of 2009 and 2010 did not emerge fully formed out of the recent economic downturn. Rather, they were rooted in a deeper and longer-term transformation of our economy and our society that has increased the economic insecurity of American workers and their families. Five years ago, in a book that attempted to draw attention to this sea change and map out a new economic path, I called this transformation the "Great Risk Shift."[3] My argument was that economic risk had increasingly shifted from the broad shoulders of government and corporations onto the backs of American workers and their families. This sea change, I argued, had occurred in nearly every area of Americans' finances, from jobs, health care, and retirement pensions to homes, personal savings, and strategies for balancing work and family. With the economic collapse that began at the end of 2007, this shift no longer seems debatable. But how to deal with this transformation given the political and budgetary constraints that our leaders face remains very much an open question.

The purpose of this volume is to provide an answer—or rather, a series of answers—to that question. In my book *The Great Risk Shift*, I sought to begin a conversation about how to adapt America's ailing economic security infrastructure to our nation's new economic and social realities. By bringing together some of the best thinkers about economic and social policy in the United States today, this book is designed to move that conversation toward concrete ideas for reform. Each of the contributors to this volume examines how economic security has changed in specific crucial areas of Americans' lives and then outlines realistic yet farsighted measures to ensure that workers and their families have the tools and policies they need to deal with unexpected shocks and to invest in their futures.

This chapter lays out the big picture that should guide these efforts. It begins by documenting and explaining the Great Risk Shift, which is rooted in the erosion of America's distinctive framework of economic security. This framework differs from the frameworks found in other nations less in terms of total *size* and more in the *form* that social protections take. Responsibilities that in other nations were handled by government, perhaps with the cooperation of non-profit mutual insurers, became the responsibility of employers and for-profit providers. Government policies that encouraged and regulated these private benefits to promote their broad distribution and stability were once at the core of America's uniquely "divided welfare state."[4] Yet this distinctive framework has crumbed over the last generation in the face of growing economic pressures on employers, as well as increasing political resistance to the ideal of economic security itself.

The chapter then turns to the question of what can be done in response to the Great Risk Shift. The legislative landmarks of 2009 and 2010 represent a major step forward. Even after their passage, however, the United States still badly needs a twenty-first-century social contract that protects families against the most severe risks they face, without clamping down on the potentially beneficial processes of change and adjustment that produce some of these risks. This will require recognizing and responding to the most fundamental source of American economic insecurity: the deep mismatch between today's economic and social realities and America's strained framework for providing economic security. It will also require recognizing that economic security and economic opportunity are not antithetical, but go hand in hand. Just as investors and entrepreneurs need basic protections to encourage them to take economic risks, so ordinary workers and their families require a foundation of economic security to confidently invest in their futures and seize the risky opportunities before them.

America's Unique—and Endangered— Framework of Economic Security

We often assume that the United States does little to provide economic security compared with other rich capitalist democracies. This is only partly true. The United States does spend less on government benefits as a share of its economy, but it also relies far more on private workplace benefits, such as health care and retirement pensions. Indeed, when these private benefits are factored into the mix, the U.S. framework of economic security is not smaller than the average system in other rich democracies—it is actually slightly larger.[5] With the help of hundreds of billions of dollars in tax breaks, American employers serve as the first line of defense for millions of workers buffeted by the winds of economic change.

The problem is that this unique employment-based system is coming undone, and, in the process, risk is shifting back onto workers and their families. Employers want out of the social contract forged in the more stable economy of the past. And with labor unions weakened and workers just worried about holding onto their jobs, employers are largely getting what they want. Meanwhile, America's framework of government support is also strained. Social Security is declining in generosity even as guaranteed private pensions evaporate. Medicare, while ever more costly, has not kept pace with skyrocketing health expenses and changing medical practices. And although the share of unemployed workers receiving unemployment benefits has risen in recent years, the long-term trend is one of declining support for Americans out of work, even as unemployment has shifted from cyclical job losses to permanent job displacements.

The history of American health insurance tells the story in miniature. After the passage of Medicare and Medicaid in 1965, health coverage peaked at roughly 90 percent of the population, with approximately 80 percent of all Americans covered by private insurance.[6] Since the late 1970s, however, employers and insurers have steadily retreated from broad-risk pooling, and the number of Americans who lack health coverage has increased with little interruption. Private health coverage now reaches just over half the American population.[7]

Employment-based health insurance has not been the only casualty. Companies have also raced away from the promise of guaranteed retirement benefits. Twenty-five years ago, 83 percent of medium and large firms offered traditional "defined-benefit" pensions that provided a fixed benefit for life; today, the share is below one-third.[8] Instead, companies that provide pensions mostly offer "defined-contribution" plans like the 401(k), in which returns are neither predictable nor assured. Moreover, despite the expansion of 401(k) plans, the share of workers with access to a pension at their current job—either a defined benefit plan or a 401(k) plan—has fallen from just over half in 1979 to under 43 percent in 2009.[9]

Defined-contribution plans are not properly seen as pensions, at least as that term has been traditionally understood. They are essentially private investment accounts sponsored by employers that can be used for building up a tax-free estate, as well as for retirement savings. As a result, they greatly increase the degree of risk and responsibility placed on individual workers in retirement planning. Traditional defined-benefit plans are generally mandatory and paid for largely by employers (in lieu of cash wages). They thus represent a form of forced savings. Defined-benefit plans are also insured by the federal government and are heavily regulated to protect participants against mismanagement. Perhaps most important, their fixed benefits protect workers against the risk of stock market downturns and the possibility of living longer than expected.

None of this is true of defined-contribution plans. Participation is voluntary, and due to the lack of generous employer contributions, many workers choose not to participate, or if they do, to contribute inadequate sums.[10] Plans are not adequately regulated to protect against poor asset allocations or corporate or personal mismanagement. The federal government does not insure defined-contribution plans. And defined-contribution accounts provide no inherent protection against asset or longevity risks. Indeed, some features of defined-contribution plans—namely, the ability to borrow against their assets, and the distribution of their accumulated savings as lump-sum payments that must be rolled over into new accounts when workers change jobs—exacerbate the risk that workers will prematurely use retirement savings, leaving inadequate income upon retirement. And, perversely, this risk falls most heavily on younger and less highly paid workers, the very workers most in need of secure retirement protection.[11]

We do not yet know how severely the market crisis that began in 2008 will reduce private pension wealth, but the signs are deeply worrisome. Just between mid-2007 and October 2008, an estimated $2 trillion in retirement wealth was lost in 401(k)s and individual retirement accounts.[12] A 2009 survey found that two-thirds of adults aged 50 to 64 years lost money during this period in mutual funds, individual stocks, or 401(k) accounts, with the vast majority losing more than 20 percent of their investments.[13] (Most who had no losses had no investments.)

But although we cannot yet know how sustained these losses will be, we do know they come after a generation of decline in the retirement-preparedness of Americans. According to researchers at Boston College, the share of working-age households that are at risk of being financially unprepared for retirement at age 65 has risen from 31 percent in 1983 to 43 percent in 2004 and a projected 51 percent in 2009.[14] Younger Americans are far more likely to be at risk than older Americans: roughly half of those born from the mid-1960s through the early 1970s are at risk of being financially unprepared, compared with 35 percent of those born in the decade after World War II.[15] In every age group, low-income Americans are the least financially prepared.[16]

In sum, as private and public support has eroded, workers and their families have been forced to bear a greater burden. This is the essence of the Great Risk

Shift. Rather than enjoying the protections of insurance that pools risk broadly, Americans are increasingly facing economic risks on their own—and often at their peril.

The New World of Work and Family

The erosion of America's distinctive framework of economic protections might be less worrisome if work and family were stable sources of security themselves. Unfortunately, they are not. The job market has grown more uncertain and risky, especially for those who were once best protected from its vagaries. Workers and their families now invest more in education to earn a middle-class living, and yet in today's postindustrial economy, these costly investments are no guarantee of a high, stable, or upward-sloping career path. For displaced workers, the prospect of gaining new jobs with relatively similar pay and benefits has fallen, and the ranks of the long-term unemployed and "shadow unemployed" (workers who have given up looking for jobs altogether) have grown.[17]

Meanwhile, the family, a sphere that was once viewed as a refuge from economic risk, has increasingly become a source of risk of its own. At first glance, this seems counterintuitive. Families are much more likely to have two earners than in the past, and a two-income family is the ultimate form of private risk sharing. To most families, however, a second income is not a luxury but a necessity in a context in which wages are relatively flat and the primary costs of raising a family (health care, education, and housing) are high and rising. According to calculations by Jared Bernstein and Karen Kornbluh, more than three-quarters of the modest 24 percent rise in real income between 1979 and 2000 experienced by families in the middle of the income spectrum was due to increased work hours (primarily the addition of a second earner) rather than rising wages.[18] In time-use surveys, both men and women who work long hours indicate they would like to work fewer hours and spend more time with their families[19]—which strongly suggests that they are not able to choose the exact mix of work and family they would prefer.

With families needing two earners to maintain a middle-class standard of living, their economic calculus has changed in ways that accentuate many of the risks they face. Precisely because it now takes more work and more income to maintain a middle-class standard of living, the questions that face families when financially threatening events occur are suddenly starker. What happens when a woman leaves the workforce to have children, when a child is chronically ill, when one spouse loses a job, or when an older parent needs assistance? In short, events within two-earner families that require the care and time of family members create special demands and strains that traditional one-earner families generally did not face.

The Rising Instability of Family Incomes

The new world of work and family has ushered in a new crop of highly leveraged investors—middle-class families. One sign of this change is the rising instability of family incomes. Although the precise magnitude of the increase depends on how income variance is measured, my own research using the Panel Study of Income Dynamics (PSID) suggests that short-term family income variance essentially doubled from 1969 to 2004.[20] Much of the rise in income volatility occurred prior to 1985, and volatility dropped substantially in the late 1990s.[21] In recent years, however, income volatility has risen to exceed its 1980s peak.[22] The proportion of working-age individuals experiencing a 50 percent or greater drop in their family income over a two-year period has climbed from less than 4 percent in the early 1970s to nearly 10 percent in the early 2000s.[23] And although less-educated and poorer Americans have less-stable family incomes than their better-educated and wealthier peers, the increase in family income volatility affects all major demographic and economic groups.[24] Indeed, over the past generation, Americans with at least four years of college experienced a larger increase in family income instability than those with only a high school education, with most of the rise occurring in the last 15 years.[25]

Understanding the causes of increased family income instability is essential if we are to reduce Americans' growing economic insecurity. Along with a team of researchers (and with funding from the Rockefeller Foundation), I have developed the "Economic Security Index," or ESI.[26] The ESI adds to research on income volatility by looking at economic instability caused by out-of-pocket medical spending as well as by income fluctuations. It also considers whether families have adequate financial safety nets to cushion these economic shocks. In a nutshell, the ESI represents the share of Americans who experience at least a 25 percent decline in their inflation-adjusted "available household income" from one year to the next and who lack an adequate financial safety net to replace this lost income until it has returned to its original level. "Available household income" is income that is reduced by nondiscretionary spending, including, most substantially, the amount of a household's out-of-pocket medical spending. (The other main form of nondiscretionary spending considered by the ESI is the cost of servicing debt.). Thus the ESI captures Americans who experience income losses of 25 percent or greater due to a decline in income, an increase in medical spending, or a combination of the two.

The ESI, available from 1985 through 2007 (with projections for 2008 and 2009) shows that economic insecurity has increased substantially over the last quarter century (see Figure 1.1). In 1985, 12 percent of Americans experienced a major economic loss sufficient to classify them as insecure in the ESI. During the recession of the early 2000s, this figure had risen to 17 percent, and projections suggest that in 2009, the level of economic insecurity experienced by Americans was greater than at any time over the past quarter century.

These stark numbers are not just a reflection of the steep economic downturn of recent years. Rather, economic security has been gradually declining since the

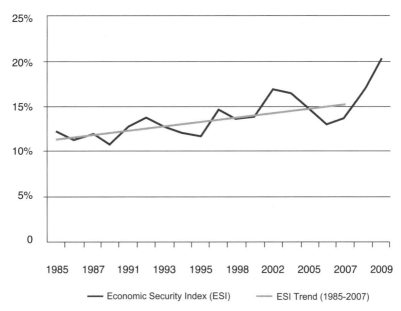

Figure 1.1: Share of Americans Who Are Insecure, 1985–2007 (with 2008–2009 Projections). Source: Jacob S. Hacker et al., *Economic Security at Risk: Findings from the Rockefeller Economic Security Index* (New York: Rockefeller Foundation, 2010), http://economicsecurityindex.org/assets/Economic%20Security%20Index%20Full%20Report.pdf

early 1980s. To see beyond short-term economic fluctuations requires calculating the longer term statistical trend in the ESI, which is shown in Figure 1.1. Based on this analysis, the ESI has increased by approximately one-third from 1985 to 2007. If the projections up to 2009 are included, the ESI has increased by almost half since 1985. To state this trend in terms of population, approximately 46 million Americans were counted as insecure in 2007, up from 28 million in 1985. Moreover, the share of Americans experiencing large drops in available household income has increased even more since the 1960s. A less complete form of the ESI available back to the late 1960s shows that large (25 percent or greater) income losses—the core component of the complete ESI—had already risen by about one-third from the 1960s to the 1980s, making subsequent increases over the past quarter century even more noteworthy.

The Indebted American Family

The rising instability of family incomes would be less troubling if families had substantial liquid savings to tide them over during periods with reduced income. Yet the ESI suggests that very few families have even modest holdings of wealth besides their home. Instead, Americans are often deeply indebted, especially families with children. As a share of income in 2004, total debt—including mortgages, credit cards, car loans, and other liabilities—was more than 125 percent of income for the median married couple with children.[27] According to a recent analysis of families with incomes between two and six times the federal poverty level and headed by working-age adults, more than half of these middle-class families have no net financial assets (excluding home equity), and nearly four in five of these families do not have sufficient assets to cover three-quarters of essential living expenses for even three months, should their income disappear.[28] And, of course, the recent economic crisis has only exacerbated the problem, causing a loss of $15 trillion in private family assets and wealth between June 2007 and December 2008.[29]

With debt levels rising, personal bankruptcy has gone from a rare occurrence to a relatively common one, with the number of households filing for bankruptcy rising from less than 300,000 in 1980 to more than two million in 2005.[30] During that period, the financial characteristics of the bankrupt have grown worse and worse (contrary to the claim that bankruptcy is increasingly being used by people with only mild financial difficulties). Strikingly, married couples with children are much more likely to file for bankruptcy than are couples without children or single individuals.[31] Otherwise, the bankrupt are much like other Americans before they file, though slightly better educated, roughly as likely to have had a good job, and modestly less likely to own a home. They are not the persistently poor or the downtrodden looking for relief: they are refugees of the middle class, frequently wondering how they fell so far so fast.[32]

Americans are also losing their homes at record rates. Even before the housing market collapsed in 2008, there had been a fivefold increase since the 1970s in the share of households that fall into foreclosure[33]—a process that begins when home owners default on their mortgages and can end with homes being auctioned to the highest bidder in local courthouses. The run-up of housing prices before the economic downturn had much less of a positive effect on Americans' net worth than might be supposed. Even as home prices rose, Americans held less and less equity in their homes. As recently as the early 1980s, home equity was around 70 percent of home values on average; in 2007, it was 43 percent—the lowest level on record.[34] In the recent downturn, approximately 20 percent of home owners have negative equity, owing more on their home than it is worth.[35] For scores of ordinary home owners—roughly one in twenty-five mortgage-owning house-holds in the past few years, a level not seen since the Great Depression—the American Dream has mutated into the American Nightmare.

The Endangered American Dream

As these examples suggest, economic insecurity is not just a problem of the poor and uneducated. It affects even educated, middle-class Americans—men and women who thought they had bought the ticket to upward mobility and economic stability by staying in school, buying a home, and investing in their 401(k)s.

Insecurity today reaches across the income spectrum, the racial divide, and lines of geography and gender. Increasingly, all Americans are riding the economic roller coaster once reserved for the working poor and, thus, are at risk of losing the secure financial foundation they need to reach for and achieve the American Dream.

Economic security matters deeply to people. When most of us contemplate the financial risks in our lives, we do not concern ourselves all that much with the upside risks—the chance that we will receive an unexpected bonus, for example. We worry about the downside risks, and worry about them intensely. In the 1970s, psychologists Daniel Kahneman and Amos Tversky gave a name to this cognitive bias: "loss aversion."[36] Most people, it turns out, are not just highly risk-averse—they prefer a bird in the hand to even a very good chance of two in the bush. They are also far more cautious when it comes to bad outcomes than when it comes to good outcomes of exactly the same magnitude. The search for economic security is, in large part, a reflection of a basic human desire for protection against losing what one already has.

This desire is surprisingly strong. Americans are famously opportunity-loving, but when asked in 2005 whether they were "more concerned with the opportunity to make money in the future, or the stability of knowing that your present sources of income are protected," 62 percent favored stability and just 29 percent favored opportunity.[37]

It should not be surprising, therefore, that recent polling shows extremely high levels of economic anxiety among all but the richest Americans. In a September 2010 poll, only half of Americans agreed that "the American Dream—that if you work hard you'll get ahead—still holds true;" more than four in ten said it no longer did.[38] In April 2009, two in three adults said that the current economy presented them with more risks than their parents confronted—six times as many as the 11 percent of those polled who said they faced fewer risks than their parents.[39] A comprehensive poll concerning economic risk that I helped design—fielded as part of the American National Election Studies with the support of the Rockefeller Foundation—asked Americans about 15 different sources of economic risk in employment, medical care, wealth, and family relations (see Figure 1.2). More than three-quarters of all Americans reported that they were very or fairly worried about at least one of these economic risks. Worries about wealth were the most frequent cause of economic unease, though concerns about medical costs were a close second.[40]

These are not idle worries. Households that experienced these economic risks between March 2008 and September 2009—especially risks that persisted for six months or more—reported much higher levels of unmet basic needs (going without food because of the cost, losing one's home or rental, or going without health care because of the expense). This was particularly true of employment and medical risks: households experiencing employment and medical spending risks were three times as likely as unaffected households to report any unmet needs and seven times as likely to report multiple unmet needs. Strikingly, even among families in the third quartile of household income (annual income between

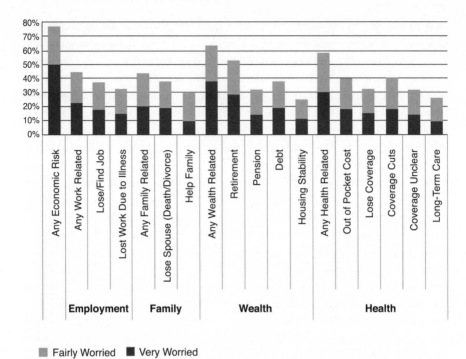

■ Fairly Worried ■ Very Worried

Figure 1.2: Scope of Concerns about Economic Security, Spring 2009. Source: Jacob S. Hacker et al., *Standing on Shaky Ground: Americans' Experiences with Economic Insecurity* (New York: Rockefeller Foundation, 2010), http://www.economicsecurityindex.org/upload/media/ESI%20report%20final_12%2013.pdf

$60,000 and $100,000), the same association between economic risks and unmet basic needs held true. More than half of families with income between $60,000 and $100,000 that experienced employment or medical disruptions reported being unable to meet at least one basic economic need.

Yet even before the economic crisis, people were already extremely worried about their economic security. In a February 2007 survey, for example, 63 percent of Americans reported feeling that the economy had become less secure in the last decade, compared to 18 percent who felt the economy had become more secure.[41] The strongest sense of rising insecurity was felt among those with family incomes between $36,000 and $92,000: respondents in this income bracket reported feeling that the economy has grown less secure rather than more secure by a margin greater than four to one (67 percent versus 17 percent, respectively).[42] In the same 2007 poll, a majority of Americans also expected things to get less secure over the next 20 years.[43]

It would be one thing if all this risk came with great reward for the middle class. After all, people will sometimes trade higher risks—a greater chance of losing their job, for example—for higher rewards. Yet this has decidedly not been the pattern. The Congressional Budget Office has put together a comprehensive measure of the distribution of income, based on actual tax records as well as on reported income in surveys (see Figure 1.3). Taking into account all government taxes and benefits, as well as private workplace health insurance and pensions, the middle quintile of households (the 20 percent of households above the bottom 40 percent and below the top 40 percent) saw their inflation-adjusted incomes rise from $44,100 to $55,300 between 1979 and 2007—a gain of 25 percent.[44] By comparison, the average after-tax incomes of the richest 1 percent of households rose from just over $346,000 a year to more than $1.3 million over the same period—an increase of more than 280

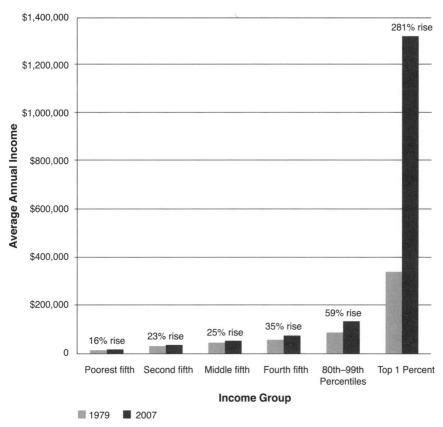

Figure 1.3: Average Household After-Tax Income Including Public and Private Benefits, 1979 and 2007. Source: Calculated from Congressional Budget Office (CBO), *Average After Tax Income for All Households, by Household Income Category, 1979–2007* (Washington, DC: CBO, June 2010), (http://www.cbo.gov/publications/collections/tax/2010/average_after-tax_income.pdf). Income includes wages, salaries, self-employment income, rents, taxable and nontaxable interest, dividends, realized capital gains, cash transfer payments, and cash retirement benefits, as well as all in-kind benefits, such as Medicare, Medicaid, employer-paid health insurance premiums, food stamps, school lunches and breakfasts, housing assistance, and energy assistance. Federal taxes are subtracted from income and account for not just income and payroll taxes paid directly by individuals and households, but also taxes paid by businesses (corporate income taxes and the employer's share of Social Security, Medicare, and federal unemployment insurance payroll taxes).

percent.[45] Recall also that most of the income gains of middle-class families are due to the fact that family members are working more hours, not that they are receiving higher pay. The risk-reward trade-off looks more like a risk-reward rip-off.

The Policy Challenge

The Great Risk Shift is not a financial hurricane beyond human control. True, sweeping changes in the global and domestic economy have helped to propel it, but America's leaders could have responded to these forces by reinforcing the flood-walls that protect families from economic risk. Instead, lacking strong political pressure to address new and newly intensified risks or to shore up dwindling pro-tections, for years those leaders have acted in ways that have further eroded the floodwalls that protect families. Proponents of these changes speak of a nirvana of individual economic management—an "ownership society" in which Americans are free to choose.[46] What they have fostered, however, is very different: a world of economic insecurity in which far too many Americans are free to lose.

Of course, we cannot turn back the clock on many of the changes that have swept through our economy and society. Nor would we always want to. Accepting our new economic and social realities does not, however, mean accepting the new economic insecurity, much less accepting the assumptions that lie behind the cur-rent assault on the ideal of security. Americans will need to do much to secure themselves in the new world of work and family, but they should be protected by an improved safety net that fills the most glaring gaps in present protections. This safety net should provide all Americans with the basic security they need as workers, as family members, and as citizens. In the remainder of this opening chapter, I will talk about some of the basic principles that should guide this effort.

The first priority for restoring security should be Hippocrates' admonition to "do no harm." Undoing what little risk pooling remains in the private sector with-out putting something better in place is harmful. Piling tax break upon tax break to allow wealthy and healthy Americans to opt out of our tattered institutions of social insurance is harmful. And though simplifying our tax code makes perfect sense, making it markedly less progressive through a flat tax or national sales tax would also be harmful. A progressive income tax, after all, is effectively a form of insurance, reducing our contribution to public goods when income falls and raising it when income rises. State and local taxes are generally regressive: accord-ing to a 2009 analysis, the richest 1 percent of households paid an effective state and local tax rate of just over 5 percent of income (after taking into account the federal tax deduction for state and local taxes), the middle fifth of households paid 9.4 percent, and the bottom fifth paid 10.9 percent.[47] Although the federal income tax has become less progressive (especially when it comes to the taxation of very high incomes), it remains one of the last major bulwarks against rising economic inequality.

Figure 1.4 shows that the Economic Security Index is higher (meaning greater insecurity) for less affluent families than for more affluent ones. Lower-income families generally have little or no wealth to protect their standard of living when income declines, and they are least likely to have access to workplace health or

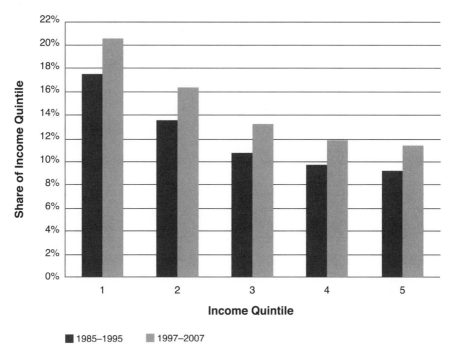

Income Quintile

■ 1985–1995   ■ 1997–2007

Figure 1.4: Share of Americans Who Are Insecure, 1985–1995, 1997–2007. Notes: The "insecure" are those whose available household income declines by at least 25 percent from one year to the next (after adjusting for inflation), as a result of a decline in household income and/ or an increase in out-of-pocket medical spending, and who lack an adequate financial safety net. Thus an individual is considered insecure if the sum of the increase in medical expenditures and lost annual income total at least 25 percent of his or her previous year's available income, as illustrated in Figure 1.3. Household income includes all private and government sources of income, including the estimated income value of defined-contribution retirement accounts, such as 401(k)s, for households with heads aged 60 or older. Household income is adjusted to reflect the economies of scale of pooling household resources and expenses. Household income is also reduced by the amount needed to pay off liquid financial debts when net financial wealth is negative. (All income is adjusted for inflation and expressed in 2009 dollars.) Individuals with adequate holdings of liquid financial wealth are not treated as insecure even when they experience 25 percent or higher income losses. We define "adequate" as enough liquid financial wealth to compensate for the lost income until typical recovery to pre-drop income or for six years, whichever comes first. Those entering retirement are also excluded from the count of the insecure even if available household income declines by 25 percent or more concurrent with retirement; once retired, however, they are counted as insecure when they experience such declines. Source: Jacob S. Hacker et al., *Economic Security at Risk: Findings from the Rockefeller Economic Security Index* (New York: Rockefeller Foundation, 2010).

disability insurance. Not surprisingly, therefore, unemployment has a much larger effect on the consumption patterns of lower-income families than it has on those of higher-income families.

Yet while we should work to preserve the best elements of existing policies, we should also recognize that the nature and causes of insecurity, as well as our understanding about how to best address it, have evolved considerably. During the New Deal, economic insecurity was largely seen as a problem of drops or interruptions in male earnings, whether due to unemployment, retirement, or other costly events. Even as working women became the norm, our programs failed to address the special economic strains on two-earner families. So too did they fail to address the distinctive unemployment patterns that became increasingly prevalent as industrial employment gave way to service work: for example, the rising prevalence of long-term unemployment (in 2010, it took an average of more than 20 weeks to find a new job—double the amount of time in the 1982–1983 recession)[48] and the shift of workers from one economic sector to another that often leads to large cuts in pay and the need for specialized retraining.

Flaws in existing policies of risk protection have also become apparent. Our framework of social protection is overwhelmingly focused on the aged, even though young adults and families with children face the greatest economic strains. It emphasizes short-term exits from the workforce, even though long-term job losses and the displacement and obsolescence of skills have become more severe. In many ways, it embodies the antiquated notion that family strains can be dealt with by a second earner—usually a woman—who can easily enter or leave the workforce as necessary. Above all, it is based on the idea that job-based private insurance can easily fill the gaps left by public programs, even though it is ever clearer that job-based private insurance is not enough.

These shortcomings suggest that an improved safety net should emphasize portable insurance to help families deal with major interruptions to income and big blows to wealth. They also mean that these promises should be mostly separate from work for a particular employer: the safety net should move from job to job. The Affordable Care Act is a step in the right direction by setting up access to health insurance for workers when they are between jobs or when their employer does not offer health insurance. But part of its success will hinge on the ease with which individuals can maintain seamless health coverage during work transitions.

By the same token, we should not force massive social risks onto institutions incapable of effectively carrying them. Bankruptcy should not be a backdoor social insurance system, private charity care should not be our main medical safety net, and credit cards should not be the main way that families get by when times are tight. To be sure, when nothing better is possible, the principle of "do no harm" may dictate protecting even incomplete and inadequate safety nets. The ultimate goal, however, should be a new framework of social insurance that revitalizes the best elements of the present system, while replacing those parts that work less effectively with stronger alternatives geared toward meeting the particular needs of today's economy and society.

This brings us to the final principle: measures to enhance economic security should also be designed to enhance economic opportunity. Most of us think of our nation's safety net as a way of helping those who have had bad fortune or have fallen on hard times. Yet providing economic security has far broader benefits for our economy and our society. Corporate law has long recognized the need to limit the downside of economic risk-taking as a way of encouraging entrepreneurs and investors to make the risky investments necessary to advance in a capitalist economy. The law of bankruptcy and the principle of limited liability—the notion that those who run a firm are not personally liable if the firm fails—allow entrepreneurs to innovate with the security of knowing they will not be financially destroyed if their risky bets fail.[49]

Just as basic protections for entrepreneurs must be in place in order to foster risk taking, families also need a basic foundation of financial security if they are to feel confident in making the investments needed to advance in a dynamic economy. All of the major wellsprings of economic opportunity in the United States—including assets, workplace skills, education, and investments in children—are costly and risky for families to cultivate. Providing security can encourage families to make these investments, aiding not just their own advancement but the economy as a whole.

Providing economic security appears even more beneficial when compared to some of the leading alternatives that insecure citizens may otherwise back. Heavy-handed regulation of the economy, strict limits on cross-border trade and financial flows, and other intrusive measures may gain widespread support from workers buffeted by economic turbulence, but these measures are likely to reduce growth overall.

The challenge, then, is to construct a twenty-first-century social contract that protects families against the most severe risks they face, without clamping down on the potentially beneficial processes of change and adjustment that produce some of these risks. Three areas of economic risk in particular cry out for attention: employment risks, retirement income risks, and health care risks. But it would be a mistake to only design economic protections narrowly around specific economic concerns. Another leading priority is to create new and flexible policies for dealing with economic risks of all kinds, such as the flexible-leave and income-maintenance policies described in later chapters of this volume.

All these changes, of course, will not come without costs, and they certainly will not come without political struggle. Yet against the cost, one must balance the savings. Americans pay billions of dollars in hidden taxes imposed by laws that facilitate bankruptcy, mandate emergency room care, and bail out the politically sympathetic when things go bad. The elimination of these expenses must be accounted for when tallying up the bill, as should the huge drain that our current system imposes when people do not change jobs, do not have kids, or do not invest in new skills because they fear the downside risks. And we should not forget that the United States already spends as much as many European nations on social benefits: we just do so in a way that is enormously wasteful, inefficient, and incapable of providing economic security to those who most need it.

New Realities, New Policies

Americans have long seen a basic foundation of economic security as essential to the nation's economic prosperity and social health. The Great Depression—widely seen as a natural disaster beyond the control or responsibility of the Americans it struck—was the watershed for many of these policies. In its wake, and especially after World War II, political and business leaders put in place new institutions designed to spread broadly the burden of key economic risks. These public and private institutions were never open to everyone. They required work, ongoing contributions, and proof of eligibility. But they were based on the notion that certain risks can only be effectively dealt with through inclusive institutions that spread costs across rich and poor, healthy and sick, able-bodied and disabled, young and old.

Over the last generation, however, this public-private framework has come undone at the same time that new economic risks are increasingly buffeting American families. We have witnessed a major transfer of economic risk from broad structures of insurance onto the balance sheets of American families. This transformation has reworked Americans' relationship to their government, their employers, and each other, with consequences for American politics and society that very much remain with us today.

In the wake of the steepest economic downturn since the Great Depression, it is time once again to retool and rebuild America's crumbling framework of economic security. Not so long ago, critics of this framework argued that government was not needed to provide basic risk protection—that private insurers could take care of health care, that private employers would ensure that everyone had a good pension, that job insecurity was becoming a thing of the past. No one can confidently hold that view today. The only question is whether new policies will be put in place to share the risks of the twenty-first century economy across Americans and between government, employers, and individual families, or whether Americans should be left to cope with these uncertainties largely on their own. Important steps were taken to broaden risk pooling in 2009 and 2010. Given the scale of the economic risks that Americans face, however, they were small steps. As this book shows, much remains to be done.

The argument for having government help pool economic risks is powerful. Designed properly, such risk pooling could provide all Americans with the financial security they need to survive and thrive in a highly uncertain economy, encouraging workers to accept the downs as well as the ups of a dynamic market.

Social insurance programs like Medicare and Social Security feature low administrative costs and broad public acceptance and popularity. And because of the public sector's formidable bargaining power and unmatched standard-setting capacity, public programs are also arguably better poised than private-sector benefits to control spending on health care and other social services in the future.

But, as the debates of 2009 and 2010 show, arguments like these are hardly universally accepted. For those who believe that risk protection interferes with the free play of competitive forces, for those who insist that government insurance merely coddles people who make the wrong choices, the only solution is to shift even more risk onto Americans' shoulders. As the following chapters show, the great debate of the twenty-first century will be whether the privatization of risk should be halted or hurried. And the outcome may well determine not just the future of U.S. social policy, but of the American model of capitalism as well.

Notes

1. See *Patient Protection and Affordable Care Act of 2010*, HR 3590, 111th Cong., 2d sess. (March 23, 2010).
2. *Dodd-Frank Wall Street Reform and Consumer Protection Act*, HR 4173, 111th Cong., 2d sess. (July 21, 2010), § 1001 et seq.; *CLASS Act*, HR 3590, 111th Cong., 2d sess., (March 23, 2010), §§ 8001–9002 (2010); *Health Care and Education Reconciliation Act*, HR 4872, 111th Cong., 2d sess. (March 30, 2010), §§ 2201–2213 (2010); *American Recovery and Reinvestment Act of 2009*, HR 1, 111th Cong., 1st sess. (February 17, 2009), § 2003.
3. Jacob S. Hacker, *The Great Risk Shift: The New Economic Insecurity and the Decline of the American Dream* (New York: Oxford University Press, 2006).
4. Jacob S. Hacker, *The Divided Welfare State: The Battle over Public and Private Social Benefits in the United States* (New York: Cambridge University Press, 2002).
5. Ibid.
6. Ibid., 186.
7. Paul Fronstin, "Tracking Health Insurance Coverage by Month: Trends in Employment-Based Coverage Among Workers, and Access to Coverage Among Uninsured Workers," *EBRI.org Notes* 31, no. 3 (2010): 8.
8. John H. Langbein, "Understanding the Death of the Private Pension Plan in the United States" (unpublished manuscript, Yale Law School, New Haven, CT, April 2006).
9. Economic Policy Institute, "Retirement Security Eroding: Private-Sector, Employer-Provided Pension Coverage, 1979–2009," in *The State of Working America* (Washington: Economic Policy Institute, 2011), http://www.stateofworkingamerica.org/charts/view/202.
10. Alicia H. Munnell and Annika Sundén, "401(k) Plans Are Still Coming Up Short," Center for Retirement Research at Boston College Issue in Brief 43 (2006): 1, http://crr.bc.edu/images/stories/Briefs/ib_43.pdf.
11. Ibid.
12. House Committee on Education and Labor, *The Effects of Recent Market Turmoil in Financial Markets on Retirement Security: Peter Orszag*, 110th Cong., 2d sess., October 7, 2008.
13. Paul Taylor et al., *Oldest Are Most Sheltered: Different Age Groups, Different Recessions* (Washington, DC: Pew Research Center Social and Demographic Trends Report, 2009), 2, http://pewsocialtrends.org/pubs/734/different-age-groups-different-recessions#pewresearch-jump.

14. Alicia H. Munnell, Anthony Webb, and Francesca Golub-Sass, "The National Retirement Risk Index: After the Crash," *Center for Retirement Research at Boston College Issue in Brief* 9–22 (2009): 4, fig. 2, http://crr.bc.edu/images/stories/Briefs/IB_9-22.pdf.

15. Ibid., 7, table 3.

16. Ibid., 4, table 1.

17. See Andrew Stettner and Sylvia A. Allegretto, "The Rising Stakes of Job Loss: Stubborn Long-Term Joblessness Amid Falling Unemployment Rates," *EPI & NELP Briefing Paper* 162 (2005): 8–9, http://www.policyarchive.org/handle/10207/bitstreams/8088.pdf.

18. Jared Bernstein and Karen Kornbluh, *Running Faster to Stay in Place: The Growth of Family Work Hours and Incomes,* Research Paper (Washington, DC: New America Foundation, 2005), 6, fig. 4, http://www.newamerica.net/publications/policy/running_faster_to_stay_in_place/.

19. Jerry Jacobs and Kathleen Gerson, *The Time Divide: Work, Family, and Gender Inequality* (Cambridge, MA: Harvard University Press, 2004), 59–79.

20. Jacob S. Hacker and Elisabeth Jacobs, "The Rising Instability of American Family Incomes, 1969–2004: Evidence from the Panel Study of Income Dynamics," *EPI Briefing Paper* 213 (2008): 2.

21. Ibid., 5, fig. A.

22. Ibid., 2.

23. Ibid., 8.

24. Ibid., 13.

25. Ibid.

26. Jacob S. Hacker et al., *Economic Security at Risk: Findings from the Rockefeller Economic Security Index* (New York: Rockefeller Foundation, 2010), http://economicsecurityindex.org/assets/Economic%20Security%20Index%20Full%20Report.pdf.

27. Hacker, *The Great Risk Shift*, 94.

28. Jennifer Wheary, Thomas A. Shapiro, and Tamara Draut, *By a Thread: The New Experience of America's Middle Class* (Waltham, MA: Institute on Assets and Social Policy, 2007), http://archive.demos.org/pub1514.cfm.

29. Christian E. Weller and Jessica Lynch, "Household Wealth in Freefall: Americans' Private Safety Net in Tatters" (Washington, DC: Center for American Progress, 2009), 9, http://www.americanprogress.org/issues/2009/04/pdf/wealth_declines.pdf.

30. The year 2005 was, of course, unusual because of the rush of filings before the 2005 bankruptcy bill took effect. The number in 2004, however, still exceeded 1.56 million, and it has been climbing back to pre-reform levels since 2006, despite the more stringent requirements that filers must now meet. In 2009, there were more than 1.4 million filings for personal bankruptcy and in 2010 the number rose to 1.5 million filing. See "Consumer Bankruptcy Filings for 2005 Are Highest on Record," Lundquist Consulting, Inc., press release, January 11, 2006, on the PRNewswire web site, http://www.prnewswire.com/news-releases/consumer-bankruptcy-filings-for-2005-are-highest-on-record-53405852.html; Ronald Mann, *National Bankruptcy Research Center 2010 Year-End Bankruptcy Filings Report* (Burlingame, CA: National Bankruptcy Research Center, 2011), http://www.nbkrc.com/Premium/NBKRC_Report_January_2011.pdf.

31. Elizabeth Warren and Amelia Warren Tyagi, *The Two-Income Trap: Why Middle-Class Mothers and Fathers Are Going Broke* (New York: Basic Books, 2003), 6.

32. Elizabeth Warren, "Financial Collapse and Class Status: Who Goes Bankrupt?," *Osgoode Hall Law Journal* 41, no. 1 (2003): 115–147.

33. Calculated from Peter J. Elmer and Steen A. Seeling, "The Rising Long-Term Trend of Single-Family Mortgage Foreclosure Rates" (Working paper 98–2, Division of Research and Statistics, Federal Deposit Insurance Corporation, Washington, DC, 1998).

34. Weller and Lynch, "Household Wealth in Freefall," 7, fig. 6.

35. Ruth Simon and James R. Hagerty, "House-Price Drops Leave More Underwater," *Wall Street Journal*, May 6, 2009.

36. Daniel Kahneman and Amos Tversky, "Prospect Theory: An Analysis of Decisions under Risk," *Econometrica* 47, no. 2 (1979): 263–291.

37. The Tarrance Group and Lake Snell Perry Mermin, *Battleground XXVII* (Washington, DC: The George Washington University, March 2005), http://www.lakeresearch.com/polls/pdf/bg305/charts.pdf.

38. Holly Bailey, "ABC News/Yahoo! News Poll: People Are Losing Faith in the American Dream," *Yahoo!NEWS*, September 21, 2010, http://news.yahoo.com/s/yblog_upshot/abc-newsyahoo-news-poll-people-are-losing-faith-in-the-american-dream.

39. Ronald Brownstein, "Financial Risk Cuts Deeper, Poll Finds," *National Journal*, April 25, 2009, http://www.nationaljournal.com/njmagazine/cs_20090425_8127.php.

40. American National Election Studies, *The American National Election Studies 2008–2009 Panel Study, Wave 15* (Ann Arbor, MI: Center for Political Studies, 2008–2009), www.electionstudies.org.

41. Rockefeller Foundation, *American Worker Survey: Complete Results* (New York: Rockefeller Foundation, 2007), http://www.rockefellerfoundation.org/news/publications/american-workers-survey-complete.

42. Calculations based on Rockefeller Foundation, "American Worker Survey."

43. Ibid.

44. Calculations based on Congressional Budget Office (CBO), *Average After Tax Income for All Households, by Household Income Category, 1979–2007* (Washington, DC: CBO, 2010), (http://www.cbo.gov/publications/collections/tax/2010/average_after-tax_income.pdf).

45. Calculations based on Congressional Budget Office, *Average Federal Taxes by Income Group.*

46. David Boaz, "Defining an Ownership Society," (Washington, DC: CATO Institute, 2004).

47. Carl Davis et al., *Who Pays? A Distributional Analysis of the Tax Systems in All 50 States* (Washington, DC: Institute on Taxation & Economic Policy, 2009), http://www.itepnet.org/whopays3.pdf

48. Ron Scherer, "Number of Long-Term Unemployed Hits Highest Rate since 1948," *Christian Science Monitor*, January 8, 2010.

49. David Moss, *When All Else Fails: Government as the Ultimate Risk Manager* (Cambridge, MA: Harvard University Press, 2002).

2

A Brief History of Risk
Management Policy

DAVID A. MOSS

Risk management has never been an entirely private affair in the United States. Public officials have frequently intervened to reduce some types of risk outright and to reallocate numerous others. These interventions have ranged from the enactment of limited liability laws in the early nineteenth century to the massive federal financial rescues that were undertaken in the early twenty-first.

In the wake of these most recent interventions, public risk management has achieved a new prominence in national policy discussions. From financial bailouts to extensions of unemployment insurance to the enactment and implementation of universal health care, government's role in managing risk has loomed large. How these debates have played out—and how they continue to play out—will undoubtedly have major implications for American workers and families and for the nation's economy going forward. Yet, equally certain, these future consequences will be rooted in our past: in the long history of public risk management in the United States and, no less important, in our *understanding* of that history. The purpose of this chapter is to inform that understanding.

Public Risk Management in Perspective

Risk management constitutes one of the fundamental ways in which government policymakers solve problems. Writing more than 2000 years ago, Cicero posited that the primary purpose of the state was to *reduce* risk by securing private property rights. "[N]othing is to be maintained in a state with such care as the civil law," he counseled. "In truth, if this is taken away, there is no possibility of any one feeling certain what is his own property or what belongs to another. . . ."[1] Eminent political philosophers regularly returned to this interpretation in later years, including Thomas Hobbes in the seventeenth century and John Stuart Mill in the nineteenth. Poorly enforced property rights, Mill explained, "means uncertainty whether they who sow shall reap, whether they who produce shall consume, and they who spare to-day shall enjoy tomorrow."[2]

In recent times, a growing body of scholarship has looked beyond property rights, exploring how the regulatory apparatus of the state has been used to *reduce* a broad array of risks that threaten personal health and safety. Policymakers can reduce risk directly by prohibiting or otherwise constraining activities that are themselves hazardous, such as driving an automobile over 65 miles per hour or handling a deadly toxin on the job. According to Supreme Court Justice Stephen Breyer, "Regulators try to make our lives safer by eliminating or reducing our exposure to certain potentially risky substances or even persons (unsafe food additives, dangerous chemicals, unqualified doctors)."[3] Economists and lawyers, including Justice Breyer himself, now commonly refer to this sort of policy as "risk regulation."[4]

But the fact is that risk-reduction strategies, whether in the form of regulation or enforceable property rights, are not the government's only means for managing risk. Policymakers have also frequently sought to reallocate risk, either by *shifting* it from one party to another or by *spreading* it across a large number of people. Risk management policy, in other words, encompasses all three of the classic risk management tools: shifting, spreading, and reduction. This simple insight allows us to bring a large number of seemingly disparate public policies under a common analytic roof.

A Short History of Risk Management Policy in the United States

Over the past few decades, risk management policies have been subjected to a steady barrage of attacks, particularly in the popular press. Countless critics have charged that government attempts to shield citizens from adverse risks are turning America into a nation of ninnies, devoid of courage and personal responsibility. One writer went so far as to complain in the *New Republic* in 1989 that the "desire for a risk-free society is one of the most debilitating influences in America today."[5]

Budget hawks, meanwhile, continually remind us just how expensive these policies can be. The major social insurance programs—Social Security, Medicare, unemployment insurance, and workers' compensation—alone cost over a trillion dollars per year.[6] Even before the 2007–2009 financial crisis, the federal government was potentially on the hook for trillions more in federal financial guarantees. By the fourth quarter of 2006, the Federal Deposit Insurance Corporation, by itself, guaranteed over $4 trillion in deposits, and it did so with the full faith and credit of the U.S. government.[7] Maximum potential liabilities stemming from the federal government's emergency response to the financial crisis were estimated to have reached nearly $10 trillion by July 31, 2009.[8] Although the financial bailout quickly became the object of intense criticism, concerns about federal guarantees were hardly new. As early as 1991, President George H. W. Bush's budget director, Richard Darman, focused particularly on the adverse fiscal implications, warning that each of the existing federal liabilities was "like a hidden Pac-Man, waiting to spring forward and consume another line of resource dots in the budget maze."[9] More recent critiques have highlighted not only the large potential fiscal burden of open-ended guarantees, but also some very troubling incentive effects, including the problem of moral hazard.

While such criticisms certainly have merit (and will be considered in greater detail below), they sometimes create the impression that public risk management is a luxury we cannot afford—the product of overindulgent and weak-willed policymakers who fail to put sufficient faith in private markets. Attacking the U.S.-led bailouts of ailing Asian economies in 1997 and 1998, an op-ed in the *New York Times* announced that the nation's leaders were "emotionally incapable of accepting capitalism's inherent risks."[10] The truth is, however, that markets themselves have not always proved capable of effectively managing capitalism's inherent risks on their own.

Some years ago, the Nobel economist Kenneth Arrow explained that missing and incomplete markets for risk represented one of capitalism's greatest failings. "Perhaps one of the strongest criticisms of a system of freely competitive markets," he wrote in a 1970 article with Robert Lind, "is that the inherent difficulty in establishing certain markets for insurance brings about a suboptimal allocation of resources."[11] Elsewhere Arrow suggested that it was up to the government to take up the slack, to "undertake insurance in those cases where [a private market for insurance], for whatever reason, has failed to emerge."[12]

A close look at American history reveals that state and federal policymakers had been heeding Arrow's "advice" long before he gave it, at least since the dawn of the Republic. Yet most accounts in the popular press foster the opposite impression, suggesting that government "meddling" with private-sector risks is of recent vintage. Articles on the subject often hearken back to some earlier time, when America was full of vigor and individualistic spirit, when every citizen faced his own risks with a sense of stoic independence and pride, and when government consistently refused to interfere with the private allocation of risk. But such a time never really existed. While public involvement in risk management changed and expanded over the years, it is impossible to locate a moment in history when policymakers were not wrestling with a variety of challenging risks. Indeed, to understand public risk management in the United States today, we must first come to terms with this long, revealing, and mostly forgotten history.

PHASE I: SECURITY FOR BUSINESS (TO 1900)

Broadly speaking, American risk management policy has passed through three phases, the first of which was already underway when the Constitution was ratified in 1788. In the late eighteenth and early nineteenth centuries, when the United States was itself a developing country, policymakers focused particular attention on risks that were thought to undermine trade and investment. Contrary to today's conventional wisdom, the historical record strongly suggests that well-conceived risk management policies can foster economic development and growth. Although risk taking lies at the heart of capitalism, the experience of this early period indicates that certain types of risk may be dysfunctional in the context of a developing country.

A good example involves the problem of unlimited liability for passive investors. Before Americans began to develop a significant manufacturing base in the early nineteenth century, the vast majority of investors were active investors—meaning that they owned and managed their own companies and farms. But the emergence of large-scale enterprises (including some textile factories and other manufacturing operations) required the participation of a new type of investor, the passive investor, who would buy shares but would not be directly involved in managing the firm. Passive investors emerged as an increasingly important source of capital as the nation industrialized.

The problem in the early nineteenth century was that many passive investors were reluctant to part with their savings so long as they faced unlimited liability. If a firm collapsed, its bankers and other creditors were entitled to seize the personal assets of any investor, whether active or passive. This meant that every single investor risked personal financial ruin—and potentially even incarceration in a debtor's prison—if his investment went bad. Such extreme liability seems almost unimaginable today, but it was the norm 200 years ago.

Although active investors had long been willing to tolerate unlimited liability, economic policymakers soon learned that passive investors were less adventurous. "The business of manufactures requires, for its successful prosecution, the employment of large capital," Governor Levi Lincoln of Massachusetts explained in 1830. "The contributions of many individuals are necessary to the creation of the fund. But men, with the admonitions they have had, will no longer consent, for the chance of profit upon a share in a concern, to put their whole property at the hazard of circumstances, which they neither can foresee, nor over which they can have any control." Unless limitations on shareholder liability were promptly established, the governor warned, "the manufacturing interest, to a great extent, must be abandoned in Massachusetts."[13] Without the enactment of limited liability laws in the first half of the nineteenth century, the development of American manufacturing might well have been impeded.

Significantly, limited liability laws required no new taxes or spending, nor did they create any new regulatory bodies. All they did was shift a portion of corporate default risk from shareholders to creditors. Several students of the subject have astutely characterized limited liability as "an implicit, creditor-provided form of insurance of the risks of business failure."[14] Remarkably, this one simple risk-shifting device was likely responsible for preserving and accelerating industrialization, particularly heavy industrialization, which came later in the nineteenth century and required far larger pools of capital. "Insofar as one associates economic progress with economies of scale," the economist Sir John Hicks wrote, "it must be regarded as a major achievement of limited liability that it has made much of our economic progress possible."[15]

Although exceedingly important, passive-investment risk was not an isolated problem in the nineteenth century. The emerging American economy was full of energy but also teeming with risks that threatened to undermine growth. Even money was far from secure as a means of payment, forcing policymakers to engage in a perennial battle to solve the problem of money risk. Senator Robert Strange of North Carolina complained in 1840 that "the paper system [of privately issued money, or bank notes] has drawn everyone irresistibly into its vortex." It had, he said, "made itself the precarious basis of all employments; it had undermined the firmest foundations, so that no man is now secure against those unforeseen accidents which were once peculiar to the trader."[16]

While policymakers recognized the need to manage a wide range of business risks, from bankruptcy to bank runs, most also understood that they operated on a razor's edge. This was particularly true in the case of money risk. Had government officials clamped down too hard on the banks (which were the primary suppliers of the nation's paper money supply at the time), they would have strangled the burgeoning economy, depriving it of vital credit and liquidity. And yet to leave this risk entirely to the market threatened to submerge the whole business community in a frenzy of speculation and fear. Finding an appropriate balance was essential.

By the end of the nineteenth century, American lawmakers had enacted a wide range of risk management policies—all intended to promote trade and investment. Most notable among them were limited liability, early banking regulation, bankruptcy law, a fixed exchange rate, and (most fundamental of all) the predictable enforcement of property rights. These policies are relevant now not only because they laid the institutional foundations of America's economic success, but also because today's developing economies face many of the very same problems. Managing economically dysfunctional risks without stopping up the wellspring of economic progress is one of the most difficult challenges facing policymakers in every developing country. Nineteenth-century America, struggling to develop its own economy, demonstrated at least one successful path through a minefield of risks on the way to industrial affluence.

PHASE II: SECURITY FOR WORKERS (1900–1960)

The dawn of the twentieth century brought an entirely new set of risks to the attention of U.S. policymakers. Industrial workers, who had once comprised but a tiny fraction of the nation's labor force, had by now grown into a large and potentially powerful social group. Although wages had increased substantially in the late nineteenth century, most workers' financial positions remained precarious. In the new industrial economy, the loss of a job—whether because of a workplace injury, illness, old age, or an economic downturn—could easily land a worker and his family in poverty. Extensive family support networks had helped to spread individual risks in older agricultural communities, but rapid urbanization left these traditional safety nets in tatters.

Progressive reformers worried that widespread worker insecurity could provoke unrest and even rebellion. John R. Commons, an academic economist and the intellectual father of the nation's Social Security system, warned ominously that "unless the capitalistic system begins to take care of the security of the laborer, begins to make jobs as secure as investments, then there is a serious question . . . whether that system can continue to exist."[17]

The focus of risk management policy thus shifted from business to labor in the early twentieth century. Workers' compensation laws, which mandated on-the-job accident insurance, were enacted in just about every state between 1911 and 1920; and compulsory unemployment and old-age insurance were introduced a generation later as part of the Social Security Act of 1935.

The man who signed the Social Security bill into law, President Franklin Roosevelt, fully appreciated the transformation that his signature helped set in motion. "Beginning in the nineteenth century," he observed in a speech about Social Security, "the United States passed protective laws designed, in the main, to give security to property owners, to industrialists, to merchants and to bankers." This was the first phase of risk management policy in the United States.

But while business-oriented policies had been sufficient in the nineteenth century, FDR insisted that the growing complexity of industrial society in the early twentieth century made it "increasingly difficult for individuals to build their own security single-handed." Government, he concluded, "must now step in and help them lay the foundation stones, just as Government in the past has helped lay the foundation of business and industry. We must face the fact that in this country we have a rich man's security and a poor man's security and that the Government owes equal obligations to both."[18] Phase II of American risk management policy was definitively underway.

At the time, many critics inveighed against the associated expansion of government authority, warning that these new social programs would choke off the dynamic spirit of American capitalism. In 1916, Ralph Easley of the powerful National Civic Federation dismissed social insurance as "largely saturated with the virus of socialism."[19] Two years later, the president of a New York trade association characterized compulsory insurance as an "absolutely un-American and paternalistic" device that would transform American workers into "spineless creatures dominated by the will of an autocracy."[20] Similarly, in 1935, one congressman bitterly attacked the Social Security bill as "simply one more step toward sovietizing our distinctive American institutions, devitalizing the self-reliance and enterprise of our people, and mortgaging our future. . . ."[21]

Despite such rhetoric, social insurance programs proved popular with the electorate—perhaps because the government appeared to be succeeding where the private market had failed. Workers' compensation and unemployment insurance grew substantially over the years, and Social Security (once so reviled by critics) became a political sacred cow, as did its younger sibling, the 1965 Medicare program. The one exception was compulsory health insurance, which was only just recently enacted, nearly one hundred years after the first attempts to introduce it in America. Still, by the dawn of the twenty-first century, Americans spent considerably more on social insurance each year than on any other budget item, including national defense. The roots had been laid in the early twentieth century, as worker security emerged as a major preoccupation of American public policy, at both the state and federal levels.

PHASE III: SECURITY FOR ALL (SINCE 1960)

The shift in emphasis from business risk to worker risk in the transition from Phase I to Phase II exerted a profound effect on the American economy and on American society. Not only did it utterly transform the nation's social welfare policy, but, for the first time, it brought a great many citizens face-to-face with the risk management function of government. Within a short period of time, nearly every member of the labor force came under the nation's social insurance umbrella. This ultimately had the effect of broadening the potential scope of new risk management policies. If the government was going to protect business people and workers against a variety of hazards, why shouldn't it also protect consumers and home owners and countless other groups? This was the question that, in the 1960s, opened a third phase of public risk management in the United States.

Risk management policy expanded suddenly and dramatically under Phase III. Federal disaster policy is a good case in point. Whereas federal disaster relief covered just 6 percent of uninsured losses from a major catastrophe in 1955, the figure had surged to nearly 50 percent by 1972.[22] Meanwhile, state and federal policymakers had launched an all-out assault on personal risk. Health, safety, and environmental regulations multiplied rapidly, and lawmakers created a broad new array of federal insurance programs and financial guarantees. Congress even established liability caps on credit cards—a sort of limited liability for consumers. First enacted in 1970, these rules required credit card issuers to act as implicit insurers, guaranteeing all cardholders against losses stemming from unauthorized use of their cards.[23]

Not to be outdone, the nation's judges turned product liability law upside down, converting it from a producer promotion program into a powerful consumer protection device. As successful product liability suits became more and more common, particularly over the 1960s and 1970s, manufacturers discovered that the doctrine of *caveat emptor* had been completely inverted. Now producers and sellers, rather than buyers, had to "beware" every time a good was sold, subject as they were to the new standard of strict liability.

One of the architects of the new liability regime, Justice Roger Traynor, acknowledged as early as 1965 that America's risk management policy was maturing along with the economy itself. "We have come a long way," he explained in a law review article. "The great expansion of a manufacturer's liability for negligence . . . marks the transition from an industrial revolution to a settled industrial society."[24] This shift was clearly reflected in the simultaneous transformations of statutory and common law approaches to risk management. Phase III—public risk management for all citizens—had arrived.

Risk Management as a Function of Government

As this brief journey back in time reveals, public risk management has deep historical roots. These roots, moreover, are grounded in actual political debates and decisions that provide powerful insights about government's strengths—and weaknesses—as a risk manager. Broadly speaking, the findings that emerge from this historical survey can be summarized in three basic arguments.

RISK MANAGEMENT AS A FLEXIBLE POLICY TOOL

The historical record reveals risk management to have been an exceedingly flexible policy tool, used to address a wide range of social problems and to serve a diverse set of social objectives. During the nineteenth century, lawmakers adopted risk management policies like limited liability and bankruptcy law to promote business development and economic growth (Phase I). But as the nineteenth century gave way to the twentieth, new policymakers increasingly targeted risks facing the nation's workers through the enactment of workers' compensation laws and other forms of social insurance (Phase II). Eventually, during the second half of the twentieth century, judges and legislators changed focus yet again, fashioning risk management policies—such as strict manufacturer liability and expansive federal disaster relief—designed to safeguard the consumer and, indeed, the citizen at large (Phase III). Reflecting a profound transformation in public priorities since the founding of the Republic, these three phases testify to the remarkable plasticity— and endurance—of risk management policy as a mode of social problem solving.

EARLY ECONOMIC SOPHISTICATION ABOUT THE
LOGIC AND LIMITS OF PUBLIC RISK MANAGEMENT

The historical record also reveals a remarkable degree of economic sophistication in the way in which leading policymakers thought about risk and the government's role in managing it. One manifestation of this was that many lawmakers— over both the nineteenth and twentieth centuries—proved suspicious of the market's capacity to solve certain risk-related problems on its own. The idea that markets for risk are far from perfect is familiar to modern economists. What the history of risk management policy demonstrates is that many public officials and social reformers were implicitly aware of this problem from a very early time and that they devoted considerable energy to addressing it.

What this history also indicates is that policymakers looked well beyond conventional market failures, such as adverse selection and moral hazard, in explaining risk-related failures in the private sector. To be sure, these concerns were often front and center. Yet policymakers also justified public risk management on the basis of other problems, including systemic threats (such as the risk of bank runs), risk-based externalities (such as pollution that can cause ill health), and—most intriguing of all—prevalent cognitive biases (such as optimistic bias), which can make it difficult for individuals to assess and respond to risks rationally on their own.

As an illustration of the focus on cognitive bias, some of the key proponents of workers' compensation laws in the early twentieth century claimed that workers failed to negotiate compensating wage differentials for hazardous work because they were overly optimistic about their own chances of escaping injury. As the economist and social reformer Henry Seager put it in 1907, each worker "thinks of himself as having a charmed life."[25] Modern behavioral economists would likely be quite comfortable with Seager's early assessment of private weaknesses in the management of accident risk.

Importantly, these same sorts of considerations implicated government's own capacity as a risk manager. Throughout U.S. history, critics consistently argued that government intervention would make matters worse, severely distorting incentives and inviting personal irresponsibility. They claimed that the availability of a discharge in bankruptcy, for example, would induce debtors to engage in reckless risk taking. Proponents countered these arguments by emphasizing the power of risk monitoring. In the case of bankruptcy discharge, a number of congressmen insisted that dangerous excess would be unlikely since creditors themselves could be expected to keep a close eye on those to whom they lent money.

The case of federal deposit insurance is similarly illustrative. Critics charged in 1933 that a government guarantee on bank liabilities would invite wild and excessive risk taking in the banking sector, since depositors would no longer have any interest in trying to avoid the riskiest banks. The authors of the enabling legislation, however, were careful to create not only federal deposit insurance but also far-reaching federal bank supervision, believing that the latter would be both necessary and sufficient to control the resulting moral hazard. Contrary to the critics' predictions, bank failures fell sharply after 1933, virtually disappearing through the postwar period. It was only when federal policymakers simultaneously deregulated depository institutions *and* increased their insurance coverage beginning in the early 1980s that failures returned on a large scale. In fact, the deregulation of federally insured depository institutions proved to be a recipe for disaster, inviting precisely the sort of wild risk taking that many critics had predicted back in the 1930s and ultimately giving rise (or at least contributing) to the so-called savings and loan crisis.

The two sides of this banking story—the virtual disappearance of bank failures after the introduction of federal deposit insurance and effective bank regulation in 1933, and the dramatic return of bank failures after the start of financial deregulation in the early 1980s—should serve as a reminder both of the constructive power of public risk management and of the absolute necessity of combining public risk management with effective mechanisms for monitoring and controlling moral hazard. In fact, this may be the single most important lesson to emerge from the history of risk management policies in the United States: namely, that these policies frequently work well when there is an associated mechanism for controlling moral hazard, but that they work far less well (and are potentially dangerous) when such a mechanism is missing.

THE SPECIAL APPEAL OF PUBLIC RISK MANAGEMENT IN THE UNITED STATES

Finally, the historical record helps us understand why public intervention in markets for risk was so prevalent in the United States, despite the country's reputation as a bastion of laissez-faire. American historians have long debated whether the nation's reputed commitment to free market principles was in fact consistent with its record of government involvement in the economy. The history of public risk management offers a valuable new perspective on this question, suggesting at least one means by which Americans reconciled their philosophical hostility to government (and their faith in the market) with their practical inclination to use the state to address social problems. Apparently willing to suspend their belief in laissez-faire when addressing certain types of risk, many policy advocates took comfort in their ability to cast risk-reallocation policies—from limited liability to social insurance—within the familiar rhetoric of contract and markets. In the case of Social Security, for example, New Dealers went to great lengths to emphasize the analogy to private insurance, believing that it would make the plan "acceptable to a society which was dominated by business ethics and which stressed individual economic responsibility."[26]

Indeed, public risk management appears to have constituted a particularly attractive form of statism for American anti-statists. Americans have long demonstrated a remarkable willingness to allow government intervention in the face of major risk-related problems, as if certain risks simply fell outside the bounds of laissez-faire. One reason for this may be that risk-reallocation policies (though not risk-reduction policies) tended to require relatively little in the way of invasive bureaucracy and could easily be cast in the rhetoric of contract. Risk-shifting policies like limited liability and bankruptcy law, for example, required no bureaucracy other than the courts themselves. The same can be said of product liability law. Even social insurance programs, which currently absorb about 8 percent of U.S. gross domestic product (GDP),[27] have proved remarkably lean from an administrative standpoint. Under Social Security, the ratio of administrative costs to total expenditures was just 6 percent in 1950, and it had fallen to an astoundingly small 0.6 percent by 2008.[28]

Of course, every government in the world has utilized a wide range of risk management policies, and most of the industrialized nations have witnessed policy shifts roughly analogous to America's three phases. Yet the United States does seem to stand out as different in several respects. In particular, more activist states elsewhere in the world have generally chosen to integrate risk management tools into broader and more aggressive policy undertakings, including programs of industrial targeting, state-sponsored capital mobilization, and far-reaching income redistribution. Such undertakings have remained comparatively rare in the United States.[29] The United States also began adopting social insurance considerably later than most of its counterparts in Europe, and its programs, once enacted, tended to involve smaller benefits, more reliance on the private sector, little if any financing out of general revenues, and (in many, but not all, cases) less of a redistributive tilt.[30]

Whatever the special role for risk management in American public policy, there is no denying that public risk management has come to play a very prominent role in American life, in all its various forms. Lawmakers have employed their power to reallocate and reduce risk to serve a wide range of social objectives, which have steadily evolved over time. Relative to their counterparts in other countries, they have shown considerable deference to the market, frequently choosing risk management policies that either augmented or simply mimicked standard contractual relationships. Relative to their reputation as champions of laissez-faire, however, they have intervened in private market transactions both often and easily, convinced that private mechanisms for allocating risk were far from perfect.

Public Risk Management at the Dawn of the Twenty-first Century

The long-standing American tension between skepticism of government on the one hand and pragmatic faith in power of government to manage major risks on the other reached a new level of intensity in the first decade of the twenty-first century. In fact, it is difficult to think of any time in American history when federal policymakers were more active in managing major risks, from natural disasters to the costs of medical care.

CRISIS MANAGEMENT

The most recent chapter of American risk management begins with a series of unprecedented crises. In the face of four massive catastrophes—the terrorist attacks of 9/11 (2001), Hurricane Katrina (2005), the financial crisis of 2007–2009, and the massive BP Gulf Coast oil spill (2010)—the federal government's role as the nation's ultimate risk manager was repeatedly confirmed, and in truly dramatic fashion. Many policymakers who had reflexively criticized "government bailouts" (and the associated moral hazard) before taking power soon found themselves overseeing some of the largest rescues in American history, from the airline bailout and the victims' compensation fund after the 9/11 attacks to the multitrillion-dollar intervention in 2008 and 2009 to save the nation's financial system from collapse. Yet with each new rescue, and particularly in the wake of the Wall Street bailout, criticism of the government's role as risk manager grew ever louder, ultimately reaching a fever pitch. The assertion that "no institution should be too big to fail" became a common refrain, and federal policymakers who had helped rescue the nation's financial system were regularly accused of having subverted the free market and, indeed, of being "socialists."

Such concerns are understandable, of course, especially after many of the biggest names on Wall Street were rescued with taxpayer funds during the recent financial crisis. But there is also a danger of self-delusion in the rush to criticize the government's response to major calamities. Once a crisis has passed, it is all too easy for critics to insist that policymakers should never have gotten involved in the first place and that government should simply stay out next time around. Not surprisingly, things often look different in the heat of a crisis.

In the fall of 2008, there was a real possibility that the entire financial system could collapse in the face of severe systemic turmoil. Without federal intervention, it is a near certainty that Bear Stearns, Fannie Mae, Freddie Mac, Lehman Brothers, AIG, and Citigroup all would have failed, most of them in fairly rapid succession. Could the rest of the financial system—and the broader American economy—have withstood such a shock? Although we can never be sure of the answer, policymakers with both the authority and the responsibility for economic policy, from Republican and Democratic administrations alike, were clearly unwilling to take the risk of inaction.

Looking ahead, the critical question is whether policymakers will decide to stay out—and not intervene—the next time there is a major disaster, terrorist attack, or financial crisis. Based on recent history, the prospect seems highly unlikely. As a result, most people (and most markets) will probably expect government bailouts and rescues in the future. The problem is not simply that this expectation will create moral hazard. As we have seen, moral hazard can generally be managed, or at least limited, through effective monitoring and regulation. The bigger problem is that if Americans reasonably expect bailouts in times of crisis, then excessive deference to the market in normal times could end up proving extremely costly, actually increasing the likelihood of large losses, by leaving moral hazard uncontrolled. This is perhaps the central challenge facing policymakers as they grapple with how best to manage the risk of major crises going forward.[31]

HEALTH CARE

In addition to unprecedented federal exercises in crisis management, the first decade of the twenty-first century also saw the largest expansion of social insurance in the United States since the enactment of Social Security in 1935. Although President Barack Obama's health care reform (the Patient Protection and Affordable Care Act of 2010) only barely made it through Congress, it did get through, and represented yet another major federal foray into public risk management. It also proved every bit as controversial as the financial bailouts of 2008 and 2009, leading critics once again to attack the underlying expansion of federal authority as "socialist" and even "totalitarian." Not surprisingly, the fight continued even after passage, with opponents pledging to eviscerate the measure in the courts and to launch a campaign for repeal in Congress.

Assuming that health care reform does survive, many of the critical policy questions will relate once again to basic principles of risk management. For example, how will policymakers deal with "adverse selection"—the tendency for those with the greatest risks, and thus most in need of insurance, to seek it out, raising the costs of coverage—now that insurers are required to accept all comers, irrespective of "preexisting conditions"? And how will they avoid the "moral hazard" of spiraling costs once coverage is assured? In 2010, President Obama and his allies in Congress achieved something that had eluded health care reformers for nearly a century. The challenge now is not to lose sight of the essential goal—namely, to help cover a set of risks that many Americans have had trouble covering on their own. Elementary risk management principles will loom large in determining the success or failure of this goal over the long term.

TOWARD THE FUTURE

If history is a guide, the furor over federal financial bailouts and health care reform will not mark the end of new experiments in public risk management. On the contrary, we are likely to see new and creative strategies employed in the future, just as we have in the past.

As an example, imagine if there were a way to help young people manage the very considerable risks associated with financing a college education. The economist Milton Friedman suggested back in the 1950s that borrowing for college is risky because the borrower cannot be sure what his or her income will be after graduating. In fact, a student loan market barely existed back then because lenders faced the same uncertainty about repayment and, as Friedman observed, there was no way to collateralize the transaction because a graduate's human capital (i.e., future earning power) could not be seized in the event of default. Student lending began in earnest once the federal government started guaranteeing lenders in the 1960s. Although this federal guarantee jump-started the market for student loans, it nonetheless left students in a precarious position—able to borrow, but unable to be sure that their future incomes would be sufficient to keep up with interest and principal payments. Lenders were now protected in case of default, but borrowers were not.

One might think it would be impossible to protect student borrowers without inviting enormous moral hazard, in the form of reckless borrowing and pervasive defaults on student loans. Yet Friedman actually suggested a simple means by which government could do this: lending directly to students and requiring them to repay not a fixed interest rate but rather a fixed percentage of their future income. Graduates who earned little after finishing college would pay little, and graduates who earned more would pay more. All one would have to do is set the percentage such that the income of the average college graduate would be sufficient to repay the loan. In fact, the economist James Tobin proposed a very similar idea and even attempted to implement it at Yale University, his home institution. Although the Yale program proved difficult to administer, one of Tobin's students would later bring the idea to Australia and show that income-contingent lending could work at the national level, so long as the national tax authority was put in charge of collection.

Here in the United States, the federal government has already taken steps in this direction, allowing income-based repayment of student loans in certain cases. Whether federal officials will ultimately go further—introducing a full-fledged income-contingent loan program for American students—remains unclear. But the idea of allowing students to invest in their human capital with more limited downside risk—a sort of limited liability educational investment—certainly deserves a closer look; and the fact that the idea was originally endorsed and promoted by both Milton Friedman and James Tobin should only add to its appeal.[32]

All of this is not to say that income-contingent lending will necessarily represent the next wave of American risk management policy. Rather, it is simply to suggest that public risk management is a powerful tool that will continue to be harnessed in new ways as social needs and priorities evolve. As with any tool, there are significant dangers if it is used improperly. The challenge is to develop policies that are consistent with the best principles of risk management, while studiously avoiding those that are not. Remarkably, over the nation's history, this challenge has been met again and again—not every time, but frequently enough to suggest that the American system of governance is ultimately capable of finding its way through the economic and political thicket, particularly when guided by the map of historical experience.

Notes

1. Marcus Tullius Cicero, "The Oration of M.T. Cicero in Behalf of Aulus Caecina," chap. 25, in *The Orations of Marcus Tullius Cicero*, trans. C. D. Yonge, vol. 2 (London: George Bell and Sons, 1891), 63. See also Neal Wood, *Cicero's Social and Political Thought* (Berkeley: University of California Press, 1988), esp. chaps. 6 and 7.

2. John Stuart Mill, *Principles of Political Economy* (London: Longmans, Green, Reader, and Dyer, 1871), bk. V, chap. 8, 531. See also Thomas Hobbes, *Leviathan* (New York: Collier Books, 1962), esp. chap. 24, par. 5, 185–186.

3. Stephen Breyer, *Breaking the Vicious Circle: Toward Effective Risk Regulation* (Cambridge, MA: Harvard University Press, 1993), 3.

4. On risk regulation, see W. Kip Viscusi, *Risk by Choice: Regulating Health and Safety in the Workplace* (Cambridge, MA: Harvard University Press, 1983); W. Kip Viscusi, *Fatal Tradeoffs: Public and Private Responsibilities for Risk* (New York: Oxford University Press, 1992); Robert A. Pollak, "Regulating Risks," *Journal of Economic Literature* 33, no. 1 (March 1995): 179–191; Walter Y. Oi, "Safety at What Price?," *American Economic Review* 85, no. 2 (May 1995): 67–71.

5. Henry Fairlie, "Fear of Living: America's Morbid Aversion to Risk," *New Republic*, January 23, 1989, 14.

6. See esp. U.S. Census Bureau, *The 2010 Statistical Abstract*, table 528, http://www.census.gov/compendia/statab/2010edition.html.

7. FDIC, *Quarterly Banking Profile, Fourth Quarter 2006*, 17, table I-B, http://www2.fdic.gov/qbp/2006dec/qbp.pdf.

8. David Moss and Cole Bolton, "Fighting a Dangerous Financial Fire: The Federal Response to the Crisis of 2007–2009," (draft, March 25, 2010), 26, exhibit 2. See also Cong. Budget Office, "The Budget and Economic Outlook: An Update," August 2009, appendix B, http://www.cbo.gov/ftpdocs/105xx/doc10521/08-25-BudgetUpdate.pdf; Gene L. Dodaro, testimony before the U.S. Senate Committee on Banking, Housing, and Urban Affairs, *Troubled Asset Relief Program: Status of Efforts to Address Transparency and Accountability Issues*, 111th Cong, 1st sess., September 24, 2009, http://www.gao.gov/new.items/d091048t.pdf; Robert A. Sunshine, testimony before the U.S. Senate Committee on the Budget, *The Budget and Economic Outlook: Fiscal Years 2009 to 2019*, appendix A, 111th Cong., 1st sess., January 8, 2009, http://www.cbo.gov/ftpdocs/99xx/doc9958/01-08-Outlook_Testimony.pdf.

9. "The 1991 Budget: Excerpts from Darman; Darman Conducts a Tour of Wonderland: The Federal Budget," *New York Times*, January 27, 1990, http://www.nytimes.com/1990/01/27/us/1991-budget-excerpts-darman-darman-conducts-tour-wonderland-federal-budget.html. See also Yair Aharoni, *No-Risk Society* (Chatham, NJ: Chatham House, 1981), 4–6, 35–36, 98–107.

10. Gerald Celente, "Capitalism for Cowards," *New York Times*, October 16, 1998.

11. Kenneth J. Arrow and Robert C. Lind, "Uncertainty and the Evaluation of Public Investment Decisions," *American Economic Review* 60, no. 3 (June 1970): 374.

12. Kenneth J. Arrow, "Uncertainty and the Welfare Economics of Medical Care," *American Economic Review* 53, no. 5 (December 1963): 961.

13. "Governor's Message," *Resolves of the General Court of the Commonwealth of Massachusetts*, January 6–March 13, 1830, 229–230.

14. Paul Halpern, Michael Trebilcock, and Stuart Turnbull, "An Economic Analysis of Limited Liability in Corporation Law," *University of Toronto Law Journal* 20 (1980): 126.

15. John Hicks, "Limited Liability: The Pros and Cons," in *Limited Liability and the Corporation*, ed. Tony Orhnial (London: Croom Helm, 1982), 11, 12.

16. Cong. Globe Appendix, 26th Cong., 1st sess., 544 (1840).

17. John R. Commons, *Industrial Relations*, address at the International Convention of Government Labor Officials, Park Hotel, Madison, WI, June 3, 1919, in *Microfilm Edition of the John R. Commons Papers*, fr. 818, 4.

18. Franklin D. Roosevelt, "A Social Security Program Must Include All Those Who Need Its Protection," August 15, 1938, Radio Address on the Third Anniversary of the Social Security Act, transcript, http://www.ssa.gov/history/fdrstmts.html.

19. Ralph Easley to Olga Halsey, April 25, 1916, *The Microfilm Edition of the Papers of the American Association for Labor Legislation, 1905–1945* (Glen Rock, NJ: Microfilming Corporation of America, 1973) [hereafter referred to as the AALL Papers], Reel #17.

20. Mark A. Daly circular letter "To All Members," February 23, 1918, AALL Papers, Reel #18.

21. 79 Cong. Rec. 5583 (1935).

22. David A. Moss, "Courting Disaster: The Transformation of Federal Disaster Policy Since 1803," in *The Financing of Catastrophe Risk*, ed. Kenneth A. Froot (Chicago: University of Chicago Press, 1999), 327–328.

23. See, e.g., *Hearings Before the Subcommittee on Financial Institutions of the Committee on Banking and Currency*, 91st Cong., 1st sess. (1969) (statement of William Proxmire).

24. Roger J. Traynor, "The Ways and Meanings of Defective Products and Strict Liability," *Tennessee Law Review* 32, no. 3 (Spring 1965): 363.

25. Henry R. Seager, "Outline of a Program of Social Reform" in *Labor and Other Economic Essays*, ed. Charles A. Gulick, Jr. (NY: Harper and Brothers, 1931), 82–83.

26. Eveline M. Burns, "Social Insurance in Evolution," *American Economic Review* 34, no. 1 (March 1944): 199. A 1940 pamphlet put out by the Social Security Board reassured workers that "[y]our Social Security Card . . . shows that you have an insurance account with the U.S. Government—Federal old-age and survivors insurance." Social Security was a "national insurance plan," the pamphlet explained, and "taxes are like the premium on any other kind of insurance . . ." Quoted in Jerry R. Cates, *Insuring Inequality: Administrative Leadership in Social Security, 1935–54* (Ann Arbor: University of Michigan Press, 1983), 33. Three years earlier, another pamphlet had emphasized that unemployment compensation was "like other types of insurance," that it was "not charity or relief but a means of preventing need for relief." *Why Social Security?* (Washington: Social Security Board, 1937), http://www.ssa.gov/history/whybook.html. See also Herbert McClosky and John Zaller, *The American Ethos: Public Attitudes toward Capitalism and Democracy* (Cambridge, MA: Harvard University Press, 1984), 275–277; Robert Y. Shapiro and John T. Young, "Public Opinion and the Welfare State: The United States in Comparative Perspective," *Political Science Quarterly* 104, no. 1 (Spring 1989): 71.

27. *Economic Report of the President 2010* (Washington: GPO, 2010), tables B1 and B80; *U.S. Statistical Abstract*, table 528 (see n. 6).

28. Social Security Board, *Annual Statistical Supplement to the Social Security Bulletin, (2009)*, table 4.A1, http://www.ssa.gov/policy/docs/statcomps/supplement/2009/4a.pdf.

29. See Moss, *When All Else Fails*, esp. pp. 321–324.

30. As one of the main authors of the Social Security Act, Edwin E. Witte, later explained, "Only to a very minor degree does [the old-age insurance program] modify the distribution of wealth and it does not alter at all the fundamentals of our capitalistic and individualistic economy. Nor does it relieve the individual of primary responsibility for his own support and that of his dependents. . . ." Quoted in Cates, *Insuring Inequality*, 24 (see n. 26). An important reason for this, which Witte alluded to in 1955, was that Social Security established "completely self-financed social insurance programs, without Government contributions, which to this day is a distinctive feature of social insurance in this country." Edwin E. Witte, "Reflections on the Beginnings of Social Security," August 15, 1955, Remarks delivered at observance of the 20th Anniversary of Social Security Act by Department of Health, Education and Welfare, transcript, http://www.ssa.gov/history/witte4.html. On welfare state regimes, see also Gøsta Esping-Andersen, *The Three Worlds of Welfare Capitalism* (Princeton: Princeton University Press, 1990); Robert E. Goodin, Bruce Heady, Ruud Muffels and Henk-Jan Dirven, *The Real*

Worlds of Welfare Capitalism (Cambridge: Cambridge University Press, 1999); Gaston V. Rimlinger, *Welfare Policy and Industrialization in Europe, America, and Russia* (New York: Wiley, 1971); Jacob S. Hacker, *The Divided Welfare State: The Battle over Public and Private Social Benefits in the United States* (New York: Cambridge University Press, 2002).

31. See esp. David Moss, "Private Risk is the Public's Business," *The American Prospect* 20, no. 4 (May 2009); David A. Moss, "An Ounce of Prevention: Financial Regulation, Moral Hazard, and the End of 'Too Big to Fail,'" *Harvard Magazine*, September–October 2009, 25–29.

32. See, e.g., David Moss, "Leave No Risk Behind," *Forbes*, July 23, 2007; David Moss and Stephanie Lo, "Financing Higher Education in Australia," (draft case study, March 1, 2010); Bruce Chapman and Yael Shavit, "A Better Way to Borrow," *Inside Higher Ed*, June 8, 2010.

3

The American Challenge in Cross-national Perspective

The economic crisis that arose in 2008 poses a formidable challenge to social welfare policymakers throughout the world. In examining the nature of this challenge and its policy implications for modern welfare states, it is useful to begin with a review of several trends that place the immediate economic predicament in a broader social context. Since the 1980s, modern welfare states have experienced a number of important policy-related developments that involve public and private expenditures, labor force participation, welfare demand, and employment measures. These developments reflect the shifting degrees of responsibility for managing economic risk among governments, individuals, and employers. This chapter analyzes these shifts from a comparative cross-national perspective, with a particular focus on how U.S. experiences compare to those of other advanced industrial democracies and the various implications for risk and insecurity therein. In conducting a wide-angle survey of the social landscape, the picture that emerges provides more of an impressionist's rendition of the world than a sharply focused photograph—which is to say that the trends I summarize may be a bit fuzzy around the edges, but nevertheless convey a reasonable approximation of the empirical experiences they seek to trace.[1]

Social Expenditure and Taxation

In order to understand the current U.S. experience from a cross-national perspective, it is important to first examine the relationship between social expenditure and taxation, which differs greatly across nations. This section will detail the history of social expenditures in the Organisation for Economic Co-operation and Development (OECD) member countries and will explore how the recent economic crisis has affected nations' abilities to spend on social welfare programs.

Public spending on social welfare is measured in various ways. The OECD's account of gross public social expenditure is one of the most frequently used estimates. According to this measure, over the two decades from 1960 to the 1980s, the average public spending on social welfare (or "social spending") in the OECD member countries, which had 21 members at that time, nearly doubled as a proportion of the gross domestic product (GDP).[2] After that period, the average rate of growth among the OECD countries slowed, increasing mildly from an average gross public social expenditure of 16 percent in 1980 to 20.4 percent in 1993.[3] From 1993 to 2005, however, as Figure 3.1 shows, the level of social spending relative to GDP remained almost flat, fluctuating by less than 1 percent a year and ending up in 2005 at 20.5 percent—virtually the same level as in 1993. The United States experienced a similar pattern of an increase in social spending as a percent of GDP between 1980 and 1993, followed by a leveling off of social spending over the following decades, though at a rate considerably below the OECD average.[4]

The leveling off of social spending as a percentage of GDP occurred just about the same time that tax revenues flattened out. As seen in Figure 3.2, the average total tax revenue for the OECD countries increased from about 26.5 percent of the GDP in 1965 to 35.3 percent in 1996, after which it appears to have leveled off, fluctuating less than 1 percent through 2006. Until recently, some social policy analysts saw the plateauing of social expenditure as a percent of GDP as signaling a potential limit on further increases in the proportional rate of social transfers.[5] The economic downturn, however, has created formidable pressures on this recent ceiling. By 2010, British, French, and German politicians were calling for a boost in taxes on high-earners to counteract the effects of the economic crisis.[6]

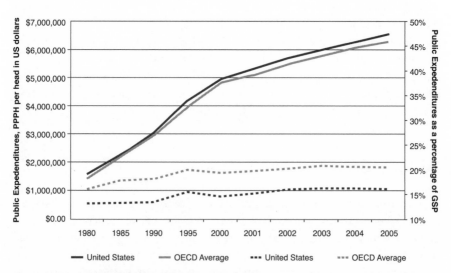

Figure 3.1:   Social Expenditures: U.S. vs. OECD Average. Source: OECD Stat data. Data extracted May 9, 2009. http://stats.oedc.org/index.aspx

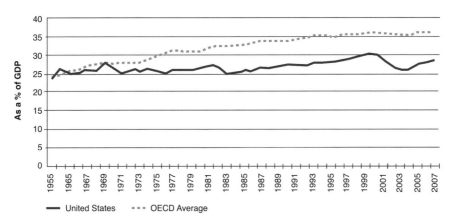

Figure 3.2:   Total Tax Revenue. Source: *OECD Factbook 2009: Economic, Environmental and Social Statistics.*

This trend, of course, does not signify that the absolute level of social spending remained constant. To the contrary, since the total real growth of GDP for the OECD countries increased by an average of 2.6 percent annually from 1994 to 2007, the actual amount of social expenditures continued to rise rather substantially—as seen when the measure of spending shifts from the percentage of GDP to per capita expenditures, controlled for purchasing power parity (PPP).[7] Under this metric, social spending not only continues to rise, but the United States emerges with the highest level of public social spending among OECD countries (as seen in Figure 3.1).

The average per capita social expenditure in the United States and other OECD countries was still rising between 1994 and 2007, despite the fact that, during this period, unemployment rates declined (see Figure 3.3). Not only did the unemployment rates in Europe and the United States fall after the mid-1990s, but the proportion of the working age population in the labor force increased among the original 15 European Union countries from 60.2 percent in 1993 to 66 percent in 2006. The rise in per capita spending was due in part to increasing demands for public spending on retirement, health services, and social care, which were being generated by the climbing number of elderly people in the OECD countries.

As illustrated in Figure 3.4, the ratio of working population to the inactive elderly is on the rise and is projected to accelerate after 2010. In 2010, the OECD countries will have, on average, close to three workers for every inactive elderly person. By 2050, this .33 ratio will climb to nearly .66—an average of one and a half workers contributing to the support of one inactive elderly person.

The growing social costs associated with the aging of the population (e.g., rising costs of medical care and retirement security) are compounded by other demographic trends. Extramarital births and divorce rates, for example, are at almost record heights.[8] The proliferation of two-income households, as well as

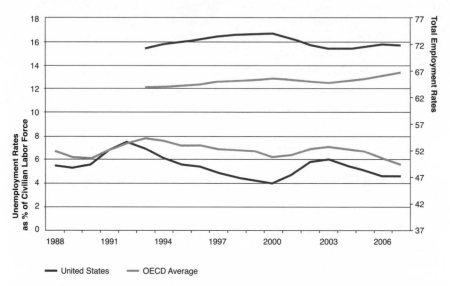

Figure 3.3:   Rates of Employment and Unemployment: U.S. vs. OECD Average.
Source: *OECD Factbook 2009: Economic, Environmental and Social Statistics.*

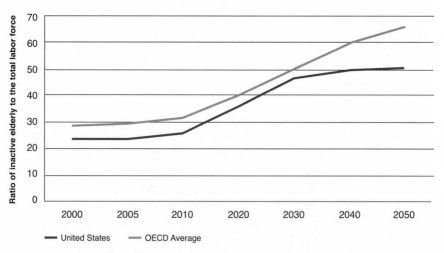

Figure 3.4:   Dependency Projections for U.S. and OECD Average. Source: *OECD Factbook 2009: Economic, Environmental and Social Statistics.*

single-parent families, have reduced the modern family's capacity to provide in-person care for children, the elderly, and other infirm relatives, which creates additional demands for the state to supply child care, financial assistance, and other supportive services. Overall, the near future forecasts illuminate a period of sociodemographic change that will generate new demands for welfare state benefits and eliminate practically no existing needs.[9] This demographic transition may help explain why social spending did not decline as might be expected when unemployment fell after the mid-1990s: although demand for unemployment benefits dropped, the need for other kinds of assistance, from child care to elderly medical benefits, grew accordingly.

Rising Levels of Privatization

The prior section detailed the dramatic increase in public social spending as a proportion of GPD in the OECD countries during the second half of the twentieth century, and its continued rise even after spending relative to total GDP leveled off in the mid-1990s.

This trend began to change as the 2000s drew near, leading to a comparative increase in the levels of private social spending. As public expenditure on social welfare as a percentage of GDP was leveling off, data from the OECD indicate that between 1990 and 2003, on average, gross private social spending showed a slight increase as a percent of GDP in a sample of 28 countries. This marks the beginning of a steeper long-term trend that is gathering momentum, particularly in pension benefits.[10]

Since 1980 the percent of pensioner households with income from private pensions climbed throughout most of the OECD countries.[11] Between 1980 and 2005, the private share of pension expenditures rose from 9 percent to 16 percent of total social expenditures for pensions in the European Union's original 27 member countries. In the United States, the United Kingdom, and the Netherlands, the private proportion accounted for about 40 percent of the total public/private pensions spending.[12] The proportion of private social expenditures will accelerate rapidly due to the fact that 30 countries have incorporated private individual accounts into their mandatory pension systems since 1992.[13]

Expenditures on private pensions in the United States represent a significantly higher proportion of the total public/private pension expenditures than the average level of private expenditure for the OECD. In 2001, for example, private benefits amounted to about 38 percent of the total public/private pension expenditures in the United States, which was two-and-a-half times the OECD (23 country) average of 14 percent.[14]

In line with the trend in pension expenditures, the private share of social expenditures for health care in the OECD countries shows a similar, though less pronounced, increase, rising between 1980 and 2005 from an average of about 4 percent to 6.5 percent of the GDP (shown in Figure 3.5). Overall, the private share of health care spending in the OECD countries accounted for slightly less than one-third of the total public/private health expenditure. By comparison, private health care spending in the United States amounted to more than 50 percent of the public/private total.[15]

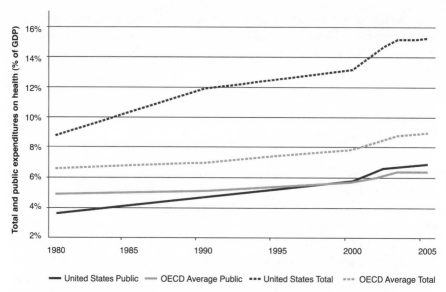

Figure 3.5: Comparison of U.S. vs. OECD Average: Public and Total Expenditures on Health (as percentage of GDP). Source: OECD Factbook 2009: Economic, Environmental and Social Statistics.

Active Labor Market Policy Reforms

The trends outlined above—changes in the public expenditures on social spending and increased privatization of certain social welfare benefits—were accompanied by one more dramatic change in social welfare benefits: the replacement of unconditional cash welfare benefits with benefits tied more strictly to work requirements.

The falling unemployment and increasing labor force participation rates in the mid-1990s were accompanied by a wave of work-oriented reforms that swept the OECD countries. Stretching across the political spectrum from Sweden to the United States, active labor market policies have created new incentives and compelling pressures for moving welfare beneficiaries into the paid labor force.

The 1996 U.S. welfare reforms were arguably the most stringent policies, introducing lifetime limits on eligibility, firmly administered incentives and sanctions, and a "work-first" approach to activating the unemployed that favored job placement over increasing human capital via skills training and education.[16] Yet the tightening of eligibility criteria and substantive direction of these reforms closely parallel the work-oriented reforms in public assistance, unemployment, and disability policies of many other OECD countries. Emphasizing the "activation" of welfare recipients, the Danish Social Assistance Reform of 1997 required that all persons receiving social assistance must participate in formulating individual action plans, which are designed to improve their working skills and to facilitate gainful employment.[17]

Just as public assistance reforms forged tighter links between benefits and work-related activities, unemployment and disability policies were trimmed and reframed to incorporate robust behavioral incentives and work requirements in countries that included Germany, France, and the Netherlands. German sociologist Jens Alber considers the current emphasis on activation as representing a new stage in the historic relationship between European social democracy and the market economy. He suggests that around the turn of the twenty-first century, the European Labor movement abandoned support of welfare policies designed to de-commodify labor by providing benefits that endowed a means of livelihood outside the market in favor of work-oriented measures to enable people to participate in the market.[18] Indeed, work-oriented reforms in public assistance, disability, and unemployment policies of the OECD countries have followed a general pattern of change that involves: (1) restricting access and accelerating exit, (2) introduction of contractual obligations and activation plans, and (3) application of diverse incentives.[19]

To sum up: these stylized facts suggest three broad patterns—of demand, privatization and activation—that characterized the context of modern welfare states during the decades immediately prior to the 2008 onset of the economic crisis.[20]

GROWING DEMAND

Public social welfare spending climbed, despite the facts that unemployment was declining and that the proportion of the working-age population entering the labor force was on the rise. This occurred because, even with falling unemployment, increasing demands for social welfare provisions were being generated by demographic changes, particularly the aging of the populations, which loomed as an immense source of fiscal pressure on health, social care, and pension provisions. Increased demand for spending was being met, not by increased taxes, which had leveled off (reaching what some considered a ceiling) but by economic growth generated by an apparently healthy economy. And over this period, social expenditures in the United States and Europe followed the same trajectory.

RISING PRIVATIZATION

Reliance on private initiatives for health and pensions was increasing among most of the OECD countries. The U.S. social welfare system has historically been distinguished by a level of privatization in these areas that is much higher than the OECD average.

ADOPTING ACTIVATION REQUIREMENTS

These policies involved work-oriented reforms that tightened eligibility and replaced the provision of unconditional cash benefits to unemployed, disabled, and elderly people with measures designed to stimulate employment and personal responsibility. The U.S. emphasis on the "work-first" approach placed less weight on building human capital through training programs and education than most of the other OECD countries and instead focused on strict work requirements.

Implications for the Division of Public and Private Responsibility

How do the trends sketched out above reflect the ways in which modern welfare states have sought to balance public and private responsibility for social risks prior to the onset of the economic downturn in 2008? And what are the implications of the increasing needs and insecurities generated by the current crisis for shifting the public and private assumption of risk in the near future?

INCREASED DEMAND IN A SHRINKING ECONOMY

Since the mid-1990s, sustained economic growth provided much of the resources allocated by modern welfare states to meet the cost of rising demand for social welfare provisions generated by the risks of aging populations, changing makeup of families, unemployment, and illness. In 2009, the GDP in OECD countries declined by an average of 3.4 percent, ranging from a decline of 5 percent in Germany to 2.2 percent in France. Estimates for 2010 show a smaller, but continuing, decline in the GDP average for OECD countries.[21] The recession is forecast to persist and unemployment rates are expected to rise well into 2010. High levels of unemployment accompanying the economic downturn have accelerated the already increasing demands for social welfare even as tax revenues fall.

The potential responses to greater demand without greater revenues or growth are relatively straightforward. Since the shrinking economies cannot rely on GDP growth to finance higher levels of social expenditure required to meet the mounting needs—as they have over the past decade—governments are left with the options of: (1) increasing or maintaining the current level of public responsibility by raising taxes or borrowing against the future; (2) increasing private responsibility by trimming public spending on social welfare benefits and shifting the costs to private recipients through increased individual co-payments (or out-of-pocket purchases) or "claw-back" taxation of public benefits (i.e., getting some of the benefits back through subsequent taxation); (3) directly cutting public spending and reducing benefits. These options are not mutually exclusive.

Although the economic downturn creates a wide range of hardships in the realms of health care, pensions, and income security in the OECD states, the character of the needs, insecurities, and policy responses in the United States are somewhat different from those of other OECD countries, and within the United

States they are differentially distributed among socioeconomic groups. The reasons for these differences have to do with how public and private responsibility and active labor policies have played out in the United States compared to other OECD countries. The needs generated by the economic downturn are magnified by the trend toward the privatization of social welfare, particularly in regard to private health insurance benefits in the United States.

HEALTH INSURANCE AND THE RISK OF UNEMPLOYMENT

In the United States and other OECD countries, the public sector assumes the major responsibility for financing the protection against social risks. But in comparison to other welfare states, the United States has placed greater emphasis on private spending (partially subsidized by the public coffer through the use of tax expenditures) to finance employee benefits, particularly health insurance and old age pensions, delivered through the private sector.

The allocation of employee benefits through the private sector has expanded over the last three decades to the point that they now constitute a significant portion of the workers' total compensation package in the major OECD countries. For example, among the eleven wealthiest countries, the average employee benefits in manufacturing climbed from 33 percent of their hourly compensation in 1975 to 40 percent in 2006.[22] The largest component of employee benefits throughout Europe and the U.S. involve the social insurances—essentially health insurance and pensions.[23] Although private expenditures on health care have increased in Europe, universal government-sponsored health insurance coverage is nevertheless widely available in the OECD countries (certainly throughout western Europe). By contrast, until 2010, government health insurance in the United States was limited to the elderly, the poor, and military personnel. In 2007, government programs insured roughly 28 percent of the U.S. population.[24] Medicare (for the elderly and disabled) covered 13.8 percent of the population; an additional 13.2 percent of the population was covered by Medicaid (for low-income people); and 3.7 percent of the population received health care through the military.[25] Private health insurance protects another 67.5 percent of the population, the vast majority (88 percent) of whom are covered through employment-based benefits, which are partially publicly subsidized via tax expenditures.[26] And the remaining 15.3 percent of the population are without any health insurance.[27] (These figures add up to more than 100 percent because the types of coverage are not mutually exclusive and people can be covered by more than one type of insurance during the year.)[28]

Although partially subsidized via public tax expenditures, the private delivery of health insurance in the United States does not provide secure coverage of the working population in times of high unemployment. Not only does rising unemployment pose a greater risk for the loss of health insurance coverage in the

United States than in other OECD countries, but within the United States, the risk to the middle and professional classes is much higher than for the elderly and the poor. (The 15.3 percent of population without health insurance, many of whom are low-income workers, have no coverage to lose. Between 1987 and 1994 the distribution of employee benefits included a disproportionate decline in health insurance for less skilled workers.)[29] Thus, in considering the relative role of public and private responsibility, it is important to bear in mind the distinction between how benefits are financed and how they are delivered.

In response to the loss of health insurance coverage that accompanies unemployment for many people, the Obama administration's stimulus package (the American Recovery and Reinvestment Act, signed into law on February 17, 2009)[30] included a provision that granted a 65 percent subsidy for the COBRA health benefit premium, which would assist unemployed workers in maintaining a continuation of their employee health care coverage for nine months. COBRA coverage can be extended to 18 months, but employees would have to pay the full premium costs after the first nine months.

The 2010 health reform bill—the Patient Protection and Affordable Care Act (ACA)—did not extend this COBRA subsidy. The ACA does, however, provide subsidies for individuals without access to employer-based coverage to purchase health insurance through the state health insurance exchanges. While this subsidy may ultimately aid unemployed workers, the transition between employer-provided coverage and coverage under the health exchange may prove challenging, leaving the unemployed with lower rates of health insurance coverage.

PRIVATE PENSIONS: DIFFERENTIAL COVERAGE

Privatization also involves employer-provided pensions, which account for a major portion of the standard costs in the employee's basic fringe benefit package. Not only have private pensions been a growing component of retirement income, but research shows that these benefits are associated with income inequality among retired households.[31] This is particularly the case in the United States, where private pensions have contributed to growing inequality.[32] While an increasing proportion of the United States population has come to rely on private pensions as a primary source of retirement income, the mix of support from public and private pensions is quite different for people in the upper, middle, and lower income groups. Among elderly people within the top 20 percent of incomes, by 1990 private retirement benefits had risen to account for more of the aggregate income than Social Security benefits. The elderly in the bottom 20 percent of the income distribution continue to remain highly dependent on Social Security, while reliance on private pensions is climbing for those in the middle and upper middle levels.[33]

The turmoil in the financial markets has negatively impacted private pensions, significantly shrinking the value of their assets. The Congressional Budget Office estimated that the value of assets held by private sector defined benefit pension plans declined by 15 percent between 2007 and 2008—and an even greater decline is estimated for the value of defined contribution plans, which are more heavily invested in equities.[34]

In an apparent response to these losses, a 2008 survey by the American Association of Retired Persons (AARP) reports that 27 percent of older workers have postponed their plans to retire.[35] (However, it should be noted that the data analyzing the impact of previous stock market declines show mixed results.[36]) Here is a specific case in which increasing privatization has been impacted by market failure, resulting in the need for greater individual effort and responsibility to protect against the economic risks of income loss in old age. In a shrinking job market, postponing retirement among elderly workers extends their personal responsibility for income maintenance at the same time that it further lowers the availability of employment for young people seeking initial entry as well as for those who have recently lost their jobs, both of which have implications for active labor policies.

ACTIVE LABOR POLICY: FROM RIGHTS TO RESPONSIBILITIES

Public efforts to rebalance social and individual responsibility in the OECD countries are most powerfully reflected in the active labor market policy reforms enacted since the mid-1990s. These reforms emerged after several decades of welfare state growth, as discussed above. The period from 1960s through the mid-1980s is often referred to as the "golden era" of welfare state expansion, due to the significant increase in public spending on social welfare relative to GDP. During this period, the political discourse on social welfare was animated by efforts to extend the range of social benefits, including health, housing, day care, family assistance, and the like. By the late 1980s, concerns about the nature of welfare entitlement shifted away from elaborating social rights to delineating the social obligations of citizenship. The long-standing acceptance of welfare as a social right was replaced by a new emphasis on the recipients' social responsibilities (namely that recipients must work for their aid), particularly for people receiving cash aid for disability, unemployment, public assistance, and even pensions. Although noted British sociologist T. H. Marshall is strongly identified as elaborating and supporting the idea of welfare provisions as social rights of citizenship, he was well aware that these rights had to be balanced by the duties of citizenship. Marshall was explicit that among these obligations, the duty to work was "of paramount importance."[37]

There are several explanations for this shifting emphasis from rights to responsibilities, concerning the structural changes in family life, a normative shift regarding women's work and the role of motherhood, and knowledge gained about the unintended consequences of generous welfare benefits.[38] For example, an OECD report on the Netherlands in the early 1990s finds:

Clear indications that the generosity of social benefits and high effective marginal tax rates implicit in income-dependent subsidies create strong disincentives to work and underlie the exceptionally high dependency ratio in the Netherlands, where one employed person supports almost one person on social benefits.[39]

There was an increasing acceptance of the idea that social welfare provisions produced "poverty traps" or "enforced dependency," phrases prudently crafted not to blame the victims.[40]

Although the United States initiated the most stringent work-oriented welfare reform policies, the policy reforms of the 1990s moved in the same direction on both sides of the Atlantic. In their 1992 *White Paper on Rehabilitation*, for example, Norwegians launched what was termed the "work approach" to social welfare policy, a basic premise of which was "that individual rights are not exclusively tied to cash benefits; each individual has, as far as possible, a right and a duty to work, to participate in rehabilitation programs or enter education."[41] The reconfiguration of social protection in the OECD countries was aptly summarized by the motto of the Dutch "purple coalition" (red Social Democrats and blue Liberals), which formed a new government in the mid-1990s—"Work, work and work again!"[42]

From the mid-1990s to 2007, both progressive and conservative policymakers were seeking to redefine and rebalance the rights and responsibilities of a new social contract, which placed greater emphasis on individual responsibility to work. The work-oriented policy reforms reduced public responsibility for maintaining the income of disabled people, unemployed workers, and single parents, and shifted the risk of income loss to those individuals, who were increasingly required to find work as quickly as possible, taking any job that was offered. But it is important to recognize that these work-focused measures were enacted during more than a decade of sustained growth and declining unemployment—an era of felicitous convergence between an increasing emphasis on individual responsibility to work and economic growth that created an environment with expanding opportunities for employment.

It is too early to provide more than a speculative view on how well work-related policies will function in an extended period of high unemployment such as the circumstances of the Great Recession of the 2000s. With that in mind, it stands to reason that services, incentives, and sanctions to move people into employment work best when there is plenty of work to be had—policies dependent on quick entry into a job stall when work is scarce. As the percentage of unemployment moves into double digits, the push and pull of incentives and sanctions are likely to produce more social frictions and stress than get-up-and-go among job seekers being thrust into a shrinking market. All this is to suggest that at this stage the balance between social rights and individual responsibilities in the welfare states is in flux.[43]

Social Risks: Convergence and Blurring of Public and Private Responsibility

During the last several decades, the balance between public and private provisions of health, unemployment, and pension benefits has shifted toward increased reliance on private efforts in almost all of the industrial democracies, blurring the line between public and private responsibility for dealing with socioeconomic risks. This trend toward privatization signifies some degree of convergence between the U.S system of social welfare and the advanced welfare states of many OECD countries, with the latter moving in the direction of the U.S. system, which has typically emphasized less public and more individual responsibility for social welfare. However, the economic crisis has introduced looming uncertainties about the path of convergence and where the shifting balance of rights and responsibilities will eventually stabilize.

On one side of the scale, some observers see the United States moving to embrace a more publicly oriented, European-style welfare state with some increase in social rights for unemployment and health insurance benefits. Under the 2009 American Recovery and Reinvestment Act, for example, federal funds are provided for several unemployment-related social welfare policies: (1) extending the duration of eligibility for unemployment benefits, (2) increasing the level of benefits by $25 per week, (3) exempting the first $2,400 of unemployment benefits from federal income taxes, and (4) providing an emergency contingency fund to help states meet the increasing costs of social assistance.[44] Eligibility for unemployment benefits was expanded to an almost unprecedented (for the United States) 99 weeks, making U.S. policy appear more like those of the western European OECD countries. In addition, U.S. health insurance coverage has been made nearly universal under the Patient Protection and Affordable Health Care Act, signed into law on March 23, 2010.[45] This brings the scope of coverage for the risk of illness more into line with that of the other OECD countries. Although some provisions of this law will come into effect in 2010, the full range of costs, benefits, and protection will not be implemented until 2014.

On the other side of the scale, publicly supported entitlements are shrinking in many of the OECD welfare states.[46] Germany has significantly reformed unemployment insurance by shifting what was once a generous long-term benefit into the system of social assistance (at a lower benefit rate) after one year of unemployment, and once-free German universities have begun to charge tuition. In France, co-payments for health care have been increasing, and in the United Kingdom, the government plans to abolish child trust funds and to stiffen work-related requirements for the unemployed. Greece, Spain, Italy and France are introducing pension reforms that lower benefits and increase individual responsibility to work for longer periods in order to be eligible, moving toward the retirement age in the

United States. Nevertheless, the U.S. pension replacement rate for median earners remains among the lowest of the OECD countries.

In sum, to date, the American and European responses to the economic downturn create a mixed picture of contradictory developments in public and private responsibility for social protection. Although the specific course of change is blurry, the general direction of welfare policy adjustments points to convergence from both sides of the Atlantic.

Notes

1. For a more detailed documentation of the trends summarized here, see Neil Gilbert, *Transformation of the Welfare State: The Silent Surrender of Public Responsibility* (New York: Oxford University Press, 2002); Neil Gilbert and Rebecca Van Voorhis, eds., *Activating the Unemployed: A Comparative Analysis of Work-Oriented Policies* (New Brunswick, NJ: Transaction Publishers, 2001); Neil Gilbert and Antoine Parent, eds., *Welfare Reform: A Comparative Assessment of the French and U.S. Experiences* (New Brunswick, NJ: Transaction Publishers, 2004).
2. Organisation for Economic Co-operation and Development, *The Future of Social Protection* (Paris: OECD, 1988).
3. The OECD membership was growing over this period and eventually climbed to 30 by 2009.
4. It is well recognized that these levels of spending change when the "gross public social expenditure" measure is adjusted for taxes, tax expenditures, as well as mandated and voluntary private benefits. A critical assessment of these measures is offered in Neil Gilbert, "Comparative Analysis of Stateness and State Action: What Can We Learn from Patterns of Expenditure?" in Jens Alber and Neil Gilbert, eds., *United in Diversity? Comparing Social Models in Europe and America* (New York: Oxford University Press, 2009).
5. Douglas J. Besharov, "Social Welfare's Twin Dilemmas: 'Universalism vs. Targeting' and 'Support vs. Dependency'" (paper, International Social Security Association Research Conference, Jerusalem, Israel, January 25–28, 1998).
6. As evidenced in Britain, where a swelling deficit of record proportions has prompted the government to propose an increase in income tax from 40 to 50 percent, but only for individuals earning over £150,000 (and couples over £250,000). Julia Werdigier, "Britain's Deficit Deepens; Its Outlook Grows Gloomier," April 22, 2009, http://www.nytimes.com/2009/04/23/business/global/23pound.html.
7. The OECD total growth rates are averages for the individual countries weighted by size and converted to dollars using PPP. Organisation for Economic Co-operation and Development, *OECD Factbook 2009* (Paris: OECD Publishing, 2009).
8. The mean increase in numbers of single-parent families over the decade from the early 1980s to the early 1990s represents a range from -10 percent in Sweden to +83 percent in France. Organisation for Economic Co-operation and Development, *A Caring World: The New Social Policy Agenda* (Paris: OECD Publishing, 1999).
9. This point is nicely documented in Bea Cantillon, "Socio-Demographic Changes and Social Security," *International Social Security Review* 43 (1990): 399–425.
10. For a more detailed analysis and documentation of the movement toward privatization of social welfare activity, see Neil Gilbert, *Transformation of the Welfare State: The Silent Surrender of Public Responsibility* (New York: Oxford University Press, 2002).
11. Axel W. Pedersen, "The Privatization of Retirement Income? Variations and Trends in the Income Packages of Old Age Pensioners," *Journal of European Social Policy* 14 (2004): 5–23.
12. Jens Alber, "Is There an Americanization of European Social Policies?" (lecture, The Future of the Welfare State: Paths of Social Policy Innovation Between Constraints and Opportunities, Espanet, Urbino, Italy, September 17, 2009).

13. Barbara E. Kritzer, "Individual Accounts in Other Countries," *Social Security Bulletin* 66 (2005): 32–36, http://www.ssa.gov/policy/docs/ssb/v66n1/v66n1p31.html.

14. Calculated from data in Chart 2, Willem Adema and Maxime Ladiaque, "Net Social Expenditures 2005 Edition: More Comprehensive Measures of Social Support," *OECD Social, Employment, and Migration Working Papers* 29 (2005), http://www.oecd.org/dataoecd/56/2/35632106.pdf.

15. Organisation for Economic Co-operation and Development, *OECD Factbook 2009*.

16. *Personal Responsibility and Work Opportunity Reconciliation Act of 1996*, Public Law 193, 104th Cong., 2d Sess. (August 22, 1996).

17. Gilbert, *Transformation of the Welfare State*.

18. Jens Alber, "What the European and American Welfare States Have in Common and Where They Differ: Facts and Fiction in Comparisons of the European Social Model and the United States," *Journal of European Social Policy* 20 (2010): 102–125.

19. Gilbert, *Transformation of the Welfare State*.

20. There are, of course, other trends such as that of growing inequality in the distribution of income and increasing competition from low-wage regions, which one might point to over this period.

21. Organisation for Economic Co-operation and Development, *OECD Interim Economic Outlook, March 2009* (Paris: OECD Publications, 2009).

22. Neil Gilbert, "Accounting for Employee Benefits: Issues of Measurement, Valuation, and Social Equivalencies" (paper, Joint OECD/University of Maryland International Conference on Measuring Poverty, Income Inequality, and Social Exclusion: Lessons from Europe, Paris, July 9, 2009).

23. Denmark's relatively low level of employee benefits in this category is due to the fact that, in comparison to other European countries, employer contributions to statutory and occupational pensions are exceptionally low because a considerable share of national pensions is financed by tax revenues. Jarna Bach, Sini Laitinen-Kuikka, and Mika Vidlund, eds., *Pension Contribution Level in Certain EU Countries* (Helsinki: Finnish Center for Pensions, 2004).

24. U.S. Bureau of the Census. *Income, Poverty, and Health Insurance Coverage in the United States: 2007*. Prepared by Carmen DeNavas-Walt, Bernadette D. Proctor, and Jessica C. Smith, Current Population Reports, Bureau of the Census. Washington, DC, 2008.

25. Ibid.

26. Ibid.

27. Ibid.

28. Ibid.

29. Wankyo Chung, "Fringe Benefits and Inequality in the Labor Market," *Economic Inquiry* 41 (2003): 517–529.

30. *The American Recovery and Reinvestment Act of 2009*, Public Law 5, 111st Cong., 1st sess. (February 17, 2009).

31. Pierre Pestieau, "The Distribution of Private Pension Benefits: How Fair Is It?" (paper, Conference on Private Pensions and Public Policy, OECD, Paris, July 1–3, 1991).

32. Chung, "Fringe Benefits and Inequality in the Labor Market."

33. Gilbert and Park, "Privatization, Provision, and Targeting"

34. House Committee on Education and Labor, Peter Orszag, *The Effects of Recent Turmoil in the Financial Markets on Retirement Security: Testimony of the Director of the Congressional Budget Office*, 110th Cong., 2d sess., October 7, 2008, http://www.cbo.gov/ftpdocs/98xx/doc9864/10-07-RetirementSecurity_Testimony.pdf.

35. Jeffrey Love, *The Economic Slowdown's Impact on Middle-Aged and Older Americans* (Washington, DC: American Association of Retired Persons, 2008), http://assets.aarp.org/rgcenter/econ/economy_survey.pdf.

36. House Committee, *The Effects of Recent Turmoil*.

37. T. H. Marshall, *Citizenship and Social Class* (Cambridge: Cambridge University Press, 1950).

38. Neil Gilbert, "U.S. Welfare Reform: Rewriting the Social Contract," *Journal of Social Policy* 38 (2009): 383–399.

39. Organisation for Economic Co-operation and Development, *Economic Surveys: The Netherlands* (Paris: OECD Publishing, 1991).

40. Jonathan Bradshaw and Jane Millar, "Lone-Parent Families in the UK: Challenges to Social Security Policy," *International Social Security Review* 43(1990): 446–459. And even in Sweden, the paragon of the modern welfare state, in the early 1990s, Prime Minister Carl Bildt declared that benefit levels had become so high as to reduce the incentives to work. Richard Stevenson, "Swedes Facing Rigors of Welfare Cuts," *New York Times*, March 14, 1993, http://www.nytimes.com/1993/03/14/world/swedes-facing-rigors-of-welfare-cuts.html.

41. Gilbert, *Transformation of the Welfare State*.

42. Ibid.

43. Neil Gilbert, "The Social Contract Revisited: Programme Appraisal" (lecture, The Foundation for Law, Justice, and Society and the Centre for Socio-Legal Studies at Oxford University, Gray's Inn, High Holborn, London, July 7, 2010).

44. Council of Economic Advisors, *Recovery Act Third Quarterly Report-Tax Relief and Income Support*, prepared by the Council of Economic Advisors, White House, 2010, http://www.white-house.gov/administration/eop/cea/factsheets-reports/economic-impact-arra-3rd-quarterly-report/section-4.

45. *Patient Protection and Affordable Care Act of 2010*, Public Law 148, 111st Cong., 2d sess. (March 23, 2010).

46. For a bleak account of this trend, see "Calling Time on Progress," *The Economist*, July 15, 2010.

4

"The Arms of Democracy"

Economic Security in the Nation's
Broader National Security Agenda

MARIANO-FLORENTINO CUÉLLAR AND CONNOR RASO

> These measures have all had only one supreme purpose—to make
> democracy work—to strengthen the arms of democracy in peace
> or war and to ensure the solid blessings of free government to
> our people in increasing measure.[1]
> —Franklin Roosevelt

Introduction

On April 8, 1952, President Truman signed an executive order that sought to seize control of a major chunk of American heavy industry—its steel mills. The nation's involvement in the Korean conflict was fueling substantial inflationary pressure, and union officials were convinced that the steel industry was achieving considerable profits at a time when workers' wages remained stagnant.[2] Because industrial power was America's defining military advantage, the president was not inclined to let a labor dispute erode this strategic asset. These circumstances help frame the conventional description of the dilemma in the famous case of *Youngstown Sheet & Tube v. Sawyer Youngstown,* which essentially turns on the extent of executive branch power to control the economy in the name of national security. When the Supreme Court issued its opinion in the case, it readily demonstrated that President Truman's dramatic action, along with the legal strategy used to defend it, was fraught with problems.[3]

The larger context in which the *Youngstown* case arose underscores a relationship between the economy and the concept of national security that neither the litigants nor the Court could afford to ignore. For the executive branch, continued steel production was at core a means to the end of sustained American industrial strength.[4] Given the federal government's priorities, the Court's decision had the potential to engender considerable further conflict about the relationship between American industry and its government. Yet the underlying labor dispute in *Youngstown* underscores an even more fundamental, and less frequently appreciated, aspect of the relationship between national security and economic policy. Far from being merely a function of material inputs to industry, a nation's economic capacity can also be shaped by the condition of its people: their health and wealth, their capacity to play productive roles in the economy, and even their belief that their country's security bears some meaningful relationship to their own. Just how, and how deeply, national security connects to individuals' ongoing sense of their own economic security, however, is rarely the subject of sustained attention.

This chapter sheds new light on the relationship between national and economic security. Though often understood as distinct spheres, the domains of economic security and national security operate in close relationship and exert powerful effects on each other within a given nation's legal, political, and economic framework. As one means of shedding light on that relationship, our focus in this chapter is primarily on the impact of economic security on national security. We define economic security in terms of a state's capacity to balance economic prosperity with measures limiting the risk of sharp discontinuities in social welfare, and we analyze national security primarily in terms of a state's ability to pursue geostrategic goals while maintaining effective domestic order and public safety.[5]

In brief, we argue that economic security policy profoundly affects the institutional, legal, economic, and political context of national security. Economic security policy affects a nation's scarce resources, impacting the fiscal environment in ways that affect both short-term and long-term national security. Decisions about economic security shape a nation's social capital and institutional capacity—both of which have played a historically important role in the capacity of nations to impact their geostrategic environment. And the long-term viability of a nation-state—depending to some extent on citizens' commitment and the capacity of interested parties to support coalitions that are consistent with a continued role for the state—is almost undeniably bound up to some extent with decisions about how to handle economic security.

In a world where nation-states manage pensions as well as peacekeepers, observers and policymakers must contend with several implications of the interrelationship between economic and national security rooted in the nature of citizens, institutions, law, and politics. First, despite some observers' insistence to the contrary, national and economic security policies heavily impact each other.[6] Economic security policies can build the sort of human capital, institutional capacity, and commitment to national goals that can strengthen a state's ability to defend against external threats and its means of promoting peace and international security. Both domains fundamentally implicate the question of how the nation-state and its citizens manage the risks of an uncertain and rapidly evolving world.

Second, the politics of economic and national security are entangled in multiple ways. Poorly conceived economic security measures can have major fiscal effects that constrain the resources available for more conventional national security activities.[7] Politicians can deliberately blur the distinctions between the two domains, as when presidents created the Federal Security Agency (in the late 1930s) and the Department of Homeland Security more recently. Internal economic dislocation can exacerbate the risk of international conflicts. National security activities, moreover, can affect the demand for economic security measures such as veterans' benefits or broadened access to health insurance.

Finally, both economic security and national security raise issues of accountability and responsibility for the evolving nation-state, some of which involve the difficulty in imposing limits on the scope of legal authorities identified with national security. The steel seizure cases provide an excellent illustration of this difficulty. Ultimately, the relationship between economic and national security underscores the practical and organizational difficulties of segregating policy-making into separate domains. This raises persistent questions about a self-contained, narrow vision of geostrategic security that purports to minimize the significance of the public's economic and social condition.

Common Roots

The Roosevelt administration's creation of the Federal Security Agency (FSA) illustrates certain underappreciated features of the relationship between economic and national security policies and, in particular, the ways in which politicians grapple with and sometimes deliberately exacerbate the entanglements between the domestic regulation of economic risk and the external defense of the nation. In the late 1930s, Roosevelt's White House created a vast agency around bureaus such as the Food and Drug Administration, the Social Security Board, and the Public Health Service. This new organization facilitated political control of these agencies and the capacity to focus their missions on administration priorities. Beginning well before World War II and continuing during and after the war, the new FSA performed critical defense-related functions. For instance, the Social Security Board placed workers in defense industry jobs and assisted families affected by World War II. Similarly, the FSA's Office of Education trained employees for industries that were important to the war effort. The administration's determination to link defense and economic security policies reflects recognition of the political value in underscoring such a connection.[8]

As the Truman administration was litigating the steel seizure cases, Federal Security Agency administrator Oscar Ewing simultaneously made a case for the FSA's expansion and for some of the core tenets of the Truman administration's

"Fair Deal." Echoing themes that he was emphasizing in speeches across the country, Ewing wrote:

> Just how secure are you at this moment? If, tomorrow, you have an acute attack . . . could you foot the bill . . . ? If a child is born in your family, are you secure in the knowledge that he will receive the best attention the medical profession can offer—that he can have the education he may set his heart upon, perhaps a college degree? Suppose you lose your job, or become disabled. What sort of world would lie ahead for you? *These personal matters of security* are the direct concern of your Federal Security Agency, of which I happen to be the Administrator. . . . As I see it, security means a sure knowledge that we shall not want for the basic necessities of life, no matter what Fate may have in store. . . . With that sure knowledge, we can proceed to go about getting the things we want from life under the American system of free choice.[9]

Ewing's pitch was delivered at a time of great concern for national security, as the United States faced the challenges of the Korean War. By the 1950s, national security was generally understood to focus on geostrategic security.[10] So how was Ewing's focus on economic security (including access to heath care) linked to national security? Ewing himself sometimes pointed out the role that his agency was prepared to play in civil defense, and sought to emphasize the extent to which citizens ought to care about all the forms of security that could affect their lives.[11] He even responded forcefully to charges that his agency, which was a focal point for the Truman administration's efforts to reform health insurance and also administered other social insurance programs, was threatening the nation's economic system:

> Some people will tell you that these advances for the good of the general welfare are approaches toward Communism. The exact opposite is true. Security is the best defense we have against Communism. When a man is provided through democratic government with the basic securities which make it possible for him to get what he wants, to stand on his own two feet, independently, he will not listen to wild "isms."[12]

While Ewing hinted at some of these potentially deeper connections between economic and national security, however, he did not explain or analyze the full range of potential connections. Neither did the man who created the Federal Security Agency, Franklin Roosevelt. Roosevelt was all too willing to underscore the interdependence between different security spheres, but he too stopped well short of offering an explicit, analytically defensible explanation.

Any attempt to develop such an explanation of the interrelationship between economic and national security policy must begin by recognizing that both domains implicate the management of risk. Under almost any defensible account of individual motivation or social organization, policymakers should expect individuals, families, and communities to harbor profound concern about risks to their well-being—whether such risks involve acute health emergencies, disasters, or external attacks. Moreover, circumstances creating stress for the nation-state, such as natural disasters or the threat of external military coercion, imperil the state's capacity to manage risks and to create the conditions for citizens to build successful and fulfilling lives.

Indeed, the question of how a society manages risk—and how common bonds are forged among individuals in addressing uncertainty in economic and national security spheres—implicates the historical trajectory of the nation-state itself. Early European states, for example, grew to a considerable degree around communities facing the possibility or the reality of violent conflict arising from external threats, and reflecting a similarly intense concern over the prospect of internal violence.[13] These proto-states depended on their capacity to raise revenue and operate an administrative apparatus to maintain their war-fighting prowess. Even today, the state's economic well-being can drive or impose drastic limits on a nation's capacity to defend itself and advance its version of its national interest.

As advanced industrialized countries emerged, individuals generally confronted an environment of increasingly complex public institutions and heightened individual expectations of personal and economic security—even as states continue to confront substantial threats to peace and to their own security. Observers and policymakers rarely grasp the full extent and precise nature of the links between economic security and national security in such societies, however; the discussion below elucidates some of these connections in greater detail.

FISCAL CONSTRAINTS

Investments meant to bolster economic security and national defense are both subject to scarcity constraints arising from limits on a nation's overall resources. Resources devoted to one area affect the level of resources available in the other realm. The argument that nations face a choice between "guns and butter" is perhaps the most pervasive conception of this trade-off.[14] Despite some complexities arising from the potential long-term relationships between national security spending and overall economic activity, the conventional account of the guns-and-butter trade-off is partially accurate. The reality of a country's fiscal constraints all but ensures that when politicians forge policies governing health insurance, social security, and other elements of economic security, they affect the resources available for national security.[15]

A key example involves health care. One of the fundamental factors capable of shaping a family's sense of economic security is the cost of health care. Rising health costs also exert an outsized effect on the federal budget. Since 1970, Medicare and Medicaid spending has increased steadily from 1.7 percent of gross domestic product (GDP) to approximately 5 percent in 2009.[16] Defense spending did not increase at this steady upward rate, declining from approximately 8 percent of GDP in 1970 to 4.7 percent in 2009.[17] As a partial response to the growing fiscal pressures created by rising health care costs, the Patient Protection and Affordable Care Act of 2010 is meant to stem this trend by curtailing rising health care expenditures. Prior to the bill's enactment, federal spending on the Medicare and Medicaid programs alone was projected to explode to 20 percent of GDP by 2050, the same share of the economy as the entire 2007 federal budget.[18] The 2010 legislation sought to curtail such growth with a combination of cost-saving reforms and reductions in Medicare payments. Although some of these projected savings are contingent upon the political will of future Congresses and presidents, even partial success in curbing growing health care costs could relieve some of the fiscal constraints affecting the country's broader economic and security priorities, including its capacity to invest in core national security functions.

The impact of health care policy on the fiscal resources available for broader national security goals is particularly severe—but not unique. The use of deficit spending to finance economic security obligations such as health care may risk undermining longer-term strategic prospects through the creation of fiscal burdens that could limit the country's capacity to address future threats to peace and security. The U.S. government has recently run particularly pronounced deficits amounting to roughly 10 percent of GDP. Deficits of this size risk diminishing presidents' power and flexibility to face unexpected threats to peace and security and may weaken the United States' global standing.[19] For these reasons, debt and defense may be difficult to disentangle. Although conventional economic assumptions suggest that countries holding U.S. Treasury bonds would seek to avoid creating instability that would reduce the value of their holdings, the recent public expression of concern by Chinese leaders regarding the safety of their Treasury bill investments on market activity underscores the potential (actual and perceived) complexities associated with U.S. government dependence on external financing.[20] The U.S. military's recently planned elaborate war game to study the threat posed by international economic interdependence on U.S. national security underscores the perceived importance of this issue within the U.S. government.[21]

SOCIAL CAPITAL

Social capital has an important but subtle impact on national security. A nation that provides economic security to its citizens builds social capital, increasing its capacity for self-defense. Conversely, a nation that neglects economic security will fail to build social capital, undermining national security.

Even conventional national security considerations, such as the capacity of a nation's armed forces, readily demonstrate the fundamental role of social capital and public health. Both considerations are integral to a nation's economic security and to national security interests. A nation that fails to provide economic security to its citizens will struggle to create and sustain strong armed forces. At the most basic level, a poor and unhealthy population will produce inadequate soldiers. For instance, research by the U.S. military on nutrition for soldiers has shown that diet is critical for individual performance.[22] As a result, the U.S. military even established a "Committee on Military Nutrition Research" to determine the nutritional regime that would maximize soldier performance under different conditions—a step underscoring the intimate relationship between a society's level of food security and the condition of its armed forces.[23] A nation that fails to provide basic economic security to a broad base of its population will struggle to produce soldiers who can perform optimally under such difficult conditions.

Reading this lesson too narrowly carries its own risks. Certain nations, such as North Korea, have historically sought to provide economic security to their armed forces while the remainder of society struggles. A RAND Institute analysis noted that militaries sometimes reflect the difficulties of their host societies, reducing security.[24] Countries may be able to maintain a strong military in the short run by devoting resources to soldiers, but a society lacking broader social capital will ultimately struggle to generate the resources and innovation necessary to sustain this dichotomy and support the military. The former Soviet Union is the most prominent recent example of this outcome.[25]

The importance of broad social capital for national defense has been recognized in the United States. Take, for example, education policy, another domain integral to economic security and long recognized as relevant to national defense in the United States. National educational achievement greatly affects whether a country has the capacity to invest in and reap rewards from research and development. By many accounts, the divergence in economic performance between East Asia and Latin American in the 1980s was widened by greater East Asian investment in education and research and development.[26]

The Sputnik scare prompted Congress to pass the National Defense Education Act of 1958 and increased interest in science and technology. Warnings such as the Hart-Rudman Commission's admonition that "the inadequacies of our systems of research and education pose a greater threat to U.S. national security over the next quarter century than any potential conventional war that we might imagine"[27] received renewed attention in the wake of the September 11 attacks. In response, policy initiatives explicitly sought to link education to national security.[28] This movement was somewhat influential, prompting prominent figures such as former House Speaker Newt Gingrich to note the importance of education to both economic and national security: "Investing in science (including math and science education) is the most important strategic investment we make in continued American leadership economically and militarily."[29]

Economic growth is only part of the picture. An educated public will also produce individuals who are more capable of undertaking sophisticated analytical tasks and advanced technology, whether in military or civilian settings. The importance of this capability has grown as advanced technology has become increasingly complex and increasingly central to military operations and strategy.[30] A military unable to attract educated soldiers will struggle to remain competitive and use such technology effectively. Indeed, the U.S. military has struggled to recruit well-qualified soldiers. A report analyzing military recruitment in Pennsylvania found that 25 percent of young adults from ages 17–24 were ineligible to serve because they lacked a high school diploma.[31] In a plea for better soldiers, a senior official of the U.S. armed forces recently highlighted the role of human capital: "The best aircraft, ships, and satellite-guided weapon systems are only as effective as the personnel the military can recruit to operate them."[32]

This problem led the military to conclude that early childhood education is integral to national security.[33] In fact, former chairman of the Joint Chiefs of Staff General Hugh Shelton and former Navy secretary John Dalton founded a non-profit agency to expand opportunities for early childhood education in order to increase the pool of individuals eligible for military service. Shelton and Dalton summarized their position by noting that "[t]he most important long-term investment we can make for a strong military is in the health and education of the American people."[34] This example underscores a recognition that a nation's erosion of social capital can impact its military capacity and strategic posture.

INSTITUTIONAL CAPACITY AND THE STATE

To understand how the concept of state institutional capacity further links national security to the management of economic risks, it is helpful to reflect on how scholars have sought to define the state and understand its evolution. In the early twenty-first century, the nation-state persists as the defining feature of international organization and domestic law, but observers consistently differ on how it should be defined. For Charles Tilly, the state is an organization that controls the population, occupying a definite territory. Steven Skowronek talks of an "integrated organization of institutions, procedures, and human talents," and Theda Skocpol describes the state in terms of a "set of administrative, policing, and military organizations."[35] These definitions capture subtly different qualities associated with nations. At their core, however, they all reference *institutional capacity*: a state's laws mean little without the organizations to honor them and to coax (or coerce) the public to do so. Institutional capacity is what lets nations and their citizens change the course of rivers to make deserts bloom, protect against crushing natural disasters, educate their children, and defend their cities. Low-capacity regimes, moreover, are less capable of limiting corruption and opportunism and thereby less capable of addressing their citizens' physical or economic insecurity.[36]

While economic security policies depend to some extent on an existing core of institutional capacity,[37] the further strengthening of a nation's organizational infrastructure can be a major consequence of new economic security arrangements. Consider, for example, the early history of the Social Security program and its associated employment services elements during the Roosevelt administration. The program grew around the goal of providing social insurance. Over time, its infrastructure of records, offices, employees, and relationships with the public facilitated the expansion of the nation's social insurance program.[38] Fairly early in its history, however, that infrastructure also facilitated planning for and implementation of the military draft. Later, as World War II loomed larger, the employment placement services became a resource for placing Americans in war-related industries.[39]

In a similar vein, state institutions that are used to administer revenue collection also have the potential to contribute to economic security policy and the more conventional national security sphere. States require substantial revenue to provide for their defense. In the United States, the federal government developed its revenue collection systems in response to the Civil War and World War I and II.[40] The state's capacity to build and maintain the institutional capacity to maintain sovereignty over its territory and provide for the common defense depended on the capacity to build institutions capable of pooling the public's resources. Such systems were later used to collect revenue for social welfare programs that provided economic security.

In more recent decades, the relationship between institutional capacity and economic security is evident in the growing concern with advanced industrialized states' capacity to protect their infrastructure. U.S. infrastructure is vulnerable to both natural disasters and terrorist attacks. A review by the American Society of Civil Engineers deemed a large portion of national infrastructure in need of significant repair.[41] State and local governments have failed to adequately plan for the risk that such vulnerable infrastructure will fail in the face of a terrorist attack or natural disaster. The Department of Homeland Security found that only 25 percent of state emergency operations plans and 10 percent of municipal plans were adequate in the face of a major terrorist attack or natural disaster.[42] Such exposure threatens the economic prospects of individuals, families, and communities at the same time that they impose potentially heightened national security vulnerabilities.[43] For instance, Hurricane Katrina disrupted core elements of economic security in the Gulf Coast region, impacting individuals' access to shelter, food, clothing, clean water, and medical care. Like the impact of the Deepwater Horizon oil spill, Katrina's impact on economic security also reflects consequences beyond the immediate affected area, as the disaster disrupted regional industry and took a toll on other sectors of the U.S. economy. The impact of a future disaster or man-made attack could prove even more severe, creating consequences not only for the state as an abstract entity but for citizens whose economic prospects depend indirectly on the nation's infrastructure. An attack on Chicago, for example, could disrupt 37 percent of total U.S. railway traffic.[44]

No doubt such examples partially reflect the complicated calculus involved in judging the normative legitimacy of national power. The institutional infrastructure necessary to provide people with access to social insurance and facilitate future employment opportunities eventually helped to ensure a steady supply of workers to war-related industries and facilitated a military draft. By the same token, the structures of domestic state power played a role in the historical episode of Japanese internment that now elicits widespread derision among Americans. In effect, a state's capacity to analyze, organize, regulate, and deploy its authority has dual consequences in the domains of economic and national security. As such, the institutional capacity that develops around robust economic security policies can facilitate coercion even as it also enables risk-spreading and the mitigation of otherwise potentially crippling natural and man-made disasters.[45]

LONGER-TERM SUPPORT FOR (AND VIABILITY OF) THE NATION-STATE

By the middle of the twentieth century, much of western Europe had embarked on an elaborate effort to create or expand the welfare state. In Britain, the creation of a National Health Service, providing the population with widespread access to health care, was emblematic of a larger trend.[46] Elsewhere in Europe, the long shadow of the Cold War coincided with renewed interest in forging the social safety nets and risk-spreading arrangements that might forestall greater domestic political conflict.[47] While these developments represented historical milestones in Europe, they shed some light on two related dilemmas of any functioning nation-state that once more link its economic security policies to its larger national security agenda: how to give individuals and groups a stake in the continuing prosperity of the nation-state, and how to dampen the fervor and potential success of those who have the least to gain from an existing national arrangement.

These dilemmas recur in the history of nation-states.[48] Though not all states share precisely the same origin,[49] they converge in their need to manage internal territory and populations in a world of scarce resources. They also frequently face a common pressure (even in relatively secure times and regions) to leverage social, physical, and economic resources to provide for common defense. In at least some depictions of the state-formation process (particularly in Europe), it is the latter imperative that drives the former and indeed that manifests itself as a core motivation for the territorial and legal scope of the state's authority in the first place.[50] States, after all, did not develop in a vacuum, and their continuing evolution reflects as much as it shapes individual human desires. People respond to their material circumstances and future prospects.[51] Individuals' capacity to act on their loyalty to the state (assuming that it already exists) is hard to separate from their economic realities, unless we make unrealistic assumptions about individual desires or responses to incentives.

The relationships between individuals, government, and the state underscore the fact that the nature and characteristics of nation-states are capable of evolving over time, though many individual states often reach a degree of stability and capacity that shapes a sense of timeless permanence. Legal and political arrangements between states and citizens evolve in a world where states thrive but also die.[52] The logic of the state depends on its capacity to create loyalty, provide incentives, and occasionally coerce. The capacity of the state to perform these functions, in turn, can falter when large proportions of the citizenry face severe, discontinuous economic and health-related risks—hence the recurring Cold War concerns, particularly in Europe, about the capacity of states to address the economic needs of their citizens.[53] Similarly, some scholars argue that states enhanced their social safety nets in response to growing public anxiety about their economic conditions in the midst of World War II.[54]

If the recent history in many developed nations reflected a willingness to invest in the creation of social safety nets following the social dislocations of war and amidst concerns about forestalling domestic political conflict, the rapid decolonization following World War II describes nearly the opposite pattern. There, colonized territories made major sacrifices to fight the war, but confronted a pattern of economic insecurity and political disenfranchisement that was all the more difficult to reconcile with domestic aspirations given their role in the war. As Niall Ferguson puts it: "No one should ever underestimate the role played by the Empire—not just the familiar stalwart fellows from the dominions but the ordinary, loyal Indians, West Indians and Africans too—in defeating the Axis powers."[55]

In short order, such unity became increasingly difficult to defend. Colonial populations had been continually exposed to a degree of economic insecurity and political marginalization that laid bare the profound practical and prescriptive limitations of colonial arrangements.[56] In contrast, within the United Kingdom and other former colonial powers, the experience of shared sacrifice turned attention to the creation of legal and financial arrangements providing greater economic security to their national populations.

These national populations tend to understand the significance of their membership in the larger political community through a process almost inevitably shaped by economic security policies. The privileges and responsibilities associated with citizenship—or lawful presence in a particular jurisdiction—help define how a society views itself and its underlying goals. Courts sometimes understandably allude to the state's role in providing the means of reducing risk when framing an individual's responsibility to society. There is a certain normative logic in passing along to individual members of society some of the reduced risk that their own participation in economic or national security activities helps to facilitate. The prescriptive power of a nation's example and its broader policy agenda are also difficult to divorce from the well-being of its citizens. For instance, concentrated poverty and inequality potentially undermine both a country's overall economic position as well as its capacity to leverage so-called "soft" power.[57]

Even leaving aside the more prescriptively oriented considerations, the only way to posit a world where economic security plays no role in encouraging people to take the state seriously is to make drastically unrealistic assumptions about human nature. The people from whom soldiers, police, teachers, doctors, farmers, and lawyers are drawn would need to be stripped of sensitivity to their material conditions. Political leaders would have to be too naïve or inhibited to respond to the potential political payoffs of mobilizing individuals adversely affected by a state that places demands on them without accounting for their needs or dignitary interests. A state burdened by sharply growing inequality and social conflict can face considerable political constraints in shaping its foreign and security policies.[58]

In part because of the political relationship between economic security policies and a nation's more conventional security challenges, national security crises can result in major turning points in the trajectory of a state's economic security policies. The United States, for example, created its first large-scale pension system for Civil War veterans.[59] Similarly, the GI Bill, a key driver of economic security, was enacted in the wake of World War II.

Scholars have yet to fully elucidate the precise dynamics through which national security threats (or efforts to face them) prompt the development of such shared national solidarity. National security crises may impact the salience of concerns that reach beyond individual interest, priming people to assign greater value to what some political scientists have labeled "sociotropic" concerns.[60] In a different vein, Kevin Narizny reviews case studies involving security expenditures in the United Kingdom, France, and the United States and finds left-leaning governments generally more willing to support the progressive taxation and public-sector economic intervention associated with major rearmament programs.[61] Once achieved, the demand for economic expenditures that benefit large segments of the public—characteristics reflected in some social insurance measures as much as in national defense spending—may persist after the political coalitions that are necessary to fight wars have overcome difficulties forging internal alliances.[62] Separately, the strains of war may forge greater interest in policies that reduce social divisions following the exertions of a national security emergency. Regardless of the precise theoretical mechanisms at work, it is far from unusual for states emerging from national security crises to face historical turning points in the development of more robust social institutions to help their citizens manage economic risks.[63]

Implications of the Relationship

The relationship between economic security and national security has significant implications for modern states and their citizens. This is true whether the focus is on historical turning points involving major changes in domestic policy such as the postwar period in the United Kingdom or the Johnson administration in the United States, or on periods of relative policy stability similar to those the United

States experienced during the 1990s. This becomes more readily apparent when discussion of national security pivots from a static focus on variables such as current force levels and postures to consider instead the implications of incentive structures, social cohesion, and national capacity in ensuring society's security and well-being.[64]

First, policymakers should think about risk across the conventional categories of economic and national security because, conceptually, economic and national security risks interact. A major natural or man-made disaster on the scale of the 9/11 attacks, for instance, can leave Americans uniquely vulnerable to further attacks coming immediately after the disaster—particularly if the initial response is inadequate. The Katrina disaster not only taxed the nation and arguably made it more vulnerable to certain national security threats at the time, it also disrupted the economic circumstances of hundreds of thousands of people. Accordingly, evaluating disaster response and mitigation policy would implicate considerations of economic security as well as national security.

Resource constraints arising because of unjustified military spending or poorly conceived mandatory spending programs can deplete available capacity for more carefully designed economic security initiatives, and national security emergencies can also accelerate interest in economic security and related measures that may be helpful in mobilizing the country for war. National security emergencies can develop a shared sense of solidarity and otherwise increase support for expanded economic security policies. Meanwhile, greater economic risk can make it more difficult for countries to build the domestic support and capacity necessary to protect national security. Indeed, countries with major domestic needs may feel pressure to cut national security spending.[65]

Second, the politics of economic and national security are closely intertwined. The public can expect new economic security policies such as veterans' benefits to follow national security crises, as occurred in the United States following World War II. In addition, the close interrelationship between economic and national security may give politicians and members of civil society a persistent reason to make public appeals that further blur the distinctions between economic and national security policy. As World War II loomed, Roosevelt emphasized the importance of an agency reorganization to bolster economic security—by creating the FSA—as having direct and indirect benefits for national security. The Obama administration's recently released *National Security Strategy* repeatedly emphasizes the national security implications of education policy and responsible stewardship of the federal deficits.[66]

A darker consequence of the entanglement between economic and national security involves, according to some scholars, the potential for internal economic dislocation to exacerbate the risk of international conflict. Governments facing hard times may engage in military activity to displace attention from domestic economic circumstances that are politically costly.[67] The leaders of nations experiencing economic dislocation may also be drawn to Keynesian fiscal initiatives involving military spending, and both leaders and the public may ascribe heightened stakes to conflicts involving international economic opportunity.[68]

Third, policy problems involving economic and national security both raise important issues of accountability and responsibility. When citizens, civil society groups, and even policymakers navigate those challenges, they must contend with the two-edged quality of state capacity. On one hand, the organization and efficiency of public agencies can help remedy collective action problems, promote public safety, and manage economic risk. On the other hand, it may also facilitate certain damaging uses of public authority, such as the internment of Japanese Americans during World War II.[69] If the American experience is any guide, societies must also confront the persistent difficulty of segregating national security and domestic policy domains. Some legal disputes, such as the *Curtiss-Wright* and *Steel Seizure* cases,[70] plainly implicate domestic policy, even as the rationale motivating presidential action originated with concern about foreign relations and defense. Such cases can affect baseline assumptions about state power that may be relevant in the domestic context, just as some cases involving domestic statutes seemingly far afield from national security may influence developments in counterterrorism or national defense.[71] Ultimately, regardless of whether a legal or policy dispute involves surveillance or Social Security benefits, both contexts implicate questions of discretion, due process, and the potential for arbitrariness. These questions arise repeatedly in agency field offices, legislatures, courtrooms, and in the public discourse. They have the potential to impact the state's legitimacy as citizens evaluate whether their government is delivering a sufficient measure of security without imposing unreasonable economic, practical, or bureaucratic burdens on society.

Conclusion

Americans confront substantial challenges to their national security in the early twenty-first century, including nuclear proliferation, potential terrorist attacks, public health emergencies, and the potential vulnerability of the nation's cyber infrastructure.[72] These threats rightly claim considerable attention because of their potential to disrupt so much of what citizens hold dear. Yet a country's economic security policies—and not just conventional security policies that address matters such as military procurement or the size of the nation's armed forces— play a role in shaping a country's capacity to address these challenges. The domain of national security policy is not self-contained. It depends on citizens, institutions, laws, and political strategies affected by—and in some cases developed in response to—to background policies involving economic security.

Our view contrasts with the presumption that national security policy is easily separable from domestic policy and also differs from those who posit one-dimensional trade-offs between guns or butter. Instead, our account provides a more complex picture. Economic security policies, whether they embody a new social insurance initiative or a de facto social decision to ignore rising health care costs, give rise to fiscal effects on available resources to support national security policies. Economic security policies also impact human and social capital, thereby affecting the performance of the armed forces, the productivity of the labor force, and a society's capacity for innovation. The institutional structures designed to advance economic security policies can affect the capacity of the nation-state in a manner that supports robust national security activities. The infrastructure of the Social Security system, for example, helped staff war-related industries. Finally, the long-term support for and viability of the nation-state is likely to be affected by economic security policy, as citizens adjust their expectations of their common responsibilities and individual circumstances in response to measures helping them manage economic uncertainty.

Although he did not map out the full extent of the common roots between economic and national security, Franklin Roosevelt readily alluded to these connections when he described domestic policies as "the arms of democracy" in announcing a powerful new Federal Security Agency to simultaneously improve the nation's economic security while strengthening the nation's capacity to fight dictatorships.[73] To neglect these links is to ignore the ways in which our nation's geostrategic capacity and resilience can be strengthened, the ways in which an economically insecure public can fuel the conflicts that gave rise to the *Youngstown* case, and the ways in which politicians navigate their environment.

The deeper issue concerns the longer-term impact of security from risks— whether external or economic—on individual and social well-being. Centuries ago, the emergence of states reflected a measure of concern over managing risks. Risks associated with armed conflict, to some degree, contributed to concerns over managing risks associated with insufficient institutional capacity and (eventually) economic and social dislocation. Societies today continue to reflect concerns about their national security, as it is conventionally understood, because wars and attacks can create sharp discontinuities in peace and prosperity. But as Oscar Ewing's words resonate well into the twenty-first century, when millions of Americans face growing economic uncertainty, it is also worth remembering that people make enormous sacrifices to protect their nation because of what they think it represents, and its role as a bulwark against economic insecurity is no small measure of what nations promise their citizens.

Notes

1. Franklin D. Roosevelt, *Reorganization Plan No. 1 of 1939*, 3 C.F.R. 1288 (1938–43 Comp.), reprinted in 5 U.S.C. app., and in 53 Stat. 1423 (1939).
2. Patricia L. Bellia, "The Story of the Steel Seizure Case," in *Presidential Power Stories*, ed. Christopher H. Schroeder and Curtis A. Bradley (New York: Foundation Press, 2008), 2–3.
3. *Youngstown Sheet & Tube v. Sawyer*, 343 U.S. 579 (1952).
4. *Youngstown*, 343 U.S. at 583 ("The indispensability of steel as a component of substantially all weapons and other war materials led the President to believe that the proposed work

stoppage would immediately jeopardize our national defense and that governmental seizure of the steel mills was necessary in order to assure the continued availability of steel.").

5. Our analysis is informed by three additional, plausible assumptions about the policymaking process. First, as a conceptual matter, domestic security policy and international security policy are closely interrelated realms that do not lend themselves to a simple, scalpel-like separation through the application of an unambiguous technical standard. Second, organizational structures shape individual incentives and aggregate policy outcomes, which means that the design of agencies will be the subject of considerable debate in the political process. Finally, individuals make reasoned policy choices, but do not always behave perfectly rationally.

6. For a contrary perspective, see, e.g., Michael Gerson, "The Promise of National Security, With a Straight Face," *Washington Post*, June 3, 2010. As we discuss below, this view consistently ignores the relationship between domestic policy generally and economic security policy in particular, and the conventional geostrategic account of national security against external threats.

7. For empirical evidence for this claim, see Alex Mintz and Chi Huang, "Guns versus Butter: The Indirect Link," *American Journal of Political Science* 35, no. 3 (August 1991): 738–757. See also Robert D. Duval, "Trading Bases: Resolving the Guns vs. Butter Tradeoff Puzzle via Full Specification" (working paper, on file with authors, 2003).

8. Mariano-Florentino Cuéllar, "'Securing' the Nation: Law, Politics, and Organization at the Federal Security Agency, 1939–1953," *University of Chicago Law Review* 76 (2009).

9. Oscar R. Ewing, "More Security For You," *American Magazine*, January 1949 (papers of Oscar R. Ewing, Federal Security Agency, Speeches and Articles, 1948–1949, Box 38, Truman Presidential Library).

10. Ewing was not the only member of the Truman administration concerned with the connection between economic and national security. For an account detailing conflict within the administration over this relationship, see Lester H. Brune, "Guns and Butter: The Pre-Korean War Dispute over Budget Allocations" *American Journal of Economics and Sociology* 48, no. 3 (1989): 357–371.

11. See, e.g., Cuéllar, "'Securing' the Nation," 625–629 (see n. 8).

12. Ewing, "More Security," 4 (see n. 9).

13. See Charles Tilly, *European Revolutions, 1492–1992* (Oxford: Blackwell Publishers, 1993). See also Douglass North, John Wallis, and Barry Weingast, *Violence and Social Orders: A Conceptual Framework for Interpreting Recorded Human History* (New York: Cambridge University Press, 2009).

14. See, e.g. Robert Gilpin, *War and Change in World Politics* (New York: Cambridge University Press 1981).

15. Political scientist Robert Duval analyzed the relationship between U.S. defense spending and social spending, and concluded that a real trade-off exists: "a dollar more for defense does indeed mean a dollar less for social or other programs, unless you go and borrow a dollar." Duval, "Trading Bases" (see n. 7).

16. Historical Budget Tables of the United States Fiscal Year 2009, http://www.gpoaccess.gov/usbudget/index.html (table 8.5: Outlays for Mandatory and Related Programs: 1962–2013, 2009).

17. Historical Budget Tables of the United States Fiscal Year 2009, http://www.gpoaccess.gov/usbudget/index.html (table 8.7: Outlays for Discretionary Programs: 1962–2009, 2009).

18. Peter Orszag, testimony before the United States Senate Committee on the Budget, *Health Care and the Budget: Issues and Challenges for Reform*, 110th Cong., 1st sess., June 21, 2007.

19. See Gerald F. Seib, "Deficit Balloons Into National Security Threat," *Wall Street Journal*, February 2, 2010.

20. Thomas Petruno, "Despite China's Jitters, Treasury Bond Market Stays Calm," *Los Angeles Times*, March 13, 2009.

21. Eamon Javers, "Pentagon Preps for Economic Warfare," *Politico*, April 9, 2009.

22. See, e.g. Donna H. Ryan, "Military Nutrition Research: Eight Tasks to Address Medical Factors Limiting Soldier Effectiveness," report prepared for the U.S. Army Medical Research and

Materiel Command (Baton Rouge, LA: Pennington Biomedical Research Center, Louisiana State University, October 2005).

23. Id.

24. Jeffrey A. Isaacson, Christopher Layne, and John Arquilla, "Predicting Military Innovation," Documented Briefing (Santa Monica, CA: RAND, 1999), 15.

25. See William Easterly and Stanley Fischer, "The Soviet Economic Decline," *The World Bank Economic Review* 9, no. 3 (1995): 341–371.

26. Chris Freeman, "The 'National System of Innovation' in Historical Perspective," *Cambridge Journal of Economics* 19 (1995): 13.

27. The U.S. Commission on National Security/21st Century, *Road Map for National Security: Imperative for Change*, Phase III Report, February 15, 2001.

28. For an example, see Association of American Universities, "National Defense Education and Innovation Initiative: Meeting America's Economic Challenges in the 21st Century" (January 2006), http://www.aau.edu/reports/NDEII.pdf.

29. Newt Gingrich, *Winning the Future: A 21st Century Contract with America* (Washington, DC: Regnery Publishing, 2005), 152.

30. For instance, the Association of American Universities noted: "As the Department of Defense has faced increasingly complex military challenges, it has relied on science and technology as a force multiplier." Association of American Universities, "National Defense Education and Innovation Initiative," 7.

31. Mission: Readiness, "Ready, Willing, and Unable to Serve" (Washington, DC: Mission Readiness, 2009), 1.

32. Id. at 6.

33. Id.

34. Hugh Shelton and John Dalton, "Strong Military Needs Early Education Focus," *Politico*, January 8, 2009.

35. Daniel Carpenter, *The Forging of Bureaucratic Autonomy: Reputations, Networks and Policy Innovation in Executive Agencies, 1862-1928* (Princeton, NJ: Princeton University Press, 2001), 18 (reviewing definitions).

36. Charles Tilly, *The Politics of Collective Violence* (Cambridge: Cambridge University Press, 2003), 134.

37. Theda Scokpol, *Protecting Soldiers and Mothers: The Political Origins of Social Welfare Policy in the United States* (Cambridge, MA: Belknap Press, 1992).

38. Cuéllar, "'Securing' the Nation," 593 (see n. 8).

39. Cuéllar, "'Securing' the Nation," 630 (see n. 8).

40. Sheldon D. Pollack, *War, Revenue, and State Building: Financing the Development of the American State* (Ithaca, NY: Cornell University Press, 2009).

41. Stephen E. Flynn, "America the Resilient," *Foreign Affairs*, March/April 2008.

42. Flynn, "America the Resilient."

43. See Stephen E. Flynn, *The Edge of Disaster* (New York: Random House, 2007).

44. Congressional Research Service, *Vulnerability of Concentrated Critical Infrastructure: Background and Policy Options*, CRS Report RL3320, 2008, 4.

45. *Cf.* Richard Polenberg, *War and Society: The United States, 1941–1945* (Philadelphia, PA: Lippincott Press, 1972), 83.

46. See Tony Judt, *Postwar: A History of Europe since 1945* (New York, NY: Penguin Books, 2005).

47. See *id.*

48. See Charles Tilly, *Coercion, Capital, and the European States* (Malden, MA: Blackwell Publishing, 1992).

49. See Karen Barkey, *Bandits and Bureaucrats: The Ottoman Route to State Centralization* (Ithaca, NY: Cornell University Press, 1997).

50. See Tilly, *Capital, Coercion, and the European States, supra* note.

51. See, e.g., Bryan Jones, *Bounded Rationality*, 2 Ann. Rev. Poli. Sci. 297 (1999).

52. See T. M. Fazal, "State Death in the International System," *International Organization* 58, no. 02 (2004): 311–344.

53. See Melvyn P. Leffler, *A Preponderance of Power* (Stanford, CA: Stanford University Press, 1991).

54. John Dryzek and Robert E. Goodin, "Risk-Sharing and Social Justice: The Motivational Foundations of the Post-War Welfare State," *British Journal of Political Science* 16, no. 1 (1986): 1–34, 11.

55. Niall Ferguson, *Empire: The Rise and Demise of the British World Order and the Lessons for Global Power* (London: Penguin Books, 2002), 289–290.

56. See David B. Abernethy, *The Dynamics of Global Dominance: European Overseas Empires, 1415–1980* (New Haven, CT: Yale University Press, 2002).

57. See Joseph S. Nye, Jr., "The Decline of America's Soft Power," *Foreign Affairs*, May/June 2004.

58. Jonathan Kirshner, *Political Economy in Security Studies after the Cold War*, 5 Rev. Int'l Pol. Econ. 64 (1998): 79.

59. See Skocpol, *Protecting Soldiers and Mothers*, chap. 2 (see n. 44).

60. See Don Kinder and Roderick Kiewiet, "Sociotropic Politics: The American Case," *British Journal of Political Science* 11 (1981): 129–161.

61. Kevin Narizny, "Both Guns and Butter, or Neither: Class Interests in the Political Economy of Rearmament," *American Political Science Review* 97 (2003): 203.

62. See Kaare Strøm and Wolfgang C. Müller, "The Keys to Togetherness: Coalition Agreements in Parliamentary Democracies," *The Journal of Legislative Studies* 5, no. 3 (1999): 255.

63. See, e.g., Niall Ferguson, *The Ascent of Money: A Financial History of the World* (New York: Penguin Group, 2008).

64. Kirshner makes this point in the context of a broader discussion of how the Cold War temporarily permitted the salience of political economy issues to recede from discussions involving national security. See Kirshner, "Political Economy" (see n. 65).

65. Mintz and Huang, "Guns versus Butter: The Indirect Link" (see n. 7).

66. For example, the *Strategy* states: "To allow each American to pursue the opportunity upon which our prosperity depends, we must . . . [achieve] access to quality, affordable health care so our people, businesses, and government are not constrained by rising costs; and the responsible management of our Federal budget so that we balance our priorities and are not burdened by debt." The White House, *National Security Strategy*, May 2010, 28.

67. See David Pion-Berlin, "The Fall of Military Rule in Argentina: 1976–1983," *Journal of Interamerican Studies and World Affairs* 27, no. 2 (1985): 55–76.

68. Kirshner, "Political Economy," 67 (see n. 65).

69. See *Polenberg, supra* note 52, at 83. See also Dorothy Swaine Thomas, "Some Social Aspects of Japanese-American Demography," *Proceedings Am. Phil. Socy.* 94 (1950): 459, 474.

70. *United States v. Curtiss-Wright Export Corp.*, 299 U.S. 304 (1936); *Youngstown Sheet & Tube Co. v. Sawyer*, 343 U.S. 579 (1952).

71. See *United States v. Comstock*, 130 S. Ct. 1949 (2010) (upholding a federal statute authorizing federal district courts to order involuntary civil commitment of sexually dangerous federal prisoners who completed their sentences). Commentators noted that this power had potentially important national security implications. See, e.g., Halerie Mahan, "*United States v. Comstock:* Justifying the Civil Commitment of Sexually Dangerous Offenders," *Duke Journal of Constitutional Law & Public Policy Sidebar* 5 (2010): 120–136.

72. See Commission on Intelligence Capabilities of the United States Regarding Weapons of Mass Destruction, *Report to the President*, March 31, 2005.

73. See Roosevelt, *Reorganization Plan* (see n. 1).

Part Two

IMPROVING ECONOMIC
SECURITY FOR WORKERS

5

The Role of Government in Ensuring Employment Security and Job Security

HEATHER BOUSHEY

Introduction

Job security provides the foundation for a family's economic security. Most Americans earn most of their income from work. Moreover, most workers are family breadwinners or co-breadwinners.[1] When a worker loses a job or cannot find suitable employment, it is not only the worker who is affected, but also the worker's family.[2] Because most Americans rely so heavily on their jobs for income and have so little in liquid financial savings, workers and their families almost invariably suffer significant hardships when unemployment hits, often even if they have access to unemployment benefits.[3]

Job security touches all aspects of social and economic life. The well-being of a community hinges on whether there are sufficient jobs at living wages for its residents. If a large employer moves out of town or many small employers close shop, there are ripple effects for all the businesses, large and small, that depended on the paychecks of that firm's employees to serve as or to bolster their customer base. The loss of jobs in a community means that unemployment lingers, rents and mortgages go unpaid, and property values fall. Schools, churches, and other institutions begin to deteriorate as citizens are unable to keep up their tithes or dues and have lowered tax liabilities, starving vital institutions of revenue. Thus widespread job insecurity threatens the integrity and well-being of communities well beyond the individual tragedies faced by workers and their families.[4,5]

A key element of job security is "employment security," the ability to find a job if you need one, which is typically measured by the unemployment rate or ratio of job openings to job seekers. In the United States since the 1940s, the federal government has played a large role in family economic security and in setting the minimum standards for job quality, including a statutory mandate to "promote maximum employment" in the Employment Act of 1946. Politicians did not need that mandate, however, to know that job security matters immensely to the electorate: Elections often hinge on "economic security" and "jobs."[6]

The near-collapse of U.S. financial markets in 2007–2008 and the resulting Great Recession[7] have amplified the public's demand for efforts to create jobs.[8] Over 7.3 million workers were laid off over the course of the recession.[9] Regaining employment security remained out of reach in the years immediately following 2008. As of the summer of 2010, there were more than five workers seeking a job for every available job opening, compared to a ratio of 1.6 in early 2007, right before the Great Recession began.[10]

The government's most fundamental role in promoting job security and job quality is to promote full employment. It is now clear that the mismanagement of the macroeconomy in recent decades posed a grave threat to employment security. The near-collapse of the U.S. financial markets, caused by the popping of the U.S. housing bubble, constrained credit, leading to a near-shutdown of borrowing and sharp layoffs, following by sustained high unemployment. Moving forward, policymakers should be acutely aware of the serious downsides of allowing asset bubbles to develop and the value of ensuring sound financial regulation. If policymakers abandon their employment mandate, job security will be eroded, as will the economic well-being of working families.

Yet job security is not simply "any job, at any wage, under any conditions." There are a set of social norms and values that define job security: Are the jobs available actually providing economic security? Is the economy generating livable middle-class jobs? The answer to these questions is more likely to be "yes" in an economy with full employment. However, there are signs that, in recent decades, even during times when the economy has been close to or at full employment, job security in terms of getting and keeping a quality job have eroded.[11]

This chapter argues that, overall, access to quality jobs has fallen in recent decades and the Great Recession is amplifying that trend. Today, the risk of unemployment is, of course, greater than it has been at any time in recent decades. Yet that is only one piece of the story. The risks of underemployment have been rising. Even during the past two decades, with relatively low unemployment, labor law enforcement was weak, while union coverage fell, and the economy saw a sharp "hollowing out" of job creation in the middle of the wage distribution (with fewer jobs created for workers in the middle of the wage distribution than those workers at the bottom), and higher wage inequality. Addressing these longer-term challenges, as well as the problem of persistently high unemployment, is critical.

High Unemployment Means
Reduced Job Security

First and foremost, job security is about whether or not a worker can find and keep gainful employment and is not subject to arbitrary or unfair dismissal. Economists typically use the unemployment rate to measure the extent to which jobs are available, but here we also examine the relationship between job seekers and job openings, which is a better indicator of whether unemployment is frictional or cyclical.[12]

For the vast majority of U.S. workers, high or rising unemployment results in the loss of employment security because it reflects the fact that labor supply (the number of people actively seeking or working in a job) outstrips labor demand (the number of workers that employers want to hire). Just because a worker needs a job does not mean that one will appear. In a capitalist economy, the private sector creates jobs when firms make investments that lead them to need to hire employees. If firms do not see a market for the goods and services they produce for either domestic or international markets, then they will not make investments to produce those goods and services. As a result, they will not hire additional workers.

Striving for full employment is not merely, however, about whether there are *enough* jobs available; it also affects the ability of workers to find high *quality* jobs. Economists have long confirmed that rising unemployment is associated with slow or falling real wage growth. In 1958, economist A. W. Phillips published his seminal work, "The Relationship between Unemployment and the Rate of Change of Money Wages in the United Kingdom 1861–1957," which showed an inverse relationship between changes in nominal wages (wages actually paid, not taking into account inflation) and changes in unemployment, a relationship that became an empirical law of economics, the "Phillips Curve."[13]

But there is not only a negative relationship between the *changes* in unemployment and wages, but also one between the *levels* of unemployment and wages. Over the past few decades, economists have amassed a body of empirical literature that documents the "wage curve," the negative relationship between the unemployment rate and wages.[14] In local economies with higher unemployment, wages will be lower, all else being equal. David Blanchflower and Andrew Oswald, along with other economists, have documented that a doubling of the unemployment rate is associated with wages that are 10 percent lower, all else being equal.[15] High unemployment disproportionately threatens job quality for disadvantaged groups. African American workers, for example, have a steeper wage curve than other U.S. workers. African American wages are *more* than 10 percent lower, with a doubling of unemployment in their communities.[16]

When an economy is close to full employment, workers have greater bargaining power vis-à-vis their employer.[17] In those circumstances, workers know that if they quit their job—or get fired—they will be able to find another place of employment. This gives workers more power to quit if an employer is abusive, unreasonable, or does not provide fair compensation, and we see that as the unemployment rate falls, the share of the unemployed who voluntarily quit a jobs rises relative to the share being laid off.[18] Furthermore, when an economy is close to full employment, there are more opportunities for workers to make the best match between their skills and preferences and a potential job. This is good for workers, as well as the economy overall, as better matches should improve productivity.

Employment security is also fundamentally and profoundly affected by whether and how government sets and enforces basic labor standards. If, for example, workers are allowed to enter the United States but are not provided with the means to work here legally, or the laws permitting their employment are not enforced, then employers have an upper hand. They can hire workers who do not have proper documentation and not only pay them less than they would U.S. citizens, but worry little about enforcement of occupational health and safety, minimum wage, or other regulations because they know that their employees do not have the same recourse to the U.S. legal system. This imbalance in negotiating power creates an unlevel playing field, heavily tilted toward employers and against employment security for immigrants first, but which ultimately pulls down labor standards for all employees.[19]

Who Bears the Brunt of the Risk When Secure Jobs Become Scarce?

Whether or not the economy is at full employment has implication for workers, communities, and the macroeconomy. Job loss threatens the economic well-being, first and foremost, of unemployed workers and their families. But the ripple effects of lower wages and reduced bargaining power magnify as the unemployment rate rises. Even in a low-unemployment economy, however, there are those who will have challenges finding a job, and thus the probability of experiencing job insecurity is not the same for everyone.

Unemployment rates vary greatly across local economies and demographic groups.[20] African American workers typically have an unemployment rate that is twice that of white workers.[21] Older workers and better educated workers typically have lower unemployment than young or less-educated workers.[22] Marital status also matters: married men typically have the lowest unemployment rate among men and women by marital status, while unmarried men typically have the highest, followed by unmarried women.[23] Other groups that may face particularly tough struggles securing employment include prisoners reentering the labor market, workers with disabilities, workers with caregiver responsibilities, and immigrants, especially those without documentation.[24]

Job loss can have lasting effects on family economic security. Research shows that workers whose job was terminated because their employer left town, outsourced production, or went out of business typically struggle longer than other workers to find employment and tend to see lower lifetime earnings after reemployment, even during relatively low-unemployment years.[25] For example, research examining long-term trends for displaced workers—those who lost a full-time job as a result of plant or company closings or moves, or abolishment of their job or shift—found that in 2004 over one-third of the reemployed full-timers took a pay cut of 20 percent or more at their new job.[26]

The costs of high long-term unemployment are especially high for the youngest workers. Yale economist Lisa Kahn has found that those who graduate from college in an economic downturn suffer persistent negative effects on their earnings. Her work examines the labor market experiences of white male college graduates as a function of economic conditions when they graduated from college. She finds that there is an initial wage loss of 6 to 7 percent for every 1 percent increase in the unemployment rate measure used in her analysis, and even 15 years after graduation, wages for this population are 2.5 percent lower (and this lower wage remains statistically significant). Taken as a whole, the results suggest that the labor market consequences of graduating from college in a bad economy are large, negative, and persistent.[27]

There is a growing body of evidence on the deleterious effects of unemployment on individual well-being, which can persist for many years after reemployment, including increased mortality, poorer health outcomes, greater probability of depression and other mental health issues, and marital instability.[28] The chief economist at the Federal Reserve Bank of Chicago, Daniel Sullivan, and Columbia professor of economics Till von Wachter have found that job displacement leads to a 15 to 20 percent increase in subject death rates for the following 20 years.[29] Overall, a worker displaced in mid-career can expect to live about two years less than a counterpart who is not displaced.[30]

Or consider the research done by Krysia Mossakowski, a sociologist at the University of Miami. She found that adults between the ages of 29 and 37 were more likely to be depressed if they were unemployed or out of the labor force, although the effects were stronger for men than for women. Longer durations of unemployment predict higher levels of depressive symptoms among young adults in the United States. These associations were measured independent of demographics, socioeconomic status, family background, and previous symptoms of depression.[31]

High unemployment can beget more high unemployment through a negative feedback loop. Consumption makes up about 70 percent of our economy, and income from employment makes up about 80 percent of the income for families earning less than $100,000 per year.[32] Without sustained job growth, especially in the credit-constrained economy that households are currently experiencing, consumption will stall, which in turn will drag down economic growth. Slower economic growth will mean lower tax revenues, which will increase the federal budget deficit and condemn millions of Americans to the devastation wrought by high unemployment and a lower standard of living. The broader community suffers when there is widespread unemployment and heightened job insecurity.

Historical Context: A Brief History of the Government's Role in Mitigating Job Insecurity

Full employment was not always at the core of the government's engagement with the economy. Until the mid-nineteenth century, families often supported themselves through farming or as craftsmen who operated their own shops. One of the unique and liberating features of the U.S. capitalist system is that workers are free to sell their labor to whomever they choose. The downside of this system, however, is that there is no guarantee that there is a job available for everyone who needs one; thus job security has become such an important issue and a priority of present-day U.S. government.

Nonetheless, the government has rarely stepped in to ensure that any particular worker has a job. Instead, the federal government focuses its monetary and fiscal policy with an eye to the general goal of full employment. This includes ensuring that macroeconomic policymaking leads to stable job creation and does not promote widening job polarization. The federal government insulates workers and their families from unemployment by setting basic labor standards that provide a minimum standard for working conditions and rules that regulate unfair dismissals. To varying degrees, in all three areas (full employment, setting minimum standards, and rules that regulate unfair dismissal) the federal government has not expanded its role of securing employment for all in recent decades. It is not that it has pared back, but rather that policies have not been updated or expanded.

The federal government is not, however, the only government entity charged with creating jobs or securing widespread full employment. State and local governments have long engaged in economic development policies that seek to boost employment, or boost certain kinds of employment within their communities, but that discussion is beyond the scope of this chapter.

THE GOAL OF FULL EMPLOYMENT

Full employment became an explicit goal of the federal government in the wake of the Great Depression. Economist John Maynard Keynes made the case that government should play a role in managing the demand for goods and services in the economy. When an economy is subject to a demand shock, that is, when firms suddenly do not have consumers for their goods and services, a negative feedback loop is created. Employers stop hiring. Fewer employed workers means less consumption, which means less overall demand for goods and services. This leads firms to continue to shed employees, which only exacerbates the problem. In this situation, government deficit spending through increasing the purchase of goods and services and/or directly hiring more employees can increase the demand for goods and services produced by the private sector. Once the private sector is back on its feet, the government can scale back and lower spending to address the buildup of government debt.[33]

Fiscal policy—that is, injecting demand into the economy through deficit spending—is not the only tool that the government has at its disposal. In many recessions, monetary policy is the most sensible policy tool with which to start. The government can reduce the cost of borrowing, which often is sufficient to spur greater investment and economic growth. But fiscal policy is an especially important policy tool when demand in the economy is too low to maintain employment even after monetary policy has lowered the cost of capital, which is the situation we have seen over the course of the Great Recession.

There are many ways for government to use fiscal policy, but one of the most efficient is through providing benefits to the unemployed. As economist Mark Zandi has shown, unemployment benefits have one of the largest multipliers of any kind of government spending: for each dollar the government spends on these benefits, there is a larger impact on the overall economy than there is with other kinds of spending.[34] Without unemployment benefits, the unemployed generally do not have cash income and they will not be able to maintain spending. Therefore, these kinds of benefits are one of the most important economic tools that policymakers can use to push the economy back toward full employment when demand is too constrained.

After the experience of the Great Depression, Congress passed the Employment Act in 1946, which created a structure and a set of rules that laid out the goal of full employment, but fell short of actually requiring it. The act established two new entities: the Council of Economic Advisors, housed in the executive branch, and the Joint Economic Committee, a bicameral congressional committee; it also called on the president to estimate and forecast the current and future level of activity in the United States. The act stated that it was the "continuing policy and responsibility" of the federal government to "coordinate and utilize all its plans, functions, and resources . . . to foster and promote free competitive enterprise and the general welfare; conditions under which *there will be afforded useful employment for those able, willing, and seeking to work*; and *to promote maximum employment*, production and purchasing power" (emphasis added).[35] As Berkeley economist Brad DeLong has noted, after the passage of this act "the shift in the cyclical behavior of the federal budget, considered as a sea-anchor for the economy's level of total spending, is impressive."[36]

The Employment Act marked a change in government policy in that it solidified the definition of the federal government's role to develop policies that would move the economy toward full employment, but it did not provide the new entities that were charged with this mission the tools to enact this policy. The power of conducting monetary policy continues to rest with the Federal Reserve System, an independent federal entity which has a dual mandate of keeping inflation low and promoting full employment. Although the 1978 Humphrey-Hawkins Act requires the chair of the Federal Reserve to testify twice a year before the Joint Economic Committee to inform Congress of the state of the economy, Congress does not have oversight over the Federal Reserve.[37]

The tenor of macroeconomic debates changed after the stagflation of the 1970s, when high unemployment existed alongside high inflation—a situation that ran counter to the widely held tenets of macroeconomics at the time. This experience led many economists and policymakers to question whether it was possible for the government to promote full employment. Monetarist and supply-side economists de-emphasized the role of government in promoting full employment, arguing that the expansion of monetary policy through either cheaper credit (lower interest rates) or increasing the money supply leads to inflation. Therefore, they concluded, monetary authorities should focus their effects on maintaining price stability, not full employment.[38]

Economists also began to focus on a more empirically grounded definition of full employment. The literature on the natural rate of unemployment came to the conclusion that because of the nonaccelerating inflation rate of unemployment (known to economists as the NAIRU), pushing the economy below 6.5 percent unemployment would lead to higher inflation.[39] However, empirical reality has invalidated this threshold: in the late 1990s and again in the 2000s, unemployment was below this threshold without rising inflation.[40] Thus, in the name of economic stability, Federal Reserve policy had focused on keeping unemployment above full employment—eroding employment security for millions of workers—even though the experience of the late 1990s showed that this was not necessarily the only policy choice.

At the end of the 1980s, the *New York Times* led a story with the title, "The Business Cycle Rolls Over and Plays Dead."[41] A decade later, macroeconomists began calling the last few decades of the twentieth century "the great moderation."[42] Business cycles had become less dramatic: recessions were weaker and job losses less severe. However, moving through the 1990s and 2000s, concerns grew about the recoveries, which were weaker as well. There has been a growing divergence between output and profits on the one hand, and employment and output on the other. The "jobless recoveries" of the 1990s and 2000s saw output and profits rise, but employment grew at a relatively slow pace, especially in the early years of the recovery.[43]

INSULATING WORKERS AND THEIR FAMILIES FROM UNEMPLOYMENT AND ITS RIPPLE EFFECTS

Basic labor standards both establish job quality and insulate workers from unemployment or the impact of unemployment on their job's quality. The federal government began taking on the issue of job quality during the Progressive Era at the turn of the twentieth century by, among other things, instituting laws against child labor and regulating hours of work. The key labor market regulations that set basic labor standards were established in the Fair Labor Standards Act (FLSA) of 1938, which set the minimum wage and hours regulations. The overtime pay provision of the FLSA requires employers to pay hourly employees 150 percent of their normal wage for any hours above 40 worked in one week.[44] Initially, the goal of this provision was twofold: to improve job quality through reducing overwork, as well as the macroeconomic goal of encouraging businesses to create more jobs rather than demanding more hours of current employees.

In the context of the Great Depression, which raised unemployment to historic highs, one original goal of the FLSA was to set a floor on wage cutting, and also to help boost consumer demand through improving wages. As President Roosevelt said at the time:

> I came to the conclusion that the present-day problem calls for action both by the government and by the people, that we suffer primarily from a failure of consumer demand because of lack of buying power. Therefore it is up to us to create an economic upturn . . . I am again expressing my hope that the Congress will enact at this session a wage and hour bill putting a floor under industrial wages and a limit on working hours—to ensure a better distribution of our prosperity, a better distribution of available work, and a *sounder distribution of buying power.*[45]

Because the goal was to boost consumer demand, Congress initially set the minimum wage at about half of the median hourly wage. But the federal minimum wage is not tied to the inflation rate and it falls in real value over time unless Congress moves to increase it. In 2010, the federal minimum wage was $7.25, but its purchasing power was 27 percent below its 1968 level, and equivalent to only 39 percent of the median hourly wage in 2009.[46] The federal minimum wage does not vary geographically to take into account differences in the cost of living. Partly in response to these flaws, many states have adopted minimum wage laws, and currently 14 states and the District of Columbia require minimum wages above the federal level and 10 states index it to the rate of inflation.[47]

Initially, the FLSA excluded some groups of workers, but in 1966, it expanded coverage to include minimum wage requirements for some farm workers and was further amended in 1974, when it was expanded to cover other state and local government employees as well as domestic workers, although it remains the case that in-home care workers are excluded.[48]

ENSURING AGAINST UNFAIR DISMISSAL

Job security hinges on workers not being unfairly dismissed by their employer. In the United States, few workers have contractual job protections, and most employees are subject to employment-at-will. Unless there is an explicit employment contract, at-will employees can be fired for any reason not explicitly prohibited through judicial or statutory exceptions. All 50 states honor employment-at-will, although all but four (Florida, Georgia, Louisiana, and Rhode Island) have statutory exceptions to the at-will doctrine.[49]

Judicial exceptions to employment-at-will began with a series of cases decided in the late 1950s.[50] The public policy exception prohibits employers from discharging their workers against an established public policy, such as for filing a worker's compensation claim after being injured.[51] The implied contract exception typically exists in the form of an employer providing oral assurance to their workers that they will not be fired unless there is just cause and/or poor performance.[52] And the good faith and fair dealing exception prohibits employee dismissals that are made in bad faith or with malice and intent.[53] Each of these exceptions provides workers with some protections, although for an individual who has been wrongfully discharged to take advantage of one of the exceptions it would likely require court action, which is costly and requires significant access to resources and information, in effect limiting its usefulness for employees.

There are also numerous statutory exemptions to at-will employment. The earliest exception was signed into law in 1987 when Montana passed the Wrongful Discharge from Employment Act, which codifies the at-will exception for violations of public policy and discharge not for "good cause" after the employee completed the employer's "probationary period." By 2007, 34 states had given some legislative protection to whistle-blowers,and 22 states had signed into law legislation making it unlawful to terminate an employee as retaliation for that employee filing a worker's compensation claim.[54]

Throughout the nation, workers covered by federal antidiscrimination protections (including Title VII of the 1964 Civil Rights Act) have job protection against wrongful discharge based on race, religion, sex, age, and national origin. Since the 1960s, federal antidiscrimination protections have also been extended to disability status through the Americans with Disabilities Act of 1990, and to those needing family and medical leave through the Family and Medical Leave Act of 1993, which gives certain workers more protection from discharge. Finally, collective bargaining agreements frequently have provisions that require just cause for adverse employment actions, as well as procedures for arbitrating employee grievances, but few workers today are covered by these agreements.

Job Security: The Trends

The trends in unemployment and employment tell a mixed story. On the one hand, unemployment has generally fallen over time, which should indicate greater job security, until the years of the Great Recession. On the other hand, the past few decades have seen slower growth in employment rates (and falling employment rates for men), slow job growth, and a greater likelihood of losing a job involuntarily during good economic times, all of which point to decreased job security. In the longer term, job quality has deteriorated as middle-income job growth has slowed alongside rising inequality and as union coverage has fallen and there has been decreased enforcement of the labor laws on the books, and U.S. trade policies have failed to support U.S. jobs and consumer and labor protections.

Job security has decreased as our macroeconomic policymaking allowed the development of asset bubbles over the past two decades. The collapse of the housing bubble left millions unemployed and lowered the value of the most important assets—homes and 401(k)—for families. This collapse came on the heels of an already bad situation as the economic recovery of the 2000s produced the weakest growth in business investment, employment, and income that the United States had seen in a half century.[55] Fundamentally, the economic policies of the past decades have weakened job security through creating asset bubbles and unsustainable debt. The Bush administration's tax cuts, which went primarily to the wealthiest families, without sound measures to promote investment or economic growth, along with fighting two unpaid-for wars, put our federal balance sheet into deficit before the financial crisis even began. At the same time, a lack of effective regulation of the financial sector allowed bad practices to fester. While these concerns may have seemed far removed from job security as they were occurring over the past two decades, now that the bubbles have burst, clearly, the lack of focus on sustained economic growth has had devastating impacts on the availability of jobs and job quality.

A basic criterion for establishing job security is that there is employment security, that there are jobs available for those who want—and need—to work. Economists often measure this by using the unemployment rate and conclude that relatively low unemployment means that most of those seeking a job can find one. Low unemployment should also improve worker bargaining power on benefits and other workplace issues because when there are fewer job seekers, workers are more difficult to replace. Thus, low unemployment should improve job security for those without a job by making it easier to find employment, as well as improving job quality for those who have jobs.[56] Looking only at the rate of unemployment, the U.S. economy was moving toward greater job security, at least until we reached the Great Recession (see Figure 5.1).

However, there are other measures of the availability of jobs that tell a more nuanced story. The employment rate measures the share of the U.S. population with a job (see Figure 5.2). Even prior to the Great Recession, adult male employment was at post–World War II lows. Another measure is the ratio of job openings to job seekers, which Figure 5.3 shows for December 2000 through October 2010 (the data on job openings have been collected only since 2000). While there is not data available to see the long-term trend, over the short term, it was the case that non-recession years showed a ratio of job openings to job seekers as less than two.

Even though unemployment overall was secularly declining over the 1990s and 2000 (until 2008), long-term unemployment has been secularly *increasing*

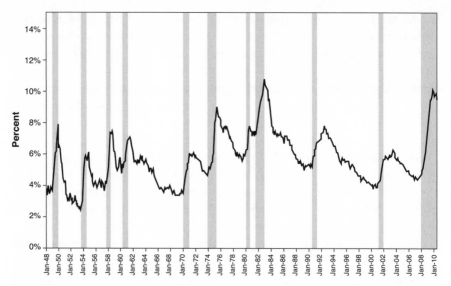

Figure 5.1:   Unemployment Rate, 1948–2010. Source: Bureau of Labor Statistics Current Population Survey, National Bureau of Economic Research Business Cycle Expansions and Contractions.

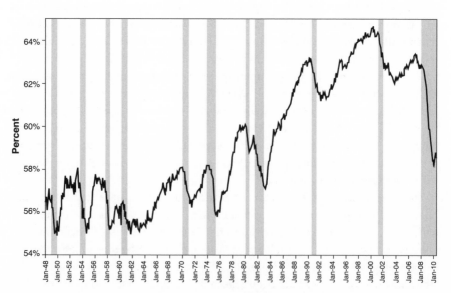

Figure 5.2:   Employment to Population Ratio, 1948–2010. Source: Bureau of Labor Statistics Current Population Survey, National Bureau of Economic Research Business Cycle Expansions and Contractions.

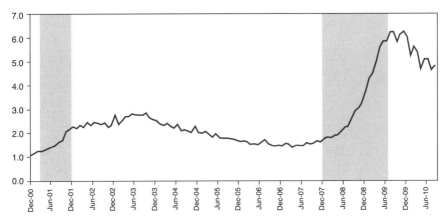

Figure 5.3:   Ratio of Job Openings to Job Seekers, 2000–2010. Source: Bureau of Labor Statistics Job Openings and Labor Turnover Survey, Bureau of Labor Statistics Current Population Survey, National Bureau of Economic Research Business Cycle Expansions and Contractions.

(see Figure 5.4). Workers are taking a longer time finding reemployment, even in low-unemployment years. Looking more closely, however, this trend may not be entirely about job insecurity, but may also rather reflect measurement and demographic changes. Economists Katharine Abraham and Robert Shimer have shown that part of the increase in the duration of unemployment is due to changes in the key survey, the Current Population Survey, which is used to measure long-term unemployment, as well the aging of the baby boomers. Once those measurement changes are accounted for, the increase in long-term unemployment is primarily among women and is accounted for by their greater labor force attachment— meaning that instead of dropping out of the labor force altogether after losing a job, women are choosing to stay in the labor force and job search, driving up overall unemployment duration figures.[57]

Another factor that points toward greater job insecurity is the share of the unemployed who involuntarily lost their jobs rather than voluntarily quitting, which has been growing over time (see Figure 5.5). Over the 2000s economic cycle, even as the economy hit relatively low unemployment rates, the share of those unemployed who had involuntarily lost their job remained relatively high. In the 1960s economic recovery, the share of the unemployed who had suffered involuntary job loss was below 35 percent, but by the 1980s and 1990s economic recoveries, that share had risen to 45 percent, and above 45 percent by the 2000s economic recovery.[58] Thus, when the economy was in recovery in recent years, more of the unemployed were "job losers." Economist Steven Davis of the University of Chicago has pointed out that the peaks of involuntarily job loss have fallen in the decades since the late 1980s, indicating a rise in job security;[59] however, the

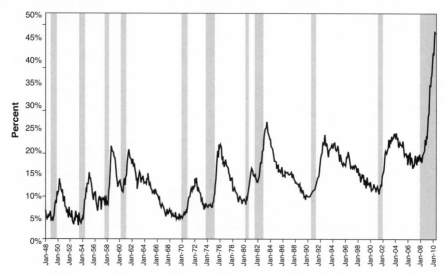

Figure 5.4: Share of the Unemployed Who Have Been Out of Work and Searching for a Job for at Least Six Months, 1948–2010. Source: Bureau of Labor Statistics Current Population Survey, National Bureau of Economic Research Business Cycle Expansions and Contractions.

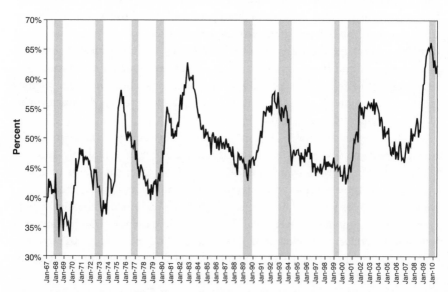

Figure 5.5: Involuntary Job Losers as a Share of All Unemployed, 1967–2010.
Source: Bureau of Labor Statistics Current Population Survey, National Bureau of Economic Research Business Cycle Expansions and Contractions.

overall trend has been a movement toward higher involuntary job loss during times of low unemployment, which moves in the opposite direction.

The data on job tenure also show that U.S. workers are staying in their jobs for shorter periods of time.[60] This does not necessarily indicate a decrease in job security, as people may be willingly switching jobs for improved opportunities. But it does mean that there are more chances that workers will be unemployed between jobs, and that traditional patterns of long-term employment are increasingly a thing of the past.

Significant changes have occurred in the overall picture of the U.S. labor market over the past four decades that affect the cost of job loss, most notably the changes in women's labor supply.[61] Women increased their labor supply sharply in the 1970s and 1980s and leveled off at a higher rate of labor supply in the late 1990s. Male labor supply fell slowly but consistently through the early 1980s, and has trended flat since then. Having two earners in most married-couple households increases incomes, but also increases the risks of job loss. A family with one male breadwinner who lost his job could have the at-home wife move into the labor force; even if she earned only two-thirds of what he earned, the family would have two-thirds of their pre–job loss income. Today, if the male earner loses his job, his wife is likely already working, and if the family is typical, then she brought home about 42 percent of the family's earnings pre–job loss, which is now what they are living on—far less than the two-thirds projected for a one-breadwinner family facing job loss.[62]

There are long-term structural factors that have played a role in eroding job security. The declining power of and membership in unions are clearly a piece of the puzzle. In recent years, unions have had less influence on establishing job security because union membership rates have fallen. Unions historically have provided a way for workers to improve job security as well as job quality. At a minimum, unions provide workers with employment contracts that typically detail how employees can be dismissed, but, just as importantly, unions create democratic institutions within workplaces to provide workers with a voice at work. Over the past few decades, however, the U.S. economy has seen a decline in the share of workers covered by a union. In 1948, nearly one-third of U.S. workers (31.8 percent) were in a union, but by 2009, fewer than one in eight workers (12.3 percent) were union members. The decline in union membership has been concentrated in the private sector, where unionization has fallen steadily since the mid-1970s, and was at 7.2 percent in 2009.[63] The cause of union decline is not only due to the loss of jobs in high-union-density industries such as manufacturing, but also concerted efforts on the part of employers to fight union organizing.

Employers are still working hard to discourage employees from exercising their democratic right to join a union. A key reason for the decline in unionization among private-sector employees is their employers' heightened anti-union campaigns. The election process has been so degraded that it is often impossible to consider union elections free and fair. Those who try to form unions are likely to get fired, even though such terminations are illegal. Economists John Schmitt and Ben Zipperer found that between 15 and 20 percent of union organizers can expect to be fired during a union organizing campaign.[64] Among firms that are found to have fired employees in violation of the National Labor Relations Act, "the average back pay award amounted to $2,749 per discharge," a relatively small amount and certainly not enough to enforce compliance.[65]

At the same time that unions, the private-sector's key mechanism for promoting job quality, were in decline, federal enforcement of U.S. labor laws has been weakened. Some weakening has been due to explicit policymaking: federal regulatory changes in 2004 reduced the reach of the overtime pay protections of the Fair Labor Standards Act by greatly expanding the definition of "executive, administrative, and professional" workers who are exempted from the rule. Analysts estimated in 2003 that this redefinition would remove an added 8 million workers (about 6 percent of the total employed workforce) from eligibility for overtime pay.[66]

There have also been cutbacks in the enforcement of basic labor standards. As sociologist Annette Bernhardt and her coauthors document, there has been a growing lack of enforcement of basic labor law, significantly weakening the power of the laws on the books. Increasing numbers of employers are breaking, bending, or evading long-established laws and standards designed to protect workers, from the minimum wage to job safety standards to the right to organize.[67] But the issue is not only employers breaking the law. As Bernhardt and her colleagues put it:

> Just as significant has been the wholesale change in expectations—the norms of the workplace. What were once considered basic elements of having a job—access to predictable and regular hours, employer-subsidized health care, pensions, vacation and sick-day accrual—have become, in effect, workplace luxuries as employers have focused more on the bottom line than social responsibility. Employees' costs have gone up as the financial burden for health coverage and retirement plans (gains won in part through post-war unionization) has shifted from owner to worker.[68]

One important exception to the trend toward decreased security for quality jobs has been a growing recognition that job security for workers with care responsibilities, an increasing segment of the labor force, is often less strong than it is for other workers. In 1993, the Family and Medical Leave Act passed, which amended the Fair Labor Standards Act to allow workers who work in business establishments with 50 or more employees to take job-protected leave to care for a new child, to care for a seriously ill family member, or to recover from one's own serious illness. Furthermore, in 2007, the Equal Employment Opportunity Commission released a new set of guidelines to help employers avoid discriminating against workers with caretaking responsibilities. These guidelines represent a strong clarification of how existing laws—Title VII and the Americans with

Disabilities Act—provide protection for families who are working to achieve a balance between the responsibilities of work and family. Nonetheless, the paucity of policies available to help workers cope with work-family conflict means that workers with care responsibilities often continue to be more vulnerable to job insecurity than other workers.[69]

Economists have argued that globalization and factory automation are to blame for a "hollowing out" of the middle of the U.S. wage distribution.[70] Economist David Autor, for example, has shown that the economy has created fewer middle-income jobs and more low-wage jobs, which has exacerbated the trend toward greater wage inequality.[71] The argument is that the middle of the wage distribution tends to have more jobs that can be automated, such as bank tellers, secretaries, and production workers, as well as jobs that can be moved more easily overseas, such as manufacturing, computer programming, or call-center staffing. In contrast, jobs at the low end of the wage distribution that require manual labor, such as child-care workers, janitors, or home health aides, and jobs at the very top of the wage distribution that often require analytic thinking, such as educators, doctors, or lawyers, are more challenging to outsource or automate out of existence.

However, other developed countries facing the same global and technological trends as the United States have seen different job security outcomes. In the United States, a factor in declining job security has been trade policy. Estimates based on the seminal work of Nobel Prize–winning economist Paul Krugman show that trade liberalization dating from the 1970s to the early 1990s accounts for about 40 percent of the observed increase in the ratio of skilled to unskilled workers' wages, and accounts for even more of that inequality in the post–North American Free Trade Agreement (NAFTA) period.[72] NAFTA created a trade area between Canada, the United States, and Mexico, but unlike the European Union, NAFTA did not establish "readiness criteria" before poorer countries could be admitted, nor did it allow for meaningful transfer of development funds.[73] This meant that NAFTA was implemented without requirements for Mexico to enforce international labor, social, or environmental standards. Moreover, investor rights and other provisions in NAFTA provided additional incentives for firms to relocate to Mexico to take advantage of a weaker labor and regulatory environment.[74] In addition to the loss of U.S. manufacturing jobs,[75] NAFTA has led to a climate in which U.S. firms increasingly invoke the threat of moving abroad, quashing job quality demands.[76] The United States has continued these kinds of policies in trade agreements following NAFTA.

Similarly, the World Trade Organization granted China membership in 2001 with a five-year grace period to comply with WTO guidelines, an exception that only exacerbated outsourcing trends. China's entry into the global trade regime resulted in massive trade imbalances with the United States as more and more U.S. companies moved their entire operations to China or outsourced manufacturing and assembly of products there. Only recently has the U.S. government acted to take China to the WTO to enforce trade rules, which is a lengthy legal process that so far has done little to help American workers protect their jobs at home.[77]

Improving Job Security for All

Clearly, at this moment, addressing the enormous employment challenges brought on by the Great Recession is the most urgent task for job security. The question is how we will lay the foundation for full employment in a political environment increasingly concerned about deficit reduction. Although concerns about the long-term deficit may be important, this chapter began by making the case that job security is key to economic security, and job security hinges most importantly on full employment. If policymakers abandon that goal, this does not bode well for the economic well-being of working families.

Although this chapter is not explicitly about job security during the Great Recession, given the immense challenges it poses, it is important to begin the discussion of public policy solutions to job insecurity by discussing how effective the federal government's response has been in addressing the issue as it has embarked on an exceptional policy response to the Great Recession. Key among these have been the Federal Reserve's actions to keep interest rates at effectively zero since the fall of 2008 and actions taken to sustain credit availability in the midst of the financial crisis. To address the fallout of the financial crisis on the real economy, policymakers enacted the largest economic stimulus funding in U.S. history through the American Recovery and Reinvestment Act of 2009.

The Recovery Act increased demand in the economy through, among other things, extending unemployment benefits to the long-term unemployed and helping states maintain spending in the face of lower tax revenues.[78] The economic stimulus provided by the Recovery Act, however, was not large enough to fill in the output gap, which is the difference between the actual output of the nation and what we could produce if all the unused productive capacity was in use, including everything from idle machines to unemployed workers. Further, the composition of spending in the Recovery Act included too many tax cuts and not enough spending with higher economic multipliers that would have done more to boost employment.[79] As of mid-2010, corporations have seen their profits recover and are sitting on large amounts of cash, but investment has not risen enough to spur sufficient job growth to start bringing the unemployment rate down.[80]

The Congressional Budget Office credits the Recovery Act with saving or creating 1.4 million to 3.3 million jobs by August 2010.[81] Even so, as of the end of the summer of 2010, there were nearly 15 million workers unemployed, nearly half of them had been out of work and searching for a job for at least six months, and there were five job seekers for every job opening available. Addressing the root causes of the Great Recession—in particular, a lack of effective financial regulation—is critical to ensuring long-term job security.

Here are some sound policy suggestions to get to full employment:

AIM FOR FULL EMPLOYMENT, NOT HALF EMPLOYMENT

One concern moving forward is that economists will begin to revisit estimates of the lower bound of the unemployment rate. Already, economist Edmund Phelps has been quoted as saying that the Great Recession has raised the natural rate of unemployment up to 7 percent, and conservative members of Congress have begun to push to eliminate the Federal Reserve's full employment mandate and to have them focus only on inflation.[82] But there is no *a priori* reason to presume that today's higher unemployment means that our economy cannot get back to the low unemployment of the past two economic recoveries, when we hit 3.8 percent unemployment in the late 1990s and 4.4 percent in the 2000s. Policymakers should focus on reducing unemployment to be only frictional, that is, creating near one-to-one ratio of job openings to job seekers. The objection to full employment often takes the form of bemoaning potential inflation, but a key factor in propagating price increases through an economy have typically been labor contracts that include cost-of-living adjustments. With so few U.S. workers in a union, there is no institutional mechanism for prices spiraling rapidly into sustained nominal wage gains.

NO MORE BUBBLES

One key lesson of the past two decades is that recoveries propped up by bubbles lead to disastrous outcomes for families. Recent research has shown that recessions following a financial crisis, such as the current recession, tend to be deeper and more protracted than other recessions.[83] The federal government, including the Federal Reserve, should focus on identifying and avoiding bubbles before they spiral out of control, including closer regulation of financial markets to ensure the stability of the financial system.

INEQUALITY THREATENS STABLE RECOVERY, WHICH THREATENS JOB SECURITY

A deeper lesson is that in the decades prior to the Great Recession, our economy became increasingly reliant on finance and incomes became increasingly unequal, with those at the very top pulling sharply away from those in the middle and bottom of the income distribution.[84] An economy that generated more equal outcomes would be more resilient because a broad consumer base leads to more stable demand, which is especially important as consumption drives the majority of our economy.[85] This is the lesson that Henry Ford tried to teach nearly a century ago: giving workers a fair day's pay means that they will be able to purchase the goods they produce.

MAKE SURE THE UNEMPLOYMENT INSURANCE SYSTEM RESPONDS TO UNEMPLOYMENT

We need to reform the unemployment insurance system so that it is more responsive to economic conditions, because that responsiveness in turn is good for the macroeconomy. The unemployment system is designed to provide a temporary income bridge as a worker searches for his or her next job. As such, the system normally provides benefits for a maximum of 26 weeks. It has long been recognized, however, that finding a job in 26 weeks may not be possible during periods of high unemployment, such as in a recession, no matter how willing and determined the worker. The program was therefore later modified to automatically extend unemployment benefits to the long-term unemployed—those who lost their job through no fault of their own and have been unable to find a new job for at least six months—if a state develops high unemployment.

Yet the "trigger" system does not work as it now exists. Few states activate the trigger quickly or at all during labor market downturns, and they extend benefits only when Congress acts separately to do so. Because the trigger system is broken, Congress has had to act repeatedly over the course of the current recession to extend the duration of unemployment benefits. Reforming the system to allow states to cycle off long-term unemployment benefits as they emerge out of the recession, rather than having an arbitrary cutoff date of a certain number of weeks, would be a good way to make the system more responsive to the labor market.[86] Among other things, implementing a state-by-state "off trigger" for extended unemployment benefits would eliminate uncertainty for the states and the cessation of benefits for the unemployed.

ENCOURAGE WORK-SHARING

When businesses need to cut back on staffing, they have two options: lay off workers or reduce hours. There are strong incentives in our labor market to simply lay off workers—benefits are often tied to the worker, not to his or her hours. But incentivizing layoffs makes no economic sense. Indeed, new evidence from Germany shows that "short-term work programs," which encourage employers to reduce hours rather than lay off workers, can significantly reduce overall unemployment rates. Although output fell more in Germany during the Great Recession than it did in the United States, the German unemployment rate actually *decreased*. Recent research by the International Monetary Fund points to the importance of the massive expansions to Germany's short-term work program, the *Kurzarbeit*, which led to reductions in hours but not higher unemployment.[87]

Currently, 17 U.S. states have opted into the "short-time compensation" or "work-sharing" program within their unemployment insurance system, which allows workers to receive partial benefits from the unemployment insurance system if their hours have been reduced, not just if they lost their job or their pay is reduced. This policy could be expanded to all states. Mark Zandi estimates that the multiplier for the short-term compensation program would be relatively high: for every dollar spent on the program, $1.69 would be added to our economy's output.[88]

TRADE POLICIES THAT PROMOTE QUALITY JOBS

Globalization and trade in general have affected nearly every aspect of the U.S. economy, and our trade policies specifically have affected how vulnerable U.S. jobs are to these transnational processes. Although other advanced economies have faced the exact same set of global competitive pressures as the United States, many of our partners have worked to create policies that have avoided greater job insecurity or higher inequality in their own countries.[89] As a case in point, trade adjustment assistance is available to U.S. workers who have lost their job or had their hours cut due to trade, but the federal government has spent too little energy developing a coherent competitiveness strategy that takes into account the need to fully utilize our human capital. In contrast, when the European Union establishes "readiness criteria" for poorer countries to be admitted to the EU, it creates a level playing field for labor, other industries, and other standards, so that trade does not become a race to the bottom with the incorporation of new countries into the Union.

There are also specific polices that focus on ensuring greater job security and job quality for individual workers:

ALLOW UNIONS TO FLOURISH WHERE EMPLOYEES WANT THEM

We need to make it easier for workers to organize unions. A recent poll shows that a record high share of workers—58 percent of those eligible—would join a union if they could. This means that there are 60 million workers in the United States who would like to join a union.[90] Buttressing this poll result is this fact: even though overall unionization has declined, union organizing drives that end with the democratic process of an election (a sporadic occurrence in recent years) are now more likely to end with a union victory.[91]

We need a new system that establishes a free and fair election process for unionization. We should allow unions to demand recognition once the majority of employees have signed authorization cards indicating that they want the union as their bargaining representative, and we should establish stronger penalties for employers who violate employee rights when workers try to organize a union or to bargain their first contract, as well as providing mediation and arbitration for first-contract disputes, as is written into the Employee Free Choice Act, which has languished in Congress.

ENFORCE THE LABOR LAWS THAT EXIST

To restore worker protections, we need to reactivate government regulation and revive unions or other elements of civil society. There are campaigns nationwide that are working to restore labor regulations, including traditional union campaigns. The living wage movement, which has successfully organized campaigns across the country, has established minimum wages and benefits for workers in municipalities and around the country. Immigrant worker centers help low-wage workers organize outside traditional unions. But, we also need to focus on legislation and federal enforcement of the laws on the books. There are a number of ways in which the administration could do this, such as using penalties to create a culture of accountability; increasing agency capabilities by strengthening relationships with community organizations, industry associations, state worker-protection agencies, and labor unions; targeting high-violation sectors with strategic initiatives; using thorough record keeping to drive enforcement priorities, enhance public accountability, and improve performance evaluation; and strengthening immigrant protections to improve job quality for all workers.[92] Another way to achieve this is through use of the federal contracting system. The federal government could do a better job screening companies based on their overall regulatory record, including the company's compliance with labor laws, and could promote higher labor standards by evaluating proposals based in part on the quality of jobs that contractors provide their workers.[93]

REFORM EMPLOYMENT-AT-WILL

In an era when many workers were covered by union contracts, employment-at-will might have made sense. But, in today's economy, this policy adds to the risk facing workers. Even if they have a job, they serve at the pleasure of their employer, creating significant power imbalances in favor of employers. Legislators could rethink this model and provide workers with the right to reasonable grounds for dismissal.

Conclusion

Over time, the U.S. government has taken a variety of steps to mitigate job insecurity, primarily through focusing macroeconomic policy on the goal of full employment. In recent years, however, economic trends have moved toward greater job insecurity, especially for some groups of workers. Outsourcing, the automation of the production process, and the decline in unions have all conspired to reduce job security for U.S. workers, as did macroeconomic policymaking.

At the same time, Congress has not updated policies that insulate workers from unemployment and job insecurity. Reimagining and reinvigorating the government's role in job security are the first steps toward an economy that works for all of us.

Notes

1. Heather Boushey and Ann O'Leary, eds., *The Shriver Report: A Woman's Nation Changes Everything* (Washington, DC: Center for American Progress,2009).
2. As part of the American Recovery and Reinvestment Act of 2009, the federal government provided unemployed workers with COBRA premium subsidies to help those workers with employer-based coverage to be able to afford their health insurance after losing their job. Unfortunately, the Patient Protection and Affordable Care Act of 2010 did not extend this subsidy. This act provides subsidies for individuals without access to employer-based coverage to purchase health insurance through the state health insurance exchanges, but the transition for unemployed workers is likely to still come with real challenges of affordability during periods of unemployment.
3. Heather Boushey and Jeffrey Wenger, "Coming up Short: Current Unemployment Insurance Benefits Fail to Meet Basic Family Needs" (Washington, DC: Economic Policy Institute, 2001), http://www.epi.org/page/-old/Issuebriefs/ib169/ib169.pdf
4. William Julius Wilson, *When Work Disappears: The World of the New Urban Poor* (New York: Knopf, 1996).
5. Katherine Edin and Laura Lein, *Making Ends Meet: How Single Mothers Survive Welfare and Low-Wage Work* (New York: Russell Sage Foundation, 1997); Katherine S. Newman, *No Shame in My Game: The Working Poor in the Inner City* (New York: Alfred A. Knopf and the Russell Sage Foundation, 1999); Robert D. Putnam, *Bowling Alone: The Collapse and Revival of American Community* (New York: Simon & Schuster, 2000).
6. Quinlan Rosner Greenberg and Public Opinion Strategies National Public Radio, "NPR Congressional Battleground Poll" (National Public Radio, 2010).
7. Although unemployment has not reached as high a level as the early 1980s peak, when we adjust for changes in the composition of the labor force in terms of age and education, the economy has surpassed prior post–World War II peaks. For more on historical levels of unemployment and underemployment, see John Schmitt and Dean Baker, "Is the U.S. Unemployment Rate Today Already as High as It Was in 1982?" (Washington, DC: Center for Economic and Policy Research, 2009).
8. Jeffrey M. Jones, "Voters Rate Economy as Top Issue for 2010" *Gallup*, April 8, 2010, available at http://www.gallup.com/poll/127247/Voters-Rate-Economy-Top-Issue-2010.aspx.
9. Bureau of Labor Statistics, "The Employment Situation: Employees on Nonfarm Payrolls by Industry Sector and Selected Industry Detail."
10. Bureau of Labor Statistics, *Job Openings and Labor Turnover Survey* (U.S. Department of Labor, 2010); Bureau of Labor Statistics, *Employment Status of the Civilian Population by Sex and Age* (U.S. Department of Labor, 2010), table A-1.
11. See, for example, Jacob S. Hacker, *The Great Risk Shift* (New York: Oxford University Press, 2006).
12. New data from the Bureau of Labor Statistics has allowed us to track this relationship since 2000, alongside the data on unemployment that goes back to the mid-1940s.
13. A. W. Phillips, "The Relationship between Unemployment and the Rate of Change of Money Wage Rates in the United Kingdom," *Economica* (1958): 283–299.
14. David G. Blanchflower and Andrew J. Oswald, *The Wage Curve* (Cambridge, MA: MIT Press, 1994).

15. Ibid.; David Blanchflower and Andrew Oswald, "The Wage Curve Reloaded," Working Paper 11338, (Cambridge, MA: National Bureau of Economic Research, 2005), http://nber.org/papers/w11338.pdf

16. Heather Boushey, "Reworking the Wage Curve: Exploring the Consistency of the Model across Time, Space and Demographic Group," *Review of Political Economy* 14 (3) (2002): 293–311.

17. Carl Shapiro and Joseph Stiglitz, "Equilibrium Unemployment as a Labor Discipline Device," *American Economic Review* 74, no. 3 (1984): 433–444.

18. Bureau of Labor Statistics, *Unemployed Persons by Reason of Unemployment* (U.S. Department of Labor, 2010), table A-11.

19. Annette Bernhardt et al., eds., *The Gloves-Off Economy: Workplace Standards at the Bottom of America's Labor Market*, An ILR Press Book LERA Research Volume (Ithaca, NY: Cornell University Press,2009).

20. Bureau of Labor Statistics, "Current Employment Statistics: Table B-1: Employees on Nonfarm Payrolls by Industry Sector and Selected Industry Detail," http://www.bls.gov/webapps/legacy/cestab1.htm

21. Alexandra Cawthorne, "Weathering the Storm: Black Men in the Recession" (Washington, DC: Center for American Progress, 2009), http://www.americanprogress.org/issues/2009/04/pdf/black_men_recession.pdf

22. Kathryn Anne Edwards and Alexander Hertel-Fernandez, "The Kids Aren't Alright—a Labor Market Analysis of Young Workers" (Washington, DC: Economic Policy Institute, 2010), http://www.epi.3cdn.net/1a64c4b106d2da34e_ulm6b5g31.pdf

23. Heather Boushey and Liz Weiss, "How Unmarried Women Continue to See High Unemployment in April" (Washington, DC: Center for American Progress, 2010), http://www.american-progress.org/issues/2010/05/unmarried_women_unemployment.html

24. See Annette Bernhardt et al., *Divergent Paths: Economic Mobility in the New American Labor Market* (New York: Russell Sage Foundation, 2001); Bruce Western, Jeffrey R. Kling, and David F. Weinman, "The Labor Market Consequences of Incarceration" (Princeton: Princeton University Industrial Relations Section, 2001); Jean-Francois Ravaud, Beatrice Madiot, and Isabelle Ville, "Discrimination Towards Disabled People Seeking Employment," *Social Science and Medicine* 35, no. 8 (1992): 951–958; Lisa Dodson, "Wage-Poor Mothers and Moral Economy," *Social Politics* (2007): 1–23.

25. Henry S. Farber, "Job Loss and the Decline in Job Security in the United States," CEPS Working Paper No. 171, (Princeton: Princeton University, Center for Economics Policy Studies and the Industrial Relations, 2007) 26, http://www.irs.princeton.edu/pubs/pdfs/520.pdf.

26. John Schmitt, "The Rise in Job Displacement, 1991–2004: The Crisis in American Manufacturing" (Washington, DC: Center for Economic and Policy Research, 2004), 16, http://cepr.net/documents/publications/labormarkets_2004_08.pdf

27. Lisa B Kahn, "The Long-Term Labor Market Consequence of Graduating from College in a Bad Economy," *Labour Economics* 17 (2010): 303–316.

28. John Irons, "Economic Scarring: The Long-Term Impacts of the Recession" (Washington, DC: Economic Policy Institute, 2009), http://www.epi.org/publications/entry/bp243/

29. Daniel Sullivan and Til Von Wachter, "Mortality, Mass-Layoffs, and Career Outcomes: An Analysis Using Administrative Data," Working Paper 13626 (Cambridge: National Bureau of Economic Research, 2007), http://www.nber.org/papers/w13626

30. Ibid.

31. Krysia Mossakowski, "The Influence of Past Unemployment Duration on Symptoms of Depression among Young Women and Men in the United States," *American Journal of Public Health* 10 (2009): 1826–32.

32. Author's analysis of Internal Revenue Service, "Individual Income Tax, All Returns: Sources of Incomes and Adjustments."

33. John Maynard Keynes, *The General Theory* (New York: Harcourt, 1956).

34. U.S. Congress, Senate Committee on Finance, *Testimony of Mark Zandi on Using Unemployment Insurance to Help Americans Get Back to Work: Creating Opportunities and Overcoming Challenges*, 111th Cong., 2d sess., 2010.

35. *Employment Act, U.S. Code* 15 (1946), § 1021, as quoted in J. Bradford DeLong, "Keynesianism, Pennsylvania Avenue Style: Some Economic Consequences of the Employment Act of 1946," *The Journal of Economic Perspectives* 10 (1996): 41, http://www.j-bradford-delong.net/teaching_folder/Econ_210c_spring_2002/Readings/delong_Pennsylvania.pdf

36. Ibid., 45.

37. This issue of Federal Reserve independence became part of the 2010 debate over financial regulation, but oversight of the Federal Reserve was not in the final legislation.

38. The most ardent proponent of this view was Milton Friedman, who, with his wife Anna Schwartz, published the seminal text *A Monetary History of the United States, 1867–1960* in 1963. See Milton Friedman and Anna Schwartz, *A Monetary History of the United States 1867–1960* (Princeton: Princeton University Press, 1963).

39. Robert Gordon, "The Time Varying NAIRU and Its Implications for Economic Policy," *Journal of Economic Perspectives* 11 (Fall 1997): 11–32.

40. David M. Gordon, "The Un-Natural Rate of Unemployment: An Econometric Critique of the NAIRU Hypothesis," *The American Economic Review* 78, no. 2 (1988): 117–123.

41. Peter T. Kilborn, "The Business Cycle Rolls over and Plays Dead," *New York Times*, January 11, 1987.

42. The phrase was first used in James H. Stock and Mark W. Watson, "Has the Business Cycle Changed and Why?," *NBER Macroeconomics Annual* 17 (2002): 159–218.

43. Erica L. Groshen and Simon Potter, "Has Structural Change Contributed to a Jobless Recovery?," *Current Issues in Economics and Finance, Federal Reserve Bank of New York* 9. no. 8 (2003).

44. Wage and Hour Division, *Overtime Pay Overview* (U.S. Department of Labor, 2009).

45. Franklin Delano Roosevelt, "Fireside Chat 12: On the Recession," (Miller Center for Public Affairs, University of Virginia, 1938).

46. Bureau of Labor Statistics, *Median Weekly Earnings of Full-Time Wage and Salary Workers by Detailed Occupation and Sex, Current Population Survey* (U.S. Department of Labor, 2010), table 39; Wage and Hour Division, *Changes in Basic Minimum Wages in Non-Farm Employment under State Law: Selected Years 1968 to 2010* (U.S. Department of Labor, 2010).

47. Bureau of Labor Statistics, *Minimum Wage Laws in the States—July 1, 2010* (U.S. Department of Labor, 2010).

48. In *Evelyn Coke vs. Long Island Care at Home*, the Supreme Court ruled that the U.S. Department of Labor could continue to exclude home care aides from the federal Fair Labor Standards Act's wage and hour protections. *Fair Labor Standards Amendments of 1966*, Public Law 601, 89th Cong., 1st sess. (September 23, 1966); *Fair Labor Standards Amendments of 1974*, Public Law 259, 93rd Cong., 2d sess. (April 8, 1984).

49. Jane Whitney Gibson and Lester Lindley, "The Evolution of Employment-at-Will: Past, Present, and Future Predictions" (paper presented at the Ninth Annual IBER and TLC Conference, Las Vegas, NC, 2009).

50. Charles J. Muhl, "The Employment-at-Will Doctrine: The Major Exceptions," *Monthly Labor Review* 124 (2001): 3–11.

51. Ibid.

52. Ibid.

53. Ibid.

54. Gibson and Lindley, "The Evolution of Employment-at-Will: Past, Present, and Future Predictions."

55. Josh Bivens and John Irons, "A Feeble Recovery: The Fundamental Economic Weaknesses of the 2001-07 Expansion" (Washington, DC: Economic Policy Institute, 2008), http://www.epi.org/publications/entry/bp214

56. Dean Baker and Jared Bernstein, *The Benefits of Full Employment: When Markets Work for People* (Washington, DC: Economic Policy Institute, 2003).

57. Katharine G. Abraham and Robert Shimer, "Changes in Unemployment Duration and Labor Force Attachment," Working Paper 8513 (Cambridge: National Bureau of Economic Research, 2001).

58. Bureau of Labor Statistics, *Unemployed Persons by Reason of Unemployment*.

59. Steven J. Davis, "The Decline of Job Loss and Why It Matters," *American Economic Review* 98. no. 2 (2008): 263–67.

60. Farber, "Job Loss and the Decline in Job Security in the United States."

61. Thomas Weisskopf, Samuel Bowles, and David Gordon, "Hearts and Minds: A Social Model of Aggregate Productivity Growth in the United States, 1948–79," *Brookings Papers on Economic Activity* 2 (1983): 381–441.

62. This issue is summarized in Elizabeth Warren and Amelia Warren Tyagi, *The Two-Income Trap: Why Middle-Class Mothers and Fathers Are Going Broke* (New York: Basic Books, 2003).

63. John Schmitt and Ben Zipperer, "Dropping the Ax: Illegal Firings during Union Election Campaigns" (Washington, DC: Center for Economic and Policy Research, 2007), http://www.cepr. net/documents/publications/dropping-the-ax-update-2009-03.pdf; Bureau of Labor Statistics, *Union Members Summary* (U.S. Department of Labor, 2010).

64. Schmitt and Zipperer, "Dropping the Ax: Illegal Firings During Union Election Campaigns"; Kate Bronfenbrenner, "Uneasy Terrain: The Impact of Capital Mobility on Workers, Wages, and Union Organizing," Research Studies and Reports, Paper 3 (Cornell University ILR School, 2000), http://www.citizenstrade.org/pdf/nafta_uneasy_terrain.pdf

65. John T. Dunlop, "Fact Finding Report: Commission on the Future of Worker-Management Relations," Federal Publications, Paper 276 (Washington, DC: Cornell University ILR School, 1994), 66, http://www.digitalcommons.ilr.cornell.edu/Ley_workplace/276.

66. Ross Eisenbrey and Jared Bernstein, "Eliminating the Right to Overtime Pay" (Washington, DC: Economic Policy Institute, 2003), http://www.epi.org/publications/entry/briefingpapers_flsa_jun03

67. Annette Bernhardt et al., eds., *The Gloves-Off Economy: Workplace Standards at the Bottom of America's Labor Market.*

68. Annette Bernhardt et al., "Confronting the Gloves-Off Economy: America's Broken Labor Standards and How to Fix Them" (UCLA Institute for Research on Labor and Employment, Center for Economic Policy Research, Center on Wisconsin Strategy, National Employment Law Project, 2009) 2, http://cepr.net/documents/publications/gloves_off_final.pdf

69. Boushey and O'Leary, eds., *The Shriver Report: A Woman's Nation Changes Everything.*

70. Lawrence F. Katz, David H. Autor, and Melissa S. Kearney, "Trends in U.S. Wage Inequality: Revising the Revisionists," *The Review of Economics and Statistics* 90 (2) (2008): 300–323; Alan S. Blinder, "How Many U.S. Jobs Might Be Offshorable?" Working Paper 142 (2007).

71. David H. Autor, "The Polarization of Job Opportunities in the U.S. Labor Market: Implications for Employment and Earnings" (Washington, DC: Center for American Progress and The Hamilton Project, 2010), http://www.brookings.edu/~/media/Files/rc/papers/2010/04_jobs_autor.pdf

72. Paul Krugman, "Trade and Inequality, Revisited" (London, UK: VoxEU.org, 2007), http://www.voxeu.org/index.php?q=node/261; Dean Baker and Mark Weisbrot, "Will New Trade Gains Make Us Rich? An Assessment of the Prospective Gains from New Trade Agreements," http://www.cepr.net/documents/publications/will_new_trade_gains_make_us_ric.htm (Washington, DC: Center for Economic Policy Research, 2001); William R. Cline, *Trade and Income Distribution* (Washington, DC: Peterson Institute for International Economics, 1997).

73. The European Union refers to these as "convergence criteria" or "Maastricht Criteria." Sarah Anderson and John Cavanagh, "Lessons of European Integration for the Americas" (Washington: Institute for Policy Studies, 2004), http://aei.pitt.edu/1436

74. Mary Bottari and Lori Wallach, "Nafta's Threat to Sovereignty and Democracy: The Record of NAFTA Chapter 11 Investor-State Cases 1994–2005," Public Citizen Publication Number: E9014, (Washington, DC: Public Citizens Global Trade Watch, 2005), http://www.citizen.org/documents/Chapter%2011%20Report%20Final.pdf

75. Josh Bivens, "Trade Deficits and Manufacturing Job Loss: Correlation and Causality" (Washington, DC: Economic Policy Institute, 2006), http://www.epi.org/publications/entry/bp171/

76. Kate Bronfenbrenner, "We'll Close! Plant Closings, Plant—Closing Threats, Union Organizing, and NAFTA," *Multinational Monitor* (1997): 56–59; Kate Bronfenbrenner, "Uneasy Terrain: The Impact of Capital Mobility on Workers, Wages, and Union Organizing."

77. Chad P. Bown, "U.S.-China Trade Conflicts and the Future of the WTO," *The Fletcher Forum of World Affairs* 33, no. 1 (2009): 27–48.

78. Heather Boushey, "A Better Way to Help the Unemployed" (Washington, DC: Center for American Progress, 2010), http://www.americanprogress.org/issues/2010/02/unemployment_insurance.html

79. Paul Krugman, "Stimulus Arithmetic (Wonkish but Important)," *New York Times* Blog: The Conscience of a Liberal, January 9, 2009, available at http://krugman.blogs.nytimes.com/2009/01/06/stimulus-arithmetic-wonkish-but-important/.

80. Christian E. Weller, "Economic Snapshot for July 2010" (Washington, DC: Center for American Progress, 2010), http://www.americanprogress.org/issues/2010/07/econsnap0710.html

81. U.S. Congressional Budget Office, *Estimated Impact of the American Recovery and Reinvestment Act on Employment and Economic Output from April 2010 through June 2010* (Washington, DC, 2010).

82. Representative Mike Pence (R-IN) has introduced a bill to eliminate the full employment mandate. See *To Amend the Federal Reserve Act to Remove the Mandate on the Board of Governors of the Federal Reserve System and the Federal Open Market Committee to Focus on Maximum Employment*, 111th Cong., 2d sess, H.R.6406

83. Carmen M. Reinharta and Kenneth S. Rogoff, "The Aftermath of Financial Crises," *American Economic Review* 100, no. 2 (2010): 466–72.

84. Thomas Piketty and Emmanuel Saez, "Income Inequality in the United States." Working Paper 8467 (Cambridge: National Bureau of Economic Research, 2001).

85. Paul Krugman, "Inequality and Crises: Coincidence or Causation?" (Princeton: Princeton University 2009), http://www.princeton.edu/~pKrugman/inequality_crises.pdf

86. Jeffrey B. Wenger and Heather Boushey, "Triggers That Work: Redesigning an Effective Unemployment Insurance Extended Benefits Program" (Washington, DC: Center for American Progress, 2010), http://www.americanprogress.org/issues/2010/02/ui_trigger.html

87. International Monetary Fund, "World Economic Outlook: Rebalancing Growth," Work Economic and Financial Surveys (Washington, DC: International Monetary Fund, April 2010), 71, http://www.imf.org/external/pubs/ft/weo/2010/01/pdf/text.pdf

88. U.S. Congress, Joint Economic Committee, *Testimony of Mark Zandi on the Impact of the Recovery Act on Economic Growth*,Cong., 111th Cong., 2d sess., 2009.

89. Francisco Rodriguez and Dani Rodrik, "Trade Policy and Economic Growth: A Skeptic's Guide to the Cross-National Evidence." Working Paper 7081 (University of Maryland, Harvard University, 1999).

90. Peter D. Hart Research Associates, "Opinion Research on Unions and Employee Free Choice Act" (Washington, DC: AFL-CIO, 2006); Committee on Education and Labor, *Strengthening America's Middle Class through the Employee Free Choice Act: Hearings on the Employee Free Choice Act*, 110th Cong., 1st sess., 2007.

91. Schmitt and Zipperer, "Dropping the Ax: Illegal Firings during Union Election Campaigns."

92. David Madland and Karla Walter, "Enforcing Change: Five Strategies for the Obama Administration to Enforce Workers' Rights at the Department of Labor" (Washington, DC: Center for American Progress, 2008), http://www.americanprogress.org/issues/2008/12/aw_enforcingchange.html

93. Committee on Armed Services, *David Madland Testimony on Promoting Higher Labor Standards in Federal Contracting Testimony for the House Committee on Armed Services*, 111th Cong., 2d sess., 2009.

6

Income Security When Temporarily Away from Work

STEPHEN D. SUGARMAN

Introduction

Suppose that you are ill or injured and temporarily unable to work. Or suppose that you are temporarily laid off or temporarily between jobs. Or suppose that you need to be away from work to care for a relative, or want to be away from work to go on a vacation. What do you do for income during periods like these? Assume that you get no income from either your employer or the government during such periods. Because you would have to engage in self-help, what might you do?

You could save money in advance to draw upon when your income temporarily stops. You could borrow money in times of temporary need and repay it later. You could seek gifts from friends, family, and/or charities. You could purchase private insurance that provides income when you are temporarily in need. In some families, if one earner is temporarily without income, perhaps another can start earning or can earn more. But this is less likely in today's world in which both adults in a two-adult household are often already working in as highly paid jobs as they can reasonably find.[1]

In the real world, all of these self-help strategies are problematic. Too many people fail to save significant sums for "rainy days";[2] most can at best cover only a couple of missed paychecks.[3] In some cases, the lack of savings is the result of short-sighted thinking that they won't ever be away from work and hence without income. Others would like to save, but have reluctantly concluded that spending on essentials eats up all of their regular income. Still others make foolish choices to spend for immediate pleasure and have nothing set aside for times of need.[4]

Relatively few buy insurance against specified risks of short-term income needs.[5] Besides, private insurance is not available to deal with several common needs for temporary income. For example, paid vacation leave is not a "risk" for which insurance is appropriate; paid sick leave for the first day or so of illness is probably administratively too expensive for a separate insurance policy to cover.

Many people temporarily away from work without adequate savings or insurance are unable to borrow enough from regular commercial sources to maintain anything like their accustomed living standard.[6] Some might be able to borrow from predatory lenders, but they would have to pay exorbitant interest rates if they do.[7] Some are able to borrow, at least for a while, from friends and relations, but many times those potential lenders themselves are financially hard-pressed.[8]

A different way to deal with a temporary loss of income would be to eat and drive less, move to cheaper housing, stop spending for recreation, and use other similar personal austerity measures, although these adjustments might significantly reduce your standard of living.[9] Besides, many people are stuck with legal obligations to pay for their current housing and vehicles, making downsizing very difficult.[10]

In the face of these realities, in order to help prevent large numbers of people from having to either rely on the kindness of others or to suffer sharp, often disruptive, drops in their standard of living, employers and government can and do play various roles:[11]

- First, government and employers can entice or require employees to save more.
- Second, they can facilitate or subsidize employee borrowing and/or relieve people from debt.
- Third, they can offer or require the purchase of insurance to cover certain risks of otherwise temporarily having no income.
- Fourth, they can redistribute income in a variety of ways to those in temporary need of income.

Acting on their own, employers presumably play these roles when they think it is good for business, including their goal of attracting and retaining well-qualified and productive employees. Employers might also play roles here because they are required (or enticed) to do so by government.

Many critics of current arrangements in the United States argue that government and employers are not doing enough to deal with people's temporary need for income replacement, or are not helping in the right ways. What is clear is that governments in many other wealthy nations do a great deal more than the government does in the United States. For example, many nations provide or require employers to provide paid sick leave, paid maternity and child-bonding leave, and paid vacation leave.[12] Almost nowhere in the United States is anything like this required.

Historical Context: What Has Been Done to Replace Wages of Those Temporarily Away from Work

ILLNESS OR INJURY (TEMPORARY DISABILITY)

Sometimes people become sick or injured and are temporarily unable to work. If the temporary disability arises out of a *work-based injury* (or illness), employees in all 50 states are entitled to claim from state-mandated and employer-funded workers' compensation programs (WC).[13] To satisfy this legal obligation, most employers either buy workers' compensation insurance or else self-insure against the risk of these claims. WC benefits permit the few who have the bad luck of being injured on the job to collect from a pool that is potentially available to everyone in their workplace.

WC income replacement benefits usually start after just a few days off work and typically replace two-thirds of past earnings on a tax-free basis (up to a modest maximum level of past earnings) for the length of the temporary disability. WC also provides medical care, rehabilitation benefits, long-term disability income replacement benefits, and death benefits. But these features will be put aside here because this chapter focuses on income replacement for temporary spells away from work.

States adopted WC plans in the Progressive Era (the time period from the 1890s to the 1920s) on the grounds that: (1) employers can control workplace dangers and hence should have financial incentives to do so, (2) the costs of workplace injuries (and illnesses) that do occur should be incorporated into the price of the product or service the employer sells, and (3) it is a fair trade-off to require this sort of employer-provided benefit because in return, in nearly all cases, WC laws preclude the injured or ill worker from suing his or her employer for money damages in tort law.

But WC covers only *work-related* disabilities. So, if workers suffer a non-occupational injury or illness, the program provides nothing to them. While this is perhaps understandable given the historic justification for the workers' compensation plans, the result is hardly satisfactory from the worker's perspective. Getting injured while at home or out on the town or at someone else's house or engaging in recreational activities, or getting sick from a disease that is not work-related, or having a child and being unable to work, can all cause the employee to have to be away from work and in need of income.

In response to this gap, many (but by no means all) employers offer "sick leave" benefits, and some offer short-term disability insurance plans.[14] These employer-provided benefits come in many different forms. The traditional sick leave plan provides employees with between 8 and 11 days a year of paid sick leave after an initial year of service.[15] In some firms, unused sick leave is accumulated and carried over from year to year. Elsewhere, sick days disappear if not used at the end of the year. Plans with an accumulation feature look more like savings plans, whereas if there is no accumulation, the plan seems more like insurance.

Employers offer sick leave for several reasons. First, some offer the benefit because they don't want workers coming to work when ill, as this condition often leads to low productivity, and could in some cases lead to infecting other employees. They also know that this is a valuable employee benefit that could help them compete against other employers to attract and retain good workers.

Although many other nations require employers to provide sick leave (or governments directly operate sick leave plans on which workers can draw),[16] in the United States, only one state requires the provision of routine sick leave.[17] Today, nearly half of American employees are not entitled to paid sick leave.[18]

Some employers do not provide sick leave because they can readily replace those who are out ill or injured and care little about having workers who have a longer term connection to them. Others may perceive keeping track of employee time off as burdensome, or may fear that too many of their employees would abuse sick leave benefits by calling in ill or injured when they are not.

For illnesses and injuries lasting more than a few days, a handful of states (California, Hawaii, New Jersey, New York, and Rhode Island) have created short-term non-occupational disability plans that provide income replacement for as long as a year after the commencement of the disability, with the benefits typically starting after a one-week waiting period.[19] These benefits tend to be less generous than workers' compensation benefits, replacing only 50–66 percent of past wages up to a statutory maximum that varies wildly from state to state: contrast the weekly maximum in New York of $170 with that of California of nearly $1,000.[20] In addition to providing assistance for non-workplace injuries and illnesses, these temporary disability insurance (TDI) plans cover pregnancy-related disability. Like all disabilities, that amount of leave time for pregnancy disabilities and childbirth is based on medical advisory guidelines used by the TDI plans (e.g., for normal births, the guidelines recommend a leave of six weeks).[21]

TDI is insurance in the sense that all employees are covered and those in need draw down the benefit. In California and Rhode Island, this insurance is fully funded by a uniform payroll tax imposed on employees (up to a designated wage ceiling).[22] TDI plans in New York, Hawaii, and New Jersey are formally funded, in part or in full, by employers,[23] but in the end, the actual economic impact of the funding (as with WC) is likely born by workers in the form of lower wages.

In states without TDI plans, some employers provide their workers with short-term disability insurance on top of sick leave (or acquire a group policy that allows their employees to elect to purchase coverage).[24] Yet in the end, fewer than half of U.S. employees have private disability insurance coverage.[25]

VACATION AND PUBLIC HOLIDAYS

Sometimes people will want to take or will be encouraged to take a vacation. Many workplaces are closed for public holidays. Again, unlike many other nations,[26] in the United States there is no requirement that employers pay their workers when the business is closed for public holidays, and American workers have no government-created legal right to paid vacation.

Of course, many employers do provide their workers with paid public holidays—although the number of such paid days off varies considerably, generally from 5 to 12 days a year, with an average of 8 days per year.[27] These paid days off can be understood as a forced savings plan, in the sense that people who might earn slightly more for the time they do work, were they not paid on public holidays, remain in pay status for those public holidays. For those paid by the month or by the week, such arrangements also make it much easier on the employer's bookkeeping since employees simply draw their normal pay on those holidays even if they are off work. Yet, 23 percent of U.S. workers with private employers are not paid for public holidays on which they are off work.[28]

Paid vacations, when provided, may also be seen as a kind of forced savings plan. The typical worker earns vacation days as he/she works—for example, one day a month, or two weeks after a year's employment. Rather than being paid slightly more when working, the employee is able to draw down consecutive paid vacation days that most workers welcome. To be sure, regardless of employee preference, some employers are eager for their workers to take vacations so as to give them a break, hoping they will come back refreshed and will be able to buckle down to work again.

But even when voluntarily provided, paid vacations in the United States tend to be quite modest in length compared to those provided (and often legally required) in other nations where a month of paid vacation leave is common. Two weeks of paid vacation is typical in the United States for those employed with a firm for a few years or less, with the length of one's paid vacation often increasing with longer service—to three or four or five, and in rare cases, even more weeks in due course.[29]

Not all employees actually take the paid vacation they earn. Perhaps they are workaholics or feel pressure from superiors not to go on vacation. In some businesses, unused vacation days simply lapse—a "use it or lose it" policy that probably prompts a substantial share of workers to take what they earn. In other employment settings, paid vacation days may be accumulated and may be drawn down in future years or cashed out as lump sum payment when leaving the firm or at retirement. Those employees whose employers allow them to accumulate paid vacation time are, in effect, saving for the future.

PAID TIME OFF (PTO)

In response to concerns about sick leave abuse (and the burdens of policing sick leave which may require invading employees' privacy), an increasing number of firms in recent years have adopted paid time off plans (PTO) that, at a minimum, merge paid sick leave and paid vacation days into a single program.[30] For example, a firm that used to give two weeks of paid vacation and eight paid sick leave days now might offer three weeks of PTO. Employees who manage their own paid time off have a strong incentive not to waste their earned days off on a pretended sick day, as that day can instead later be used for a more extended vacation (or for some other preference of the employee, such as going to see a child's performance at school). A few firms have merged other kinds of paid time off into their PTO plan as well, such as folding in paid public holidays at enterprises like hospitals that operate and require staffing every day of the year. In such a setting an employee might well have more than five weeks a year of PTO.

FAMILY CARE

Sometimes family members will need someone who normally would be at work to stay home and provide them care, typically because the family member is ill. Those in need of care might be children, spouses, parents (including in-laws), or an even wider range of relatives and close friends. The period that the employee must be away from work to provide such care can vary enormously, from a day or two to several months. The need to be away to provide care is sometimes predictable, though at other times it is not; this need is sometimes recurrent and other times not. In the United States today, most of this sort of time off is taken by women.[31]

For short increments of leave, some workers are able to use vacation days (or PTO days) to provide care to an ailing family member, and in some firms, employees are able to use their sick days to care for ill loved ones. In California and seven other states, employers who provide paid sick days to their employees are required to allow employees to use up to half of their accrued sick leave benefits to care for a sick family member, including a child, parent, spouse, or registered domestic partner.[32]

For more serious illnesses requiring longer absences, generally speaking, there is no right in the United States to paid time off in such circumstances. However, California and New Jersey have extended their TDI plans to cover this sort of need (calling it paid family leave, or PFL, in California, and family leave insurance, or FLI, in New Jersey).[33,34] To be sure, some employers provide special paid leave arrangements for employees to care for their children immediately before and after birth.[35] But, apart from the exceptions noted, all of those are voluntary arrangements, and a large share of employees must simply go without pay if they take time off to provide necessary care to kin.

What is "necessary care" is not always clear, and existing paid family leave programs contain safeguards to prevent abuse. California, for example, requires physicians to certify the relative's serious health condition before the caretaker can be paid for leave.[36] Yet requiring one's kin to have a serious health problem is arguably too narrow a rule, as it prevents, for example, adult children from claiming paid time off when it is essential for them to resettle their elderly parents (who don't meet the definition of seriously ill) in a new living situation.

SPECIAL DUTIES

Sometimes a special occasion will arise that will draw a person away from work (e.g., a special event in a child's life, or a funeral of a loved one). Other times, people are called away from work to perform public service, such as jury duty or temporary military service. Again, U.S. workers have no legal right to be paid for time off of this sort, although some employers voluntarily keep employees in full pay status for at least some of these sorts of leaves.[37] Moreover, some specifically provide several days a year as paid "personal days" to be taken whenever the employee wishes, and those days could be used for these sorts of purposes.[38]

UNEMPLOYMENT

For a variety of reasons, some employees are temporarily laid off work or discharged from their jobs. Other employees choose to leave a job and then find themselves temporarily between jobs. During this period of unemployment the worker might be actively seeking another position, retraining for a new kind of work, or may simply be off work (which might facially resemble vacation, although the employee might not feel as if it is "vacation" unless she or he already has a new job set to start at a specific time in the future).

The unemployment insurance (UI) system that exists in every state provides partial income replacement for those who are unemployed for some statutorily enumerated reasons.[39] States are effectively coerced by federal tax policy to offer such benefits, although states have some leeway in the details. Simply put, to claim unemployment benefits you must not have voluntarily quit your job or have been discharged for misconduct, and you must be available to take a new job and must be actively searching for new work.

UI traditionally replaces 40–50 percent of prior wages up to a moderate statutory ceiling. That low benefit level itself helps prod claimants to search for a new job. Yet it also makes it difficult for the unemployed to retain their past living standard for very long.[40] Traditionally, these benefits are available after a week of unemployment and can continue for up to six months. In times of high national unemployment, Congress often extends unemployment benefits for longer periods.[41]

Employers pay into their state UI fund based on the past claims history of their own employees, subject to minimum and maximum contributions.[42] State UI plans came into effect in the 1920s, and the federal program was adopted in 1935 as part of the Social Security Act.[43] The thinking behind the federal unemployment insurance program was similar to that underlying WC: employers should have financial incentives to keep people employed once they have been hired, and, in turn, they should take responsibility for providing short-term income support for those whom they hire and then choose to let go (but they should not be responsible for the income needs of those whom they discharge for misconduct or who voluntarily quit). As with WC, the federal government has utilized employers to fund employees' insurance protection against unemployment risks that could leave them (and their families) in serious financial trouble.

Both WC and UI premiums likely have the economic effect of ultimately reducing the wages that would be paid in the absence of such plans. Thus, speaking generally, these plans may be thought of as ways of forcing employees to insure themselves. The existence of such plans surely makes many workers believe (or would do so if they thought about it) that they need not save money (or as much money) to prepare for these possible risks (or try to buy private insurance to cover these risks on their own).

BANKRUPTCY AND WELFARE

Brief mention should also be made of other roles that governments play for the temporarily unemployed. People who are without income for temporary periods and borrow money they cannot later pay back (or who have already borrowed in the past and must default on their loans when they are temporarily without income) might, by choice or by feeling they have no other choice, declare bankruptcy. Rather than putting people in debtors' prison (or other such harsh penalties) as was the practice in the early nineteenth century, bankruptcy laws allow debtors, at least to some extent, to discharge their obligations without paying them off in full.[44] However, the government limits individual bankruptcy filings to once every eight years,[45] and doing so may seriously harm credit ratings.[46] Bankruptcy might be viewed as a kind of redistribution mechanism from creditors to debtors.

Yet, knowing of the bankruptcy escape hatch, creditors presumably charge interest and fees on the funds they extend to consumers that allow the creditors to absorb losses when debts are discharged in bankruptcy. On that understanding, it might be said that bankruptcy is a kind of insurance plan in which borrowers in general pay more for credit to cover the risk that some of them might become bankrupt. These days, because creditors are increasingly sophisticated in the way they segment classes of borrowers, those who are at greater risk of bankruptcy pay more for credit based on that risk, which may be thought of as analogous to risk-rated insurance premiums.

In any event, most people would probably agree that, while perhaps serving in a back-stop role, our bankruptcy system is hardly the best way to plan for the need for income when temporarily away from work.

Another role that the government plays for those temporarily without income is in the provision of means-tested cash assistance (TANF, or welfare) and related programs (such as food stamps, public housing, and Medicaid). But to qualify, people usually must have lost or spent most of their assets, and the benefits provided support only an extremely modest living standard.[47] Clearly, one strong policy reason for making other arrangements for temporary income replacement available on a local, state, or national level is to prevent workers from falling into welfare status, given both the stigma and typically sharply reduced living standards that usually accompany welfare enrollment.

Models Underlying Paid Leave Arrangements; Saving/Borrowing, Insurance, and Redistribution

FORCED SAVINGS

From the libertarian perspective, workers should be left to bear the negative consequences of failing to provide for their own future if that was their choice. But many people would reject this line of argument, not only because they understand that some workers, if left to their own devices, will fail to protect their own interests, but also because they fear that too many could wind up not on the street, but on welfare.

Moreover, from a pragmatic perspective, we have seen that a variety of programs are already in place to force people to plan ahead.[48] For example, paid vacations, paid public holidays, PTO plans, and certain sorts of paid sick leave plans are, as noted above, readily understood as arrangements by which employees are forced to save up for future periods of absence from work.

Given existing arrangements, some scholars and policymakers believe that workers could be pressed to save up as well for temporary unemployment, temporary disability, and the temporary need to care for kin.[49] Even if those events are less predictable than routine occurrences like public holidays and vacations, across a lifetime of employment, modest sums could regularly be put away to cover these other risks. And if these events do not occur, that would simply mean a higher standard of living in retirement (or more money to leave to one's heirs). Clearly, government could create such a forced savings plan and require all workers to participate. It could run such a regime through public agencies or make employers manage it. A less aggressive approach would be to provide a financial incentive for this sort of plan—perhaps analogous to the tax incentives that government now provides in an effort to entice workers to save (beyond Social Security) for their retirement (e.g., 401(k) plans).

From the savings perspective, the different reasons that people have for temporarily needing income might seem ill-served by having separate savings accounts for each different purpose, as is generally the practice today. With one, presumably larger, account, people could draw down from it for vacation, having a baby, being ill, being between jobs, and so on. As a result, people would be less likely than today to have, for example, unused unemployment benefits while running out of paid sick leave. However, if people could draw down all of their savings any time in order to go on vacation, then the idea of coerced savings for various less predictable needs is undermined. This suggests that some paternalistic restrictions on the draw-down of savings might be included in any forced saving plan. For example, part of a worker's account might be earmarked exclusively, say, for disability or unemployment lasting more than two weeks.[50] Furthermore, workers might be permitted to borrow against this portion of their account at reasonable interest rates if unplanned/involuntary contingencies occurred early in their career and before adequate savings have been created.

REQUIRED PRIVATE INSURANCE

Rather than coercing people to save for occasions that create a need for temporary income replacement, they might instead be required to obtain insurance from the private insurance market for certain events. The idea here is that the bad luck of getting ill, being injured, or losing a job, or having to provide extended care for an ill loved one will be unevenly felt, in contrast to the general need to take off work on public holidays or to take vacations. From this perspective, the vision is that nearly all of us would prefer to pay a small sum on a regular basis that in turn gave us the right to draw down a substantial sum when we suffer one (or more) of these bad luck life events. Put differently, it may seem unfair that people who, without fault, lose jobs or become ill or are injured or have to provide kin care receive less paid vacation than those who do not, which would be the case were time away from work owing to those unplanned events to be funded from a forced savings plan of the sort described above.

REDISTRIBUTION

Forced savings and forced insurance plans are based on the idea that workers should be coerced into taking care of their own needs. But some may believe that certain needs for paid time off are specially entitled to public support. Paid time off to deliver and then to bond with a newborn baby is a benefit that likely falls in this category, based on the belief that such supported time off is good for both the child and the rest of society. From this perspective, to make would-be parents individually save up for such paid time off is the wrong solution. Of course, providing this benefit for such workers need not be part of any special temporary income replacement plan, but could come directly via tax law. Indeed, the existing federal child tax credit ($1,000 annually) does exactly this—providing funding from society at large to those who have children (albeit without any requirement that they use the funds to provide care or any requirement of prior workforce attachment).[51] Hence, one could imagine a much larger tax credit going to those who care for their newborns—especially those who temporarily take time away from work to do so.

Note also that another way to promote redistribution is to adopt a coerced insurance plan that does not charge premiums on the basis of risk even when it would be administratively efficient to do so. In such case, the funding mechanism serves to redistribute from low-risk to high-risk participants in the plan. Putting an arbitrary cap on UI premiums illustrates this phenomenon.

OVERALL

Those who reject libertarian calls for self-sufficiency and instead favor government intervention to help provide employees with income support when they are temporarily away from work may rest their recommended policy solutions on quite different underlying ideas about the public purpose(s) behind any such plan—forced savings, required insurance, or redistribution.

Our feelings about the appropriateness of drawing down income support when away from work for certain reasons may vary, depending on the model underlying the plan being tapped. For example, if you are understood to have saved up beforehand, then we are much more likely to accept your choice to draw down from your account when you are between jobs if you left voluntarily and want time to find new work. But if someone did not save individually and seeks to draw from an insurance pool, we are much less likely to favor allowing claims from those who have chosen to be out of work.

Thus the details of any plan are extremely important, such as the income replacement rate, any waiting period, the behaviors that disqualify one from obtaining the benefit, the prior workforce attachment required to obtain a benefit, the maximum duration of the benefit, the funding mechanism used to pay for the plan, and the party who will administer the plan (e.g., the employer, a government agency, or an insurance company).

But unless one is clear about whether coerced savings will suffice, whether insurance for some risks is essential, and whether certain grounds exist for claiming deserve special redistributive support, it is difficult to make sensible judgments about what those details should be.

Current Policy Proposals

Many people advocate reforming the way in which income is provided to those temporarily away from work, but reformers envision very different solutions. I group them under two headings.

MAINTAIN SILOS BUT MAKE CHANGES

The most common reform proposals build on what we have now. Needs for income when temporarily away from work are identified based on the reason for the need, and each type of need is dealt with by a separate program (or silo).

Despite structural similarities, reform proposals in this vein can differ wildly from one another. On the one hand, some seek to expand the amount of the benefit provided by one or more existing silos. In the 1970s, for example, a reasonably successful national effort was made to increase the share of lost income that is replaced by WC.[52] But increasing the wage replacement rate is not the only way to improve benefits.

CONSIDER POSSIBLE UI REFORM

The basic UI benefit could be expanded to routinely cover a year of unemployment, the maximum wage level to which the benefit applies could be raised to twice the average weekly wage, and/or the amount of prior labor force attachment (or prior earnings) needed to qualify for any UI could be reduced. One could also liberalize the plan's eligibility requirements; for example, perhaps pregnancy-related leave could be covered (as was proposed during the Clinton administration).[53]

On the other hand, some reformers seek to create new silos by making mandatory some benefits that are now almost entirely voluntarily provided by employers, if at all. San Francisco, for example, has mandated that all employers in the city provide paid sick leave, and many would like this solution imposed by Congress nationwide.[54] Making the current five-state TDI program a nationwide program is another example in this vein.

The likely impact of these silo reform proposals depends on the details. For example, imagine that employers were required to give all workers a two-week paid vacation after a year of service. That would make mandatory something that a very large number of employers already provide, so that only a minority of businesses would be impacted. By contrast, if the mandatory paid vacation were extended to, say, a month, as is common in Europe, that expansion would impose a larger obligation on nearly all employers.

Many women's groups are currently focused especially on creating new paid time off benefit plans for workers who care for seriously ill or injured relatives and/or their newborn children (while the proposals are gender-neutral, we know from the experience of European programs and California's Paid Family Leave program that mainly women benefit from such programs). In essence, advocates want to turn the unpaid leave now guaranteed to qualified employees by the Family and Medical Leave Act (FMLA) into a paid leave plan. Many advocates of this idea would also like a changed cultural climate in which male workers would just as frequently take on this caregiving role.[55] This reform responds to a specific issue that is clearly important to women and much touted by those who see such benefits as facilitating ongoing female labor force participation rates.[56]

MORE SWEEPING REFORMS

In the 1970s there was talk (that amounted to nothing) of expanding WC coverage to injuries incurred around the clock. Twenty-four-hour workers' compensation would have provided new protections for workers suffering from non-occupational disabilities (sickness or injury). Focusing just on temporary income replacement, 24-hour WC would have brought the 45 states that do not have TDI broadly into line with the few states that do. From the worker's perspective, this makes sense. To be sure, off-work injuries and illness are generally beyond the control of the employer and their coverage by employers might be difficult, given the level at which WC insurance premiums are currently set. Employers successfully fought this initiative, which some thought was short-sighted, as the additional cost of this reform would likely have been passed on to the worker in the form of more slowly rising wages.[57]

As noted earlier, starting in the 1990s, a substantial number of employers began to offer paid time off (PTO) in lieu of certain earmarked (silo) benefits. One strong motivation for such a plan is the belief by some employers that policing sick leave is an unnecessarily difficult problem. Underlying PTO is the belief that if employees are in charge of their own paid time off, they will be more responsible with that time, such as being more likely to give notice before they will take that time off, allowing firms to plan better for absence. The typical PTO plan provides more paid vacation days for the majority of workers, who are generally out sick fewer than five days a year. However, a person who has the bad luck of actually being sick for longer, such as eight work days, could be worse off under the PTO plan than under the firm's former sick leave policy (although even that person might be better off over time if that sickness is simply an unusual bad luck experience). Those who are most harmed by combining silos into PTO are those who are regularly and genuinely out ill for more than five days. This comparison vividly shows the contrast between the "savings" model that underlies PTO and the "insurance" model that at least some sick leave plans reflect: the former imposes costs on the less fortunate, who must spend their savings on illness instead of vacation, while the latter imposes costs on the more fortunate, who must pay for sick benefits they might rarely use, if ever.

Some have written about converting UI into a coerced savings plan akin to PTO.[58] Their idea is that over their career, most people can cover their own occasional unemployment (if any) via required savings (especially if one may also occasionally draw one's "time off" savings account into debt). This approach not only denies the need for "insurance" for most people, but also seeks to end what are seen as many of the undesirable features of today's unemployment plan—intrusion into employee privacy by supervising work searches; denying benefits to those who quit voluntarily but with good reason (even if the reason is not good enough to qualify them for benefits under existing rules), providing only a modest level of income replacement, and requiring a substantial deductible before benefits flow (typically, the first week of unemployment is uncompensated). Moreover, given that it would be the employee's own savings fund that was being drawn upon, this would provide a clear incentive for the claimant to quickly find a new job.

More than 20 years ago, I proposed an even more sweeping reform that would create a substantially non-siloed forced-savings plan intended to cover all of the needs for income for those temporarily away from work.[59] I called that plan "short term paid leave." Under my proposal, employees would earn one paid day of leave for every five days worked. This paid leave bank could be drawn from to pay for time off for the full range of reasons discussed earlier. My plan would be accompanied by the ending of all of today's silo programs—paid public holidays, paid vacation, paid sick leave, paid maternity leave, paid leave to care for family members, unemployment insurance (UI), paid occupational disability compensation (WC), and paid non-occupational disability compensation (TDI). My plan is intended to deal with temporary periods away from work of up to six months.

My proposal includes a modest insurance or redistribution feature—allowing a moderate amount of "borrowing" against future Social Security retirement benefits, combined with a partial forgiveness of such loans in some cases. My plan also has a paternalistic semi-silo feature—requiring some banking of paid days off for use on the occasion of more extended unemployment or illness/injury (lasting more than two weeks). The proposal requires employers to fund all end-of-year unused paid leave beyond two weeks by depositing appropriate amounts in employees' accounts at designated financial institutions—analogous to the way in which 401(k) retirement plans are funded. This not only helps protect employees against the risk of the possible bankruptcy of employers who might leave their workers with now-worthless accrued paid time off, but also it assures the effective "portability" of accrued benefits from job to job.

Some employers feared the added costs of this plan, but many of those already providing generous paid leave warmed to the idea, seeing that at worst it might cost them slightly more in payroll costs, which could well be offset by slowing the rate of wage increases. Typical workers in these firms might well, in effect, be trading somewhat lower wages for an extra week of paid vacation each year. But employers are helpless to implement such an idea on their own, as government-required WC, UI, and TDI benefits would have to be eliminated as this sort of substitute plan were put in place. That would require special government waivers that have not been forthcoming so far.

I appreciate that some people oppose my plan because they place a higher value on the insurance and redistribution features of both existing and proposed schemes. They are often put off by the idea that at least some of those with repeated bad luck requiring time away from work because of joblessness, disability, child-bearing, and kin care could be worse off than under an imagined series of separate silos.

As a compromise, I suggest combining my proposal with, for example, a separate plan that uses federal income tax revenues to fund six weeks of baby-bonding leave, on the theory that in taking such leave the parent is performing a public service that should be funded by society at large.

Conclusion

In sum, as a policy matter, the advantage of the silo approach to temporary income replacement is that special terms and conditions can be applied as appropriate to the different reasons for which income is to be replaced. This approach can also readily combine insurance for some income losses, savings arrangements for others, and redistribution features for yet others. And it can mix and match employer, government, and required employee roles and responsibilities in saving as seems appropriate. On the other hand, unless the system of silos covers all employee needs, workers can find themselves with many protections that they cannot call upon because the reason they are temporarily away from work does not have its own silo, or the worker's claim on that silo is exhausted. Moreover, employee benefits that require meeting silo-specific eligibility conditions often are expensive to administer and require intrusion into the employee's private life (to obtain eligibility verification and to be sure the employee is engaging, or not engaging, in certain behaviors).

A non-silo approach could be easier to administer and more protective of employee privacy, and could be largely indifferent to the reason the employee temporarily needs income replacement. Yet, unless additional features are attached, a single "forced savings" approach for dealing with short-term paid leave precludes handling some risks of income loss via insurance and openly subsidizing some reasons for being away from work on redistribution grounds.

The politics of these competing reforms is complex. The silo approach so far has left us with many missing silos, and even the existing silos often look incoherently different from each other. Still, special interest groups with a concern about one type of temporary income loss are likely to focus attention on creating or improving a silo that deals with that specific problem, and as a result, they might be able to create a coalition for what is pitched as a narrow reform. Getting rid of silos altogether is a far more ambitious strategy. Yet, if the benefit costs of the two approaches to employers were largely the same, business might get behind the non-silo strategy on the basis of the simplification of administration and in the name of employee autonomy.

Notes

1. In 2006, 41 percent of married-couple families had both spouses in the workforce. Stella Potter Cromartie, "Labor Force Status of Families: A Visual Essay," *Bureau of Labor Statistics* (July/August 2007), http://www.bls.gov/opub/mlr/2007/07/ressum.pdf.
2. During unemployment, personal savings only account for around 25 percent of earnings loss smoothing, making it a significantly smaller source of smoothing than government support, which makes up over 50 percent of earnings loss compensation. Susan Dynarski, Jonathan Gruber, Robert A. Moffitt, and Gary Burtless, "Can Families Smooth Variable Earnings?" *Brookings Papers on Economic Activity* (1997): 230.
3. Discover Financial Services, "Discover U.S. Spending Monitor Falls to New Low," *Business Wire*, March 4, 2009, http://investorrelations.discoverfinancial.com/phoenix.zhtml?c=204177&p=irol-newsArticle&ID=1262399&;highlight=; James X. Sullivan, "Borrowing during Unemployment: Unsecured Debt as Safety Net," *Journal of Human Resources* 43 (2008): 386. ("The median 25–64-year-old worker only has enough financial assets to cover three weeks of pre-separation earnings. This falls far short of the average unemployment spell, which lasts about 13 weeks").
4. Savings or assets are only used to smooth about one-quarter of the loss of income from unemployment, and only over one-third of households have assets worth more than their entire

income loss. Dynarski, Gruber, Moffitt, and Burtless, "Can Families Smooth Variable Earnings?" 270–271; a growth in frequency of transitory income shocks in the United States has led to increasing consumption inequality. Richard Blundell, Luigi Pistaferri, and Ian Preston, "Consumption Inequality and Partial Insurance," *American Economic Review* 98, no. 5 (2008): 1913.

5. Older and better-educated cohorts are more likely to purchase partial insurance to guard against temporary income shocks, though lower-income households are far more sensitive to these shifting circumstances. However, none of these populations self-insure fully and comprehensively. Blundell, Pistaferri, and Preston, "Consumption Inequality," 1914.

6. Unemployment has a stronger effect on food consumption, housing, and durables expenditures than other kinds of income shocks. Dynarski, Gruber, Moffitt, and Burtless, "Can Families Smooth Variable Earnings?" 265–266; Sullivan, "Borrowing during Unemployment," 384–385, 406 ("very low-asset households do not borrow . . . these households are not able to fully smooth consumption over these temporary income shocks . . . [they] tend to have very low credit limits and their applications for credit are frequently denied . . . Half of all very low-asset households that have applied for credit have been denied within the past five years").

7. Predatory lenders are estimated to cost families $3.4 billion each year, and approximately 5 million payday loan recipients find themselves caught in a cycle of non-repayable debt each year through debt extension programs such as rollovers, extensions, or back-to-back transactions. Keith Ernst, John Farris, and Uriah King, "Quantifying the Economic Cost of Predatory Payday Lending," *Center for Responsible Lending* (2004): 2–4.

8. Borrowing from family and friends plays a relatively small role in U.S. temporary income relief. Sullivan, "Borrowing during Unemployment," 405; an extensive literature on the "added worker effect" shows little evidence of a statistically significant financial benefit to additional household member employment. Dynarski, Gruber, Moffitt, and Burtless, "Can Families Smooth Variable Earnings?" 266–267.

9. Households across the income spectrum are, to some extent, able to use postponing durable goods purchasing in order to smooth consumption across temporary income shocks. Sullivan, "Borrowing during Unemployment," 386.

10. Karen E. Dynan, "Changing Household Financial Opportunities and Economic Security," *Journal of Economic Perspectives* 23, no. 4 (2009): 59–60; Katherine Porter and Tara Twomey, "Risk Allocation in Home Ownership: Revisiting the Role of Mortgage Contract Terms," chapter 8 of this volume.

11. Private transfers (such as between family members), additional work by other household members, and household savings play a small role in smoothing consumption during temporary income shocks, especially when compared to the relatively strong role that government programs, particularly unemployment insurance, can play. Sullivan, "Borrowing during Unemployment," 383–386.

12. E.g., Australia, Canada, New Zealand, the United Kingdom.

13. For a history of the development of workers' compensation programs, see Richard Epstein, *The Historical Origins and Economic Structure of Workers' Compensation Law*, 7 Workmen's Comp. L. Rev. 1 (1983–1984).

14. See Table 19, Bureau of Labor Statistics, U.S. Department of Labor, *National Compensation Survey: Employee Benefits in Private Industry in the United States*. Prepared by the Bureau of Labor Statistics, 2007, 28, http://www.bls.gov/ncs/ebs/sp/ebsm0006.pdf.

15. On average, private workers receive 8 days of paid sick leave annually, and state and local government workers receive 11 days of paid sick leave annually. Bureau of Labor Statistics, U.S. Department of Labor, *Paid Sick Leave in the United States*. Prepared by the Bureau of Labor Statistics, 2010, 28, http://www.bls.gov/opub/perspectives/program_perspectives_vol2_issue2.pdf.

16. See, e.g., *New Zealand Holidays Act, Revised Statutes,* (2003), §§129–63–71; *Australia Fair Work Act, Commonwealth Numbered Acts,* (2009), § 87; *Canada Labour Code, Revised Statutes* (1985), § 183.

17. In 2011, Connecticut became the first state to require employers with 50 or more employees to provide up to 40 hours of paid sick time each year to certain hourly employees who accrue

such time. *See* 2011 Conn. Pub. Acts 0052. In addition, two cities have enacted paid sick days requirements—San Francisco and Washington, DC (Milwaukee, Wisconsin passed a local ordinance by ballot, but it was overturned)—and according to the National Partnership for Women and Families, in 2011, there are 20 states and cities that have introduced paid sick day legislation or have active campaigns to promote legislation. *See* National Partnership for Women and Families, "State and Local Action on Paid Sick Days," June 2011.

18. See Table 19, "National Compensation Survey.," 2007, 28.

19. See relevant Disability Program statutes: *Cal. Unemp. Ins. Code* § 2627(b) (1993); *N.J. Stat. Ann.* § 43:21–38 (2004); *N.Y. Workers' Comp. Law* § 208 (McKinney's 2006); *R.I. Gen. Laws* § 28–41–12 (2008); *Haw. Rev. Stat.* § 392–324 (West's 2009); *P.R. Laws Ann.* 11 § 203(c)(1) (1995).

20. State of California Employment Development Department, "Disability Insurance (DI) and Paid Family Leave (PFL) Weekly Benefit Amounts in Dollar Increments (2009), DE 2589 Rev. 3 (1–10), http://www.edd.ca.gov/pdf_pub_ctr/de2589.pdf; *N.Y. Workers' Comp. Law* § 204 (McKinney's 1989).

21. See Jonathan Borak, MD, "Book Reviews: *The Medical Disability Advisor and Official Disability Guidelines,*" *J. Occup. Environ. Med* 49, no. 3 (2007): 346–347.

22. Rhode Island Department of Labor & Training, "About TDI," http://www.dlt.state.ri.us/tdi/; State of California Employment Development Department, "About the Program," http://www.edd.ca.gov/Disability/About_the_Program.htm.

23. New York State Insurance Fund, "About Disability Benefits," http://ww3.nysif.com/Home/DisabilityBenefits/AboutDisabilityBenefits.aspx; New Jersey Department of Labor and Workforce Development, "Cost to the Worker-State Plan," http://lwd.dol.state.nj.us/labor/tdi/worker/state/sp_cost.html.

24. The majority of private insurance companies offer short-term disability insurance programs. For an overview of the percentage of workers with access to such programs, see Table 16, U.S. Department of Labor, *National Compensation Survey, March 2009,* Prepared by the Bureau of Labor Statistics, 60, http://www.bls.gov/ncs/ebs/benefits/2009/ebbl0044.pdf.

25. Ibid.

26. For instance, workers in Australia are entitled to four weeks of annual paid leave, while Canadian workers are entitled to at least two weeks of paid vacation. Both countries give longer leave entitlements to workers who have been with their company for longer periods. See *Australia Fair Work Act, Commonwealth Numbered Acts,* (2009), § 87; *Canada Labour Code, Revised Statutes* (1985), § 183.

27. See Table 20, U.S. Department of Labor, *National Compensation Survey: Employee Benefits in Private Industry in the United States, March 2007,* Prepared by the Bureau of Labor Statistics, 29, http://www.bls.gov/ncs/ebs/sp/ebsm0006.pdf.

28. Ibid. at 28.

29. Jessica Yang, "Paid Time Off from Work," *Salary.com,* November 12, 2004, http://www.salary.com/personal/layoutscripts/psnl_articles.asp?tab=psn&cat=cat011&ser=ser031&part=par088.

30. Forty-two percent of private companies now offer PTO rather than a traditional vacation plan. Society for Human Resource Management, "2009 Employee Benefit Survey," Table D-1, 26, Society for Human Resource Management, http://www.shrm.org/Research/SurveyFindings/Articles/Documents/09–0295_Employee_Benefits_Survey_Report_spread_FNL.pdf. X employers say they switched to this to avoid moral hazard and administrative burden problems.

31. National Partnership for Women and Families, "Facts about the FMLA: What Does It Do, Who Uses It, and How?" National Partnership for Women and Families, http://www.nationalpartnership.org/site/DocServer/FMLAWhatWhoHow.pdf?docID=965.

32. See *Cal. Lab. Code*§233. See also *Conn. Gen. Stat.* § 31–51ll; *Haw. Rev. Stat.* § 398–3 (2010); *Md. Code Ann., Lab. & Empl.* § 3–802; *Maine Rev. Stat Ann. Tit.* 26, § 636; *Minn. Stat.* § 181.9413; *Wash. Rev. Code Ann.* § 49.12.270; *Wis. Stat.* § 103.10.

33. State of California Employment Development Department, "Paid Family Leave Fact Sheet," DE 8714CF Rev. 10 (12–09), http://www.edd.ca.gov/pdf_pub_ctr/de8714cf.pdf.

34. New Jersey Department of Labor and Workforce Development, "Family Leave Insurance-General Information," http://lwd.dol.state.nj.us/labor/fli/worker/program_info_menu.html.

35. See Table 19, Bureau of Labor Statistics, "National Compensation Survey: 2007," 28.

36. Employment Development Department, "Paid Family Leave Fact Sheet," 2009.

37. A 2009 Survey of selected private companies found that 62 percent offered pay during jury duty and 24 percent offered pay during periods of military leave. Society for Human Resource Management, "2009 Employee Benefit Survey," Table D-3, 57

38. Ibid.

39. U.S. Department of Labor, *State Unemployment Insurance Benefits*. Prepared by the Employment and Training Administration, 2010, http://workforcesecurity.doleta.gov/unemploy/uifactsheet.asp. List reasons.

40. Sullivan, "Borrowing during Unemployment: Unsecured Debt as Safety Net," 386.

41. For a recent example, see Michael Luo, "99 Weeks Later, Jobless Only Have Desperation," *New York Times*, August 2, 2010.

42. U.S. Department of Labor, *Significant Provisions of State Unemployment Insurance Laws Effective July 2009*. Prepared by the Employment and Training Administration, http://www.ows.doleta.gov/unemploy/content/sigpros/2000–2009/July2009.pdf.

43. *Social Security Act of 1935*, U.S. Code 42 (1960), §§501 et seq.

44. U.S. Courts, *Bankruptcy Basics Third Edition: Chapter 13*, Administrative Office of the U.S. Courts on behalf of the Federal Judiciary, http://www.uscourts.gov/bankruptcycourts/bankruptcybasics/chapter13.html.

45. *Bankruptcy Act of 1978*, U.S. Code 11 (2010), § 727(a)(8).

46. Interestingly, some lenders are eager to loan money to those who just emerged from bankruptcy, thinking that such people won't be able to once more avoid their obligations in that way for some time in the future. See Katherine M. Porter, *Bankrupt Profits: The Credit Industry's Business Model for Post-Bankruptcy Lending*, Iowa Law Review, Vol. 94 (2008).

47. In 2004, a household composed of one caretaker and two children received, on average, $397.41 per month. See Table 9.G1, Office of Policy, U.S. Social Security Administration, *Annual Statistical Supplement 2005: Other Social Insurance, Veterans' Benefits, and Public Assistance*. Prepared by the Office of Policy, 2007528, http://www.ssa.gov/policy/docs/statcomps/supplement/2005/9g.html.

48. For examples, see Cass Sunstein and Richard Thaler, *Nudge: Improving Decisions about Health, Wealth, and Happiness* (New Haven: Yale University Press, 2008).

49. See Hazel Bateman, Geoffrey Kingston, and John Piggott, *Forced Saving*, (Cambridge: Cambridge University Press, 2001).

50. Note the comparison with 401(k) retirement plans, which carry tax penalties if the funds are drawn down before retirement, but which have special exceptions for specified earlier unpenalized draw downs

51. Child Tax Credit, *Taxpayer Relief Act of 1997*, U.S. Code 26 (2009), §§ 24, 152.

52. Daria Kiselica, Bruce Sibson, and Judith Green-McKenzie, "Workers' Compensation: A Historical Review and Description of a Legal and Social Insurance System," *Clinics in Occupational and Environmental Medicine* 4, no. 2 (2004): 237.

53. Jill Hamburg Copland, "Here Comes Paid Parental Leave," *Business Week*, 2000, http://www.businessweek.com/smallbiz/0007/sb000703.htm.

54. Ilana DeBare, "Law Now Entitles All Workers in S.F. to Paid Sick Leave," *San Francisco Chronicle*, February 6, 2007, http://articles.sfgate.com/2007–02–06/news/17232369_1_sick-leave-sick-time-mission-district.

55. Rebecca Ray, Janet Gornick, and John Schmitt, *Parental Leave Policies in 21 Countries: Assessing Generosity and Gender Equality*, Center for Economic and Policy Research, 2009, 1–2, http://www.cepr.net/documents/publications/parental_2008_09.pdf.

56. Gillian Lester, "In Defense of Paid Family Leave," *Harv. J. L. & Gender* 28, no. 1 (2005): 79–82, http://www.law.harvard.edu/students/orgs/jlg/vol28/lester.pdf. This perspective fears that

the absence of such benefits now causes women to drop out of the workforce entirely when such needs for temporary time away from work occur (and also perhaps discourages some women from joining the labor force in the first place on the understanding that, absent such income replacement programs, women will later have to withdraw from the force when such needs arise.

57. Depending on the funding mechanism, employers might have an incentive to hire employees who are less likely to be harmed off the job (e.g, younger, married people, perhaps, who don't play football or skydive). Even so, any resultant discrimination could be handled through new antidiscrimination laws already in place in a few states that forbid discrimination by employers against workers based on their off-work recreational activities. Stephen D. Sugarman, "'Lifestyle' Discrimination in Employment," *Berkeley J. Emp. & Lab. L.* 24 (2003): 377, http://www.law.berkeley.edu/faculty/sugarmans/Sugarman%20lifestyle%20090303.pdf.

58. Joseph E. Stiglitz and Jungyoll Yun, "Integration of Unemployment Insurance with Retirement Insurance," *Journal of Public Economics, Elsevier* 89, no. 11–12 (December 2005): 2037–2067.

59. Stephen D. Sugarman, "Short Term Paid Leave: A New Approach to Social Insurance and Employee Benefits," *Cal. L. Rev.* 75 (1987): 465.

Part Three

IMPROVING ECONOMIC
SECURITY FOR FAMILIES

7

Public Policy Options to Build Wealth for America's Middle Class

CHRISTIAN E. WELLER AND AMY HELBURN

Introduction

The economic crisis of 2007 and thereafter—the Great Recession—took a heavy toll on family wealth. Wealth declined by about $20 trillion (in 2010 dollars) from its peak in June 2007 to its trough in March 2009. This was the sharpest wealth drop since the Federal Reserve started to collect these data in 1952.[1]

This unprecedented wealth decrease is worrisome in itself. Yet it is all the more troubling in light of the increasing economic risk that Americans have faced in recent decades. Wealth is a store of future income that can be drawn upon in the case of retirement, unemployment, illness, or injury. It allows families to smooth consumption over their lifetime, even when incomes and expenses change. The chance that families will have to rely on their wealth for such smoothing has risen substantially as Americans have taken on more and more economic risks in their lives.

A sharp drop in wealth can also mean that many families are caught in a vicious cycle of low wealth. Families with little wealth are poorly situated to send kids to college and to choose a degree that suits their abilities. They cannot easily switch jobs to match their particular skills or let their creative spirits take hold and start a business. The level of wealth that is necessary to invest in a secure future has grown over time as the responsibility for the costs of education, health care, and retirement has shifted onto individuals. Many families had to put off exploring a new career, starting their own business, or sending their kids to college when wealth dropped sharply in the Great Recession.

Wealth is at the heart of economic security and opportunity. Yet the long-term shift of risk from employers and the government onto workers and their families has made it harder for Americans to build wealth. Workers face slower income growth and longer unemployment spells, and families have to pay for an increasing share of the growing costs of such big-ticket items as health care, housing, energy, and transportation, leaving less money to save. And employers have cut health and pension benefits, further reducing saving. Government incentives encourage savings by higher-income earners, but they give little help to low- and moderate-income savers. And what help there is comes in the form of support for costly and risky individualized accounts that do not serve these less-affluent savers well.

Overcoming these challenges requires new comprehensive measures to increase savings rates, especially among lower-income families; to lower the costs of building wealth; and to reduce individual risk exposure. We lay out a range of principles for public policies and offer specific examples that could do just that. Families could rebuild wealth a lot more quickly if policymakers turned tax deductions for personal savings into refundable tax credits, streamlined tax incentives for savings, further automated many savings decisions, increased financial market transparency, offered incentives for more financial market competition, and directly supported loans, where private financial markets are either underdeveloped or nonexistent.

Historical Context

Wealth building in the United States has always relied heavily on the private sector, with employers and families expected to build wealth outside government arrangements. Nonetheless, Americans have not always relied as heavily on individual efforts as they do today. Public and private policies have encouraged a shift away from social insurance arrangements—both public and private—for wealth building.

As Alicia Munnell reports in chapter 11 of this volume, this shift is especially apparent in retirement savings. Retirement savings have changed dramatically from social insurance arrangements, such as employer provided pensions, to individual savings accounts, such as 401(k)s and IRAs. In 1975, 39 percent of private sector workers were covered by a traditional defined benefit pension, while the share of private sector workers with an individual retirement savings plan (defined contribution plan) was only 6 percent.[2] By 2006, only 20 percent of private sector workers participated in a traditional defined benefit pension plan and 43 percent of private sector workers had an individual savings retirement account.[3]

This risk shift has come about due to employer pressures to cut costs and reduce long-term commitments as well as increasing tax incentives for individualized wealth-building efforts. Starting in the 1970s and accelerating in the early 1980s, employers started to shed traditional defined benefit pension plans. The costs of providing these benefits had risen in the wake of the Employee Retirement Income Security Act of 1974 (ERISA), which required employers to better protect their employees' pensions in the eventuality of an employer bankruptcy.[4] Also, starting in the late 1970s and early 1980s, a greater emphasis on short-term corporate profit seeking led large corporate employers to start shedding long-term commitments to their employees, particularly pensions.[5] Moreover, the IRS clarified the rules on 401(k) plans in 1981, which gave individual retirement savings a boost.[6] Contributions to retirement savings accounts are tax deductible up to predetermined limits. This is especially valuable for taxpayers with higher marginal income tax rates since their implicit subsidy is higher than for taxpayers with lower marginal tax rates. Individual savings accounts have thus contributed to rising wealth inequality.[7] Other, similarly skewed tax incentives for personal wealth have followed suit for homeownership, education, and health care. Changes in wealth building policies over the past three decades have thus prioritized individual savings with the concomitant individual risks and costs and they have contributed to rising wealth inequality.

Features of Risk

Recent patterns of wealth-holding in the United States have three salient characteristics: inequality, little saving, and concentration in risky assets.

INEQUALITY

Wealth inequality increased even before the recent economic crisis, laying the foundation for further increases after 2007. During the 2000s, wealth grew faster for higher-income households than for lower-income households, faster for older families than for younger families, faster for whites than for nonwhites, and faster for single individuals than for married couples.[8] Moreover, data from the Survey of Consumer Finances (SCF) show that wealth in each demographic subcategory became more concentrated between 2004 and 2007.[9]

LITTLE SAVING

Two additional factors exacerbated the risks of the housing and stock market crash for less affluent Americans. The first was wealth inadequacy. The personal saving rate—one measure of the rate at which families build wealth to deal with economic shocks—fell to historic lows. For the entire last business cycle, from March 2001 through December 2007, the personal saving rate averaged 1.4 percent—less than one-third of the 1990s.[10]

Families had also heaped on massive amounts of debt since the 1980s.[11] This leverage magnified the effect of price changes on the original investment. When asset prices fall, for instance, what little equity stake a family has in an investment is quickly wiped out. In 2007, over 77 percent of families owed some type of debt.[12] Debt grew substantially faster in the 2000s than during previous business cycles.[13] This debt boom was largely fueled by a growth in debt secured by private homes,[14] such that the share of home equity as a percent of home values has, with few exceptions, steadily declined from 70 percent in 1982 to 43 percent in 2008.[15]

In addition, families frequently incurred high costs in building wealth, due to substantial fees for borrowing debt and managing assets that can increase debt and lower savings. Very high cost loans include payday lending, car title loans, and overdraft loans. Interest rates on payday loans typically average about 400 percent.[16] The median annual interest rate for a car title loan is about 300 percent, while overdraft fees can quickly translate into triple-digit annualized interest rates.[17] Moreover, credit card debt often costs more than other forms of credit due to higher interest rates and additional fees.[18] Finally, subprime mortgages are by definition higher-cost loans. The evidence indicates that all these forms of higher-cost credit are more prevalent among minorities and lower-income families than among their counterparts in other groups.[19]

Additional costs exist for assets. A broadly studied example is the so-called 401(k) plan.[20] Fees of 401(k) plans can substantially reduce the savings that will be available for retirement. Even fees as low as 1 percent of assets annually—typical for 401(k) plans—can lower total savings over a career by more than 20 percent.[21] Larger plans offer fewer investment choices, or feature passively managed assets that may have lower fees.[22]

As a consequence of these trends, many lower- and middle-income families simply did not have sufficient wealth to protect themselves during the Great Recession.

CONCENTRATION IN RISKY ASSETS

Finally, wealth has also become increasingly insecure—the third troubling pattern. Because their assets were often insufficiently diversified, families were exposed to substantial market risk. Families invested an ever larger share of their assets in their homes as prices rose rapidly.[23] The simultaneous rise in stock prices led to a concentration of financial wealth in stocks.[24] Historically, real estate and corporate equities made up 43 percent of total assets on average, as compared to more than 50 percent during the 2000s.[25]

When the housing and stock markets fell, Americans' already fragile personal safety nets were ripped asunder. Literally trillions in personal wealth disappeared almost overnight. By 2008, total wealth to after-tax income was more than 30 percentage points lower than it had been, on average, during the previous business cycle—from March 2001 to December 2007.[26]

Causes of Increased Risk Burden

Growing wealth inequality, low savings, and large concentration of risk were driven by powerful forces, including technological change. But public policies were a consistently crucial factor.

INEQUALITY

The tax code is one determinant of wealth equality and low savings. The primary savings incentive in American tax law is the tax deductibility of contributions to tax advantaged savings, such as retirement savings, and also of mortgage interest. These saving incentives are skewed toward higher-income earners.[27] These earners are most likely to be offered tax-advantaged accounts and to use them, or to own an expensive home with a large mortgage, and they face the highest marginal income tax rates and thus receive the largest benefit from tax deductions.[28] The Tax Policy Center, for instance, reports that the top income quintile could expect to receive 72.2 percent of the benefits of ongoing changes in the federal retirement savings incentives in 2006.[29]

Cost differences of asset building between higher- and lower-income families may also arise due to segmented markets and limited services for less affluent consumers. Markets may be segmented due to lenders tailoring their products to specific groups; lenders restricting their geographic scope due to limited resources or discriminatory practices such as red-lining; and regulatory restrictions such as limits on credit union activities.[30]

LOW SAVINGS

A low personal savings rate prior to 2007 further exacerbated the factors just mentioned. Another partial explanation for America's low personal savings rate is the wealth effect, whereby families save less because they feel wealthier due to unexpected increases in asset prices.[31] The asset market booms of the 1990s and 2000s propelled people's wealth beyond expectation and thus they saved less. Large swings in asset prices can hence have an adverse impact on wealth creation by inducing people to save less than they otherwise would have.

Another aspect of declining wealth is of course rising debt. Consumer credit has increased because both credit demand and supply have grown.[32] Household debt, for instance, has grown because income has not kept up with consumption needs.[33] Lenders were willing to extend more credit to previously credit-constrained borrowers since they could simultaneously shift risk to other stakeholders due to debt securitization.[34]

CONCENTRATION IN RISKY ASSETS

Economic research has long documented that savers do not optimally diversify their assets. Savers can thus become exposed to greater market risk than is appropriate given their circumstances and preferences. Participants in retirement savings plans, such as 401(k)s, often do not rebalance their assets, even after large price changes in one asset class have led to increasing asset concentration.[35] Many participants also use "naïve diversification" when making investment decisions. For example, participants often divide their assets evenly across all available options.[36] Alternatively, if there are many available investment options, participants seem to choose one item from each category and then evenly diversify across categories.[37] In fact, if the range of available options becomes too confusing, participants in 401(k) plans may reduce their equity exposure.[38] Finally, 401(k) participants tend to hold a relatively high share of their assets in their employer's stock, often because they feel that they know the company.[39]

Policy Responses to Date

Existing policy responses have often been ineffective since they do not fully address the underlying causes of wealth inequality, inadequacy, and insecurity.

SAVINGS INCENTIVES

Shifting more savings tax incentives to lower-income earners could increase total personal savings since existing incentives have the largest positive effect among lower-income families.[40] Consider the retirement Savings Contributions Credit, also known as the Saver's Credit, which was enacted in 2002 as a temporary provision and became permanent in 2006. The Saver's Credit tries to compensate for the skewed nature of other savings incentives by focusing primarily on lower-income savers. However, its success is limited since its take-up rate was only 50.5 percent—that is, just half of those eligible claimed it.[41] This low take-up rate follows because the credit is nonrefundable; it is not provided as a cash incentive to those with little or no federal income tax liabilities.[42] Many low-income filers therefore cannot receive the credit at all.

The splintered nature of savings incentives—for home ownership, health care, retirement, and education, among others—adds more complications that impede wealth building. Savers, who have maxed out on their incentives to save for retirement, but not on their other incentives, cannot mix and match incentives across savings categories.[43]

Automated Savings

Many of the existing savings policies expect substantial financial acumen from individuals. Individuals have to decide when to save, how much to save, where to invest their savings, how to invest their savings, and how and when to withdraw their savings. All of these decisions are complex and fraught with opportunities to make costly mistakes.

Behavioral economics has taught us that policy can instead use people's inherent inertia to build wealth.[44] Congress attempted to follow this approach and make it easier for employers to automatically enroll employees in defined contribution plans in passing the Pension Protection Act of 2006 (PPA). PPA required that the Department of Labor establish rules that guide default investment options to increase diversification.[45] Early figures show that automatic enrollment is a feature of a growing share of defined contribution plans. For instance, a survey by Hewitt Associates LLC showed that 44 percent of responding firms offered automatic enrollment and 30 percent of those that did not yet offer it were considering implementing it in 2008.[46] Also, managed portfolios, such as life-cycle funds and model portfolios, have grown quickly, which should improve asset diversification in the future. These efforts to overcome behavioral obstacles could be expanded to other savings and investment decisions.

FINANCIAL MARKET TRANSPARENCY

Comprehensive, concise, and comparable information on the costs and risks of different forms of wealth needs to be made available to all consumers. Currently, required information is often presented in a way that makes it harder for consumers to comparison shop, for example by presenting some costs as a percent of assets and others as dollar fees. Moreover, some financial information is presented in legal and technical jargon, as is often the case on credit card statements, and hidden in the fine print of lengthy documents, such as mortgage documents.

FINANCIAL MARKET COMPETITION

Much of the financial service industry today is an uneven playing field that is skewed against the consumer. Financial markets are often segmented, given rise to quasi-monopolies among banks because of limited competition. The primary policy approach is to increase the number of banks that operate in underserved market segments. Two examples of such a policy approach are: (1) industrial loan banks, which are sometimes referred to as "Wal-Mart banks" since this retailer has in the past sought a charter to operate such a bank; and (2) expanded operations of credit unions. Both of these examples face regulatory limits.

Industrial loan banks (ILB) and industrial loan companies (ILC) are financial institutions supervised by the Federal Deposit Insurance Corporation (FDIC) that may be owned by commercial firms, such as GM, Target, Nordstrom's, and Harley-Davidson. Such financial institutions have existed since the turn of the twentieth century, and the ILC management—the parent corporation—is held accountable for ensuring that bank operations and business functions are performed in compliance with banking regulations imposed by the state and the FDIC.[47] Other corporations, namely Home Depot and Wal-Mart, have also previously tried to obtain an ILC charter.

There are regulatory challenges to increasing the reach of ILCs. These entities would be exempt from consolidated supervision and regulation.[48] The lack of proper regulatory oversight opens the door to greater systemic risk and conflicts of interest between the retail and the banking business.

Credit unions are an alternative venue to more financial market competition. Credit unions may be chartered at the federal or state level. Most credit unions are organized as nonprofits to serve a particular community, groups of employees, or members of an organization or association. Since profit is not the primary motivation, interest rates have been historically more favorable for consumers at credit unions, as compared to banks.[49] Even if families are not credit union members, they may enjoy the benefits of their growth since competition with credit unions has lowered the costs of financial services at other banks.[50]

Limitations on credit unions' scope with respect to personal finance have decreased over time, but some remain. Beginning in the 1980s, credit unions were permitted to offer first mortgages, and they have been allowed to offer membership to multiple groups since the late 1990s.[51] However, limits remain, particularly in the ability of credit unions to make business loans.[52]

NONEXISTENT AND UNDERDEVELOPED MARKETS

Public policy has also created incentives for financial institutions to fill gaps in the market. Some credit markets do not exist or involve large costs, such as markets for new technologies, affordable student loans, and infrastructure financing. Historically, three approaches have been used to fill such gaps: loan guarantees by the public in the event of borrower default, direct loans underwritten by the public, and lending requirements for private sector lenders to extend credit to particular types of projects and borrowers.

Loan guarantees, the first approach, exist for a wide variety of special industries and particular types of business. The result, however, is considerable complexity and administrative cost. Moreover, many loan guarantees exist as temporary budget items that require regular reauthorization by Congress, making them vulnerable to political swings over time.

The most notable example of the second approach, direct government loans, is student loans. Direct government lending received a major overhaul to increase the amount available in loans and to lower the costs to consumers as part of the health care legislation passed in early 2010. This new provision will expand the total amount of Pell grants and the eligibility for undergraduate college students and it will eliminate fees paid to banks acting as intermediaries in providing student loans.[53]

The Community Reinvestment Act (CRA) is a typical example of the third approach, lending requirements. It serves to encourage depository institutions, such as banks, to meet the credit needs of surrounding communities, particularly low- and moderate-income neighbooods.[54] The CRA, in conjunction with other measures, seems to have increased credit access and reduced the costs of credit for previously underserved communities, especially minorities and lower-income borrowers.[55] CRA's reach, though, has decreased as new regulations in 2005 exempted a large number of banks from its requirements.[56]

Solutions

The following discussion presents a few principles and examples that should guide policy efforts to make wealth-holding more equal, adequate, and secure. Several principles address more than one of these three goals.

TURN TAX DEDUCTIONS INTO CREDITS

Savings incentives are more likely to be effective if they are designed as refundable tax credits instead of deductions. For instance, existing tax deductions could be replaced with a uniform savings credit or with a flat government-matching contribution.[57,58] In the latter proposal, which has been suggested in the context of employment-based retirement savings, the match would comprise 30 percent of both employer and employee contributions to retirement saving accounts, regardless of employees' level of income. The employer's contribution would be taxed as employee income. This proposal would be roughly revenue neutral, in comparison with current tax deductions.[59]

Policymakers may want to move gradually in replacing existing tax deductions with credits. Initial improvements could center on the aforementioned Saver's Credit. Currently, nonrefundable income tax credits are given on the first $2,000 that filers contribute to a Roth IRA, traditional IRA, or voluntary pension plan.[60] The credit rate is 50 percent for very low-income earners, 20 percent for filers with slightly higher incomes, and 10 percent for moderate-income earners. The income limits are inflation adjusted.[61] Proposed improvements to the Saver's Credit go toward making the credit refundable and making more people eligible for the credit. Raising the income limits, such that middle-income families whose retirement wealth has been decimated by the crisis could also benefit, may also represent a compelling policy change.[62]

Other saving incentives could be similarly restructured. Mortgage interest payments, for instance, are also tax deductible, favoring owning over renting, particularly for higher-income families. A first step toward turning tax deductions for owner-occupied housing into tax credits could be a mortgage credit as proposed by President Barack Obama in 2008. The proposal would give those taxpayers who do not itemize their mortgage interest payments as tax deductions a flat credit of 10 percent of the interest payment, up to a maximum credit of $800.[63]

STREAMLINE SAVINGS INCENTIVES

Wealth building incentives should be streamlined. There should be one incentive to save for current needs and one for future needs, rather than a wide range of incentives. Current needs include such near-term issues as income replacement during an emergency, education, business formation, and housing, while future needs refer to retirement savings.

Streamlined savings incentives would promote efficiency by offering savers more choice to use their savings as they see fit. The efficiency gains—more savings for the same amount of tax incentives—arise for three reasons. First, people can determine their own savings goals. Home ownership would not be prioritized over renting, education over working, and so on. Second, savers may be inclined to save more if they have more choice over what to do with their savings. For instance, research on 401(k) plans indicates that savers will contribute slightly more if such plans offer a loan option.[64] Third, streamlined incentives reduce the complexity of the current system and would thus likely reduce administrative costs and increase participation.[65]

A number of experts have discussed streamlining retirement savings. President George W. Bush's Advisory Panel on Federal Tax Reform, for instance, met in 2005 to develop and recommend tax reforms in order to remove obstacles to saving, among other aims.[66] The panel recommended several reform options for savings incentives, including consolidating tax incentives into three programs: Save at Work, Save for Retirement, and Save for Family. Defined contribution plans would be consolidated into Save at Work plans with simple rules and then-current 401(k) contribution limits.[67] In a similar vein, Pamela Perun and C. Eugene Steuerle propose to streamline and simplify the rules governing retirement savings plans at work and increase available government matches for savers.[68] Save for Retirement accounts, proposed by President Bush's tax panel, would replace retirement savings plans, such as IRAs, Roth IRAs, nondeductible IRAs, deferred executive compensation plans, and tax-free "inside buildup" of life insurance and annuities cash values, in exchange for higher contribution limits than existing retirement savings plans allow and expanded availability to all taxpayers.[69] Streamlining savings options is desirable, while higher contribution limits typically favor only high-income earners. These proposals to simplify savings incentives should thus only be adopted with modifications.

The logic of streamlined savings incentives can be extended to establish another tax credit for nonretirement, universal, and unrestricted savings. Families can decide how to use their wealth to fit their needs. Save for Family accounts, as proposed by President Bush's tax panel, for example, would be available to all Americans to save $10,000 annually for a range of goals, including health care, education, training, and home purchase.[70] This incentive could replace the plethora of existing savings incentives for a range of purposes, including 529 accounts for education and mortgage interest deductions to promote home ownership. The previous point about the need to turn tax deductions into credits also applies here.

More streamlined savings incentives shift some of the responsibility for saving for particular long-term goals back onto the individual. Individuals will have to decide how much money they will need for current consumption needs and for retirement, rather than the government providing specific incentives for each socially desired savings goal. This creates the potential pitfall that families may miss their savings targets. This pitfall is even greater with a whole array of savings incentives. And automating savings and investment decisions can further reduce the chance of saving too little or too much.

AUTOMATED SAVINGS AND INVESTMENT DECISIONS TO MAKE IT EASIER TO SAVE

A number of policy proposals would expand so-called "auto solutions" to workers who do not work for an employer who offers a retirement savings plan. These solutions can take several forms. The first and most familiar is automatic enrollment. Mark Iwry and David John, for instance, suggest that every employer with ten or more employees should offer employees the opportunity of automatic payroll deductions into designated IRAs.[71] A second option is to have participating workers automatically save more as their incomes increase, known as automatic escalation.[72] In addition, retirement savings plans can be set up so that savings are automatically invested in a low-cost and limited-risk default investment option, unless the saver decides otherwise. Finally, withdrawals from retirement savings plans could also be automated. William Gale, Jonathan Gruber, and Peter Orszag, for example, propose an approach similar to the Thrift Savings Plan, under which the federal government facilitates an arrangement between private insurers and employees to establish annuities that keep pace with inflation.[73]

Most proposals to automate savings also include another provision that could lower the costs of savings: offering publicly administered but privately managed investment options to private sector employers. Such an investment option could reduce the fees and risks associated with individual accounts for smaller employers with low-income workers.[74]

The options so far may not encourage savers to contribute enough to their accounts. Public policy could mandate contributions or offer new incentives for employers and employees to contribute to retirement savings. Several experts have proposed a mandate on employers and employees (with some including an opt-out provision), to contribute at least a minimum of earnings, typically 2 to 5 percent, to their retirement savings plans.[75] (Munnell offers a proposal along these lines in her chapter.) Alternatively, there could be new incentives for voluntary contributions, such as tax form check-off boxes. Savers could check a box on their tax returns that indicates they want their tax refunds to go to a designated savings account.[76] This type of proposal could be expanded to direct tax refunds into low-cost savings options, such as savings bonds. It could also be used to couple savings from tax refunds with existing savings matches, such as the Saver's Credit or individual development accounts.

INCREASED TRANSPARENCY FOR SAVINGS AND CREDIT PRODUCTS

A number of existing measures aim to increase financial market transparency and consumer protections. Lawmakers, however, correctly decided in 2010 that these efforts have not brought about the desired changes. The financial regulatory reform passed by Congress establishes a consumer protection agency with an independent funding stream and an independent leadership. The agency is modeled on a proposal by Elizabeth Warren that envisioned a Financial Products Safety Commission that would set disclosure rules for all regulated consumer financial products.[77] The newly created agency will set and enforce guidelines on information disclosure for a wide range of consumer financial products offered by a broad swath of financial institutions.

INCREASED CREDIT MARKET COMPETITION

Policymakers could take additional steps to encourage financial market competition through industrial loan companies (ILCs) and credit unions. Expanding financial services through retailers, such as Wal-Mart, reaches communities where such services may be limited. At the time of the Wal-Mart ILC attempt in 2006, Wal-Mart CEO Lee Scott estimated that 20 percent of Wal-Mart shoppers did not have a checking account. ILCs typically cannot offer checking accounts, but they can take deposits and make loans.[78] The flipside, though, is that banking through a retailer can build an affinity relationship that retailers could exploit.

Wal-Mart already offers check-cashing services, money order and money transfer services, and even an Easy Investing program that consists of stock market investing and a money market fund, provided via *ShareBuilder* of ING Direct. The typical minimums and fees apply. An ILC charter, if permitted, would handle Wal-Mart's credit card, debit card, and electronic transactions, which would save Wal-Mart fees that it currently pays to a third party.

Greater emphasis on ILCs will have to address the primary objection from its opponents that these entities would be exempt from consolidated supervision and regulation.[79] The lack of proper regulatory oversight opens the door to greater systemic risk and conflicts of interest between the retail and the banking business. The new financial regulatory framework strengthens consumer protections for all financial products but creates a loophole for ILCs. The newly created systemic risk regulator—a council of regulators intended to monitor and intervene preemptively if too much risk is building up—could potentially monitor and regulate ILCs, but this issue was not addressed in the financial regulatory reform effort of 2010. The Obama administration had called for ILCs to be regulated in the same manner as banks, especially since a number of Wall Street firms, including Lehman Brothers, Merrill Lynch, Goldman Sachs, and Morgan Stanley, held ILC charters. Yet the Senate preserved their charter, continuing a major gap in regulatory oversight. The Senate instead placed a three-year moratorium on the approval of new ILC charters while the Government Accountability Office further studies ILC regulation.[80]

Regulation could also expand credit unions' scope. This could take the form, for example, of increasing their ability to make small business loans by raising existing limits on the share of total assets that a credit union can hold in business loans.[81] The total size of credit union loans will likely remain relatively small because credit unions tend to be small. Raising the limits on the share of credit union assets that are invested in small business loans may make it easier for some communities to build more wealth by reducing the costs of starting and expanding a business.

PUBLIC SUPPORT FOR UNDERDEVELOPED CREDIT MARKETS

Some holes in credit markets may persist even after implementing the measures just discussed. Credit markets are typically underdeveloped when lenders assess the expected return and risks involved in financing a project, as in the case of financing new, untested technologies, such as the Internet. Alternatively, the rate of return and risk that are involved in a project may be known, but these rewards and risks are so distant in the future that lenders are unwilling to commit their money for long periods of time, as is often the case with infrastructure projects. Finally, some markets do not exist because lenders cannot write loan contracts that will ensure that they will get repaid with a relatively high degree of certainty because borrowers' incomes are comparatively predictable or lenders hold reasonable collateral. Lenders, who extend education loans, for instance, cannot enforce a borrower's promise to complete a degree and earn the expected higher income necessary to repay the loan. Policymakers then should apply one of the three tools available to fill these gaps: loan guarantees, direct loans, and lending requirements.

All three tools could be expanded. A recent concrete example is the National Infrastructure Development Bank proposed by the Obama administration for fiscal year 2010 and reiterated as a key proposal by President Obama in his 2011 State of the Union address.[82] The proposal offers seed funding of $5 billion in 2010 and total funding of $25 billion from 2010 to 2014 for guarantees and loans to infrastructure projects. This approach envisions a self-financing entity to support a broad swath of activities that generally face trouble in securing adequate financing.

A challenge in designing policies to fill credit market gaps is to know when such measures should cease. New technologies will not always remain new, the time horizon of infrastructure projects may be shortened, and institutional changes may make it possible to write more complete contracts. In such circumstances the rationale for public policy intervention disappears and public support for particular credit markets could be reduced or eliminated. Policymakers should regularly consider the circumstances under which their involvement may be reduced or eliminated in response to the inception of a new public financial product.

Conclusion

Wealth has always played a critical role in ensuring economic security and opportunity. Yet this has only become more true as responsibility for accessing education, health care, and retirement security has increasingly shifted onto individuals. Against this backdrop, the recent financial crisis and ongoing economic slowdown could represent a painful wake-up call. American families have lost $20 trillion during the first year and a half of the current financial crisis that began in 2007. Public policy should intervene to help families repair their private safety net by increasing their assets and reducing their debts. The specific policy goals to be achieved include increased saving rates, reduced risk exposure, and lower costs associated with saving and investing.

We propose six broad steps to achieve these goals and help families regain their economic security as quickly as possible. Public policy can turn tax deductions for savings into refundable tax credits to offer greater benefits to lower-income families than is currently the case. Policy could also streamline savings incentives to lower the complexity and thus the costs of saving. We propose specifically two incentives—one for current needs, such as education and emergencies, and one for future needs, such as retirement. The new incentives will be particularly effective if policymakers further help to automate savings and investment decisions, for example by making it easier for savers to automatically save a share of their paycheck. And, savers will get to keep a larger share of their savings, if the costs of saving, investing, and borrowing are reduced with greater financial market transparency and competition. Finally, policy should support loan products where private financial markets are inadequate—too little for too much money—or are completely missing. This will make it easier for families to borrow when they want to invest in their future, for example by furthering their education.

There is no silver bullet to bring back trillions of dollars in lost wealth. American families will need all the help that they can get. Policymakers should not shy away from comprehensive wealth-building policies. A piecemeal approach will not reach many families and will delay their much-needed recovery in economic security.

Notes

1. Authors' calculations based on Federal Reserve Statistical Release: Statistics and Historical Data, http://www.federalreserve.gov/releases/chargeoff/(Charge Off and Deliquency Rates on Loans and Leases and Commercial Banks, 2009). Our data discussion includes data through the end of 2008, although many trends continued afterward. The end of 2008 marks the end of the sharpest downturn in financial wealth and the end of the first year of the economic recession.

2. U.S. Department of Labor, Pension and Welfare Benefits Administration, *Private Pension Bulletin 1993: Abstract of 1993 Form 5500*, no. 6, 1996.

3. U.S. Department of Labor, Bureau of Labor Statistics, National Compensation Survey, http://www.bls.gov/eci/2010.

4. Alicia Munnell and Annika Sunden, *Coming Up Short: The Challenge of 401(k) Plans* (Washington, DC: Brookings Institution Press, 2004), 26–27; Theresa Ghilarducci, "Guaranteed Retirement Accounts: Toward Retirement Income Security," EPI Briefing Paper, no. 204 (Washington, DC: Economic Policy Institute, 2007), http://www.sharedprosperity.org/bp204/bp204.pdf.

5. Mary O' Sullivan, *Contests for Corporate Control: Corporate Governance and Economic Performance in the United States and Germany* (New York: Oxford University Press, 2000).

6. Munnell and Sunden, *Coming Up Short*, 2, n. 2.

7. Edward Wolff and Christian Weller, "Buyer Beware: Pension Wealth Inequality Rises as 401(k) Plans Become More Popular," Center for American Progress, http://www.americanprogress.org/issues/2004/01/b22329.html (January 16, 2004).

8. Brian K. Bucks, et al., "Changes in U.S. Family Finances from 2004 to 2007: Evidence from the Survey of Consumer Finances," *Federal Reserve Bulletin*, February 2009: A7–8, http://www.federalreserve.gov/pubs/bulletin/2009/pdf/scf09.pdf.

9. Ibid.

10. Christian E. Weller and Jessica Lynch, "Household Wealth in Freefall: Americans' Private Safety Net in Tatters," (Washington, DC: Center for American Progress, 2009), 4, http://www.americanprogress.org/issues/2009/04/household_wealth.html.

11. Weller and Lynch, "Household Wealth in Freefall," 5.

12. Weller and Lynch, "Household Wealth in Freefall," 5.

13. Weller and Lynch, "Household Wealth in Freefall," 5.

14. Weller and Lynch, "Household Wealth in Freefall," 5.

15. Weller and Lynch, "Household Wealth in Freefall," 7.

16. Uriah King, Leslie Parrish and Ozlem Tanik, "Financial Quicksand: Payday Lending Sinks Borrowers in Debt with $4.2 Billion in Predatory Fees Every Year," (Durham, NC: Center for Responsible Lending, 2006), 2, http://www.responsiblelending.org/payday-lending/research-analysis/financial-quicksand-payday-lending-sinks-borrowers-in-debt-with-4-2-billion-in-predatory-fees-every-year.html.

17. Jean Fox and Elizabeth Guy, "Driven into Debt: CFA Car Title Loan Store and Online Survey," (Washington, DC: Consumer Federation of America, 2005), 2, http://www.consumerfed.org/finance/payday.asp; Jacqueline Duby, Eric Halperin and Lisa James, "High Cost and Hidden From View: The $10 Billion Overdraft Loan Market," Center for Responsible Lending Issue Paper, no. 9 (Durham, NC: Center for Responsible Lending, 2005), 2, http://www.responsiblelending.org/overdraft-loans/research-analysis/high-cost-and-hidden-from-view-the-10-billion-overdraft-loan-market.html.

18. Robert Manning, *Credit Card Nation: The Consequences of America's Addiction to Credit* (New York: Basic Books, 2000); Tim Westrich and Malcolm Bush, "Blindfolded into Debt: A Comparison of Credit Card Costs and Conditions at Banks and Credit Unions" (Chicago: Woodstock Institute, 2005), http://www.fdic.gov/news/conferences/affordable/woodstock2.pdf.

19. For a detailed literature review see Christian Weller, "Access Denied: Low-Income and Minority Families Face More Credit Constraints and Higher Borrowing Costs" (Washington, DC:

Center for American Progress, 2007), http://www.americanprogress.org/issues/2007/08/access_denied.html.

20. For a detailed recent discussion of the fees associated with 401(k) plans, see Sarah Holden and Michael Hadley, "The Economics of Providing 401(k) Plans: Services, Fees, and Expenses," *Research Fundamentals* 15, no. 7 (Washington, DC: Investment Company Institute, 2008), http://www.ici.org/pdf/fm-v15n7.pdf.

21. Christian Weller and Shana Jenkins, "Building 401(k) Wealth One Percent at a Time: Fees Chip Away at People's Retirement Nest Eggs" (Washington, DC: Center for American Progress, 2007), 6; Munnell and Sunden, *Coming Up Short* (see n. 5); Government Accountability Office, testimony of Barbara D. Bovbjerg before the United States Senate Special Committee on Aging, *Private Pensions: 401(k) Plan Participants and Sponsors Need Better Information on Fees*, 2007.

22. Council of Institutional Investors, "Protecting the Nest Egg: A Primer on Defined Benefit and Defined Contribution Retirement Plans" (Washington, DC: Council of Institutional Investors, 2006); Sean Collins, "The Expenses of Defined Benefit Pension Plans and Mutual Funds," *Investment Company Institute Perspective* 9, no. 6 (Washington, DC: Investment Company Institute, 2003); Holden and Hadley, "The Economics of Providing 401(k) Plans" (see n. 27).

23. Weller and Lynch, "Household Wealth in Freefall," 2–3.

24. Weller and Lynch, "Household Wealth in Freefall," 8.

25. Weller and Lynch, "Household Wealth in Freefall," 8.

26. Weller and Lynch, "Household Wealth in Freefall," 3–4.

27. There is evidence, however, that while all families save more in tax advantaged savings due to the tax incentives, only low-income families actually save more money overall. By contrast, high-income families simply shift savings from non-tax-advantaged savings to tax-advantaged savings. If this is true, then the savings incentives do not so much exacerbate wealth inequality as perpetuate it. Eric Engen and William Gale, "The Effects of 401(k) Plans on Household Wealth: Differences across Earnings Groups," NBER Working Paper, no. 8032 (Washington, DC: National Bureau of Economic Research, 2000); James Poterba, Joshua Rauh, Steven Venti and David Wise, "Defined Contribution Plans, Defined Benefit Plans, and the Accumulation of Retirement Wealth," *Journal of Public Economics* 91, no. 10 (2007): 2062–2086.

28. Peter Orszag, testimony before the U.S. House of Representatives Committee on Education and Labor, *The Effects of Recent Market Turmoil in Financial Markets on Retirement Security*, 110th Cong., 2d sess., October 7, 2008.

29. Tax Policy Center, "Table T07–0290, Tax Benefits of the Exclusions and Deductions for Retirement Savings, Distribution of Federal Tax Changes by Cash Income Percentile, 2006" (Washington, DC: Tax Policy Center, 2007), http://www.taxpolicycenter.org/numbers/displayatab.cfm?DocID=1955.

30. Alicia Munnell, Geoffrey Tootell, Lynn Browne, and James McEneaney, "Mortgage Lending in Boston: Interpreting HMDA Data," *American Economic Review* 86, no. 1 (1996): 25–53; Kathe Newman and Elvin Wyly, "Geographies of Mortgage Market Segmentation: The Case of Essex County, New Jersey," *Housing Studies* 19, no. 1 (2004): 53–83.

31. Congressional Budget Office, *Housing Wealth and Consumer Spending* (2007); James Poterba, "Stock Market Wealth and Consumption," *Journal of Economic Perspectives* 14, no. 2 (2000): 99–118.

32. Matt Fellows and Mia Mabanta, "Borrowing to Get Ahead, and Behind: The Credit Boom and Bust in Lower-Income Markets" (Washington, DC: The Brookings Institution, 2007), http://www.brookings.edu/papers/2007/0511metropolitanpolicy_fellowes.aspx.

33. Elizabeth Warren and Amelia Warren Tyagi, *The Two-Income Trap: Why Middle-Class Mothers and Fathers Are Going Broke* (New York: Basic Books, 2003).

34. Martin Baily, Douglas Elmendorf, and Robert Litan, "The Great Credit Squeeze: How It Happened, How to Prevent Another," (discussion paper, Washington, DC: Brookings Institution, 2008), http://www.brookings.edu/papers/2008/0516_credit_squeeze.aspx.

35. Olivia Mitchell, Gary Mottola, and Stephen Utkus, "The Inattentive Participant: Portfolio Trading Behavior in 401(k) Behavior," Pension Research Council Working Paper 2006–2

(Philadelphia: Pension Research Council, Wharton School, University of Pennsylvania, 2005), http://knowledge.wharton.upenn.edu/paper.cfm?paperID=1319.

36. Shlomo Benartzi and Richard Thaler, "Heuristics and Biases in Retirement Savings Behavior," *Journal of Economic Perspectives* 21, no. 3 (2007): 81–104; Gur Huberman and Wei Jiang, "Offering versus Choice in 401(K) Plans: Equity Exposure and Number of Funds," *Journal of Finance* 61, no. 2 (2006): 763–801.

37. Sheena Iyengar and Emir Kamenica, "Choice Overload and Simplicity Seeking," (working paper, New York: Columbia University, 2006).

38. Iyengar and Kamenica, "Choice Overload."

39. Iyengar and Kamenica, "Choice Overload."

40. Engen and Gale, "The Effects of 401(k) Plans on Household Wealth" (see n. 27).

41. William Gale, Mark Iwry, and Peter Orszag, "The Saver's Credit: Issues and Options," *Tax Notes* 103, no. 5 (2004): 605.

42. Esther Duflo, William Gale, Jeffrey Liebman, Peter Orszag, and Emmanuel Saez, "Saving Incentives for Low-and Middle-Income Families: Evidence from a Field Experiment with H and R Block," *The Quarterly Journal of Economics* 121, no. 4 (2006): 1334–1335.

43. President's Advisory Panel on Federal Tax Reform, *Simple, Fair, and Pro-Growth: Proposals to Fix America's Tax System*, 2005, http://www.taxpolicycenter.org/taxtopics/upload/tax-panel-2.pdf

44. Shlomo Benartzi and Richard Thaler, "Heuristics and Biases in Retirement Savings Behavior," *Journal of Economic Perspectives* 21, no. 3 (2007): 81–104.

45. *The Pension Protection Act of 2006*, Public Law 109–280, 109th Cong., 2d sess. (January 3, 2006).

46. Hewitt Associates LLC, "Survey Findings: Hot Topics in Retirement 2008" (Lincolnshire, IL: Hewitt Associates LLC, 2008).

47. Mindy West, "The FDIC's Supervision of Industrial Loan Companies: A Historical Perspective," Federal Deposit Insurance Corporation, http://www.fdic.gov/regulations/examinations/supervisory/insights/sisum04/industrial_loans.html (2004).

48. Randall Dodd, testimony before the Federal Deposit Insurance Corporation, Washington, DC, April 11, 2006.

49. CommonBond Communications, Inc., "Credit Unions Compared to Banks," Credit Unions Online, http://www.creditunionsonline.com/ (accessed July 22, 2009).

50. William Emmons and Frank Schmid, "Bank Competition and Concentration: Do Credit Unions Matter?," *Federal Reserve Bank of St. Louis Review* 82, no. 3 (2000): 29–42; Robert Feinberg, "The Competitive Role of Credit Unions in Small Local Financial Services Markets," *Review of Economics and Statistics* 83, no. 3 (2001): 560–563; Robert Feinberg and A.F.M. Ataur Rahman, "A Causality Test of the Relationship between Bank and Credit Union Lending Rates in Local Markets," *Economics Letters* 71, no. 2 (2001): 271–275.

51. Keith Leggett and Robert Strand, "Membership Growth, Multiple Membership Groups and Agency Control at Credit Unions," *Review of Financial Economics* 11, no 1 (2002): 37–46; James Tripp and Stanley Smith, "U.S. Credit Union Motivation for Involvement in the First-Mortgage Market," *Journal of Real Estate Finance and Economics* 7, no. 3 (1993): 229–236.

52. Eli Lehrer, "Taxicab Medallions and Heirloom Tomatoes to the Rescue: How Expanding Credit Union Lending Can Help Small Business to Survive the Credit Crunch" (Washington, DC: Competitive Enterprise Institute, 2007), http://cei.org/studies-point/taxicab-medallions-and-heirloom-tomatoes-rescue; Eli Lehrer, "Let Credit Unions Lend More: A Modest Proposal to Increase the Availability of Capital to Small Businesses," (Washington, DC: Competitive Enterprise Institute, 2009).

53. Peter Baker and David Herszenhorn, "Obama signs Bill on Student Loans and Health Care," *New York Times*, March 30, 2010.

54. Raphael Bostic, Hamid Mehran, Anna Paulson, and Marc Saidenberg, "Regulatory Incentives and Consolidation: The Case of Commercial Bank Mergers and the Community Reinvestment Act," Working Paper Series WP-02–06 (Chicago: Federal Reserve Bank of Chicago, 2002).

55. Timothy Bates, "Financing the Development of Urban Minority Communities: Lessons of History," *Economic Development Quarterly* 14, no. 3 (2000): 227–241; Bostic, Mehran, Paulson, and Saidenberg, "Regulatory Incentives and Consolidation: The Case of Commercial Bank Mergers and the Community Reinvestment Act."

56. Office of Thrift Supervision, "OTS Announces Final CRA Rule," February 28, 2005, http://www.ots.treasury.gov (accessed May 30, 2010).

57. Gene Sperling, "A Progressive Framework for Social Security Reform" (Washington, DC: Center for American Progress, 2004), http://www.americanprogress.org/issues/2004/01/b289151.html.

58. William Gale, Jonathon Gruber, and Peter Orszag, "Improving Opportunities and Incentives for Saving by Middle and Low-Income Households," The Hamilton Project Discussion Paper 2006–02 (Washington, DC: The Bookings Institution, 2006), http://www.brookings.edu/papers/2006/04saving_gale.aspx.

59. Lily Batchelder, Fred Goldberg, and Peter Orszag, "Efficiency and Tax Incentives: The Case for Refundable Tax Credits," *Stanford Law Review* 59, no. 1 (2006): 23–76.

60. Duflo, Gale, Liebman, Orszag and Saez, "Saving Incentives for Low-and Middle-Income Families" (see n. 42).

61. Internal Revenue Service, "Retirement Savings Contributions Credit," 2008, http://www.irs.gov/publications/p.590/ch05.html.

62. William Gale, Mark Iwry, and Spencer Walters, "Retirement Saving for Middle-and Lower-Income Households: The Pension Protection Act of 2006 and the Unfinished Agenda" (Washington, DC: Retirement Security Project, 2007).

63. Leonard Burman, Surachai Khitatrakun, Greg Leiserson, Jeff Rohaly, Eric Toder, and Roberton Williams, "A Preliminary Analysis of the 2008 Presidential Candidates' Tax Plans" (2008) (Washington, DC: Tax Policy Center, 2008).

64. Government Accountability Office,"401(k) Pension Plans: Loan Provisions Enhance Participation But May Affect Income Security for Some," (Washington, DC, 2008); Jack VanDerhei, "Contribution Behavior of 401(k) Participants," EBRI Issue Brief 238 (Washington, DC: Employee Benefits Research Institute, 2001).

65. President's Advisory Panel on Federal Tax Reform, *Simple, Fair, and Pro-Growth* (see n. 43).

66. President's Advisory Panel on Federal Tax Reform, *Simple, Fair, and Pro-Growth*.

67. President's Advisory Panel on Federal Tax Reform, *Simple, Fair, and Pro-Growth*.

68. Pamela Perun and C. Eugene Steuerle, "Why Not a 'Super Simple' Saving Plan for the United States?," (Washington, DC: Urban Institute, 2008).

69. President's Advisory Panel on Federal Tax Reform, *Simple, Fair, and Pro-Growth*.

70. President Bush's tax panel largely maintained the tax deductibility of contributions to savings accounts and added tax-free withdrawals from savings accounts. Such a move would exacerbate the existing inequality of savings incentives and thus likely make savings incentives less efficient. The tax panel's proposals are mentioned here to highlight the fact that experts generally agree that simplification of savings incentives is a worthwhile policy goal. See text accompanying note 66 above.

71. Mark Iwry and David John, "Pursuing Universal Retirement Security through Automatic IRAs," (Washington, DC: The Retirement Security Project of the Brookings Institution, 2006).

72. William Gale, Mark Iwry, and Peter Orszag, "The Automatic 401(K): A Simple Way to Strengthen Retirement Saving," *Tax Notes* 106, no. 10 (2005): 1207–1214.

73. Gale, Gruber, and Orszag, "Improving Opportunities and Incentives for Saving by Middle and Low-Income Households" (see n. 58).

74. Dean Baker, "Universal Voluntary Accounts: A Step Towards Fixing the Retirement System," (Washington, DC: Center for Economic and Policy Research, 2006).

75. Rahm Emmanuel, "Supplementing Social Security," *Wall Street Journal*, September 13, 2007; Theresa Ghilarducci, "Guaranteed Retirement Accounts: Toward Retirement Accounts," EPI Briefing Paper, no. 204 (Washington, DC: EPI, 2007); Christian Weller, "PURE: A Proposal for More Retirement Income Security," *Journal of Aging and Social Policy* 19, no. 1 (2007): 21–38.

76. Mark Iwry, "Using Tax Refunds to Increase Savings and Retirement Security," Policy Brief, no. 2005–9 (Washington, DC: Retirement Security Project, 2005).
77. Elizabeth Warren, "Unsafe at Any Rate," *Democracy: A Journal of Ideas* 5 (2007): 8–19.
78. Liz Pulliam-Weston "National Bank of Wal-Mart?," MSN Money, http://moneycentral.msn.com/content/Banking/Betterbanking/P109171.asp. (accessed May 31, 2009).
79. Randall Dodd, testimony before the Federal Deposit Insurance Corporation, Washington, DC, April 11, 2006.
80. David Cho, "Bank Loophole for Wall Street Remains in Financial Regulation Bill," *Washington Post*, May 19, 2010.
81. Eli Lehrer, "Taxi Cab Medallions and Heirloom Tomatoes to the Rescue," (see n. 58); Eli Lehrer, "Let Credit Unions Lend More" (see n. 52).
82. Office of Budget and Management, *A New Era of Responsibility: Renewing America's Promise*, 2009, 19, http://www.gpoaccess.gov/usbudget/fy10/pdf/fy10-newera.pdf

8

Risk Allocation in Home Ownership

Revisiting the Role of Mortgage Contract Terms

KATHERINE PORTER AND TARA TWOMEY

Introduction

Home ownership is the main mechanism that American families use to build wealth[1] and strongly associated with middle-class financial security and prosperity.[2] Indeed, for most of the twentieth century, home ownership was touted as the "American dream." In the twenty-first century, however, home ownership is proving for millions of families to be the American nightmare.

The current foreclosure crisis has wiped out all the increase in the home ownership rate achieved in the last decade.[3] The rate is expected to fall further, with millions of families already facing foreclosure and millions more struggling with delinquent loans.[4] As of 2010, nearly one in four home borrowers owed more on their mortgages than their homes were worth.[5] Even before housing prices plunged, the steep run-up in mortgage debt in the years preceding the foreclosure crisis had severely eroded the net worth of American families. Between 1983 and 2007, the debt-to-equity ratio of middle-class families grew by 165 percent, with much of this change coming from increased mortgage debt.[6] This loss of wealth makes home owners more vulnerable to financial distress triggered by unanticipated changes in income or expenses, such as job loss or medical bills. The plight of these families and the reverberating effects on neighborhoods, governments, and the economy are powerful reminders of the risks that accompany home ownership.[7]

The current crisis has sparked interest in reexamining America's policies aimed at promoting home ownership.[8] Laws as divergent as the Internal Revenue Code and the Community Reinvestment Act have been criticized for contributing to the foreclosure crisis.[9] Some scholars have proposed alternate ownership structures that would unlink housing consumption and housing investment.[10] Others have focused on the lawlessness of actors in the mortgage market and advocated for reforms such as the registration and licensing of mortgage brokers.[11] These approaches are sharply divergent, but all reflect a fundamental concern with identifying and recalibrating the risks of home ownership.[12]

This chapter takes a more narrow approach to that problem, but one that is complementary to these larger efforts and surprisingly neglected within them. We argue that policymakers have not focused sufficiently on how changes in mortgage contract terms increased home ownership risk for families. We trace the development of mortgages and illustrate how the terms of mortgage loans are crucial levers of risk.

The mortgage contract is crucial not just because it establishes the affordability of the loan but also, and less recognized, because it determines the overall risk associated with the home purchase and allocates those risks between the borrower and lender.[13] Government is a key player in mortgage risk management alongside lenders and borrowers because of its ability to regulate the terms of mortgage contracts.

After exposing how the recent decades of mortgage product innovation both increased the risk of home ownership and shifted more of that risk to borrowers, we develop three core principles that should guide future regulation of mortgages. First, the government should collect comprehensive and reliable data on mortgage products and should monitor the way in which those products allocate the risks between borrowers and lenders. Second, any effort to rebalance the risks inherent in the mortgage process must consider consumers' limited abilities to evaluate complex financial products. Third, any successful regulation of mortgage products requires the development and deployment of effective enforcement tools for consumer protection laws. Together, these three principles provide a broad and flexible framework for balancing policy concerns about advancing opportunity for home ownership, on the one hand, and limiting the risks of mortgage markets, on the other.

Historical Context

In 1900, less than half of the households in the United States owned their homes.[14] Property acquisition typically required a large down payment. Financing was largely unregulated and often took the form of short-term, interest-only balloon notes. These loans typically lasted only five years and had monthly payments equal to the accrued interest. Because the payments did not include any amounts to pay off the principal, the borrower was required to pay a large lump sum payment at the loan's maturity.[15] Repayment typically was achieved through refinancing. The Great Depression led to unprecedented levels of foreclosures as credit markets constricted, and borrowers were unable to refinance their short-term obligations. Nonfarm foreclosure rates more than tripled between 1926 and 1933.[16] By the beginning of 1934, as many as half of urban home mortgages were delinquent.[17] Home ownership rates, which had been relatively flat until the 1930s, dropped over 4 percentage points to a record low of 43.6 percent by 1940.[18]

In an effort to stabilize the mortgage markets, Congress created the Federal Housing Administration in 1934.[19] The FHA's primary tool for reinvigorating the decimated housing market was insurance that would protect lenders against losses from mortgage defaults. Along with the insurance program came the development of the long-term, fixed-rate mortgage. Figure 8.1 shows these and other major developments in the U.S. mortgage market.

Initially, FHA insurance was limited to mortgages that had principal balances of $16,000 or less, that had down payments of at least 20 percent,[20] that fully amortized over the term of the loan which was not to exceed 20 years (later 30 years),[21] and that had a maximum interest rate of 5–6 percent.[22] Eligible mortgages also had to have periodic payments that did not exceed the borrowers' "reasonable ability to pay."[23]

The standardization of a long-term, fixed-rate product—the "plain vanilla" mortgage—dramatically reduced borrowers' risk in financing a home purchase. The fixed rate insulated borrowers from the risk of increases in interest rates and protected them from payment shock during inflationary periods. The risk that the borrower would be unable to pay or refinance a balloon payment note—the "refinance risk"—was eliminated by the fully amortizing feature of the loan. The extended term of 30 years made the loan affordable to more potential home buyers, and the 20 percent down payment requirement reduced barriers for first-time home buyers while still serving as a hedge for lenders against fluctuations in home prices. With this plain vanilla product, the primary risk of default lay in unexpected and significant decreases in borrowers' income that hindered the borrower from making timely payments on the loan. (e.g., job loss). Critical terms of the mortgage were limited to the interest rate and the amount of the loan, which together determined the level monthly payment for thirty-year loan. The paucity of terms and the simple relationship between the terms made it relatively easy for borrowers to understand the risks associated with financing a home purchase.

The plain vanilla loan product was the workhorse of the mortgage industry for more than half a century. But rapidly rising interest rates during the 1970s drove

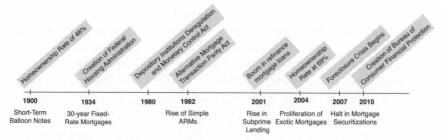

Figure 8.1:   Timeline of Major Developments in U.S. Homeownership.
Source: Author's illustration.

lending institutions, with government support, to create alternative mortgage products.[24] With interest rates climbing into the double digits, many lenders, particularly savings and loan institutions, were squeezed by a growing disparity between high short-term interest rates payable on deposits and the lower return being generated by fixed-rate mortgage loans.[25] Potential new home owners faced affordability problems as the average interest rate on 30-year fixed-rate mortgages rose steeply and topped 18 percent in 1981.[26]

As mortgage interest rates neared their peak, the federal government relaxed statutory and regulatory constraints on the lending industry. In 1980, Congress eliminated state usury caps for most loans secured by first liens on residential real estate.[27] Regulators liberalized rules for federal depository institutions by allowing them to issue variable-rate mortgages and nonamortizing loan products.[28] This deregulation of the residential mortgage market was extended to almost all lenders with the passage of the Alternative Mortgage Transaction Parity Act of 1982,[29] which preempted many state laws that restricted mortgage terms, including prohibitions on variable interest rates, balloon payments, and negative amortization.[30] While the intent of this deregulation was to increase the supply of mortgage credit and the profitability of mortgage loans,[31] an attendant effect was to permit lenders to increase the overall risk of mortgage loans and shift more risk onto borrowers.

Conditions/Features of Risk

The mortgage market in the three decades leading up to the foreclosure crisis that began in 2007 was characterized by the introduction of new loan products. Product innovation was always toward complexity; the new loans added features that complicated the plain vanilla model and provided more options to home owners. These changes complicated the calculus of a home owner trying to select the best home loan.

THE RISE OF ADJUSTABLE RATE MORTGAGES

Adjustable-rate mortgages (ARMs) were developed to reduce the interest rate risk borne by lenders and to address the affordability problem faced by borrowers. An ARM is characterized by interest rate changes based on fluctuations in an index. Borrowers' payments adjust in relation to interest rate change. The five key components of the basic ARM are: the initial interest rate, the index, the margin, the adjustment period, and caps. The initial interest rate is the rate in effect at the origination of the loan. The value of the index varies over time and determines the starting point for calculating any change in the interest rate.[32] The margin is a constant spread or fixed premium added to the value of the index by the lender to generate profit on the loan. For example, if on the day that the interest rate is adjusted, the value of the designated index is 5.5 percent and the margin specified in the loan documents is 2 percent, then the new interest rate on the loan will be 7.5 percent. The adjustment period is the time between mortgage interest rate changes. Periodic caps limit the amount of interest rate change in any given period, and the lifetime cap establishes the loan's maximum interest rate.[33] Each of these components allocates risk between the consumer and the note holder.

The adjustable nature of the interest rate transfers more interest rate risk to the borrower. In theory, borrowers are compensated for assuming the long-term interest rate risk with lower initial interest rates. To some degree, periodic caps counteract the variability of the interest rate. They also reduce borrowers' default risk because they decrease the possibility of significant interest rate and payment increases (also known as payment shock). Shorter adjustment periods and higher periodic or lifetime caps increase borrowers' interest rate risk because they more fully subject the borrower to current market conditions.

Even a basic ARM presents borrowers with many more terms to evaluate than a fixed-rate loan. Consumers must not only consider the initial affordability of the loan and their own income expectations but must also determine whether their incomes will be sufficient if interest rates and payments increase. Fundamentally, ARM loans require borrowers to make a guess, educated or otherwise, about the direction of market interest rate change. This is a complex calculation, even for lenders with sophisticated modeling and billions of dollars at stake.

The high interest rates of the early 1980s, combined with mortgage lenders' aversion to interest rate risk, made ARMs a mainstream mortgage product even for the most creditworthy borrowers. As interest rates subsequently declined, so too did the share of ARMs. By 2003, mortgage interest rates were at a historical low, but ARMs nevertheless found new life within the nonprime mortgage market.

GROWTH OF THE SUBPRIME MORTGAGE MARKET

The U.S. mortgage market has two main categories: prime and nonprime. Prime borrowers are typically those with excellent credit and a demonstrated ability to repay the loan. Nonprime borrowers are generally divided into two subgroups: Alt-A and subprime. Alt-A loans were generally made to borrowers who fell just short of qualifying for prime loans because of some loan or borrower characteristic (e.g., no income documentation or no down payment). Subprime loans theoretically are made to borrowers with blemished credit or with limited repayment capacity (e.g., too many other debts or a housing payment that is too large relative to the borrower's income).[34] The subprime mortgage market expanded significantly between 2004 and 2006, peaking at approximately 20 percent of all mortgage originations. Much of the increase in subprime lending during these boom years is attributable to the growth of ARMs. In 2000, ARM loans just marginally outnumbered fixed-rate loans in the subprime and Alt-A markets. But by 2005, the peak of the lending frenzy, subprime and Alt-A loan originations consisted of 2.8 times as many ARM loans as fixed-rate loans.[35]

In addition to adjustable rates, other risk-shifting features that were rarely found in prime loans, such as prepayment penalties and teaser rates, were ubiquitous in the growing nonprime market.[36] Prepayment refers to the payment of a loan's principal before it is due. Penalties may apply when the borrower prepays a mortgage loan in full or in part during the penalty period (typically the first three to five years after the origination of the loan). Borrowers have an incentive to prepay and refinance if interest rates fall below the rate on their loan or if they qualify for lower interest rate loans. Prepayment penalties compensate lenders for the risk that loan proceeds will have to be reinvested at lower interest rates than the borrowers were paying. While limiting risk to the holders of the mortgage loans, prepayment penalties can trap borrowers in uneconomical loans because they increase the cost of refinancing. Borrowers, in theory, are compensated for assuming this risk by receiving a lower interest rate.[37] In this way, prepayment penalties allocate risk and affect the price of loans.

Ratchet rate loans layer a risk-shifting feature on top of the basic ARM model. Ratchet rate loans are adjustable-rate loans that only adjust upward from the initial interest rate. By the loan terms, the interest rate can never drop below the initial rate, even if the index goes down from its value at the loan's origination. Ratchet rate loans force borrowers to bear the burden of interest rate increases but bar them from the benefit of interest rate reductions.

Teaser rate loans also build on the basic ARM model, with the effect of increasing payment shocks that can lead to default. Teaser rates were a common feature of the adjustable-rate mortgages that dominated the subprime mortgage market between 2004 and 2006.[38] Teaser rate loans have an initial interest rate that is below the fully indexed rate. That is, the starting interest rate for the loan is below the composite rate obtained by adding the margin to the index rate. At the end of the first adjustment period, the discounted rate is typically replaced by a fully indexed rate, subject to any periodic caps. Even if the index rate has not changed, borrowers with teaser rates will nevertheless experience payment increases because the original discount is no longer applicable. If the value of the index rate also has increased, the payment increase will be even greater. If the periodic cap limits the initial rate adjustment, the payable interest rate will continue to increase at each subsequent adjustment period until it reaches the fully indexed rate. While low initial teaser rates temporarily improve the affordability of the loan, they can have serious negative consequences for borrowers if they do not have sufficient income to cover the payment increases. Not only do borrowers bear the risk of interest rate changes, but the payment increase that occurs after the teaser rate expires heightens the likelihood that borrowers will default on the loan.

CONTINUED INNOVATION: EXOTIC LOANS

The complexity of these variants on the basic ARM loan pales in comparison to the "exotic" mortgage products that had gained significant market share by 2006.[39] A new version of the interest-only loan that once reigned in the 1920s emerged again during the subprime boom. These interest-only loans were typically long-term loans (e.g., 30 years) that allowed borrowers to make interest-only payments for a certain portion of that term (typically the first 5 or 10 years after loan origination). At the end of the interest-only period, the loan recasts such that it amortizes fully over the remainder of the term. The re-amortizing of the loan results in a significantly higher payments.

A second exotic mortgage product was the payment option ARM. This loan typically had four payment options: the minimum payment, the interest-only payment, the 30-year fully amortizing payment, and the 15-year fully amortizing payment. The minimum payment is insufficient to pay for all the interest that accrued the previous month, and unpaid interest is added to the principal balance. Thus, for borrowers making only the minimum payment, the loan balance on a pay-option ARM grows (negatively amortizes) instead of being paid down. This product ostensibly offered flexibility to borrowers who could choose a payment to match their needs. It is estimated that in reality more than 75 percent of pay-option ARM borrowers made only the minimum payment.[40] Most pay-option ARM loans have a trigger term that would cause the loans to "recast" and become fully amortizing if the principal balance exceeded a certain percentage (typically 110–125 percent) of the loan balance. The vast majority of pay-option ARMs also have a five-year recasting trigger. If the principal balance trigger is not reached in the first five years of the loan, the loan will still reamortize based on this time trigger. Recasting, whether as a result of the principal balance or time trigger, causes a significant increase in borrowers' payments.

Like teaser rate loans, these exotic loans appear less expensive because they reduce the initial payments. The terms of the loans, however, make borrowers more vulnerable to interest rate increases, housing price depreciation, and stagnant wages. The interest-only and negative amortization features that were commonly layered on top of an ARM loan with a prepayment penalty not only had the effect of shifting risks to borrowers but also compounding the risk of default. Deferred payments of interest and principal built into these exotic products necessarily resulted in higher monthly payments—potentially two to three times the previous payment amount—when the loans recast. To meet higher payment obligations, borrowers needed to either increase their income or refinance. Most pay-option ARM borrowers had little prospect of significantly increasing their income. As a result, lenders and borrowers relied almost exclusively on the ability to refinance these loans to manage the risk of the loan becoming unaffordable. Such a model adds the risk of changes in housing values and the availability of credit to the risk factors for default.

Causes of Increased Risk Burden

Most economists hailed these innovative mortgage products. From their perspective, the one-size-fits-all approach to mortgages represented by the 30-year fixed-rate mortgage misallocates resources. Alan Greenspan captured this sentiment when he praised the virtues of adjustable-rate mortgages and noted that fixed-rate mortgages "effectively charge home owners high fees for protection against rising interest rates and for the right to refinance."[41] In this view, the plain vanilla mortgage is an expensive method of financing a home; instead, consumers should use adjustable-rate mortgages and put the savings from lower initial payments to more productive use. For example, Piskorski and Tchistyi recently posited that the best possible loan between home buyers and lending institutions is an ARM loan with flexible payments that permit negative amortization and prepayment restrictions. In essence, they opine that the optimal mortgage loan is a pay-option ARM.[42] This loan earns the accolades of many economists, in part, because it gives borrowers the flexibility to pay down mortgage debt when they have excess income or to finance the interest when their income is short. The authors find that "[g]ains from the optimal contract relative to simpler mortgages are substantial and are the biggest for those who face substantial income variability, buy pricey houses given their income level or make little or no down payment."[43]

Works such as this are useful in thinking theoretically about mortgage contract terms, but they do not incorporate actual borrower and lender behavior. The theoretical world in which such economic models are constructed is based on a "rational" consumer and competitive, full-information markets. Yet these conditions do not really exist. Theoretical models such as these should be used cautiously by policymakers because they do not contain all the information needed to design a regulatory framework necessary to monitor the allocation of risk between borrowers and lenders in the real world.

Historically, much of our consumer protection law has been based on the rational actor model. The success of this economic model depends on borrowers understanding the terms of various mortgage products. The model assumes that if borrowers fully understand the contract terms, then they will make the best (most rational) choices for themselves in selecting mortgage products. These rational actors, armed with a rich knowledge of the comparative risks of different products, are fully capable of comparative shopping for products, thus ensuring that the lending market reaches a competitive equilibrium. In this vein, the major policy objective has been to counter borrowers' lack of understanding and financial illiteracy through education or its sidekick, disclosure.

The burgeoning field of behavioral economics has undermined the rational actor model. While some of this work is theoretical, its focus is on identifying how behavior in real markets may deviate from the assumptions of traditional economics.[44] Behavioral economic research suggests that knowledge cannot always trump the behavioral biases that often unconsciously shape consumers' mortgage decisions.[45] Consequently, education and disclosure are likely to be of limited utility.[46] For example, borrowers often focus on the affordability of the initial monthly payments, rather than the terms that contribute to the loan's total cost and risk such as its length, balloon payments, and prepayment penalties.[47] This is because they underweight the future, relative to the present, thus making a miscalculation about the relative benefits of lower initial payments in exchange for more risk and higher costs later in the loan's life. Alternatively, borrowers may be overly optimistic in believing that their payments will not increase because market interest rates will not increase.[48] Evidence suggests that financial education is relatively ineffective in combating behavioral biases such as these.[49]

Consumers are particularly apt to make cognitive errors when products are complex.[50] When nearly all loans were plain vanilla, consumers could more easily shop for the lowest price. Product innovation increased the number of products severalfold but, more important, meant that each product required sophisticated analyses of terms and their accompanying risk. As three behavioral scholars ask rhetorically, "How many home owners really understand how the teaser rate, the introductory rate, and the reset rate really relate to the London interbank offered rate plus some specified margin . . . ?"[51] In these situations, shortcuts in decision making are used to cope with the overwhelming interplay of relevant factors.[52] Thus behavioral economics research highlights the limits of consumer cognition, even if paired with improved financial literacy and disclosure.[53] The market can, and will, design product attributes that manipulate consumer behavior or, worse, actively mislead consumers.[54]

Policy Responses to Date

During the period of product innovation and subprime lending, the regulatory framework for mortgage loans was weak and fractured. This diffusion of responsibility aided the innovation of mortgage products while simultaneously thwarting the careful monitoring of such products' risks. Many mortgage origination companies were not traditional financial institutions and operated outside regulatory oversight. Until the financial reforms enacted in 2010, a lender's regulator was determined by the nature of the entity, not the nature of the financial product. For example, a nationally chartered depository bank and a state-chartered savings and loan, even when making identical mortgage loans, had different regulators. This structure produced inconsistent standards between regulators. Because lenders could determine their regulators by institutional design, it also encouraged regulatory arbitrage with a race to fewer restrictions on product terms. Because the core mission of financial agencies is to protect the regulated entity and its depositors or shareholders, concerns of institutional safety and soundness led to a focus on profitability and portfolio risk management. From this perspective, mortgage products that move risks from lenders and onto consumers are largely positive because they increase profits and off-load risk.

As mortgage instruments shifted more risk to home owners, however, the government failed to expand its regulatory focus to measure consumer risk. The result was a massive underestimation of the amount of total risk generated by mortgage product innovations and, crucially, a lack of knowledge of where such risks lay.[55] The former chairman of the Federal Reserve was purportedly shocked to learn the number of subprime mortgages originated in his tenure.[56] The inability of consumers to understand product terms and calculate the interaction of market risks and default risks posed by those terms simply was not on the federal regulatory agenda. After staunchly defending the benefits of uninhibited product innovation for years, former Treasury secretary Henry Paulson admitted in March 2008 that "regulation needs to catch up with innovation."[57] Regulators did a poor job of monitoring the risks of nontraditional home mortgages to institutional lenders and were not even focused on consumers as a constituency of concern.

The current crisis has sparked momentum for fundamental reform of the financial industry. Such efforts are multilayered. Much of the debate has centered on assertions that subprime lending creates unbearably high risks and that the government should impose a return to the underwriting criteria of the 1970s. We caution against equating the default rate and predatory practices that characterized swaths of the subprime marketing with carefully orchestrated efforts to expand home ownership into low-and moderate-income households. Dan Immergluck's book *Foreclosed* (2009) carefully separates efforts to address lending discrimination and red-lining and problems with high-risk lending in mortgage markets, cautioning that a failure to focus on disparate access to home ownership can lead to "naïve nostalgia" for prior lending practices.[58] And while the spike in defaults may have begun in the subprime market, the foreclosure crisis has clearly revealed that the prime market also was deeply distorted by 2007.

The data suggest that the eradication of subprime lending is too large a target for substantive regulation. Figure 8.2 shows the percentage of loans that were seriously delinquent when the foreclosure crisis emerged. Months after the mortgage markets froze and home prices began to decline, default rates on 30-year fixed-rate subprime loans were less than half those on subprime ARMs. Indeed, the delinquency rate in early 2009 for fixed-rate subprime loans was close to that for ARM loans made to prime borrowers. Creditworthiness did reduce risk, but the type of mortgage may be nearly as important in controlling default risk.

The prime market also reveals the role of contract terms in delinquency risk. Prime borrowers with an adjustable-rate loan are three times more likely to be delinquent than if their mortgage has a fixed-rate. The default rates on pay-option ARMs, which were made primarily to borrowers with good credit scores, stand at nearly 37 percent and are climbing.[59] These data signal the importance of loan

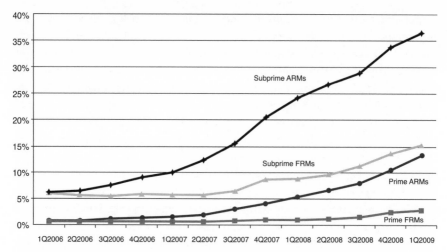

Figure 8.2:   Seriously Delinquent Loans. Source: Mortgage Bankers Association
Delinquency Survey.

features in risk management. To date in the current crisis, the terms of the loan
have been a crucial determinant of default, notwithstanding the general creditworthiness of the borrower. Regulation of mortgage terms can curb default risk
without limiting access to credit for subprime borrowers as sharply as would
alternatives such as imposing required minimum down payments.

Regulators need to remember that risk is inherent in lending. Imposing constraints on the incentives of brokers or other actors or requiring more conservative underwriting can limit the quantity of risk. But the residual risk of the loan
must still be allocated between the consumer and lender (or more precisely, the
holders of the mortgage note). Product terms are crucial levers in that allocation
process—a point somewhat lost in the recent panoply of reform efforts that
take broad aim at the past decade's subprime borrowing market. The real culprit,
in our view, was product innovation without corresponding innovations in regulation. The effect of this dynamic was to shift risk from lenders onto consumers, and ultimately onto the government when the risks overwhelmed the
entire private market.

SOLUTIONS

A major question in the aftermath of the financial crisis will be how to manage
home ownership risk. We use the term "manage" rather than "mitigate" to emphasize that risk inheres in credit transactions. Short of requiring people to pay up-
front cash for the entire purchase price of their homes, the home ownership
process will continue to be characterized by risk—for both borrowers and lenders.
The task is to curb risks when they do not benefit home ownership policy, to be

acutely aware of the amount of risk and where it resides, and to allocate the remaining risk in a sensible way.

Before turning to the substantive regulation of mortgage terms, we pause to comment on the importance of the procedural framework for risk allocation decisions. Because the historic regulatory structure is entity driven rather than product driven, it cannot comprehensively govern the terms of consumer financial transactions. The financial reform bill created a new Bureau of Consumer Financial Protection to focus on risks from the consumers' perspective.[60] Critically, it has authority over all mortgages, regardless of the lending entity. This consolidation of authority will sharpen awareness of risk allocation decisions, and the consumer-oriented perspective will improve awareness of the degree to which loan products push risk onto home buyers. Such a structure is a necessary framework for developing responsive and intelligent product regulation.

The Bureau of Consumer Financial Protection is charged with promulgating rules that govern products and product features, including mortgage loan contracts. Its authority permits it to either ban or place reasonable restrictions on product terms.[61] Substantive regulation of the terms of consumer mortgages is not a novel power. Indeed, an early response of the Federal Reserve to the mortgage crisis was to create a new set of rules governing higher-priced loans, including a two-year ban on prepayment penalties, a requirement that the creditor consider the borrower's ability to repay the loan, and an escrow account requirement.[62] And for decades, the Home Ownership Equity Protection Act has restricted the terms that may be included in high-cost loans.[63] The new regulator, however, is unusual in having a clearly identified focus on assessing risk from consumers' perspectives.[64]

We have identified the terms of mortgage loans as an important tool for risk management and have championed the idea of a consumer-oriented regulator as a key player in that process. We do not wish to minimize the challenges of determining the permissible attributes for mortgage loans, and we do not purport to have the necessary data or experience to proscribe product attributes.[65] We do, however, develop three principles for regulating mortgage product terms. The principles focus on missing aspects of past regulatory approaches and can serve as a guide for upcoming policy debate on mortgage market regulation.

As a first principle, we observe that the government itself must monitor the risk-shifting aspects of mortgage finance. Lenders and home buyers each would prefer that the other bear the risk; in a robust market, we should see these actors developing and selecting products that push risk back and forth between banks and borrowers. The government has a poor track record of monitoring risk in home ownership, as evidenced by the savings and loan crisis in the 1970s and the recent financial meltdown. As a first matter, the government needs to collect better data about mortgage markets.[66] The dedicated research unit within the Bureau of Consumer Financial Protection could greatly aid in improving data about mortgage markets.[67]

The government then needs to invest in risk modeling for mortgages as part of the costs of promoting home ownership. Empirical data and analytical models are themselves valuable public goods. They permit regulators to police lenders to ensure that they are pricing for risk and to monitor the financial reserves of lending institutions. And they permit government to protect families who put their assets, such as home equity and future income streams, on the line to attempt home ownership. The government should not be permitted to promote home ownership without taking on responsibility for monitoring the risks of that policy.

One way to ease the task of monitoring the amount and allocation of risk is to limit the number of types of mortgage products. In its strongest form, government could effectively return the mortgage industry to a single product market consisting of 30-year fixed-rate loans. Indeed, some have openly argued for a dominant role for plain vanilla loans,[68] while others may be trying to effectively produce such an outcome by imposing hefty underwriting duties on lenders offering any alternate product.[69] This medicine may be too strong, but some curb on lenders' ability to complicate risk calculations with new products may be necessary.

One possibility is that the Bureau of Consumer Financial Protection could require the lender to test products before widespread introduction in the market. The goal would be to produce data on how innovative contract terms alter default risk. One could measure how well consumers understand those risks and gauge whether the lender's predicted rate of default holds up. This is not unlike the Federal Drug Administration's model for collecting data on drug side effects before approving products. Given its role in the mortgage markets as guarantor and ultimate insurer of last resort, the government cannot protect itself without reasonably accurate data on product terms and their risk allocation effects.

The second principle is that any fruitful rebalancing of the risks of home ownership between lenders, consumers, and government must be mindful of the limits of consumers to assess and manage risks. We argue that governments and lenders are better risk bearers for the types of market-wide mortgage risks that are not idiosyncratic to a given consumer, such changes in interest rate indices. Regulations that limit risks on consumers should also limit the complexity of mortgage products that overwhelm consumers' ability to assess the risks of home ownership.

The counterparties to a mortgage loan have dramatically different tools for understanding product features and calculating risk. Consumers are ill suited to assess the number and variety of risks in exotic mortgages, even if they are more adequately prepared with counseling or financial education. The pay-option ARM is a prime example of a product with too many moving parts and too much complexity. Empirical data show that consumers with ARM loans underestimate how much the interest rate can increase and the lifetime cap on the loan.[70] Regulators must take into account the limits of consumer cognition and not be deterred by unsupported claims that product innovation is always an advance for home ownership.

In this vein, lenders should be required to underwrite mortgages to certain standards, rather than leaving consumers free to assess risk without any external checks. Federal law now requires lenders to consider a consumer's ability to pay when issuing a mortgage.[71] Models developed in an econometric vacuum, such as those that mathematically model why pay-option ARMs are the ideal mortgage loan, should be left in the academic sphere. Policymakers need to rely on empirical data when they exist, and supplement those data with theories of risk that account for the realities of consumer behavior. This is true both for consumer-oriented and lender-oriented regulation. The government's failure to force lenders to confront the realities of consumer behavior allowed the industry to perpetuate and to rely on inaccurate risk models.

Assuming the risks are correctly assessed, it is the duty of government to supervise the allocation of such risks. In most instances, consumers will be worse at bearing market-based risks of home ownership such as interest rate risk. They cannot spread such risks and have less sophisticated analyses to predict interest rate change. On the other hand, consumers should bear property-specific risks to avoid moral hazard concerns.[72] As we explain above, the effect of product term change is to shift many market risks away from the note holders and onto consumers. ARMs shift the risk of higher interest rates onto consumers, particularly when those products set the floor interest rate at the level of the teaser rate (as is typical). That is, the interest rate at origination is usually the lowest rate permitted, while an interest rate increase of several percentage points is possible. The steady pattern of lengthening mortgage loans from 15 to 30 to 40 years increases the period of interest rate fluctuation that the home owner must bear.[73] Prepayment penalties are another risk-allocation term. Eliminating some of these terms reduces the number of tools that lenders and consumers can use to divide risk. Streamlining products reduces the difficulties that consumers face in evaluating their risks and that note holders face in developing accurate risk models.

The final principle is that regulation of home ownership must imbed effective enforcement tools to prevent the lawlessness that characterized the lending boom of the late 1990s and early 2000s. This principle recognizes the difficulty in effective regulatory enforcement. The mortgage market is huge and diffuse. An attractive feature of product term regulation is that it is relatively easy to enforce. Provided that every entity making loans is covered by the same regulation (a problem ostensibly solved by the Bureau of Consumer Financial Protection), the policing obligation involves examining loans in the marketplace and comparing their terms against regulations. This is surely more complex than the bare description suggests, but it also a substantially easier task than alternatives, such as imposing a duty of suitability for making mortgage loans.[74]

Product term regulation has relatively stark boundaries. While that bluntness may be a substantive disadvantage, it is a corresponding procedural advantage. Making violations easier to identify will prevent evasion and will increase the likelihood that regulators will actually undertake enforcement activity and pursue sanctions. The penalties for offering mortgages that contain nonsanctioned terms must be steep. They should be sufficient to deter, as well as punish, because relatively few consumers will have the sophistication or resources to identify or pursue violations. In determining the permissible contract terms, regulators should strongly weigh practical enforcement concerns. Clear and tangible standards, such as prohibitions on prepayment penalties, lend themselves to robust enforcement. Despite the hand-wringing of politicians, the financial reform law largely avoids substantive regulation of mortgage terms.

At the current moment, the risks of home ownership and the hardships of failing to manage such risks are laid bare. This economic disaster provides a powerful opportunity to reshape the fundamentals of home ownership policy. This chapter has argued that the substantive terms of mortgage loans are a key tool to allocate home ownership risk. After exposing the limits of alternate approaches to product complexity, such as theoretical risk modeling and consumer education, we have suggested principles to guide policymakers in regulating the terms of future mortgage contracts.

Acknowledgments

Porter is Professor of Law, University of California Irvine School of Law. Twomey is Of Counsel to the National Consumer Law Center. We thank Diane Thompson, Steve Sugarman, and Alan White for helpful comments

Notes

1. Eric Belsky and Joel Prakken, *Housing Wealth Effects: Housing's Impact on Wealth Accumulation, Wealth Distribution and Consumer Spending*, (Cambridge, MA: Joint Center for Housing Studies, 2004), 3, http://www.jchs.harvard.edu/publications/finance/w04–13.pdf.
2. "Homeownership is the status to which most Americans aspire . . . Homeownership is nearly always treated as desirable—symbolizing wealth and status through the society." Teresa A. Sullivan, Elizabeth Warren, and Jay Lawrence Westbrook, *The Fragile Middle Class: Americans in Debt* (New Haven: Yale University Press, 2000), 199.
3. The current home ownership rate, as reported for the first quarter of 2010, is 67.1 percent. This 2010 level is below that of 2001. U.S. Census Bureau, *Housing Vacancy Survey, Homeownership Rates 1968–2010*, http://www.census.gov/hhes/www/housing/hvs/qtr109/q109tab5.html.
4. The Mortgage Bankers Association reports that 4.6 percent of loans are in foreclosure proceedings and more than 9 percent of home loans are delinquent. Mortgage Bankers Association, *National Delinquency Survey Q1 2010*, (May 2010), http://www.mbaa.org/files/Research/NDSQ110flyer.pdf.
5. CoreLogic, *Real Estate News and Trends*, accessed May 10, 2010, http://www.corelogic.com/; Paul S. Calem, Susan M. Wachter, and Marsha Courchane, "Sustainable Homeownership" (paper presented at Housing after the Fall: Reassessing the Future of the American Dream, Irvine, CA, March, 2009), 25, http://ssrn.com/abstract =1365436.

6. Calculations from Survey of Consumer Finances data show that the debt-to-equity ratio for the middle three quintiles of households by net worth went from 37.4 in 1983 to 61.1 in 2007. Edward N. Wolff, "Recent Trends in Household Wealth in the United States: Rising Debt and the Middle-Class Squeeze—An Update to 2007," Levy Economics Institute Working Paper, no. 589, (Levy Economics Institute of Bard College, 2010), 50, table 8, http://www.levyinstitute.org/pubs/wp_589.pdf. Wolff also calculates that households in these middle three wealth quintiles had significant declines in the ratio of net home equity to total assets, and significant increases in the ratio of mortgage debt to home values during the decade before the foreclosure crisis began in 2007.

7. Dan Immergluck, *Foreclosed: High-Risk Lending, Deregulation, and the Undermining of America's Mortgage Market* (Ithaca, NY: Cornell University Press, 2009), 133–168.

8. A. Mechele Dickerson, "The Myth of Home Ownership and Why Home Ownership Is Not Always a Good Thing," *Indiana Law Journal* 84 (2009): 189.

9. "[The Internal Revenue Code is] perhaps the single most important cause of the financial crisis." Bert Ely, "Bad Rules Produce Bad Outcomes: Underlying Public Policy Causes of the U.S. Financial Crisis," *The Cato Journal* 29, no. 1 (Winter 2009): 99. The CRA is one of the crucial reasons for the subprime mortgage meltdown because it "forced lenders to make loans to low-income borrowers, regardless of credit." Vernon W. Hill, "Viewpoint: Counterpoint—Many Roads to the Subprime Debacle," *American Banker*, March 7, 2008.

10. See, e.g., Lee Ann Fennell, "Homeownership 2.0," *Northwestern University Law Review* 102 (2008): 1047; Robert J. Shiller, *Macro Markets: Creating Institutions for Managing Society's Largest Economic Risks* (Oxford: Oxford University Press, 1993), 207–208.

11. *Secure and Fair Enforcement for Mortgage Licensing Act of 2008*, Pub. L. No. 110–289, 122 Stat. 2659 (2008).

12. For an overview of dimensions for possible regulation of the mortgage market, see Kathleen C. Engel and Thomas J. Fitzpatrick IV, "A Framework for Consumer Protection in Home Mortgage Lending" (2010), http://ssrn.com/abstract=1669540.

13. A variety of other players also bear mortgage risks, including investors and governments, but we focus on the initial parties in mortgage originations (consumers and lenders) in this chapter.

14. U.S. Census Bureau, Housing and Household Economic Statistics Division, *Historical Census of Housing Tables: Homeownership*, last revised December 2, 2004, http://www.census.gov/hhes/www/housing/census/historic/owner.html.

15. Michael J. Lea, "Innovation and the Cost of Mortgage Credit: A Historical Perspective," *Housing Policy Debate* 7 (1996): 147; Richard K. Green and Susan M. Wachter, "The American Mortgage in Historical and International Context," *Journal of Economic Perspectives* 19 (2005): 93–94.

16. David C. Wheelock, "Changing the Rules: State Mortgage Foreclosure Moratoria during the Great Depression," *Federal Reserve Bank of St. Louis Review* 90, no.6 (November/December 2008): 569–570.

17. Ibid., 569.

18. U.S. Census Bureau, *Historical Census of Housing Tables* (see n. 13).

19. Congress created several other entities during the 1930s with the purpose, at least in part, to preserve and encourage home ownership. These entities include the Federal Home Loan Bank Board (1932), the Home Owners' Loan Corporation (1933), the Federal Deposit Insurance Corporation (1933), the Federal Savings and Loan Insurance Corporation (1934), and the Federal National Mortgage Association (1937).

20. *Act of Aug. 2, 1954*, ch. 649, Title I, §§ 104–110, 68 Stat. 591, 592; Pub. L. No. 85–104, Title I, § 101(c), 71 Stat. 294, 295 (1957).

21. *Housing Act of 1948*, 80 Pub. L. No. 901, ch. 832, § 101(j)(2), 62 Stat. 1268, 1272.

22. *National Housing Act of 1934*, § 203(b), 48 Stat. 1248 (1934). Statutory interest rate caps were removed in 1983. Pub. L. 98–181, Sec. 404(b)(2)(1983).

23. *National Housing Act of 1934*, 73 Pub. L. No. 479, § 203(b)(4), 48 Stat. 1246, 1248 (1934).

24. See Immergluck, *Foreclosed*, 41–45 (see n. 7).

25. See Green and Wachter, "The American Mortgage in Historical and International Context" (see n. 15); see also Senate Committee on Banking, Housing, and Urban Affairs, *Garn-St Germain Depository Institutions Act of 1982*, S. Rep. No. 97–536 (1982), reprinted in U.S.C.C.A.N 3054, 3059.

26. Freddie Mac, "30-year Fixed-Rate Mortgages Since 1971," http://www.freddiemac.com/pmms/pmms30.htm.

27. *Depository Institutions Deregulation and Monetary Control Act of 1980*, Pub. L. No. 96–221, § 501(a), 94 Stat. 132, 161.

28. Adjustable Mortgage Loan Instruments, 46 Fed. Reg. 24,148[-01] (April 23, 1981) (codified at 12 C.F.R. pt. 545); Adjustable-Rate Mortgages, 46 Fed. Reg. 18,932 (March 27, 1981) (codified at 12 C.F.R. pt. 29).

29. *Garn-St Germain Depository Institutions Act of 1982*, Pub. L. No. 97–320, 96 Stat. 1469 (codified in various sections of 12 USC).

30. 12 U.S.C. § 3802(1) (2006).

31. The Congressional findings and purpose in enacting ATMPA states that "alternative mortgage transactions are essential to the provision of an adequate supply of credit secured by residential property necessary to meet the demand expected during the 1980's." 12 U.S.C. § 3801(a)(2) (2006).

32. There are several indices that are commonly used in ARMs, including LIBOR (the London Interbank Offer Rate), the one-year constant-maturity Treasury (CMT), and the Cost of Funds Index (COFI).

33. 12 U.S.C. § 3806 (2006); Reg. Z., 12 C.F.R. § 226.30 (2010).

34. A study by Freddie Mac found that 15 to 35 percent of all subprime loans it bought in 2005 could have qualified for prime-rate loans, and a study by Fannie Mae found that up to 50 percent of subprime loans it bought in 2005 had credit profiles that could have qualified them for prime rates. Les Christie, "Wow, I Could've Had a Prime Mortgage," CNNMoney.com, May 30, 2007, http://money.cnn.com/2007/05/29/real_estate/could_have_had_a_prime/index.htm.

35. Government Accountability Office, *Characteristics and Performance of Nonprime Mortgages*, table 4, 25–6 (Washington, DC: GAO, 2009).

36. A 2003 study by the Center for Responsible Lending noted that 80 percent of subprime loans contained prepayment penalties compared to 2 percent of prime loans. Debbie Goldstein and Stacy Strohauer Son, "Why Prepayment Penalties are Abusive in Subprime Home Loans," Center for Responsible Lending Policy Paper, no. 4 (Durham, NC: Center for Responsible Lending, 2003). Short-term hybrid loans made up 78 percent of subprime loans at the market's zenith in 2005. GAO, *Characteristics and Performance of Nonprime Mortgages*, table 5, 26 (2009). Short-term hybrid ARMs were majority of subprime loan originations from 2000 to 2007. Ibid.

37. There is some evidence that prepayment penalties simply reduced lenders' exposure to risk without a concomitant financial benefit for home owners. See Keith S. Ernst, *Borrowers Gain No Interest Rate Benefits from Prepayment Penalties on Subprime Mortgages* (Durham, NC: Center for Responsible Lending, 2005), http://www.responsiblelending.org/media-center/press-releases/archives/rr005-PPP_Interest_Rate-0105.pdf.

38. In those years, short-term hybrid ARMs were about three-quarters of subprime loan originations. GAO, *Characteristics and Performance of Nonprime Mortgages*, table 4, 25–26 (2009).

39. From 2003 to 2005, nontraditional mortgage product originations increased from less than 10 percent of residential mortgages to over 30 percent. Government Accountability Office, testimony before the United States Senate Subcommittees on Housing and Transportation and Economic Policy, Committee on Banking, Housing, and Urban Affairs, *Alternative Mortgage Products: Impact on Defaults Remains Unclear, but Disclosure of Risks to Borrowers Could be Improved*, GAO-06-1112T, 2006, 6.

40. Bob Tedeschi, "A Reckoning on Option ARMs," *New York Times*, September 18, 2009. An estimate by UBS found that 70 percent of borrowers with pay-option ARMs were making only the minimum payment in late 2005. Ruth Simon, "A Trendy Mortgage Falls from Favor," *Wall Street Journal*, November 29, 2005.

41. Alan Greenspan, Chairman, Fed. Res. Bd., "Understanding Household Debt Obligations," speech, Credit Union National Association 2004 Governmental Affairs Conference, February 23, 2004, http://www.federalreserve.gov/boarddocs/speeches/2004/20040223/.

42. Tomasz Piskorski and Alexei Tchistyi, "Optimal Mortgage Design," (2007): 4–5, http://papers.ssrn.com/sol3/papers.cfm?abstract_id=971223.

43. Ibid., 6.

44. Alan M. White, "Behavior and Contract," *Law and Inequality* 27 (2009): 135. White describes some of the challenges that behavioral economics has made to rational choice theory in area of consumer law.

45. Patricia A. McCoy, "A Behavioral Analysis of Predatory Lending," *Akron Law Review* 38 (2005): 725–738.

46. Lauren Willis, "Against Financial Literacy Education," *Iowa Law Review* 94 (2008): 197.

47. Framing, a type of psychological consideration, refers to the contexts in which choices are presented and made. See Amos Tversky and Daniel Kahneman, *Science* 211, (1981): 453–458. "The frame that a decision-maker adopts is controlled partly by the formulation of the problem and partly by the norms, habits, and personal characteristics of the decision-maker." Ibid.

48. Optimism bias is the tendency to overweight the likelihood of positive events (such as an increase in future income) and underweight the likelihood of negative events (such as a decline in future income). See Dan Arialy, "The Curious Paradox of 'Optimism Bias," *Business-week*, Aug. 13, 2009.

49. Abdighani Hirad and Peter Zorn, "Pre-Purchase Homeownership Counseling: A Little Knowledge Is a Good Thing," in *Low-Income Homeownership: Examining the Unexamined Goal*, eds. Nicholas P. Retsinas and Eric S. Belsky (Washington, DC: Brookings Institution Press, 2002), 146–174.

50. "With product proliferation and multiple origination channels, consumers often face information overload. In such cases, as the number of choices available rises, decision making performance declines due to the difficulties consumers have in ordering their own priorities and recalling relevant information." Ren S. Essene and William Apgar, *Understanding Mortgage Market Behavior: Creating Good Mortgage Options for All Americans* (Cambridge, MA: Joint Center for Housing Studies, 2007), 11, http://www.jchs.harvard.edu/publications/finance/mm07-1_mortgage_market_behavior.pdf.

51. Michael S. Barr, Sendhil Mullainathan, and Eldar Shafir, "Behaviorally Informed Home Mortgage Regulation," in *Borrowing to Live: Consumer and Mortgage Credit Revisited*, eds. Nicolas P. Retsinas and Eric S. Belsky (Washington, DC: Brookings Institution Press, 2008), 193.

52. "Consumers considering obtaining a typically complex subprime mortgage loan may simplify their decision by focusing on a few attributes of the product or service that seem most important." Truth in Lending, 73 Fed. Reg. 44,522, 44,525 (July 30, 2008) (to be codified at 12 C.F.R. pt. 226).

53. For an effort to use disclosure to circumvent the adverse effects of imperfect rationality, see Oren Bar-Gill, "The Law, Economics, and Psychology of Subprime Mortgage Contracts," *Cornell Law Review* 94 (2009): 1073.

54. Consumers can never perform their demand function sufficiently to correct mortgage market problems because of transaction and information barriers. Lauren E. Willis, "Will the Mortgage Market Correct? How Households and Communities Would Faire if Risk Were Priced Well," *Connecticut Law Review* 41 (2009): 1229–1230.

55. Neither the Federal Reserve nor any other agency in Washington examined the consequences of housing price decline. Edmund L. Andrews, "Fed Shrugged as Subprime Crisis Spread," *New York Times*, December 18, 2007.

56. "Greenspan puzzled over one piece of data a Fed employee showed him in his final weeks. A trade publication reported that subprime mortgages had ballooned to 20 percent of all loans, triple the level of a few years earlier. 'I looked at the numbers . . . and said, 'Where did they get these numbers from?' Greenspan recalled in a recent interview. He was skeptical that such loans had grown in a short period 'to such gargantuan proportions.'" Alec Klein and Zachary

Goldfarb, "The Bubble: How Homeowners, Speculators and Wall Street Dealmakers Rode a Wave of Easy Money with Crippling Consequences," *Washington Post*, June 15, 2008.

57. U.S. Department of the Treasury, "Remarks by Secretary Henry M. Paulson, Jr. on Recommendations from the President's Working Group on Financial Markets," news release, March 13, 2008, http://www.ustreas.gov/press/releases/hp872.htm.

58. Immergluck, *Foreclosed*, 47 (see n. 7).

59. Marshall Eckbland, "Pick-A-Pay Loans: Worse Than Subprime," *Wall Street Journal*, July 14, 2009.

60. *Dodd-Frank Wall Street Reform and Consumer Protection Act*, Pub. L. No. 111–203, § 1001 et seq., 127 Stat. 1376 (2010).

61. Ibid. 1022, 1033.

62. Higher-cost loans are defined as mortgage loans secured by the consumer's principal residence with an annual percentage rate that exceeds the average prime offer rate for a comparable transaction by 1.5 percent for first lien loans or 3.5 percent for subordinate liens. 73 Fed. Reg. 44,522, 44,603 (July 30, 2008) (to be codified in 12 C.F.R pt. 226); 12 C.F.R. § 226.35 (2010).

63. 15 U.S.C. § 1639 (2010); 12 C.F.R. § 226.32 (2010)

64. 15 U.S.C. § 1021 (2006).

65. Ren S. Essene and William Apgar, *Understanding Mortgage Market Behavior: Creating Good Mortgage Options for All Americans*, (Cambridge, MA: Joint Center for Housing Studies, 2007), 50, http://www.jchs.harvard.edu/publications/finance/mm07–1_mortgage_market_behavior.pdf. There is no consensus as to what constitutes a "good loan product." Ibid.

66. Greenspan explained that his first knowledge of the spark in subprime mortgage originations came in 2005 from data estimated by a private vendor that the Federal Reserve later worked to confirm. Greg Ip, "His Legacy Tarnished, Greenspan Goes on Defensive," *Wall Street Journal*, April 8, 2008.

67. *Dodd-Frank Wall Street Reform and Consumer Protection Act*, Pub. L. No. 111–203, § 1013(b)(1), 127 Stat. 1376 (2010).

68. One model would be to require lenders to offer plain vanilla mortgage products and then allowing borrowers to opt out of the basic product with heightened disclosures and additional legal liability for lenders. See, e.g., Michael S. Barr, Sendhil Mullainathan, and Eldar Shafir, "Behaviorally Informed Home Mortgage Regulation," in *Borrowing to Live: Consumer and Mortgage Credit Revisited*, eds. Nicolas P. Retsinas and Eric S. Belsky (Washington, DC: Brookings Institution Press, 2008), 194–195.

69. *Mortgage Reform and Predatory Lending Act of 2009*, H.R. 1728, 111 Cong., 1st sess. (2009) (amends the Truth in Lending Act to specify duty of care standards for originators of residential mortgages).

70. Brian Bucks and Karen Pence, "Do Homeowners Know Their House Values and Mortgage Terms?" Finance and Economics Discussion Series, no. 2006–3, (Washington, DC: Board of Governors of the Federal Reserve, 2006), 18–19, http://www.federalreserve.gov/pubs/feds/2006/200603/200603pap.pdf.

71. *Dodd-Frank Wall Street Reform and Consumer Protection Act*, Pub. L. No. 111–203, § 1411, 127 Stat. 1376, (2010).

72. For example, home owners must pay the costs of insuring against the risk of casualty loss to the property.

73. Even among fixed-rate first-lien loans, the share of loans 30 years or longer increased more than 7 percentage points between 2004 and 2007 to reach 65.1 percent in 2007. See Brian K. Bucks, Arthur B. Kennickell, Traci L. Mach, and Kevin B. Moore, "Changes in U.S. Family Finances from 2004 to 2007: Evidence from Survey of Consumer Finances," *Federal Reserve Bulletin* 95 (2009): A44, table 14.2, http://www.federalreserve.gov/pubs/bulletin/2009/pdf/scf09.pdf.

74. Kathleen C. Engel and Patricia McCoy, "A Tale of Three Markets: The Law and Economics of Predatory Lending," *Texas Law Review* 82 (2002): 439.

9

Risk Sharing When Work and Family Clash

The Need for Government and Employer Innovation

ANN O'LEARY

Introduction

Family caregiving needs, which force workers to leave the workforce or downscale their commitment to work, are unlike most of the other risks described in this volume. Unlike health insurance and retirement pensions, this risk has never rested primarily with employers or the government. Instead, the responsibility of caring for children and ailing relatives traditionally has resided within the family. Public policies—from social insurance to labor and health laws—presume that when a child needs care or a family member is ill, someone in the family is able and available to provide that care.

This does not mean, however, that the risks associated with family care have remained constant. Quite the contrary: changes in family composition, shifts in the demographics of the workforce, and the lack of government and employer action to comprehensively address the needs of modern families and workers have meant that caregiving poses sharply increased risks for many families.

Changes in family composition have had the most impact on increasing family caregiving risks. Today, just 25 percent of families consist of two parents with one parent at home and one parent in the labor force. But in 1975, nearly half (48 percent) of families consisted of two parents with one in the workforce and one who stayed at home to care for the family.[1] With few adults left at home to attend to unexpected family caregiving needs—such as caring for an ill child or taking an elderly parent to the doctor—workers often now need to exit the labor market to provide that care, which can impose economic harm on families as well as the entire economy.

These caregiving risks have profoundly reshaped the needs, demands, and wishes of workers. A recent poll conducted by the Rockefeller Foundation and *Time* magazine found that an overwhelming majority of Americans believe— across genders as well as political and religious affiliations—that employers should be required to provide employees with greater workplace flexibility and with paid family and medical leave, and that businesses should team up with government to provide more funding for child care for parents who work.[2]

Yet the United States has no laws mandating that employers provide workers with a right to receive or even request flexible work hours.[3] Only half of the American workforce has the right to take unpaid family and medical leave with a guarantee that they will not be fired for doing so.[4] We have no national social insurance to provide wage replacement when a worker needs to take leave for family or medical reasons, and employers that offer these benefits tend to provide them almost exclusively to professional and high-end workers.[5] Despite increased federal investments in the last several years, direct support for child care and elder care reaches few families, and provides limited assistance for those it does reach.[6] And our government health programs—Medicare for the elderly and disabled and Medicaid for the poor—have policies that favor family care over institutional care, operating on the assumption that family members are available to provide such care.[7]

The political rhetoric and policy proposals to address "work-family conflict" have been strikingly similar across the decades. Since the 1960s, presidential commissions and reports have recommended various forms of workplace flexibility. Commissions convened during Democratic presidencies have also recommended increased government investments in child care and paid maternity or paid family leave.[8] President Barack Obama's commitment to help solve the work-care clash has focused on these same issues. Using his bully pulpit and the federal government as a model employer, President Obama has called for voluntary action on the part of employers to improve workplace flexibility.[9] He has also increased federal investment in child care and has called for a small amount of federal dollars to be used to incentivize states to develop paid family leave programs.[10]

Despite many years of consistent recommendations—workplace flexibility, improved access to child care, and paid family leave—there are no comprehensive government policies to address the mismatch between workplace rules and family responsibilities. Instead, as explained in this chapter, the government has addressed problems of work-care conflict in two divergent ways. First, as the family model of separate spheres of breadwinning and caregiving has broken down, so too has the government's willingness to provide cash assistance to impoverished caregivers who are without a breadwinner. The government ratcheted down its safety net for poor caregivers, ending "welfare as we know it," and sending a message that these caregivers should work to earn their family income rather than rely on the government as a substitute for a family breadwinner.[11] Second, the government has squeezed protection against the risk of lost wages from caregiving needs into other laws, policies, and programs whose missions were never aimed at these problems and, as a result, may not be able to provide comprehensive protection to working caregivers. A prime example, as discussed below, is the increasing use of unemployment insurance to provide income protection for workers who lose their jobs due to work-care conflicts.

Some scholars and advocates have suggested that our government should have robust policies in place that allow parents, particularly mothers, of all incomes to stay out of the workforce in order to dedicate themselves as caregivers (at least for some time).[12] Others argue that we need gender-neutral policies that encourage workers to stay attached to the labor force while meeting the caregiving needs of families, including paid family leave, child care, and workplace flexibility (including part-time parity and overall reductions in hours).[13]

My goal in this chapter is to extend the latter body of work by proposing ways in which the government and employers can support women and men in combining work and care throughout their lives and, in turn, can help families increase their economic security. While there has been limited scholarly or advocacy attention paid to how our existing social insurance programs are transforming to meet the needs of working caregivers, I argue that policy makers should innovate by more effectively using Temporary Assistance for Needy Families (TANF) and unemployment insurance (UI) to provide wage replacement when family caregiving responsibilities clash with work. These social programs can provide crucial economic protection for working caregivers, shielding them from the harshest consequences of job disruption, such as a total loss of all family income. I recognize that these programs have serious limitations and that ultimately our government needs to consider comprehensive policies, such as social insurance that offers wage replacement during family leave and employer mandates to improve workplace flexibility. These programs will increase shared responsibility between employers and the government and relieve families from the weight of solely shouldering caregiving risk.

Current Features of Risk Allocation

The primary risk to families when work and care clash is the loss of steady income that workers experience when they lose their job or cut back their hours to address family caregiving needs. Many workers are unable to replace earned income with employer-provided paid leave, a government benefit, or family savings. An additional risk that families face is the high cost of purchasing services that substitute for family care—for example, a spot at a child care center or a paid caregiver to assist with an ailing parent. Of course, families with lower incomes experience greater risks both because they have less access to income replacement and because they often cannot afford to purchase substitute care.

DECREASE IN FAMILY INCOMES
DUE TO WORK-FAMILY CLASHES

Families use different strategies for managing work and care, many of which lead to lower incomes (and sometimes no income). For some families negotiating work and caregiving, one member works part-time—more often the woman in a two-parent family.[14] Other workers adjust their work schedules to deal with care-giving conflicts that may ultimately reduce their income, including going to work late or leaving early.[15] Other strategies directly lead to lower incomes, including refusing overtime work or turning down a promotion.[16] Finally, some workers simply leave their jobs because they cannot combine work and care.[17]

These downward shifts in labor market participation have short-term and long-term consequences for family economic security, including loss of income, loss of health insurance, loss in retirement earnings, and negative impacts on future earnings potential. Research shows that significant family care obliga-tions often lead to reduced labor force attachment, which in turn leads to lower lifetime incomes.[18]

For workers who must take a leave of absence from work or work fewer hours due to family care, wage replacement—in the form of employer-based paid leave, government benefits, or family savings—is a critical economic stabilizer for fam-ilies. Unfortunately, access to wage replacement is not universally available. Low-income employees have dramatically less access than higher earners to the employer-based benefits of job-protected family leave and paid time off.[19] As other chapters of this book document, families who face a drop in income due to caregiving conflicts are also less able to rely on family savings and are more likely to be in debt than families of the past.[20] The next section will detail the patchwork of government benefits available to caregivers, which are both less available than in the past and not universal for the purposes of paid family leave. Researchers have concluded that this decrease in the availability of government benefits is a major contributing factor to the insecurity that American families experience in their family incomes.[21]

INABILITY TO PURCHASE SUBSTITUTE CARE

The additional risk that workers face in combining work and care is the inability to afford paid care for children, sick family members, or aging relatives. In chapter 12 of this volume, Andrew Scharlach and Amanda Lehning provide a detailed ac-count of the financial risks associated with providing paid care for a seriously ill or elderly family member, due in large part to a lack of shared responsibility on the part of government and employers.

Like paid care for ill family members, paying for child care is extraordinarily expensive and there is little government aid to ameliorate the expense. Low-income workers are much more likely to spend a significant percentage of their income on child care expenses. Families living in poverty spend 32 percent of their family income on child care expenses, whereas families living at 200 percent of the poverty line or higher spend only an average of 7 percent of their family income on child care expenses.[22] Low-income families are also much more likely to rely on child care provided by relatives, including another working parent—termed "tag-team parenting," as one person provides care to the children while the other works, and then they trade shifts.[23] These informal or within-family child care arrangements are more prone to break down, causing workers to miss work.

As part of the economic stimulus package passed at the start of the Obama administration, the federal government infused federally supported child care programs with $4.1 billion. But this increase in funding barely brought the program back to the number of families it was serving in 2001. With more and more states unable to provide state funding to support child care, many workers struggle to afford child care while they work.[24]

History and Current Role of Government

The federal government's commitment to insuring families against income losses from caregiving has changed dramatically over the years. Gone is the fairly robust social safety net that allowed low-income caregivers to stay out of the workforce. Today, there is a set of disconnected programs and policies to provide wage replacement for workers who fulfill caregiving responsibilities.

THE DISMANTLING OF WELFARE—OUR COUNTRY'S ORIGINAL SOCIAL INSURANCE FOR CAREGIVERS

When the Social Security Act was enacted in 1935 to protect workers and families against unforeseen risks, policymakers were mindful of protecting children and families against the financial devastation caused by the loss of a breadwinner's income. The act included not only wage replacement for the unemployed and for retirees, but also cash assistance to mothers who were raising children with no breadwinner in the home (primarily widows). This program, Aid to Dependent Children (later renamed Aid to Families with Dependent Children [AFDC]), was based on the notion that there was only one family breadwinner—most often the man in the family—and that in the absence of financial support from any male breadwinner, the government should provide aid and assistance to mothers so that they would not need to enter the workforce if they had children at home.[25] From its inception, there was no requirement that recipients of AFDC participate in the labor market. In practice, welfare benefits were so low that many recipients used the benefits as an income supplement while doing some work in the labor market.[26] With no work requirement, however, recipients could manage on an individual basis how they combined work and care. Welfare benefits gave them a safety net to rely on if family needs prohibited work.

As women's entry into the labor force increased, and as the majority of the population receiving welfare benefits shifted from "deserving" widows to divorced and never-married women, AFDC was continually amended to encourage recipients to work or to receive job training while receiving cash assistance. For decades, however, parents caring for young children were exempted from these work requirements.[27] In 1996, Congress passed the most significant overhaul of the U.S. welfare system in its history, eliminating AFDC and replacing it with the Temporary Assistance for Needy Families (TANF) program. TANF allows parents to collect up to five years of cash aid to support children, but requires parents to work for these benefits and to permanently leave the welfare system for the labor market after five years of aid.[28] There are no federal exemptions for parents caring for young children or for sick or disabled relatives, although states can adopt such exemptions.[29] Nor are there any legal rights or assurance of job protection—such as family and medical leave, paid sick days, or even protections against firing pregnant workers—for many low-wage working caregivers struggling to combine this minimum welfare benefit with work requirements (simply because they don't meet the eligibility requirements for legal protections or are not offered such benefits from their employers).[30]

Thus the federal government's provision of insurance to caregivers against the loss of a family breadwinner was seriously constrained starting in 1996. Today, nearly everyone receiving welfare is required to work, including, in some states, parents of very young children. Yet the federal government has developed no alternative form of short-term social insurance to replace wages when work disruptions occur as a result of major caregiving demands like a new baby or a very sick child or relative. Nor has the government placed responsibility on employers to provide protection for workers who face work friction due to more minor caregiving events like a child with a fever or the sudden unavailability of a babysitter.[31]

REBUILDING WELFARE TO MEET THE NEEDS OF WORKING CAREGIVERS?

Despite the constraints of the current program and the lack of employer protections, TANF should not be entirely dismissed as a possible mechanism to replace wages for caregivers. In one state—Wisconsin—low-income working mothers can use the state's welfare program, Wisconsin Works (W-2), as a form of means-tested paid maternity leave during the first three months of the child's life.[32] Wisconsin is one of very few states that exempts parents of infants from work requirements and does not count the time against the recipients' five-year TANF time limit.[33]

Wisconsin's program, called the "Custodial Parent of an Infant" program, was modeled on the Family and Medical Leave Act, and intended to provide income support when a worker was on FMLA leave for the first twelve weeks of the child's life.[34] After this program was created in 1999, custodial parents of infants newly enrolling in W-2 increased from 8.5 percent of all claims in 1998 to nearly 50 percent in the first six months of 2004, showing an increased enrollment of women who were not previously using welfare but who may now be using it as a form of paid family leave.[35] A handful of other states also exempt recipients from work requirements and from the ticking of the time-limit clock while the recipient is caring for an ill or incapacitated family member.[36] With public education and encouragement from states, these exemptions could allow low-income workers to use TANF as a safety net for income replacement when they are temporarily out of work due to clashes between work and care.

In addition to innovative uses of TANF, other states are finding ways to fit work risks associated with caregiving conflicts into the framework of their other existing social insurance programs. Perhaps the most notable example is the use of unemployment insurance as a safety net for workers who lose their job due to work-care conflicts.

UNEMPLOYMENT INSURANCE: THE NEW INSURANCE FOR CAREGIVERS?

In 1999, President Clinton proposed allowing states to use their unemployment insurance (UI) programs to provide benefits to parents of newborns or newly adopted children so that they could receive partial wage replacement during these critical times of parental care.[37] However, this proposed change to UI was abandoned before it was ever implemented.[38]

Today, UI may not be used to provide wage replacement for new parents, but in many states it is quietly being transformed into a source of support for workers who lose their job due to caregiving conflicts. In order to receive UI, workers must have lost their jobs through no fault of their own and must be able, available, and actively seeking work.[39] If a worker is fired or laid off from his or her job, he or she will generally qualify for UI. If the worker is fired for misconduct or voluntarily quits, the worker is generally disqualified. Starting in the late 1970s, states began considering whether workers would qualify for UI if they were fired for misconduct because they were faced with a serious family caregiving conflict and chose to care for family rather than work.[40] By the 1990s most states allowed workers to receive UI if they were fired due to a family caregiving conflict that was serious in nature.[41] Until very recently, states were less consistent on the question of whether workers who didn't wait to be fired, but instead voluntarily quit when faced with a caregiving conflict, would qualify for UI.[42]

In the past several years, spurred by the federal government, more and more states are allowing workers to use UI as a safety net for caregiving conflicts. The American Recovery and Reinvestment Act (ARRA)—the economic stimulus package passed in the first month of the Obama administration—included financial incentives to states to modernize their UI programs to meet increased demands caused by the recession and to update the program to meet the needs of the modern workforce.[43] In order to qualify for two-thirds of these financial incentives, states could choose from a menu of modernization reforms, including updating their UI program to allow workers to qualify for UI when they voluntary leave their job due to "compelling family reasons," which is defined to include care for an immediate family member with an illness or a disability.[44] As of November 2010, 19 states and the District of Columbia had amended their UI laws to incorporate the ARRA's "compelling family reasons" qualification for benefits.[45] At least four other states do not meet the specific definition required by the ARRA but have laws allowing workers to qualify for UI benefits due to caregiving conflicts.[46]

PAID FAMILY LEAVE: THE WAVE OF THE FUTURE?

In addition to UI, some states are building on their unique state-based social insurance programs. Five states and one territory—California, Hawaii, Rhode Island, New York, New Jersey, and Puerto Rico—have statewide temporary disability insurance programs. These government insurance programs provide benefits to workers who are unable to work because of their own non-work-related illnesses or injuries, including disabilities related to pregnancy, childbirth and recovery from childbirth.[47] Two states—California and New Jersey—have amended their state temporary disability insurance programs to set up paid family leave. These programs, financed solely through an employee payroll tax, provide nearly all private-sector workers in the state with partial wage replacement when they are away from work due to the birth or adoption of a child or to care for a seriously ill family member.[48]

As it did with UI, the federal government may soon provide financial incentives to encourage more states to set up paid family leave programs. President Obama's Fiscal Year 2011 budget included a request that Congress provide funds for a "State Paid Leave Fund" to help states with start-up costs associated with paid family leave programs.[49] If this funding is made available, a number of states will be poised to take advantage of it. For example, Washington State has passed, but not yet implemented, a paid parental leave program.[50] State legislatures elsewhere are also considering paid family leave legislation.[51]

EMPLOYER-PROVIDED BENEFITS
FOR CAREGIVING RISKS

In addition to directly sponsoring caregiving insurance, the government plays an active role in incentivizing and mandating certain employer-provided benefits. While the government does not require employers to provide paid family leave, it forbids employers from discriminating on the basis of gender in the provision of employee benefits.

This antidiscrimination law—Title VII of the Civil Rights Act of 1964, as amended by the Pregnancy Discrimination Act of 1978 (PDA)[52]—has had its strongest impact on the provision of paid leave for pregnancy and childbirth for highly educated female workers. Title VII only requires employers to offer benefits to all employees on the same terms; it does not proactively require employers to provide paid maternity leave or paid family leave. For college-educated women

workers, the law has made a big difference because many employers of professional workers were already offering short-term disability insurance and paid sick
days. The PDA effectively required those benefits to be made available for the purposes of pregnancy and childbirth. From 1961 to 1965, only 14 percent of college-
educated women workers received paid leave before or after the birth of their first
child.[53] This number dramatically increased to 59 percent of college-educated
women workers in the immediate period after passage of the PDA.[54] For
less-educated workers, the law has made little difference with regard to employee
benefits because these workers are less likely to have access to any paid leave.[55] For
workers with less than a high school degree, the increase in paid leave after childbirth was only 3 percentage points from 1961 to 2003 (19 percent to 22 percent).[56]
Title VII is also used today as a tool to combat discrimination against men and
women who are denied access to employment benefits because of gender stereotypes associated with caregiving.[57]

In addition to the Title VII requirement of equal access to employer-sponsored
benefits required, the government also affirmatively requires some employers to
offer job-protected family leave to workers. The Family and Medical Leave Act of
1993 (FMLA) mandates that certain employers provide unpaid leave, regardless
of gender, to care for family or medical needs. FMLA provides qualified employees
with the right to take up to 12 weeks each year of job-protected unpaid leave for
the birth or care of the employee's child, the care of an immediate family member
with a serious health condition, or for the employee's own serious health condition.[58] This law provides critical economic security to eligible workers because it
requires that the worker get his or her job back upon returning from leave. It also
prevents employers from dropping or reducing an employee's health insurance
benefits because the worker took FMLA leave: employers are required to maintain
the same group health plan coverage before and after a worker has taken FMLA
leave.[59] As important as these benefits are, only about half of the workforce is
covered under FMLA.[60]

Causes of Increased Risk Burden on Families

In addition to the shortcomings of workplace policies and the patchwork of government benefits and protections, the family unit has become less able to insure
against the risk of lost income from caregiving.

THE FAMILY AS INSURER AGAINST LOSS OF INCOME
RESULTING FROM CAREGIVING

Recent changes to family composition—with more single parents and dual-
earning families than ever before—have resulted in a breakdown of our system
of family insurance along two fronts. Most families no longer have a stay-at-home

caregiver who can provide care and aid when an unexpected illness or accident strikes the family. In the past, if the breadwinner became temporarily disabled or unemployed, the stay-at-home caregiver could enter the labor force to partially replace the lost family income. Today, with most adults in families working, very few families have a labor market substitute in waiting who can partially fill the void of lost wages.[61] Instead, each of these unanticipated events means that a working family member must adjust his or her schedule, take a leave of absence, or leave his or her job. Harvard Law professor Elizabeth Warren estimates that two-income families in the 2000s were 10 times more likely than a one-income family of the 1970s to have a wage earner who needed to miss work to care for a sick child.[62] These downward adjustments of work to perform caregiving often directly lead to a decrease in future hours and pay and a severe hit to the family income.

For single-parent families, the loss of income due to a caregiving conflict is a direct hit. If only one parent is supporting the family, any loss in income can be devastating, and the risk that caregiving will conflict with work is greater. Single parents, who are predominately women, have historically had higher rates of unemployment than other workers.[63] During the recent Great Recession, the unemployment rate of women in female-headed households rose much faster than it did for all other women.[64] In fact, single-parent households have the highest level of income insecurity.[65]

For two-parent families, the increase in reliance on women's contribution to the family income, combined with the fact that women generally have less access to benefits that allow them to combine work with care, has meant that the caregiving risks to families have increased. In 2008, employed wives in two-earner families contributed 36 percent of total family earnings.[66] During the Great Recession, as men lost jobs at higher rates than women, the share of the family income contributed by wives accelerated rapidly.[67] Despite their greater propensity to do caregiving for a family, women have less access to policies allowing them to combine work and care than men. For example, 25 percent of working mothers compared to 17 percent of working fathers have no access to any form of paid time off.[68] Similarly, men have greater access to workplace flexibility and feel less worried than women that using paid time off would put their job in jeopardy.[69]

These risks of income loss due to caregiving are real. In 2001, 25 percent of two-income couples who filed for bankruptcy did so after missing work because of the illness of the worker or another family member.[70]

This is not to say that the risk experienced by two-income families means that families should move back to the era of separate spheres for breadwinners and caregivers. In fact, research suggests that the risk is worth it. Only two-earner families have seen their families incomes increase since the 1970s,[71] and two-earner families have lower family income volatility overall than married couples with only one earner.[72]

Policy Responses to Date

Despite these increased risks, the responses to the problems have been haphazard and insufficient on the part of both government and employers. This failure to respond is partly due to ambivalence among Americans about who should bear the responsibility for caring for children and ill relatives. Only in recent years have many Americans changed their traditional viewpoint that the family should bear sole responsibility for family caregiving needs.[73] And despite their prevalence and importance to millions of Americans, the issues of work-family conflict have also never risen to the level of a national call to action. Even in 1992, after President George H.W. Bush twice vetoed the Family and Medical Leave Act and just before President Clinton signed it into law, these issues were not among the top ten that voters cared about (and they have not been in any subsequent presidential election).[74]

Given this lack of a clarion call, government has avoided passing any comprehensive legislation to create new social insurance programs or broadly requiring employers to take more responsibility for the problem. Instead, it has quietly acted to mold and fit existing programs, laws, and policies to respond to the work-family clash. But there are four primary weaknesses with fitting the work-family clash into the existing social safety net and social insurance programs: (1) the existing programs have challenges meeting their stated missions even without expanding to cover caregiving clashes; (2) none of the current programs encourage or require continued labor force attachment (and some prohibit it); (3) the role of the employer in sharing responsibility is weak at best; and (4) the cobbled-together programs are far from universal.

WEAKENED PROGRAMS

Today, both UI and TANF are facing real challenges in meeting their core missions. The biggest potential threat to state unemployment insurance systems is insolvency. In 2010, there were 34 states that had to take loans from the U.S. Department of Labor to remain solvent, and no state in the country had enough funds on reserve to maintain the program for 12 months in the face of high unemployment.[75] In addition, UI has been under political attack, as those on the Left have tried to extend its coverage during the Great Recession and those on the Right have worried that such extensions discourage individuals from finding work.[76] With these threats to both the financial stability and the political popularity of the program, expanding it to address the work-care clash, a problem not traditionally covered, could face resistance from states and from traditional supporters of UI.

At the same time, TANF is facing severe budget cutbacks at both the federal and state level.[77] But a call to use TANF as a much more temporary paid leave program for low-income workers could have resonance in this climate.

LABOR FORCE ATTACHMENT

Aiding workers in remaining attached to a steady stream of income from the labor market provides workers and families with greater economic stability in the short and long run.[78] But all three existing forms of social insurance being used to provide wage replacement when care clashes with work—welfare (TANF), unemployment insurance, and state-based paid family leave programs—provide no protection for workers to get their jobs back after the caregiving crisis subsides or after an alternative care situation can be arranged (workers must separately qualify for the Family and Medical Leave Act [FMLA] to be afforded job protection). Each program also has features that could encourage (or require) the worker to sever his or her ties to employment. The possibility that the worker could be out of work longer than providing the needed family care requires could lead to greater income insecurity in the short run and to decreases in family income in the long run. It also leads to an inefficient use of human capital as workers are sidelined for longer than necessary.

Of the three wage replacement programs, unemployment insurance requires the greatest detachment from the labor market. In order to qualify for UI benefits when care clashes with work, the worker must have left his or her job entirely. When a worker is fired due to a work-care clash or voluntarily quits due to the clash, the employer is under no obligation to take the worker back after the care crisis ends. In fact, a worker who takes job-protected FMLA leave cannot qualify for UI during the leave. Only if the worker is not covered by FMLA, or is forced to quit after an FMLA leave because the worker's dependent is still in need of care, may the worker be able to qualify for UI in those states that offer it for caregiving. When the worker is receiving UI, the worker must be able and available for work and must demonstrate that he or she is seeking work. Seeking work and being "available" for work while providing care to a seriously ill family member can sometimes prove challenging, making reentry into the labor market difficult. In fact, some workers may even lose eligibility for UI if the state does not allow the worker to take into account his or her family care obligations when seeking a job.[79]

For workers who qualify for job protection under the FMLA, state-based paid family leave programs in California and New Jersey offer the greatest possibility of staying attached to the labor market. However, for workers not covered by FMLA, the paid family leave programs can end up being used as an off-ramp from the labor market because the programs do not require employers to allow workers to take the leave and return to their jobs afterward. Unlike UI or TANF, the paid family leave programs impose no requirements to reenter the labor market.

Using TANF as a form of paid parental leave may be the most promising avenue to ensure continued attachment to the labor force after a leave from work (or a reduction in work hours) due to caregiving, but it is only available to the poorest workers. Although TANF requires no prior labor force attachment—a feature that does weaken the likelihood of consistent post-TANF work for those entering the program with no work history—it does have strong incentives to encourage work in the future. For low-income workers coming to the program with a strong work history, these incentives could get the recipient back to work, as the program intends. This is more likely when TANF is coupled with crucial supports. Consider a worker in one of the states that does not condition receipt of TANF assistance on work during the period of parental care or caregiving of a sick relative. After the caregiving period is complete, the worker will be required to find work or participate in an activity that meets the work requirements, such as job training or education. During this transition period, the worker may be able to access additional supports, such as child care subsidies or transportation subsidies, to assist in his or her move back into the labor market. In one study of "worker mothers" who used Wisconsin's welfare program as a form of paid maternity leave, 80 percent returned to work immediately after the expiration of the three months of welfare without work requirements.[80]

Consider also a worker who reduces his or her hours of work in order to provide care. TANF is based on income and parental status rather than employment and does not require that workers involuntarily sever their labor market ties. Certain features of TANF cash benefits, including the provision in some states of allowing workers to retain a portion of their earned income, encourage the combination of work and care.

Of course, encouraging or requiring work will not be sufficient when approximately 40 percent of all unemployed workers are considered long-term unemployed because they have been looking for a job for six or more months.[81] Unless these social insurance programs are coupled with some sort of job-protected leave from the worker's current employer, many workers will struggle to reenter the labor market—simply because jobs will not exist.

EMPLOYER SHARE IN RESPONSIBILITY AND RISK

Government policies to insure against income drops due to work-family clashes will be insufficient if employers do not take greater responsibility in proactively helping workers to manage work and family obligations. It does not matter if the insurance program is one like UI, which is squeezing family care into its mission, or one like paid family leave, which was specifically designed to address the work-care clash. If employers do not accept their responsibility to help employees manage caregiving risk, workers will be able to temporarily rely on government programs, but may still face a great risk of being out of work and out of income for longer than necessary. It does not make sense from an employer- or employee-efficiency perspective to encourage workers to leave the workforce when caregiving temporarily clashes with work. For businesses and workers alike, policies to promote labor market attachment, which necessarily must include employer incentives or directives, will increase economic stability.

Right now, employers have little obligation to aid workers in mixing work and care. As described above, large employers must comply with the FMLA, and most employers cannot discriminate against workers based on gender stereotypes about caregiving. But there is no federal law restricting the number of hours that an employer can require an employee to work, and there are no prohibitions against unpredictable work hours. Requiring mandatory overtime or suddenly switching a work shift can mean that a worker must choose between keeping a job or caring for a child.

The UI system has some mechanisms to discourage employers from firing workers with care obligations in states that allow UI to be collected for work-care clashes, including basing the employer UI tax in part on the employers' past experience of layoffs. Some scholars doubt whether employers should properly bear this risk of an increased tax when the work-care clash is not a result of employer action, and others believe that the threat of increased taxation actually deters responsible employer behavior by discouraging firms from hiring workers who might take advantage of UI in the future.[82]

LACK OF UNIVERSALITY

The final shortcoming of the existing system is the unevenness in worker access to the existing forms of social insurance for family caregiving, which exacerbates income volatility for those workers with no access. Eligibility for each program differs widely. TANF is a means-tested program, so at most it will serve only the lowest-income workers. UI is universal, but it requires a level of labor force attachment that some workers with care responsibilities may not meet. The use of UI as a form of paid family leave is also limited only to those workers who are caring for an ill family member and cannot be used as a form of paid family leave for new parents. Paid family leave without job protection and with low levels of wage replacement often leaves out low-wage workers, even though they are the workers it is intended to help, and it is only available in a limited number of states. Eligibility for these programs differs not only across states but also from year to year as a result of state budget cuts and federal action. As a result, the provision of wage replacement is far from universal.

Solutions

Perhaps the most promising—and ambitious—long-term solution would be to create a system of national paid family leave and to couple it with job protection that covers a greater portion of the workforce. A well-designed system would allow workers to take time off from work at critical life junctions—such as the birth of a child or the serious illness of a loved one—without losing their job or all of their income.[83] Its advantages would be that it would be aimed directly at in-suring against a clash of work and care and so could be designed to encourage temporary spells away from work as well as reattachment to the labor force imme-diately thereafter, so as to ensure a continuity of work and income derived from work over one's lifetime.

In the short run, however, advocates and scholars should not focus solely on creating a comprehensive system of national paid family leave (building up to such a system will take more political agreement that such a program is needed). Instead, I recommend two immediate concrete steps: (1) help states to innovate and to create wage replacement for work leaves resulting from caregiving through our existing social insurance programs, and (2) increase the share of responsi-bility and risk assumed by employers.

STATES SHOULD INNOVATE AND CREATE
WAGE REPLACEMENT

Already a number of states have taken critical steps to update their social insur-ance systems to provide wage replacement for working caregivers. Discussions of wage replacement for family leave tend to focus on the two states with paid family leave programs—California and New Jersey. Less well known is that there are 26 states plus the District of Columbia that offer some form of wage replacement when work and care clash, either through unemployment insurance or TANF. In addition, nine of these states have family and medical leave laws in place that are more expansive than the FMLA.[84] Three additional states and the District of Columbia offer protections against discrimination against workers based on parental status or family responsibilities.[85] None of these programs alone can solve the problem, but together they can begin to create some form of insurance for workers and thereby foster state innovation that could ultimately lead to a universal system of paid family leave.

States that have taken these innovative steps should consider promoting these programs as an integrated web of support to provide access to wage re-placement for workers with caregiving conflicts. Some workers may receive wage replacement through the means-tested program of TANF, just as low-income in-dividuals receive health care insurance through the means-tested program of Medicaid. Some may receive it through the unemployment insurance system where the worker has sufficient attachment to the labor force and where the worker's state allows collection of UI when the job loss occurred as a result of the need to provide care to an ill or disabled family member. Others may not qualify for social insurance programs, but may discover that they have a right to the voluntary benefits provided by their employer because of federal and state anti-discrimination requirements.[86] Finally, some may not qualify for wage replace-ment, but may qualify for job protection under the FMLA or the state's own family and medical leave law.

This web of social insurance programs and employment laws is difficult to comprehend and access for those who are not familiar with the fine print. States could do a great service to workers by simply increasing transparency on how to use these programs and laws. States should consider creating a one-stop information portal for workers to learn about how to protect their jobs and wages when care clashes with work. In doing so, states would provide increased economic stability to families, smoothing out the financial impact that the work-care clash causes on both families and state economies.

States that have not innovatively updated their TANF and UI programs and have not enacted paid family leave should learn from these other states and begin to set up such programs. The federal government can continue to help on this front by providing financial incentives for states to update their TANF and UI programs or to start new paid family leave programs.

EMPLOYERS NEED TO STEP UP

Despite the loud protests of many employers upon the passage of FMLA and upon the state passage of paid family leave laws, employers today face few requirements with regard to helping workers manage work and care. The states that are already on the edge of innovation in using their social insurance system for working caregivers should consider ways to encourage employers to improve workplace flexibility and job security for working caregivers.

One idea, adopted in the United Kingdom, New Zealand, and Australia, is to adopt "right to request flexibility" laws and policies.[87] These laws do not mandate that employers provide every worker with the schedule they desire, but they do require that employers set up a process to discuss and negotiate workplace flexibility and only allow the employer to turn down the requests for certain business reasons. This would be an improvement over the current situation, in which an employee could be disciplined for even asking about a flexible work arrangement or predictable work schedule. Putting in place a "right to request flexibility and predictability" would enable workers to seek these key accommodations for caregiving without the fear of retaliation.[88]

An alternative, stronger model can be found in the Australian state of New South Wales, where employees are protected against discrimination based on care responsibilities and employers are required to affirmatively provide reasonable, flexible work schedules unless doing so would cause the employer undue hardship.[89]

As of 2010, only one state—New Hampshire—has introduced legislation that would allow employees the right to request flexibility.[90] Other states could begin consideration of how to improve workplace flexibility and predictability through similar legislation. This idea could be of particular interest to states that allow UI to provide wage replacement when care clashes with work. Setting up a system that addresses work-care conflicts at the front end could decrease the number of workers who need to sever their work ties and collect unemployment insurance.

Conclusion

Recent changes to existing social insurance programs that allow greater access to working caretakers offer some promise for building a better system for workers who need economic security when work and care clash. These changes, however, will be insufficient without greater responsibility on the part of employers and greater planning and purpose on the part of government. In the end, the federal government should develop a national paid family leave program, and employers should be required to offer employees job protection and the right to request flexibility and predictability without losing their jobs or facing retaliation. But these long-term goals should not blind us to the short-term steps that states could take to improve income security for working caregivers by offering benefits through existing social insurance programs.

Acknowledgments

The author would like to thank the faculty affiliated with the Berkeley Center on Health, Economic & Family Security at UC Berkeley School of Law for providing invaluable feedback, including Jacob Hacker, Gillian Lester, Mary Ann Mason, Katie Porter, and Steve Sugarman. Thank you, too, to Goodwin Liu for his feedback and to Ellen Bravo for her assistance in uncovering Wisconsin's innovative use of welfare to support working caregivers. Finally, thank you to Angela Clements and Zoe Savitsky for their excellent research assistance and comments throughout.

Notes

1. See Bureau of Labor Statistics, *Economic News Release: Table 4. Families with Own Children: Employment Status of Parents by Age of Youngest Child and Family Type, 2008–09 Annual Averages*, prepared by the Bureau of Labor Statistics, U.S. Department of Labor, 2010; Institute of Education Sciences, *Indicator 18: Parent's Employment, Employment Status of Parents with Own Children under 18 Years Old, by Type of Family: 1975 to 1993*, prepared by the Institute of Education Sciences, U.S. Department of Education, 1996.
2. Heather Boushey, *It's Time for Policies to Match Family Needs: New Polling Data Shows Widespread Support for an Agenda to Match Work-Family Conflict* (Washington, DC: Center for American Progress, 2010).
3. Ann O'Leary and Karen Kornbluh, "Family Friendly for All Families," in *The Shriver Report: A Woman's Nation Changes Everything*, eds. Heather Boushey and Ann O'Leary (Washington, DC: Center for American Progress, 2009), 91–93.
4. *Family and Medical Leave Act*, U.S. Code 29 (2000), §§ 2601–2654; Jane Waldfogel, "Family and Medical Leave: Evidence from the 2000 Surveys," *Monthly Labor Review* 124, no. 9 (2001): 19–20.
5. Workplace Flexibility 2010 and Berkeley CHEFS, "Chapter 2: Temporary Disability Insurance," in *Family Security Insurance: A New Foundation for Economic Security* (Washington, DC: Workplace Flexibility 2010 and Berkeley CHEFS, 2010) (hereinafter "Family Security Insurance Report").
6. Peter S. Goodman, "Cuts to Child Care Subsidy Thwart More Job Seekers," *New York Times*, May 23, 2010.

7. See Andrew E. Scharlach and Amanda J. Lehning, "Government's Role in Aging and Long-Term Care," chapter 12 of this volume.

8. For a review of government action, see O'Leary and Kornbluh, "Family Friendly for All Families," 78.

9. "President and First Lady Host White House Forum on Workplace Flexibility," White House press release, March 31, 2010.

10. Ibid.

11. Barbara Vobejda, "Clinton Signs Welfare Bill Amid Division," *Washington Post*, August 23, 1996.

12. See, e.g., Neil Gilbert, *A Mother's Work: How Feminism, the Market, and Policy Shape Family Life* (New Haven: Yale University Press, 2008) (proposing that the government adopt policies that would allow mothers to choose a sequential pattern of work and care, including providing at-home care allowance for full-time homemakers; transitional policies for reentering mothers; Social Security caregiving credits; and an increase in community property laws).

13. See, e.g., Gillian Lester, "A Defense of Paid Family Leave," *Harvard Women's Law Journal* 28 (2005): 21–22 (calling for the government to develop a paid family leave program to allow women to stay attached to the labor force); Vicki Schultz, "Life's Work," *Columbia Law Review* 100 (2000): 1881 (calling for the remaking of culture and laws to allow everyone to participate in life-sustaining work, including laws to reduce the work hours that all employees must work).

14. Bureau of Labor Statistics, *Women in the Labor Force: A Databook*, prepared by the Bureau of Labor Statistics, U.S. Department of Labor, 2009, "Employed Persons by Full- and Part-time Status and Sex, 1970–2008 Annual Averages, Table 20," (showing that just under 25 percent of women work part-time compared to just over 17 percent of men).

15. MetLife Mature Market Institute, National Alliance for Caregiving, and Center for Productive Aging at Towson University, *The MetLife Study of Sons at Work Balancing Employment and Elder-care* (Westport, CT: Mature Market Institute MetLife, 2003) (showing that 78 percent of men and 84 percent of women reported coming in late or leaving early as a result of an elder care conflict) (hereinafter Sons at Work Study); "Alzheimer's Association Women & Alzheimer's Poll, 2010," Ann O'Leary, "What's the Workplace Impact?," in *The Shriver Report: A Woman's Nation Take on Alzheimer's*, eds. Angela Timashenka Geiger et al. (Washington, DC: Alzheimer's Association, 2010) (hereinafter Women & Alzheimer's Poll) (finding that 61 percent of female and 70 percent of male working Alzheimer's caregivers reported needed to go in late or leave early from work as a result of caregiving conflict).

16. MetLife, *Sons at Work Study* (showing 8 percent of women and 8 percent of men turned down a promotion due to an elder caregiving conflict; and showing that 16 percent of men and 24 percent of women turned down overtime work as a result of caregiving responsibilities); "Women & Alzheimer's Poll" (showing that 11 percent of women and 14 percent of men turned down promotion due to caregiving conflict; and showing that 11 percent of women and 8 percent of men lost a job benefit as a result of caregiving).

17. *Sons at Work Study* (showing 20 percent of women and 11 percent of men considered quitting their jobs due to an elder caregiving conflict); "Women & Alzheimer's Poll" (showing that 12 percent of women and 8 percent of men had to give up working entirely due to caregiving conflict).

18. Lester, "A Defense of Paid Family Leave," 21–22.

19. O'Leary, "How Family Leave Laws Left Out Low-Income Workers"; Workplace Flexibility 2010 and Berkeley CHEFS, *Family Security Insurance Report*, Chapter 2.

20. See Christian E. Weller and Amy Helburn, "Public Policy Options to Build Wealth for America's Middle Class," chapter 7 of this volume; and Stephen D. Sugarman, "Income Security When Temporarily Away from Work," chapter 6 of this volume.

21. Jacob S. Hacker et al., *Economic Security at Risk: Findings from the Economic Security Index* (New York: The Rockefeller Foundation, 2010), 17.

22. Kristin Smith and Kristi Gozjolko, *Low Income and Impoverished Families Pay More Disproportionately for Child Care* (Durham, NH: Carsey Institute at the University of New Hampshire Policy Brief No. 16, 2010).

23. "Nearly Half of Preschoolers Receive Child Care from Relatives," U.S. Census Bureau press release, February 28, 2008 (noting that among the 11.8 million children younger than 5 whose mothers were employed, 30 percent were cared for on a regular basis by a grandparent during their mother's working hours and another 25 percent received care from their fathers during the mother's working hours).

24. Goodman, "Cuts to Child Care Subsidy Thwart More Job Seekers."

25. This national scheme was based on mother's pensions that had developed in many states. Both the early mother's pension programs and the federal Aid to Dependent Children excluded women who were not considered "morally deserving" of such aid and these rules often fell disproportionately on women of color. See Theda Skocpol, *Protecting Soldiers and Mothers: The Political Origins of Social Policy in the United States* (Cambridge, MA: Harvard University Press, 1992), 471–72, 535–36.

26. Joel J. Handler and Yeheskel Hasenfeld, *We the Poor People: Work, Poverty, and Welfare* (New Haven: Yale University Press, 1997), 47–48 (citing quantitative research demonstrating that the majority of welfare recipients under AFDC combined work and welfare).

27. Ann O'Leary, "How Family Leave Laws Left Out Low-Income Workers," *Berkeley Journal of Employment and Labor Law* 28 (2007): 1, 48–50 (recounting history of work requirements and exemptions for parents).

28. See *Personal Responsibility and Work Opportunity Reconciliation Act*, U.S. Code 42 (1996) § 601.

29. See Mary Farrell et al., *Welfare Time Limits: An Update on State Policies, Implementation, and Effects on Families* (New York: The Lewin Group and MDRC, 2008), 13 (Table 1.3) (49 states provide either an exemption to welfare time limits or extensions of time for individuals who are either disabled or caring for a disabled family member; 14 states offer exemptions or extensions for parents caring for young children; and 16 states offer exemptions or extensions for recipients who lack either child care or transportation); see also Gretchen Rowe and Mary Murphy, *Welfare Rules Databook: State TANF Policies as of July 2006* (Washington, DC: The Urban Institute, 2006), Table III.B.1. (33 states exempt single parents from working while caring for an ill or incapacitated person and 43 states exempt single parents who are caring for an infant with varying definitions of the age of the infant ranging from 3 months to 24 months).

30. O'Leary, "How Family Leave Laws Left Out Low-Income Workers," 53–56.

31. Bills to require employers to provide a minimum number of sick days have been introduced in Congress, but have made little progress towards passage. *Healthy Families Act*, S 1152 § 5, 111 Cong., 1st sess. (May 21, 2009); *Healthy Families Act*, HR 2460 § 5, 111 Cong., 1st sess. (May 18, 2009).

32. Wis. Stat. § 49.148(1m) (2009); Wisconsin Department of Children and Families, *Wisconsin Works (W-2) Manual* (Madison, WI: Department of Children and Families, 2010), 24 (Chapter 7, Section 7.5.0).

33. Rowe and Murphy, *Welfare Rules Databook*, Table III.B.1. and Table IV.C.3 (Arkansas, Connecticut, Florida, Hawaii, Tennessee, and Wisconsin exempt parents of young infants from work requirements and do not count the time toward the five-year time limit).

34. Wisconsin Department of Children and Families, *Wisconsin Works (W-2) Manual*, 24.

35. Wisconsin Department of Workforce Development, *An Evaluation: Wisconsin Works (W-2) Program, Report 05–6* (Madison, WI: Legislative Audit Bureau, 2005), 4, 25, 55. The program was created through *Assembly Bill 133*, WI Legis. 9 (1999) (Part II), § 1237m.

36. Rowe and Murphy, *Welfare Rules Databook*, Table III.B.1. and Table IV.C.3 (Arkansas, California, Connecticut, Hawaii, Missouri, New Jersey, and Rhode Island exempt recipients who are caring for an ill or incapacitated family member from work requirements and do not count the time toward their five-year time limit).

37. John M. Broder, "Clinton Proposes Using Surpluses to Extend Family Leave Benefits," *New York Times*, May 24, 1999. For the final rule, see Employment and Training Administration, *Birth and Adoption Unemployment Compensation*, prepared by the Employment and Training Administration, U.S. Department of Labor, June 13, 2000 (codified at *Code of Federal Regulations*, title 20, pt. 604).

38. Employment and Training Administration, *Unemployment Compensation—Trust Fund Integrity Rule: Birth and Adoption Unemployment Compensation; Removal of Regulations*, prepared by the Employment and Training Administration, U.S. Department of Labor, Oct. 9, 2003 (codified at *Code of Federal Regulations*, Title 20, pt. 604).

39. Employment and Training Administration, "Chapter 5: Nonmonetary Eligibility," in *Comparison of State Unemployment Laws* (Washington, DC: U.S. Department of Labor, 2010), 1–42.

40. Martin H. Malin, "Unemployment Compensation in a Time of Increasing Work-Family Conflicts," *University of Michigan Journal of Law Reform* 29 (1996): 131, 136–139.

41. Ibid.

42. Ibid., 139–147 (explaining that the three states that allowed workers to claim UI for voluntary quits with good cause due to family reasons had restrictive statutory allowances for such claims and that the other states that allowed such claims only did so if the employer was the cause of the work-family conflict).

43. For more details about the modernization provisions, see National Employment Law Project, *The American Reinvestment and Recovery Act's Modernization Provisions: Benefit Funding and Workers to Benefit in States That Adopt ARRA Incentive Reforms* (New York: NELP, 2009).

44. States must include in their definition of compelling family reason at least the following three reasons: leaving a job due to domestic violence or sexual harassment, to accompany a spouse to a new location due to a change in the spouse's employment location from which it is impractical to commute, and to care for an immediate family member with an illness or a disability. *Social Security Act, U.S. Code* 42 (2009) § 1103(f)(3)(B)(i-iii); see also Douglas F. Small, *Special Transfers for Unemployment Compensation Modernization and Administration and Relief from Interests on Advances* (Washington, DC: U.S. Department of Labor, Feb. 26, 2009), Attachment III, III-9–III-17 (explaining what will satisfy the definition of "compelling family reason").

45. The 19 states are: Alaska, Arkansas, Colorado, Connecticut, Delaware, Hawaii, Illinois, Maine, Minnesota, Missouri, Nevada, New Hampshire, New York, North Carolina, Oklahoma, Oregon, Rhode Island, South Carolina, and Wisconsin. See "Unemployment Insurance Modernization Incentive Payment State Certifications," U.S. Department of Labor, accessed November 30, 2010.

46. Other states that include caring for an ill or disabled family member as an allowable reason to voluntarily quit a job and still qualify for UI are: California, Massachusetts, Pennsylvania, and Texas. See Employment and Training Administration, "Chapter 5: Nonmonetary Eligibility," 5-3–5-5.

47. For more information about state temporary disability insurance programs, see Workplace Flexibility 2010 and Berkeley CHEFS, *Family Security Insurance Report*, Chapter 2.

48. *Cal. Unemp. Ins. Code* §§ 3300–3306 (Deering 2003); *N.J. STAT. ANN.* § 43:21–39.1–3 (West 2008).

49. The White House, *Proposed Budget for the Department of Labor, FY 2011 797*, prepared by the Executive Office of the President, 2010.

50. Rev. Code Wash. §§ 49.86.005–.903 (2010).

51. National Partnership for Women and Families, *2010 State Action on Paid Family Leave* (Washington, DC: National Partnership for Women and Families, 2010).

52. *Civil Rights Act of 1964, U.S. Code* 42 (2006) § 2000e–2; *Pregnancy Discrimination Act, U.S. Code* 42 (2006) § 2000-e(k).

53. Tallese D. Johnson, *Maternity Leave and Employment Patterns of First Time Mothers: 1961–2003*, (Washington, DC: U.S. Census Bureau, February 2008), 12 (Figure 3).

54. Ibid.

55. Workplace Flexibility 2010 and Berkeley CHEFS, *Family Security Insurance Report*, Chapter 2.

56. Ibid.

57. Naomi C. Earp, *Enforcement Guidance: Unlawful Disparate Treatment of Workers with Caregiving Responsibilities* (Washington, DC: Equal Employment Opportunity Commission, 2007).

58. *Family and Medical Leave Act, U.S. Code* 29 (2000) §§ 2601–2654.

59. Ibid., §§ 2601, 2614(c).

60. Waldfogel, "Family and Medical Leave."

61. For those families with one stay-at-home parent, this option remains an important form of self-structured family insurance. During the Great Recession, the percentage of two-parent families with only the mother employed rose from 3.4 percent in 2007 to 5.1 percent in 2009, suggesting that as men lost their jobs, stay-at-home mothers did enter the workforce. For more information on this form of family insurance, see generally, Chinhui Juhn and Simon Potter, *Is There Still an Added-Worker Effect?* (New York: Federal Reserve Bank of New York Staff Report no. 310, 2007).

62. Elizabeth Warren and Amelia Warren Tyagi, *The Two-Income Trap: Why Middle-Class Mothers and Fathers Are Going Broke* (New York: Basic Books, 2003), 88, Figure 4.3.

63. Institute for Women's Policy Research, *Unemployment among Single Mother* Families (Washington, DC: IWPR, 2009).

64. Joint Economic Committee, *Women in the Recession: Mothers and Families Hit Hard*, 111 Cong., 2d sess., 2010, Committee Print.

65. Hacker et al., *Economic Security at Risk*.

66. Bureau of Labor Statistics, *Women in the Labor Force: A Databook*, prepared by the Bureau of Labor Statistics, U.S. Department of Labor, 2008, Table 24.

67. Kristin Smith, *Wives as Breadwinners: Wives' Share of Family Earnings Hits Historic High during the Second Year of the Great Recession* (Durham, NH: Carsey Institute at the University of New Hampshire, 2010).

68. Katherin Ross-Phillips, *Getting Time Off: Access to Leave among Working Parents* (Washington, DC: the Urban Institute, 2004), 2.

69. Workplace Flexibility 2010 and the Urban Institute, *A Comparison of Men's and Women's Access to and Use of FWAs* (Washington, DC: Workplace Flexibility and the Urban Institute, 2008).

70. Warren and Tyagi, *The Two-Income Trap*, 85, n. 47.

71. Heather Boushey, "The New Breadwinners," in *The Shriver Report: A Woman's Nation Changes Everything*, eds. Ann O'Leary and Heather Boushey (Washington, DC: Center for American Progress, 2009).

72. Jacob S. Hacker and Elisabeth Jacobs, *The Rising Instability of American Family Incomes, 1969–2004, Evidence from the Panel Study of Income Dynamics* (Washington, DC: Economic Policy Institute, 2008).

73. Ellen Galinsky, Kerstin Aumann, and James T. Bond, *Times are Changing: Gender and Generation at Work and at Home* (New York: Families and Work Institute, 2008); Pew Research Center for the People & the Press, *Trends in Political Vales and Core Attitudes: 1987–2007* (Wavwshington, DC: Pew Research Center for the People & the Press, 2007).

74. *US Public Opinion on Election 1992–Most Important Problem* (Washington, DC: Gallup/CNN/Knight Ridder Poll, August 1992); *US Public Opinion on Election 1996–Most Important Problem* (Washington, DC: Gallup Poll, July 1996); *US Public Opinion on Election 2000–Most Important Problem* (Washington, DC: Gallup Poll, October 2000); *US Public Opinion on Election 2004–Most Important Problem* (Washington, DC: Gallup Poll, October 2004); *US Public Opinion on Election 2008–Most Important Problem* (Washington, DC: Gallup Poll, October 2008).

75. U.S. Government Accountability Office, *Unemployment Insurance Trust Funds: Long-Standing State Financing Policies Have Increased Risk of Insolvency*, Report to the Chairman, Subcommittee on Income Security and Family Support, Committee on Ways and Means, House of Representatives, April 2010.

76. Michael Luo, "99 Weeks Later, Jobless Have Only Desperation," *New York Times*, August 2, 2010.

77. Liz Schott and LaDonna Pavetti, *Federal TANF Funding Shrinking While Need Remains High* (Washington, DC: Center on Budget and Policy Priorities, 2010). As an example of state cuts, see Governor Jerry Brown's proposed cuts to CalWorks, California's TANF program. See California Budget Project, *Governor's Proposed Budget Balances Spending Reductions with Additional Revenues, Includes Deep Cuts to Health and Human Services Programs* (Sacramento, CA, Budget Project, 2011).

78. Lester, "A Defense of Paid Family Leave," 21–22.

79. Malin, "Unemployment Compensation In a Time of Increasing Work," 151.

80. Marci Ybarra, "The Implications of Paid Family Leave Policies for New Mother Participants: Evidence from Wisconsin" (Conference paper. Presented at the Society for Social Work Research Annual Conference, 2011) (finding that 40 percent of W-2 New Mothers were employed across four consecutive quarters prior to enrollment in welfare (referred to as "workers") and 80 percent of "worker" New Mothers returned to work immediately following New Mother benefit expiration confirming a substantial minority (32 percent) utilize W-2 as a means-tested PFL program).

81. Randy Ilg, *Long-Term Unemployment Experience of the Jobless*, prepared at the request of the Bureau of Labor Statistics, U.S. Department of Labor, June 2010.

82. Lester, "Unemployment Insurance and Wealth Distribution"; Malin, "Unemployment Compensation in a Time of Increasing Work-Family Conflicts"; Michael J. Graetz and Jerry L. Mashaw, *True Security: Rethinking American Social Insurance* (New Haven: Yale University Press, 1999), 76.

83. Workplace Flexibility 2010 and Berkeley CHEFS, *Family Security Insurance Report*.

84. National Partnership for Women and Families, *State Family and Medical Leave Laws That Are More Expansive Than the Federal FMLA* (Washington, DC: National Partnership for Women and Families, 2008).

85. Bornstein and Rathmell, *Caregivers as a Protected Class*, 4.

86. Stephanie Bornstein and Robert J. Rathmell, *Caregivers as a Protected Class: The Growth of State and Local Laws Prohibiting Family Responsibilities Discrimination* (San Francisco: The Center for WorkLife Law, 2009).

87. Karen Kornbluh, "The Joy of Flex," *Washington Monthly*, December 2005.

88. This paragraph and the next are drawn from work I coauthored with Heather Boushey. See Heather Boushey and Ann O'Leary, *Our Working Nation: How Working Women Are Reshaping America's Families and Economy and What it Means for Policymakers* (Washington, DC: Center for American Progress, March 2010).

89. Georgetown Federal Legislation Clinic, *The New South Wales Carers' Responsibilities Act* (Washington, DC: Workplace Flexibility 2010, Georgetown University Law Center, 2006).

90. An Act Relative to Working Families' Flexibility, HB 663, sess. 2010 (New Hampshire 2010).

Part Four

INCREASING HEALTH AND RETIREMENT SECURITY

10

Health Care Reform 2.0

Fulfilling the Promise of the Affordable Care Act

JACOB S. HACKER

Arnold Dorsett was an American success story. An air conditioner repairman, he earned almost $70,000 a year, owned a good home in the suburbs, and was married with three children. He was also, it turned out, the father of a young boy who was sick and getting sicker.

Zachary, his oldest child, had not been healthy since his birth. But it was not until Zachary was eight that he was diagnosed with an immune system disorder that promised even bigger medical costs down the road. By then, the bills had crushed the family's finances. Despite having health insurance and refinancing their home, the Dorsetts had run up nearly $30,000 in outstanding credit-card balances and could no longer make their car or mortgage payments. In March 2005, they filed for bankruptcy, becoming one of the roughly two million households filing that year. The choice was not easy. "I make good money, and I work hard for it," Arnold Dorsett said. "When I filed for bankruptcy, I felt I failed."[1]

For years, the health care insecurities of millions of ordinary Americans like the Dorsetts were seen as insoluble in our polarized partisan climate. In 2010, however, the U.S. Congress passed and President Barack Obama signed the Patient Protection and Affordable Care Act (hereafter, ACA).[2] A remarkable policy breakthrough, the law involves: (1) extensive new regulation of private health insurance, (2) the public creation of new insurance-purchasing organizations called "exchanges," (3) the reorganization and expansion of Medicaid for the poor, and (4) major reductions in spending growth within and substantial changes to the Medicare program for the aged and disabled.[3] According to the Congressional Budget Office, more than 30 million Americans will be newly covered by 2019.[4] In addition, new federal subsidies for coverage, greater economies of scale in administration, and new insurance rules that prohibit price discrimination against higher-risk patients will substantially reduce the cost of insurance for those who buy it through the exchanges.

To be sure, the ACA falls well short of the international health policy standard of universal coverage and robust efforts to restrain medical costs. The affluent democracy closest to us in terms of the structure and history of health insurance,

Switzerland, has featured subsidized universal insurance since the mid-1990s and its per-capita spending is roughly 60 percent of ours. But in light of the long history of health care reform's defeat, the ACA represents a decisive departure from the past politics and policy of American health care.[5] The destination of that departure, however, is not yet clear. Enacting a new law is only part of the challenge of social reform. The other, more daunting, part is building support for the successful implementation, improvement, and expansion of the inevitably jerry-rigged programs that can be passed through America's fragmented and deeply polarized legislative process. Democratic senator Tom Harkin of Iowa rightly calls the health care law a "starter home." Unfortunately, the home is not yet built (the main parts of the framework go up in 2014), and the construction zone is in the path of a hurricane: a perfect storm of runaway costs and unbridled conservative attacks on the law.[6]

The greatest threat to the ACA is not repeal. Notwithstanding the fierce assault on the legislation and ongoing court challenges, the basic building blocks of the law will almost certainly be put in place unless the White House changes hands after 2012. And even were Republicans to capture the presidency in 2012, the reversal of several core elements, such as the creation of the exchanges and establishment of individual subsidies for coverage, would be difficult, though certainly not impossible. If these core elements are put in place, millions of Americans who are uninsured today will obtain coverage under the ACA. Meanwhile, those who already have coverage will enjoy the security of knowing they can more easily obtain it even if they lose or change jobs, become sick or disabled, or live in a family with someone who experiences such events.

And yet these successes will also be incomplete. Although millions will be newly insured, millions more will still lack basic protections: they will fall through the law's cracks, or they will be exempted from its requirement to buy coverage because they cannot afford the premium. Medical costs will still represent a painful, growing hit to family incomes. And families who don't qualify for generous subsidies will still find insurance shockingly expensive.[7]

In short, the reforms launched with the ACA will need to be strengthened or they will fall increasingly short. Every crucial aspect of the act—the reach and affordability of insurance, the degree of security that this insurance provides, the cooperation of states and employers, the promise of federal savings—will rise or fall on reformers' ability to strengthen the act to ensure that it delivers on its promises. This chapter explains why this must be done and how it can be.

Historical Context

The United States is the only rich democracy without guaranteed health coverage for all (or virtually all) citizens or measures that aim to contain costs at a high level of aggregation.[8] As Table 10.1 shows, America's distinctive position

Table 10.1 **American Health Care and Social Policy in Cross-National Relief**

Country	Share of Population Covered by Government Health Programs (2004)	Total Government and Private Health Spending Per Capita (2004)	Government Health Spending Per Capita, Including Tax Breaks (1998/99)	Annual Medical Inflation in Excess of Population Growth and Aging, 1985–2002	Public and Private Spending on Health and Economic Security after Taxes as a Share of GDP, 2001
Australia	100%	$3,120	$1,300	0.88%	24.00%
Austria	98%	$3,124		0.65%	24.80%
Belgium	99%	$3,044		1.10%	26.30%
Canada	100%	$3,165	$1,500	0.43%	23.30%
Denmark	100%	$2,881		-0.10%	26.40%
Finland	100%	$2,235		-0.43%	22.60%
France	99.90%	$3,159	$1,400	0.61%	31.20%
Germany	89.80%	$3,043	$1,600	0.76%	30.80%
Greece	100%	$2,162		1.31%	
Iceland	100%	$ 331		1.52%	21.70%
Ireland	100%	$2,596		-0.65%	13.90%
Italy	100%	$2,467	$1,150		25.30%
Japan	100%	$2,249	$1,200	-0.03%	22.10%
Netherlands	62.50%	$3,041		0.88%	25.00%
New Zealand	100%	$2,083			18.20%
Norway	100%	$3,966		1.50%	23.60%
Spain		$2,094		1.25%	18.90%
Sweden	100%	$2,825	$1,300	0.19%	30.60%
Switzerland	100%	$4,077	$2,100	1.88%	
United Kingdom	100%	$2,508	$1,100	1.43%	27.10%

continued

Table 10.1 (continued)

Country	Share of Population Covered by Government Health Programs (2004)	Total Government and Private Health Spending Per Capita (2004)	Government Health Spending Per Capita, Including Tax Breaks (1998/99)	Annual Medical Inflation in Excess of Population Growth and Aging, 1985–2002	Public and Private Spending on Health and Economic Security after Taxes as a Share of GDP, 2001
Non-US Average	97.30%	$2,859	$1,405.50	0.73%	24.20%
United States	27.30%	$6,102	$2,500	2%	24.50%

* This table appeared in Jacob S. Hacker, *Health at Risk: America's Ailing Health System—and How to Heal It* (New York: Columbia University Press, 2008), 110.

Sources: OECD Health Data 2007, "Share of Population Eligible for a Defined Set of Health Care Goods and Services under Public Programmes," *OECD Health Data 2007* (Paris: OECD, 2008); Gerard F. Anderson, Bianca K. Frogner, and Uwe E. Reinhardt, "Health Spending in OECD Countries in 2004: An Update," *Health Affairs* 26 (2007): 1481–1489; Steffie Woolhandler and David U. Himmelstein, "Paying For National Health Insurance—And Not Getting It," *Health Affairs* 21 (2002): 88–98; Chapin White, "Health Care Spending Growth: How Different Is the United States from the Rest of the OECD?" *Health Affairs* 26 (2007): 154–161; Willem Adema and Maxime Ladaique, "Net Social Expenditure, 2005," *OECD Social, Employment, and Migration Working Papers* 29 (Paris: OECD, 2005), http://www.oecd.org/dataoecd/56/2/35632106.pdf.

cannot easily be chalked up to the penuriousness of its government. Yes, public health insurance in the United States covers just over 27 percent of Americans, whereas virtually all other rich nations cover their entire citizenry (column 1). But because American medical costs are so much higher than health costs in other nations (column 2), total U.S. public spending on health care per capita (including tax breaks for coverage and coverage for public employees) is actually the highest in the world (column 3). As the fourth column of the table shows, moreover, U.S. health spending (both public and private) is also growing much more quickly. (The reasons for this are discussed later in this chapter; for now it suffices to say that it reflects the fragmentation of the American system and, in particular, the lack of strong, coordinated efforts by those financing care to foster cost-effectiveness.)

What is particularly distinctive about American health care is that a large share of the United States' very high spending is financed by voluntary private health insurance, sponsored by employers and heavily (and regressively) subsidized by the federal government through the tax code. (In 2004, the cost of exempting health benefits from taxation in terms of forgone tax revenues was

$188.5 billion, with nearly 27 percent of this benefit going to the 16 percent of the population with annual family incomes in excess of $100,000.) This point holds more generally: private employment-based benefits (mainly health insurance and retirement pensions) play a much larger role in the United States than in other rich nations—so much more so that, as the final column of Table 1 shows, accounting for these private benefits raises U.S. spending on health and economic security as a share of the economy to something close to the average for advanced industrial democracies.

A legacy of policy decisions and battles of the mid-twentieth century, America's distinctive reliance on employment-based health insurance has created powerful hurdles to an expanded public role in the financing of health care. Americans have come to depend on the private system, and powerful vested interests have arisen within and around it. Attempts to enact major legislative changes to that system, even changes that would make Americans as a whole better off, have again and again run headlong into the specific dislocations that reforms threaten for both private interest groups and well-insured Americans. It is this basic political reality—that most Americans *have* coverage, however costly and insecure, and could be easily frightened into believing that they would lose what they have by defenders of the present system—that best explains why the ACA was so much more limited than the health policy precedents set abroad.[9]

Health at Risk

The problems that the ACA was designed to address—rampant uninsurance and underinsurance, runaway medical debt, crippling benefit costs—are hardly new. Yet all of them grew much more prevalent and troubling from the late 1970s on, and all of them increasingly affected the politically crucial middle class. The ranks of the uninsured have grown substantially since the 1970s—among the middle class as well as lower income groups (though the poorest Americans have been somewhat cushioned by the major expansion of public health care coverage for low-income groups). Everyone has heard the sobering numbers: more than 50 million Americans without health insurance (compared with fewer than 30 million in 1980), the vast majority of them in working families.[10] But the uninsured are a constantly shifting group that includes many more people than that. Between 2007 and 2009, nearly 87 million people—one out of three non-elderly Americans—went without health insurance at some point. Almost three-quarters of this population were uninsured for at least half a year; three in five were uninsured for at least nine months.[11] Even those whose spells without insurance are short could have found themselves facing an unexpected disaster and might have ended up not just with huge bills but also future denials of coverage for "preexisting conditions."

Medical bankruptcy is also a major, troubling, and almost certainly growing problem—one that affects those who have health coverage as well as those without it. The Dorsetts, whose story was told in the first pages of this chapter, are hardly unique.[12] Indeed, if the overriding problem of the 1990s was lack of health insurance—a problem that has, of course, worsened—the problem of the 2000s and future may well be "underinsurance," the lack of *adequate* health insurance. In the twelve months prior to May 2007, according to a survey by *Consumer Reports*, around three in ten non-elderly adults who had health insurance lacked adequate coverage.[13] Nearly six in ten of the *under*insured postponed needed medical care because of the cost, nearly four in ten had to put off home or car maintenance or repairs due to medical expenses, a third had to dig into their savings or borrow to pay for medical care, and more than one in five made job-related decisions based mainly on their health care needs.[14] Strikingly, the median family income of the *under*insured is $58,000—almost exactly the same as the median income of those with adequate coverage.[15] The *under*insured are just as likely to be white as the well-insured, nearly as well-educated, and just as likely to work full-time and in large or medium-sized companies. The only consistent way in which they differ from those who are better protected is that they are at grave, and growing, economic risk.[16]

The main reason for these worrisome trends is simple: as medical costs and health premiums continue to skyrocket, traditional employment-based coverage is declining. Some surveys suggest that its reach has plummeted by as much as 9 percentage points between 2000 and 2005, while others indicate a steadier and somewhat smaller drop.[17] What is not in dispute is that Americans are ever less likely to be covered by their employers, and that employers are consistently asking workers to pay a larger share of the cost of their coverage and care.[18] With health premiums growing by roughly 50 percent in inflation-adjusted terms between 2000 and 2006, over a period in which median family income actually declined, it is hardly surprising that health care costs and coverage have risen in prominence as stated concerns of Americans in opinion surveys.[19]

Nor is this simply a matter of dollars and cents. It is a matter of life and death. Researchers at Harvard University estimate that 45,000 working-age Americans die each year because of the lack of universal health insurance in the United States.[20] But that is not even the most startling statistic. According to a recent study, the United States ranks 19th out of 19 rich nations in the rate of "amenable mortality"—deaths before age 75 that could have been prevented with the provision of timely and effective care.[21] A decade ago, we were five places higher on the list. But we are nowhere near the nations with the best rates, all of which provide affordable, quality care to all of their citizens. If, for example, the United States had the same rate of amenable mortality as the three nations with the lowest rates of preventable death, more than 100,000 fewer people would die in the United States each year.[22] These are risks that all Americans face because of the costly, fragmented, and inadequate American framework of medical financing.

The Affordable Care Act

Most of the text of this section appeared previously in Hacker, "Health-Care Reform, 2015," 10–14.

The ACA represents a dramatic response to these risks. Yet it is a response that bears the marks of the serious constraints imposed by America's distinctive policy structure and polarized politics. Compared to Medicare, a simple public program that provides insurance (paying private providers) to virtually all the aged and disabled, the ACA looks like a Rube Goldberg contraption. Its basic structure mixes state and federal responsibilities, competing administrative centers of authority, and public and private activities in a manner that can be charitably described as complex. The most Medicare-like, and thus straightforward, aspect of the original legislative package was the so-called public option—a public insurance plan competing with private plans for the business of non-elderly Americans, an idea I have long championed.[23] However, the public option was stripped from the legislation in the Senate to batten down wavering Democratic votes and overcome a GOP filibuster. Thus, a simple, popular element that could have provided a major tool of cost containment was lost.

The simplest way to describe the new ACA is as a structure consisting of three pillars of coverage, supported by a foundation of regulations and spending. The first pillar is an expansion and upgrade of Medicaid to cover all poor people under 133 percent of the federal poverty level. (Currently, Medicaid, which varies greatly from state to state, provides health coverage to only certain poor people, such as pregnant women and children, and excludes most poor childless adults.) Even though the federal government will finance virtually all of the expansion of Medicaid mandated under the ACA, states will have to reach those who are eligible and ensure that coverage on paper means in fact that doctors and hospitals will be willing to take often-penurious payments—something many states do poorly now and will continue to do poorly after reform.

The second pillar of the ACA is the creation of new health-insurance "exchanges" that will allow small employers and Americans who do not receive employer-based coverage to choose from a range of regulated private plans, with much of the cost of the premiums for middle-and lower-income Americans borne by the federal government. The plan is to have these exchanges set up by the states by 2014, but the federal government will establish them directly if states do not. Moreover, states can also establish exchanges in cooperation with other states, an option that might be attractive in less populated regions or where multistate metropolises exist (such as the St. Louis–Kansas City area). And the statute requires that the federal government contract with at least two private health plans directly—at least one of which must be a nonprofit—to provide coverage on a nationwide basis. These national plans will also be offered through the exchanges.

The third—and, in terms of the number of Americans covered, the broadest—pillar of the new health care law will be newly regulated and mandated private coverage through employers. Large employers (those with 50 or more workers) will be required to provide minimum coverage to their workers or pay a fine. The terms of employment-based plans will be more strictly regulated than they are today. (For example, if employers offer employer-based coverage whose employee premium cost exceeds around a tenth of the workers' household income, the worker will qualify for federal subsidies and the employer will pay a penalty.) And, eventually, the favorable tax treatment of those plans will be limited. In essence, the ACA will gradually transform the present voluntary, semi-regulated, subsidized system of workplace insurance into a less voluntary, more regulated, and somewhat less subsidized system.

Each of these three pillars raises distinct implementation challenges and significant unknowns. This is in part because, at the insistence of the Senate, the law leans so heavily on the states for the expansion of coverage and regulation of insurers, making the ACA in essence not one reform law, but a set of basic requirements within which as many as 51 systems could blossom—or wilt. Even if the current full-throated state challenges to the constitutionality of the law crumble, that will not stop many states from fumbling the establishment of the exchanges, the regulation of insurers, and the expansion of Medicaid. Across the states, the administrative capacities of public officials vary enormously, as does the will of those officials to use the capacities they have. Some state political leaders—mostly in so-called "Red States" dominated by conservative politicians—will do all they can to drag their feet. Yet even in states where leaders wish to properly implement the law, state regulators are often badly outgunned by insurers and providers tenaciously defending their economic turf. As a result, the initial rollout of the law is destined to be one of mixed success.

Much will hinge, therefore, on whether and how the federal government uses the fallback authority at its disposal.[24] If and when states fail to develop plans for workable exchanges, or fail to carry out those plans, the federal government needs to step in, as it did in setting up temporary high-risk insurance pools (a stopgap measure in the law until the exchanges go live in 2014) in the nearly two dozen states without their own plans in July 2010.[25] Indeed, a paradox of the law is that in states where political leaders are dragging their feet, reform's strongest advocates at the state level should be willing to encourage state leaders *not* to set up their own exchanges, pressing instead for state officials to conserve resources and enlist the federal government to contract with and oversee private plans directly.

On the other hand, in states where political leaders are eager to create their own frameworks (up to and including a single state plan to cover all residents), there should be support for experimentation. Plans that would integrate coverage under some kind of "public option" have received serious consideration in a number of states (most, not surprisingly, are "Blue States" like Connecticut and

Vermont). Such experimentation should not, however, be a cover for failure to make serious progress in implementing the law and fulfilling its spirit. States should only be allowed to depart from the basic exchange approach when they can credibly demonstrate that at least as many residents will be provided high-quality insurance under their proposal as under the exchange framework.

At the federal level, the prospects for successful implementation remain far better than at the state level, not least because of the consistent support for the law that will be forthcoming from Washington so long as President Obama holds office. Nevertheless, the range of complex decisions and responsibilities that the ACA places in the hands of federal officials all but guarantees that some decisions will be made poorly or will turn out badly, while others will pose difficult trade-offs and substantial uncertainties.

In particular, while the states grapple with the thorny problem of creating exchanges, the federal government will face its own challenges in regulating employment-based plans. The Congressional Budget Office's prediction of 32 million newly insured Americans at relatively modest federal cost (or at least modest by health care's inflated pricing standards) rests heavily on the assumption that most employers now providing insurance will continue to do so, even if their plans are subject to new rules. That, however, is an assumption worth interrogating.

The problem here is not political will or administrative skill. The problem is that the third pillar of the law—the less voluntary, more regulated, less subsidized system of workplace insurance—creates a basic structural dilemma: trying to improve the generosity or security of private employment-based insurance will create costs and administrative hassles for employers that could reduce their willingness to provide insurance at all, notwithstanding the penalty that larger employers will pay if they fail to sponsor coverage. Put bluntly, the primary tool that the act grants federal officials—enforcing the rules for employment-based plans—can be used aggressively only at the risk of undermining the primary means of coverage in the law.

The structural bind raised by the reliance on employment-based insurance only hints at the deeper dilemma: effective implementation and administration of the ACA will not, by themselves, ensure that the key goals of the legislation are met. Even if every step envisioned by the law is successfully taken by 2015—a big "if"—there will still be large gaps in coverage and weak restraints on costs. Insurers will not be able to blatantly turn people away, or price the sickest out of the market altogether. But they will still be able to charge premiums that exceed many people's means and, as discussed later in this chapter, those premiums will still be rising far too rapidly. Although regulators overseeing private plans will know much more about what they offer and what they spend their money on, getting insurers to change what they offer and what they spend their money on will be another matter. In short, Senator Harkin's "starter home" needs to be renovated and improved.

Renovating and Improving
the "Starter Home"

Most of the text of this section appeared previously in Hacker, "Health-Care Reform, 2015," 16–18.

If reformers just play defense, they will be stuck protecting a law that has two notable problems: it is not designed to ensure that everyone is covered, and it is not capable of seriously reining in medical inflation.

The first problem is the easier of the two to tackle, at least in policy terms. In our predominantly employment-based insurance system, there are only two routes to seamlessly guaranteed coverage—either (1) requiring that employers provide coverage or contribute toward its costs, or (2) severing the financial link between employment and health benefits by raising the funds for subsidized coverage through alternative means. The ACA embodies an uneasy hybrid of these two approaches: somewhat weak coverage requirements on the largest employers, but none on those with fewer than 50 workers, and no guarantee that those without coverage through employment will receive insurance through the exchanges or Medicaid.

From a policy standpoint, the creation of a new insurance funding stream outside employment—say, a value-added tax whose revenues are dedicated to subsidizing health coverage—has a lot going for it: it could ensure a stable revenue stream, serve other policy goals (such as encouraging savings), and de-link health insurance from its connection to employment. Yet developing a new source of health insurance funds also has notable drawbacks. First, it requires frontally challenging the GOP's long-standing anti-tax crusade. Given the controversy already surrounding reform, this may be a bridge too far. Second, a separate revenue source will not have any direct, tangible connection to the benefits of reform, which would make it more difficult to explain to the public why such a tax is necessary. Consider the comparison to another famous tax, the Social Security payroll tax, about which President Franklin Roosevelt famously said, "We put those payroll contributions there so as to give the contributors a legal, moral, and political right to collect their pensions and their unemployment benefits. With those taxes in there, no damn politician can ever scrap my Social Security program."[26]

For these reasons, a more promising route may be to build on the existing law to fill in its gaps. The first step would be to strengthen the employer requirements to turn them into an automatic source of affordable coverage for workers. In practice, this would mean extending the employer coverage requirement to employers with fewer than 50 workers, eventually reaching all employers, including the self-employed. It would also mean transforming the penalty—currently $2,000 per full-time employee (excluding the first 30 employees) for most employers—into something closer to a "play-or-pay" mandate in which uninsured workers' coverage is automatic through the exchange (or Medicaid) when their employer pays a dedicated payroll-based contribution.

Exempting small employers entirely from the coverage requirement, as the current law does, has two salient drawbacks. First, it means that millions of Americans do not receive automatic coverage at their place of work. More than half of the working uninsured are either self-employed or work in firms with fewer than 50 employees.[27] Because these firms are not required to contribute even a token amount on behalf of their workers, coverage for these workers has to come through Medicaid outreach and enforcement of the individual mandate, neither of which is likely to work as well as simply signing workers up for employer- or government-sponsored coverage at their place of work.

Second, a blanket small-business exemption is ill-targeted, since it exempts small high-wage firms with substantial financial capacity to provide coverage (such as law firms) in a way that is identical to the treatment of small low-wage firms without such capacity. Instead, employers that do not sponsor coverage should be required to contribute to the cost of their workers' coverage on a sliding scale based on firm payroll, which is a better measure of a firm's ability to provide coverage than the number of employees. Moreover, such a change would still take into account firm size as well as wages, easing the burden on the smallest firms. For example, firms could be required to pay 1 percent on the first $250,000 of payroll, 4 percent on the next $750,000, and so on, up to a full levy of, say, 7 percent. The lower contributions required of low-wage firms could be subsidized by redirecting the law's ill-targeted tax breaks for small businesses—breaks that would no longer be necessary to encourage these firms to participate.

This approach would have three benefits. First, the payroll contribution would be a dedicated amount that firms and workers could perceive as "purchasing" their benefits through the exchange. Second, this approach would mean that everyone working or living in the family of a worker (including the self-employed, who, as with Social Security, would be required to make the contribution on their own behalf) would be automatically covered, either directly through an employment-based plan or through the exchange when their employer pays the contribution. Third, a true play-or-pay approach would lessen reliance on the highly controversial individual mandate, which is viewed with skepticism by a majority of Americans and is the target of a vigorous GOP assault. At least before the recent downturn, an approach requiring that all firms (including the self-employed) either play or pay would have guaranteed coverage to more than 95 percent of Americans younger than 65. If no one was allowed to exit coverage without showing proof of an alternative source, this number would rise to 100 percent in short order, as very few non-elderly Americans have no tie to the workforce for an extended period.

Given the resistance of employers to the ACA's existing rules, it may seem fanciful to think that the employer requirements could be strengthened. But as the new law goes into effect, employers playing by the rules may become more supportive, recognizing that their less responsible competitors gain a competitive advantage by not providing insurance, while raising the costs of all employer plans when their uninsured workers receive uncompensated care. To be sure, this logic would work only for firms actually providing coverage, and it is likely to be persuasive only for those coverage-providing firms (such as unionized supermarkets) that have aggressive low-wage competitors. But firms not providing insurance could see advantages in a broader employer requirement as well. If the cost of allowing their workers to buy into the exchanges was affordable, small and large firms alike could see it as beneficial to buy coverage through the exchanges rather than on their own. Indeed, the exchanges should eventually be opened up to all employers, not just the smallest—a step that states have the authority to take.

This is yet another reason that states and the federal government must be vigilant in ensuring that the exchanges are set up on solid foundations, and why cost-control tools have to be used actively and strengthened over time. If the exchanges function effectively to provide lower-cost coverage, they are likely to become more and more attractive to employers, especially the smallest among them. The exchanges, after all, will provide a menu of health-plan options, and they will remove from employers' shoulders the administrative burden of picking and monitoring health plans and managing enrollment in them (this, incidentally, might be another allure to small firms to participate). So long as firms are required to pay a reasonable amount to fund workers' coverage, there is no reason to insist that firms provide insurance on their own when they and their workers would prefer to buy it through the exchange.

Controlling Costs

> Most of the text of this section appeared previously in Hacker, "Health-Care Reform, 2015," 19–23.

None of this will matter much, however, if costs are not contained. The long-term budget challenge faced by the United States is almost entirely a medical cost challenge: take out Medicare and Medicaid and the federal fiscal forecast looks surprisingly rosy. At the same time, if costs are not restrained, politicians and corporations will be pressed to shift more and more of the health care tab onto Americans' already burdened finances. Families, businesses, state governments, and the federal government alike—all of them will suffer if costs continue to rise at the rate of recent decades.

And here we reach the weakest foundational aspect of Senator Harkin's starter home. All the reform ideas that would have provided big direct savings—from serious administrative streamlining through a single national exchange to the public insurance option I have advocated—were either sidelined or neutered as they ran the gauntlet of affected interests. Indeed, the public option debate was a case study in why cost control is so hard: conservative Democrats first effectively stripped out the tools of cost control that would have allowed the public option to compete aggressively with private insurers, most notably the use of provider rates based on Medicare's payment schedule. Then, they complained that the public option wouldn't control costs.

Virtually everyone who has studied the private medical market in recent years has noted its unhealthy consolidation on both the demand (insurer) and supply (provider) sides. A revealing indicator of the problem: just as the health care bill neared passage, the American Medical Association (AMA) released a report finding that 99 percent of metropolitan areas studied had "highly concentrated" insurance markets.[28] Equally striking, a single private insurer held 70 percent or more of the private market in 24 of the 43 states examined (up from 18 of 42 states just a year earlier).

The AMA was understandably less eager to point out the simultaneous consolidation of medical providers—with large physicians' groups and flagship hospital systems gaining enormous leverage to drive up prices, even when faced with dominant insurers. As one health plan executive recently complained to researchers studying California's escalating medical costs, "I am shocked there isn't an outcry over the fact that our costs are driven out of control. We would like to establish some sort of boundary, beyond which these guys can't go. We'd welcome some regulatory intervention to break up these monopolies, because they are just killing us."[29]

Yet "regulatory intervention"—pushing back against consolidated health plans, or "breaking up" dominant provider groups—is not in the cards in most states. The federal government has the leverage to hold down price increases. Medicare, for example, has held annual spending growth for comparable services at a level two to three percentage points below private insurance over the past 15 years or so. In contrast, as the recent report on California notes, private insurers' "payment rates to hospitals and powerful physician groups approach and exceed 200 percent of what Medicare pays, with annual negotiated double-digit increases in recent years."[30]

After dramatic private premium increases in early 2010, California's senior senator, Dianne Feinstein, called for requiring insurers seeking increases in health-plan premiums to get approval from states before doing so. Although Feinstein's amendment didn't make it into the ACA, states do have the authority to establish such procedures under the new law. Unfortunately, prior approval for premium increases is unlikely to have much effect on the long-term trajectory of costs. The majority of states already require prior approval of premiums for at least some insurers and some specific markets. And although regulators sometimes insist on and receive lower premium increases, the overall trajectory of medical costs has continued sharply upward. To be sure, prior approval might be more effective when insurers are constrained from changing what and whom they cover. But even with reform, insurers will be able to lower premiums by restricting (within regulatory bounds) provider networks, the conditions under which they pay for needed care, or coverage terms.

The ACA does, however, include a new requirement with greater potential teeth. Under the law, insurers are required to spend at least 80 percent of premiums on medical care, as opposed to administrative costs and profits (the standard is 85 percent for large group plans and 80 percent for small group and individual plans).[31] More significant still, insurers that do not meet this 80 percent standard—known within the industry, revealingly, as the "medical-loss ratio," or MLR—will have to provide rebates to consumers equal to the difference between 80 percent and their actual spending on care.[32] MLRs have been falling since the 1990s, but on average, insurers still exceed this 80 percent threshold: in 2007 the industry-average MLR was 81 percent.[33] Yet many insurers spend less than 80 percent of premiums on care, and in the individual and small-group markets the share can be as low as *60 percent*.[34] According to the advocacy group Health Care for America Now!, the six largest for-profit insurance companies would have had to provide nearly $2 billion in rebates if the requirement had been effect in 2009 (it actually takes effect in 2011).[35]

The MLR requirement represents an important step in encouraging private insurer transparency. If properly implemented, it could ensure that a higher share of premiums is spent on care rather than administrative costs or profits, and it might even lead to one-time premium rebates. Like prior approval, however, it will not do much to slow the growth in costs over time. The MLR is a ratio—care versus administration. It says nothing about whether overall spending is excessive or not. What's more, insurers are doing everything within their power to gut the MLR rules even before they take effect, arguing that scores of functions historically treated as administration—such as the costs of denying care ("loss adjustment expenses," in insurance terminology), fraud prevention, network management, and provider credentialing—are actually "care."[36] The Obama administration is currently standing firm. But some state regulators are already saying that they will exempt categories of insurers or phase in the requirements over an extended period.[37] It is safe to assume that the final MLR rules will be even weaker than those envisioned in the ACA.

By far the most promising approach for state leaders may be to institute "all-payer" rate setting.[38] Under an all-payer system, payments for specific services or for treatment of patients with particular diagnoses would be set through a negotiated process in which insurers, providers, and state governments, as well as consumer representatives, had a seat at the table. These rates would then be used by all payers (hence the name), and they could be extended to more complex payment methods, such as payment for entire episodes of care (e.g., treatment of a heart attack). By consolidating bargaining power on the demand side and limiting the ability of providers to play one payer off another, all-payer systems have the potential to both create lower, more uniform payments and to restrain the increase in service prices over time.

The key to controlling costs over the long term, however, is reviving the public option. In addition to the savings created by a public option—which, by its nature, has no need to earn a profit and will have large numbers of subscribers over which to spread administrative expenses—the public option would restrain costs in two additional ways. The first and simplest is by building on Medicare's success in restraining prices. Indeed, the public option could be the prime means for extending to non-elderly Americans the innovations in payment and care management that will be used to slow Medicare spending growth in the coming years.

The second means by which the public option would hold down costs is by serving as a competitive benchmark for private plans. The public plan would represent a simple, affordable plan available on similar terms throughout the nation, reassuring Americans newly required to have insurance that they can gain access to a transparent product with a broad choice of providers. As such, the public option is likely to be an attractive alternative to private plans, pressing insurers to work harder to restrain their own premiums and to showcase their own distinctive merits. In today's weakly competitive market, even a modest spillover of the public plan's cost-control efforts into the private sector could have major effects.

In theory, states could create a Medicare-like public option of their own under the new law—and a handful may well do so before the exchanges become operational in 2014, including Oregon, Vermont, and Connecticut.[39] A state public option would create greater accountability for private insurers, especially in states where a single insurer dominates the market. But a state public option would, of course, be available only to those who live within the states that offer it. If only a handful of states move forward, most Americans will be shut out. For the same reason, the cost-control potential of state public plans will be limited. States have far less market leverage than the federal government: a national public option, if equally attractive in substance and coverage, would have 500 times as many subscribers as a Vermont-only plan.

More important, individual states also have far less political leverage. State public officials—often less closely monitored by constituents than national leaders, possessing fewer administrative tools and more limited budgets, and frequently term-limited—are a weak match for a determined, consolidated private medical insurance industry. As a prominent consumer representative working to influence state insurance commissioners recently explained, "Insurers spend tens of millions of policyholder-supplied funds to lobby for insurer interests. In contrast, consumer interests have few such resources."[40] The entire consumer participation budget at the National Association of Insurance Commissioners—the organization of state insurance regulators—is dwarfed by the salary of a single insurance lobbyist.[41] In the face of the industry's political onslaught, many states whose leaders are contemplating a state public option may not end up with one at all.

Hence the need for a national plan. A simple Medicare-like public option could build on the provisions of the law that establish at least two national plans offered within state exchanges (at least one of which must be a nonprofit). Offered within every state exchange, a national public option could provide simple, predictable coverage and use its enormous bargaining power to obtain better rates. Moreover, administrators of a national public option would have the incentive and ability to invest in innovative payment and care-management strategies, building on the improvements in Medicare envisioned under the ACA. As poll after poll during the health care debate showed, the public option is popular.[42] And unlike many popular ideas, it will actually save serious money.

The public option is often seen—by detractors as well as some supporters—as an alternative to relying on private insurance. Although it will certainly cover some Americans who would otherwise enroll in private plans, it is best thought of as an alternative to relying exclusively on *regulation* to make private plans act in the public interest. The public option is a means of allowing the private and public sectors to operate in cooperative tension with each other, as in any dynamic market system, without putting excessive faith in the ability of regulators to make the private sector behave in fundamentally different ways.

Above all, the public option is the renovation that solidifies Harkin's starter home in the face of a perfect storm. What the advocates of Social Security recognized and fought for in the 1930s and beyond was the strongest *structure*. They understood that a firm foundation could be built on, and that a popular, capable program could attract more financing and greater institutional resources. The public option is a crucial and popular addition to the institutional architecture of the law, filling in the weakest aspect of the home's foundation—its anemic cost-control measures—so that the other reforms discussed in this chapter can expand that home to include more Americans over time.

Organizing for American Health Care

Most of the text of this section appeared previously in Hacker, "Health-Care Reform, 2015," 23–24.

Reformers are planning to spend the next few years trying to make sure the ACA is properly implemented and to convince Americans that the ACA was in their interest. But they should not be afraid at the same time to point out where the law needs to be strengthened, and nowhere is this more true than when it comes to the public option.

This was the approach taken with the Social Security Act of 1935, whose champions celebrated the law's achievements, yet never ceased to point out how the law still failed to provide the foundation of economic security initially promised. On the third anniversary of the Social Security Act in 1938, President Roosevelt delivered a stirring reminder of the law's achievements—and its unmet promise:

We have come a long way. But we still have a long way to go. There is still today a frontier that remains unconquered—an America unclaimed. This is the great, the nationwide frontier of insecurity, of human want and fear. This is the frontier—the America—we have set ourselves to reclaim.[43]

We have come a long way in achieving health security. But we will still have a long way to go. Making the case for the changes that are needed—from strengthening the relatively weak employer requirements in the law, to opening up the exchanges to larger employers, to creating a national public option to bring down escalating costs—will require more than incremental steps to build trust in the law. It will also require a broader vision of how the overarching goal of affordable, quality care for all can be achieved, backed up by an ongoing, organized movement. Like President Roosevelt in 1938, reformers in the coming years will have to identify the next "unclaimed frontier of insecurity," and show Americans how and why to cross it. They owe families like the Dorsetts, struggling with the continuing threat of health insecurity, at least that much.

Notes

1. This story first appeared in Jacob S. Hacker, *The Great Risk Shift* (New York: Oxford University Press, 2006), 137–138.
2. *Patient Protection and Affordable Care Act of 2010*, Public Law 148, 111th Cong., 2d sess. (March 23, 2010).
3. Although Medicare is primarily designed to provide health care for Americans age 65 and over, the entitlement program also provides care for certain disabled members of the under-65 population. *Social Security Act*, U.S. Code 42 (2009), § 1395i-2a.
4. Douglas W. Elmendorf, "Direct Spending and Revenue Effects of the Patient Protection and Affordable Care Act," prepared by the Congressional Budget Office, United States Congress, 2009, http://www.cbo.gov/ftpdocs/108xx/doc10868/12–19-Reid_Letter_Managers_Correction_Noted.pdf.
5. The first part of this paragraph appeared in Jacob Hacker, "The Road to Somewhere: Why Health Reform Happened; Or Why Political Scientists Who Write about Public Policy Shouldn't Assume They Know How to Shape It," *Perspectives on Politics* 8 (2010): 863.
6. Jacob Hacker, "Health Reform 2.0," *The American Prospect*, August 17, 2010, http://www.prospect.org/cs/articles?article=health_reform_20.
7. Drawn from Jacob S. Hacker, "Health-Care Reform, 2015," *Democracy* 18 (2010): 8–24, http://democracyjournal.org/pdf/18/Hacker.pdf.
8. This section draws on Jacob S. Hacker, "Dismantling the Health Care State? Political Institutions, Public Policies, and the Comparative Politics of Health Reform," *British Journal of Political Science* 34 (2004): 693–724.
9. Parts of these two preceding paragraphs appeared in Jacob S. Hacker, "Yes We Can? The New Push for American Health Security," *Politics & Society* 37 (2009): 3–31.
10. Carmen DeNavas-Walt, Bernadette D. Proctor, and Jessica C. Smith, *Income, Poverty, and Health Insurance Coverage in the United States: 2009*, prepared by the Economics and Statistics Administration, U.S. Census Bureau, 2010, http://www.census.gov/prod/2010pubs/p.60-238.pdf.
11. Families USA, *Americans at Risk: One in Three Uninsured* (Washington, DC: Families USA, 2009), http://www.familiesusa.org/assets/pdfs/americans-at-risk.pdf.

12. David U. Himmelstein, Deborah Thorne, Elizabeth Warren, and Steffie Woolhandler, "Medical Bankruptcy in the United States, 2007: Results of a National Study," *The American Journal of Medicine* 20 (2009): 1–6.

13. Consumer Reports, "Health Care Survey—May 2007," *Consumer Reports* 2007, http://www.consumerreports.org/health/insurance/health-insurance-9-07/overview/0709_health_ov.htm.

14. Consumers Union, "Consumer Reports Health Insurance Survey Reveals 1 in 4 People Insured but Not Adequately Covered," *Consumer's Union*, August 6, 2007, http://www.consumersunion.org/pub/core_health_care/004798.html.

15. Id.

16. Hacker, *The Great Risk Shift*, 138–139.

17. The Kaiser Family Foundation and Health Research and Educational Trust, *Employer Health Benefits: 2007 Summary of Findings* (Washington: The Henry J. Kaiser Foundation and Health Research and Education Trust, 2007), http://www.kff.org/insurance/7672/upload/Summary-of-Findings-EHBS-2007.pdf; Jared Bernstein and Heidi Shierholz, "A Decade of Decline: The Erosion of Employer-Provided Health Care in the United States and California, 1995–2006," *EPI Briefing Paper* 209 (2008), http://www.epi.org/publications/entry/bp209/.

18. Kaiser, *Employer Health Benefits*, 2.

19. Kaiser, *Employer Health Benefits*, 1.

20. Andrew P. Wilper et al., "Health Insurance and Mortality in US Adults," *American Journal of Public Health* 99 (2009): 1–7.

21. Jacob S. Hacker, "Sharing Risks in a New Era of Responsibility," *National Academy of Social Insurance Health and Income Security Brief* 13 (2009): 1–6.

22. Ellen Nolte and C. Martin McKee, "Measuring The Health of Nations: Updating an Earlier Analysis," *Health Affairs* 27 (2008): 58–71.

23. Jacob S. Hacker, "Medicare Plus: Increasing Health Coverage by Expanding Medicare," in *Covering America: Real Remedies for the Uninsured*, ed. E. K. Wicks (Washington, DC: Economic and Social Research Institute, 2001), 73–100.

24. *Patient Protection and Affordable Care Act*, §§ 1311–1321.

25. Kaiser Family Foundation, "Explaining Health Reform: Questions about the Temporary High-Risk Pool," *Kaiser Family Foundation Publication 8066* (2010), http://www.kff.org/healthreform/upload/8066.pdf.

26. Quote attributed to President Franklin Delano Roosevelt in Arthur M. Schlesinger, Jr., *The Age of Roosevelt: The Coming of the New Deal* (New York: Houghton Mifflin, 1988), 308–309.

27. Ken Jacobs and Dave Graham-Squire, "Calculations on the Working Uninsured Based on the 2007 California Health Interview Survey" (unpublished calculations, U.C. Berkeley Labor Center, University of California, Berkeley, 2010).

28. David W. Emmons, José R. Guardado, and Carol K. Kane, *Competition in Health Insurance: A Comprehensive Study of U.S. Markets* (Chicago: American Medical Association Division of Economic and Health Policy Research, 2010).

29. Quoted in Robert A. Berenson, Paul B. Ginsburg, and Nicole Kemper, "Unchecked Provider Clout in California Foreshadows Challenges to Health Reform," *Health Affairs* 29 (2010): 1–7.

30. Id. at 2.

31. *Patient Protection and Affordable Care Act*, § 2718.

32. Id.

33. Wendell Potter, "The Insurance Industry's Lethal Bottom Line—and a Solution from Sens. Franken and Rockefeller," *Huffington Post*, December 6, 2009, http://www.huffingtonpost.com/wendell-potter/the-insurance-industrys-l_b_382001.html.

34. FamiliesUSA, *Medical Loss Ratios: Evidence from the States* (Washington, DC: Health Policy Memo, 2008), http://www.familiesusa.org/assets/pdfs/medical-loss-ratio.pdf.

35. Health Care for America Now, *New Federal Health Law's Insurance Premium Rules Will Control Costs for Families, Businesses* (Washington, DC: Health Care for America Now, 2010), http://hcfan.3cdn.net/415b606e9dc7b1655c_w2m6ibgwg.pdf.

36. Senate Committee on Commerce, Science, and Transportation, Office of Oversight and Investigations, Majority Staff, *Implementing Health Insurance Reform: New Medical Loss Ratio Infor-*

mation for Policymakers and Consumers, report prepared by Chairman Rockefeller's Staff, 111th Cong., 2d sess., 2010, Committee Print, 6.

37. See, e.g., Rebecca Adams, "Maine Seeks Exemption from Medical Loss Ratio (MLR) Requirement," *CQ HealthBeat*, July 13, 2010.

38. This is the dominant form of cost control in the advanced industrial world, and it is one that has been pursued by some states and localities in the past. Canada, for example, has used all-payer rate setting for decades, and not only features medical spending roughly half that of the United States on a per-person basis, but has also seen that spending rise substantially less quickly since the mid-1980s. Just across the border from Canada, Rochester, New York, pursued an innovative all-payer system for its hospitals in the 1980s—with apparent success in restraining cost increases and improving participating hospitals' financial stability.

39. April Baer, "State Senator Seeks Public Health Care Option for Oregon," *OPB News*, April 1, 2010, http://news.opb.org/article/7041-state-senator-seeks-public-health-care-option-oregon/;   Igor Volsky, "Vermont House Passes Single Payer Bill: Why It Can't Opt-Out of Federal Health Reform to Implement It," *Think Progress*, April 27, 2010, http://wonkroom.thinkprogress.org/2010/04/27/single-payer-erisa-vermont/; Joanne Kenen, "A Public Plan for Connecticut?" *The American Prospect*, August 2, 2010, http://www.prospect.org/cs/articles?article=a_public_plan_for_connecticut.

40. Phil Gusman, "Consumer Rep: We're Outgunned," *Life & Health*, December 8, 2009, http://www.lifeandhealthinsurancenews.com/News/2009/12/Pages/Consumer-Rep-Were-Outgunned.aspx.

41. Id.

42. See Dan Balz and Jon Cohen, "Public Option Gains Support: Clear Majority Now Backs Plan," *Washington Post*, October 20, 2009, http://www.washingtonpost.com/wp-dyn/content/article/2009/10/19/AR2009101902451.html; Igor Volsky, "POLL: 59% Of Those In Favor Of Repeal Want Congress To Pursue The Public Option," *Think Progress*, April 14, 2010, http://wonkroom.thinkprogress.org/?p=29943.

43. President Franklin Delano Roosevelt, "Radio Address on the Third Anniversary of the Social Security Act," August 14, 1938.

11

Bigger and Better

Redesigning Our Retirement System in the

Wake of the Financial Collapse

ALICIA H. MUNNELL

The financial crisis has dramatically demonstrated how a collapse in equity prices can decimate retirement savings. The crisis has also highlighted the fragility of the existing retirement system, where 401(k) plans serve as the primary supplement to Social Security. Investing a portion of these 401(k) accounts in equities is a central tenet of any effective retirement saving strategy, because the higher expected return (higher than standard interest-bearing savings accounts) offers the potential for lower required contributions. But the upside of investing in equities comes with the risk of sudden and steep declines or extended periods of sluggish returns. Absorbing such blows is difficult in any circumstances. It is especially difficult given the large-scale shift in risk associated with retirement savings from employers to individuals that has occurred over the past quarter century.

This chapter describes what would be involved in building a bigger and better retirement income system. The first section describes the evolution of today's retirement programs, including the decline in Social Security replacement rates and the shift from defined benefit to defined contribution plans. The second section explores the challenges that individuals face when it comes to retirement saving decisions. The third section provides an overview of the impact of the financial collapse on the nation's retirement plans. The fourth section describes recent public policy efforts to reform the existing system and concludes that they have had relatively little impact; the following section argues that the United States needs a new tier of retirement savings between Social Security and employer-sponsored plans, discusses what such an additional tier might look like, and describes the challenges of providing return guarantees as part of this new tier. The concluding section suggests that a better place to invest equities in an expanded retirement income system may be Social Security rather than the new tier. This section argues that with the ability to spread risk over a number of generations, Social Security can improve the expected return. Higher returns for Social Security would reduce the need for contributions, thereby freeing up resources for the new tier, which could be as conservatively invested as risk-averse individuals might want.

The Evolution of Today's Retirement Savings System

The challenges facing today's workers as they plan for retirement are unprecedented. Never before have individuals been required to make such complicated decisions that will have such a profound effect over such an extended period of retirement.

THE EVOLUTION OF RETIREMENT

During the pre-industrial period, the elderly generally continued to work for as long as they could. Family farms and handicraft businesses were natural vehicles for accumulating wealth as part of a worker's routine, and many elderly were able to retire from active labor by selling or leasing these assets.[1]

This pattern changed in the nineteenth century, when urbanization and industrialization transformed the economics of aging. Urbanization concentrated the population in the large labor and product markets, which eliminated the traditional sources of family or communal assistance. Industrialization undermined the ability of the elderly to support themselves through work or the ownership of income-producing assets. These nineteenth-century workers should have saved for retirement, but their parents and grandparents had not, and neither did they.[2]

The failure to save caught up with early industrial workers. Around the turn of the century, the labor force participation of older men dropped sharply, in large measure due to their inability to find work at a reasonable wage. The elderly became the subject of public and private charity.[3]

The response to a growing number of distressed older workers in every industrial nation was the creation of retirement income programs by large employers and national governments.[4] In the United States, however, by the beginning of the 1930s employer-sponsored plans covered only 15 percent of the workforce.[5] The severity of the Great Depression, combined with a surge in the supply of older workers, dramatically worsened the employment and income problems of the elderly. In response, Congress enacted Social Security in 1935.[6]

The elderly nevertheless remained a distinctly poor population. The critical 1950 Social Security Amendments substantially expanded coverage and restored retirement benefits that had been seriously eroded by inflation during the war, but wage replacement rates—benefits relative to pre-retirement earnings—remained very low at 30 percent for the average worker. Given the widespread acceptance of retirement as a legitimate period of rest after a lifetime of work and the low level of government benefits, a significant expansion of the retirement income system was essential. In 1972, Congress sharply increased Social Security benefits, to roughly a 40 percent earnings replacement rate for the benchmark average earner.[7]

Employer-sponsored pensions—primarily defined benefit plans that specify a regular and repeating benefit at retirement—also expanded in the postwar period.[8] The combination of Social Security and employer-sponsored defined benefit plans provided covered workers with long service a predictable, secure, and comfortable retirement in the 1960s, 1970s, and 1980s.

FROM EASY TO HARD

Everything began to change in the early 1980s. On the pension side, the shift began from defined benefit to defined contribution plans—specifically 401(k) plans. Congress had enacted the Employee Retirement Income Security Act (ERISA) of 1974, which imposed vesting, funding, and governance requirements and required employers to purchase insurance from the new Pension Benefit Guaranty Corporation. This legislation raised the costs to employers of sponsoring defined benefit plans. And beginning in the early 1980s, globalization and sharp increases in the educational attainment of the labor force, in the technical level of production, and in the employment of married women had various corrosive effects. First, these forces undermined the power of unions, a major factor in the postwar expansion of employer plans. Second, these forces undermined the financial stability of large corporate employers, making the assumption of long-term pension obligations a more risky undertaking. Finally, the changing labor force—more female, educated, and young—diminished the appeal of lifelong careers, especially for higher-paid workers that employer plans primarily serve. As employment in industries with defined benefit plans—namely, heavily unionized manufacturing industries—declined and new companies adopted defined contribution plans, overall pension coverage shifted to 401(k)s (see Figure 11.1).

Originally, 401(k) plans were viewed mainly as supplements to employer-sponsored pensions and profit-sharing plans. Since 401(k) participants were presumed to have their basic retirement needs covered, they were given substantial discretion over 401(k) choices, including whether to participate, how much to contribute, how to invest, and when and in what form to withdraw the funds.

On the Social Security front, it became clear that the cost of pay-as-you-go government plans, where benefits are paid primarily from current taxes, would dramatically rise in the future as the ratio of retirees to workers increased. Moreover, the program faced a short-term funding crisis in the early 1980s. In response, the National Commission on Social Security Reform presented a series of reforms that enabled the system to pay immediate benefits and supposedly restored

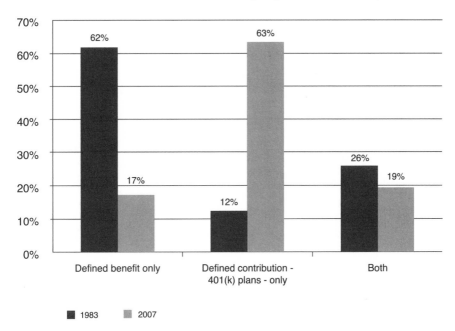

Figure 11.1: Percent of Workers with Pension Coverage by Type of Plan, from Survey of Consumer Finances, 1983 and 2007. Source: Author's calculations based on the U.S. Board of Governors of the Federal Reserve System, *Survey of Consumer Finances*, 2007.

solvency over the 75-year horizon.[9] One component of the 1983 reform package was the extension of the full retirement age from 65 to 67. This change meant that at any given age of retirement, Social Security was slated to replace a smaller percentage of pre-retirement earnings.

THE SITUATION TODAY

Today, most Americans face retirement dependent on 401(k) plans and a contracting Social Security program. At the same time, life expectancy has risen dramatically. A couple retiring today faces a 50 percent chance of having at least one member live to 92.[10]

Social Security's contraction results not only from the extension of the full retirement age from 65 to 67, but also from the deduction of rapidly rising Medicare premiums and from the taxation of benefits for a rising share of the income distribution. As shown in Figure 11.2, these three factors will reduce the net wage replacement rate for the median worker, who claims at age 65, from 39 percent in 2002 to 28 percent in 2030. Note that this figure does not include any additional benefit cuts that might be enacted to shore up the solvency of the Social Security program.[11]

401(k) plans also create enormous challenges. As noted above, when 401(k) plans first emerged in the early 1980s they were viewed mainly as supplements to

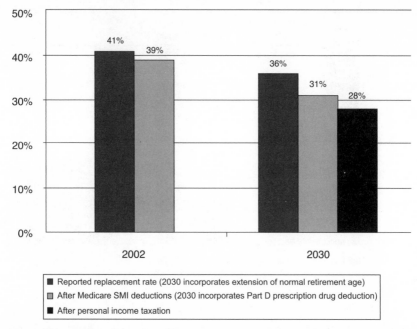

Figure 11.2: Social Security Replacement Rates for the Median Earner, 2002 and 2030. Source: Author's calculations based on Munnell (2003).

employer-funded pension and profit-sharing plans, so participants were given substantial discretion over 401(k) choices. As these plans replaced traditional pensions, however, the impact was to shift all the risk for retirement savings from the employer to the employee. The individual had to decide whether or not to join the plan, how much to contribute, how to invest the contributions and when to re-balance, what to do about company stock, whether to roll over accumulations when changing jobs, and how to withdraw the money at retirement. The evidence indicates that, at every step along the way, a significant fraction of participants make serious mistakes.[12]

Despite the passage of the Pension Protection Act of 2006, many of today's workers are at risk of having insufficient resources in retirement.[13] Balances in 401(k) plans are modest ($78,000 for the typical individual approaching retirement, according to the Federal Reserve's 2007 *Survey of Consumer Finances*).[14] Moreover, 401(k) plans provide workers with lump-sum payments at retirement. Lump sums mean that individuals risk either spending too rapidly and outliving their resources or spending too conservatively and consuming too little. These risks could be eliminated with the purchase of annuities—insurance contracts that, in exchange for an up-front payment, provide monthly income for life, usually following retirement—but the annuity market in the United States is tiny.

In addition, less than half of private-sector workers—at any moment in time—participates in any form of employer-sponsored plan. Since median job tenure for Americans 25 years and older is only five years, many workers will move in and out of coverage.[15] As a result, while two-thirds of households will end up with some pension accumulations at retirement, those without continuous coverage will often have only small balances. And the one-third of households with no 401(k) assets will be forced to rely only on Social Security.

The Psychological Challenge

Not only has the retirement income system changed in ways that force individuals to make complex decisions, but many people are unprepared to tackle these tasks and generally lack knowledge about financial concepts and instruments.

The saving and investing process requires a good deal of foresight, discipline, and skill. To properly forecast both retirement needs and how much they should save each year, people need to predict their earnings over their lifetime, how long they will be able to work, how much they will earn on their assets, and their life expectancy. Making these projections is extremely difficult. And recent work in behavioral economics suggests that people are disinclined to even try.[16]

Myopia is a major barrier. People are absorbed in their daily routines, or prefer not to think of their own old age, and fail to see what lies in the future. People also tend to place a low value on their future well-being. One explanation offered by psychologists and economists is that people are "hyperbolic" discounters, in that their near-term discount rates are much higher than their long-term discount rates.[17] That is, individuals state a preference for consuming today but saving tomorrow, and then, when tomorrow arrives, they again postpone saving. The result of this tension is that hyperbolic individuals tend to save less than they feel they should, are overly reliant on debt, and make purchases that they later regret. Self-control is another issue.[18] Many people say they should be saving for retirement, but find it very difficult to act on that knowledge. Inertia and procrastination are major components of the discipline problem with regard to saving behavior. One common response of workers as to why they do not participate in savings plans is, "I never get around to it." Some reasons that people never get around to it are obvious: a secure retirement tomorrow involves sacrificing consumption today; postponing the start of saving has no immediate penalty; and the process is complicated.

One manifestation of the difficulty for individuals to save is their response to the changing retirement landscape. Given the decline in Social Security and employer-provided pensions and the rise in longevity, workers should have been accumulating more wealth on their own to generate an equivalent retirement income. But that does not appear to be the case. Repeated *Surveys of Consumer Finances* indicate that median household wealth, *excluding* Social Security and employer defined benefit pensions but including 401(k)/IRA assets and home equity, has remained remarkably constant relative to household income. That is, as shown in Figure 11.3, the wealth-to-income ratios for each survey lie on top of one another. The implication is that households have not increased their accumulation

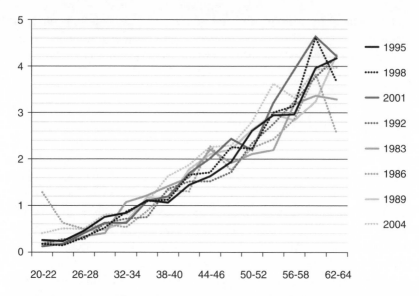

Figure 11.3: Ratio of Wealth to Income from Survey of Consumer Finances, by Age Group, Selected Years 1983–2004. Source: Authors' update from Delorme, Munnell, and Webb (2006) based on U.S. Federal Reserve Board (1983–2004) and *Survey of Consumer Finances*.

of wealth to offset the demise of defined benefit plans or the scheduled reduction in Social Security replacement rates.[19]

Recent surveys confirm that people have a hard time saving for retirement. In response to a 2010 questionnaire, only 19 percent of respondents indicated that they were very confident that they had put aside enough for retirement, 31 percent had not saved anything for retirement, and 54 percent had not even tried to figure out how much they might need.[20] The Center for Retirement Research's National Retirement Risk Index indicated, before the financial collapse, that 43 percent of today's households will be unlikely to maintain their pre-retirement living standards in retirement.[21]

The Impact of the Collapse in Equity Prices on Retirement Plans

The recent financial collapse highlighted the fragility of the U.S. retirement system. Equity prices fell 57 percent between the peak of the stock market on October 9, 2007, and March 9, 2009. Over that 18-month period, the value of equities in pension plans and household portfolios fell by $15.5 trillion. Of that $15.5 trillion decline, $2.8 trillion occurred in 401(k)s and individual retirement accounts (IRAs), $2.4 trillion in public and private defined benefit plans, and the rest in areas other than pensions.[22] By the fall of 2010, equity prices were still 23 percent below their 2007 peak.

Defined benefit and defined contribution plans were affected similarly by the market collapse because both types of plans had about two-thirds of their assets invested in equities.[23] But the impact on participants differed dramatically.

In defined benefit plans, participants were sheltered from the immediate impact of the $1.8 trillion of losses; plan sponsors bore the brunt. Private sector sponsors faced large increases in contributions to amortize losses as required under the Pension Protection Act of 2006. Congress relieved some of the pressure in December 2008, by easing the transition rules for plans that fail to meet their funding targets.[24] In the public sector, where defined benefit plans dominate, the tradition of using a five-year moving average for valuing assets means that required increases will be phased in, but, given that benefits are virtually guaranteed in most states, taxpayers and employees will eventually have to ante up.[25]

In the case of 401(k) plans, participants took an immediate direct hit from the financial crisis. Individuals saw the value of equities in their 401(k) plans or IRAs, whose balances consist largely of rollovers from employer-sponsored plans, decline by $2.0 trillion. Those approaching retirement with a substantial portion of their 401(k) balances in equities suffered the largest losses and have the least time to recover.[26] But the historical pattern of boom and bust has also created a situation in which younger cohorts could be in even worse shape unless the stock market soars going forward.

Consider the outcome of 401(k) saving for three hypothetical employees, ages 30, 40, and 50 in 1999, who all began contributing 6 percent to their 401(k) at age 30, and received an employer matching contribution of 3 percent. Those approaching retirement clearly saw their balances plummet in the wake of the financial crisis. But this group actually fared quite well over their lifetime. The problem is that they, lulled into a false sense of security, had made plans based on large balances that disappeared. Younger participants, unlike their older counterparts, never enjoyed the full run-up in the stock market from 1982–2000 and will need high annual returns—11 to 13 percent—to end up with assets anywhere near those of current pre-retirees.

In short, the recent financial crisis has demonstrated the devastating effects of the privatization of financial risk for individuals who rely on 401(k) plans as their primary supplement to Social Security. But the inadequacies of our current retirement system go beyond the vulnerabilities revealed by the current economic crisis. As discussed above, even without the stock market collapse, future retirees were projected to end up with too little retirement income because the system is contracting while people are living ever longer. The challenge is to design a more substantial, efficient, and resilient retirement income system, one that ensures adequate incomes in retirement and distributes risk more effectively.

Efforts to Date

To date, efforts to reform the retirement system have focused on three areas: replacing a portion or all of Social Security with individual accounts; automating 401(k) plans so that they work more effectively; and expanding coverage through simplified plans and "automatic IRAs" for those without employer-sponsored plans.

PRIVATIZE SOCIAL SECURITY

Between the mid-1990s and the financial crisis of 2008, proposals abounded to replace part or all of Social Security with individual accounts. Some proponents were simply misguided and thought that such a transfer would provide higher returns for current and future workers and solve Social Security's financial shortfall. Others understood that solving the financing problem required an increase in contributions and/or a reduction in benefits, but still supported individual accounts because of different values or political projections. These proponents placed different weights on individual control versus shared responsibility. They had different assessments of the long-term stability of the current system versus that of a combined defined benefit/defined contribution approach. They had different assessments of the ability to protect accumulations in the Social Security Trust Fund versus individual accounts from political pressures to use them for other purposes. And they had fundamentally different views about the appropriate size of the defined benefit versus defined contribution components of the nation's retirement system.[27]

But the facts are clear on how individual Social Security accounts affect individuals. These accounts would expose individuals to several risks: market risk, the risk of using their savings before retirement, and the risk of outliving their retirement income. They would also involve higher administrative costs, which would reduce net benefits. And individual accounts would hurt the disabled, women, and low earners. Fortunately, enthusiasm for privatizing Social Security appears to have waned in the wake of the financial crisis.

IMPROVE 401(K)S

Over the past 10 years, policymakers and business leaders came to recognize the challenges inherent in 401(k) plans and began to take steps to make these plans easier and more automatic. Many of the efforts built on a series of studies by behavioral economists who demonstrated that inertia plays a major role in how workers participate and invest in 401(k)s.[28] The lessons learned by individual employers were reflected in the provisions of the Pension Protection Act of 2006 (PPA).[29] The PPA encouraged automatic enrollment by removing obstacles that had kept some employers from adopting these arrangements and established a safe harbor whereby employers that adopt automatic enrollment are deemed to have met the "top heavy" and discrimination rules.[30] It also encouraged the automatic escalation of default rates so that participants would not be stuck at low contribution rates, and allowed employers to default participants into qualified higher-yielding investments without being exposed to fiduciary liability.

With the passage of the PPA, hopes were high that many of the problems associated with the accumulation phase in 401(k) plans had been addressed. But despite the benefits associated with automatic provisions in 401(k) plans, surveys have found that only about 40 percent of plans offer automatic enrollment, and the large majority of these plans only apply the policy to new hires; and even fewer plans offer automatic escalation of default contribution rates.[31] The cost of these policies to the employer is clearly one factor affecting these decisions, but employers are also apparently concerned that their employees would not like automatic enrollment.

EXPAND COVERAGE

As noted above, at any moment in time, only half the private sector workforce is covered by an employer-sponsored plan of any sort. For decades, policymakers have tried to solve the coverage problem, primarily by introducing simpler products, such as the SIMPLE (Savings Incentive Match Plan for Employees of Small Employers), that could be adopted by small business.[32] The trend data on coverage, however, clearly indicates that simplifying plan design will never lead to a major expansion of coverage.[33]

Recognizing the difficulty in getting small employers to introduce employer-sponsored retirement savings plans, the Obama administration has proposed "automatic IRAs." IRAs are savings vehicles designed to provide those without an employer-sponsored plan an opportunity to save on a tax-deferred basis, yet fewer than 10 percent of eligible workers make a tax-favored contribution to an IRA.[34] The administration's recent proposal would automatically enroll those workers without workplace retirement plans in IRAs through payroll contributions. The contributions would be voluntary—employees would be free to opt out—and would be matched by the Savers Tax Credit for eligible workers.

The key deficiency of the "automatic IRA" proposal is that it provides additional savings opportunities *only* for those without coverage, on the assumption that those who currently work for employers with a 401(k) plan will end up with adequate retirement resources. As noted above, such a presumption is incorrect: 401(k) balances were inadequate before the financial crisis and are clearly inadequate now.

Adding a New Tier of Retirement Saving

One way to make the nation's retirement income system larger and safer would be to add a new tier of individual retirement saving accounts that comes as close as possible to duplicating the best aspects of the defined benefit model (see Figure 11.4). This tier would bolster retirement security both for low-wage workers facing declining Social Security replacement rates and for middle- and upper-wage workers who must increasingly rely on voluntary and inadequate 401(k) plans as their only supplement to Social Security.

This additional tier would aim to provide a stream of annuity income that replaces about 20 percent of pre-retirement income once the system matures. Since contributions would take decades to produce this level of replacement, the new tier would not provide much in relief to those currently approaching retirement, but would be of great value to middle-age and younger future retirees who are

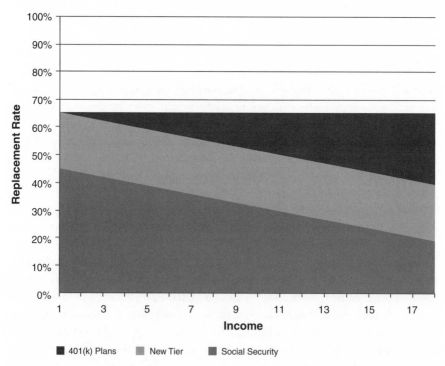

Figure 11.4: Additional Tier of Funded, Privately Managed Retirement Saving.
Note: Ages are as of 1999. 401(k)s did not exist in their current form in 1975, so we assume that annual contributions of 9 percent of salary went to a profit-sharing plan that was converted to a 401(k) after 1981. Sources: Author's calculations based on Center for Research in Security Prices (2009); Ibbotson Associates (2006); Barclay's Capital (2009); U.S. Board of Governors of the Federal Reserve System, *Survey of Consumer Finances*, 1995; U.S. Bureau of Labor Statistics (2009); and Standard & Poor's Index Services (2009).

unlikely to do as well on their investments as baby boomers have done, even with the recent market collapse. This proposed 20 percent wage replacement rate from the new tier, combined with 36 percent (before Medicare deductions and taxes) from Social Security, would produce 56 percent of pre-retirement earnings for the average earner at age 65. Middle- and high-income workers would also want to save more through 401(k)s and other mechanisms.

The new tier should be funded and should reside in the private sector. As we have just learned, funded and pay-as-you-go systems are subject to different kinds of risks. While 401(k) plans were decimated by the financial collapse, the pay-as-you-go Social Security system continued to send out checks and suffered only a modest increase in its long-run costs due to the recession-induced decline in pay-roll taxes. Thus, adding a funded tier would allow the retirement income system to diversify the risks.

Politically, it seems important for the new tier to reside in the private sector. (A question remains whether it would be better for the system to be employer-based or to be set up as a system of regional cooperatives.)[35] If financial services firms do not see some potential gain from the new system, they will have every incentive to resist change. Even if the opportunity for profit were minimal in the new tier—funded with low-cost index equity funds and inexpensive bond funds—financial firms could be supportive if they viewed participation as a way to get their foot in the door with sponsors (i.e., the employers or regional co-ops offering the plans), hoping to sell them higher-profit products down the line.

Participation should be by default at a minimum and perhaps be made mandatory. As with 401(k)s, contributions would be paid by employees, and per-haps employers. Low-income workers would need some form of government sub-sidy. Participants should have very limited access to money before retirement, and benefits should be paid as annuities.

The introduction of a new tier should probably also be accompanied by revision in the tax treatment of retirement saving. Experts have suggested replacing existing tax deductions for retirement savings with a government matching contribution in order to end the regressivity of the current tax treatment. That is, workers' contributions to retirement plans would no longer be tax deductible and any *employer* contributions would be treated as taxable income. Under one proposal, the government would make a 30 percent matching contribution for contributions of up to $20,000 per person into a 401(k) account and up to $5,000 into an IRA.[36] The same match could apply to a new tier account. As under current law, earnings would continue to accrue tax-free, and withdrawals at retirement would continue to be taxed as regular income. While the proposal would be roughly revenue-neutral for the federal government, it would provide—unlike the current system—the same matching grant per dollar of saving to low-wage workers as to the higher paid.

The hard question is how these monies should be invested. The challenge hinges on the trade-off between lifetime returns and the required contribution.

Equities offer a higher return, but they also bring greater risk, as the recent financial crisis proved. If accounts yielded a real return of 7 percent, as equities have done in the past, the contribution rate could be as low as 2 to 3 percent. If the assets were invested in bonds yielding 3 percent, the required contribution rate would be about 6 percent (see Table 11.1). The natural response is to try to take advantage of the equity premium and also protect the participant by offering guarantees. The question is whether guarantees are feasible and cost-effective. The message from standard financial theory is that private insurers cannot guarantee anything more than the riskless rate—between 1.5 and 2 percent.[37] And, at least historically, a riskless rate guarantee would have done nothing to smooth out fluctuations, since no cohort fully invested in equities would have received a lifetime return of less than 3.2 percent.

Indeed, looking around the world, private sector guarantees for defined contribution plans have been at very low rates.[38] In Germany and Japan, sponsors must offer participants an investment option that guarantees the nominal value of contributions.[39] That is, participants must be able to get back at least what they put in. Preserving the principal is equivalent to a zero percent nominal rate-of-return guarantee. Switzerland requires a guarantee of 2 percent nominal on employee contributions.[40] None of these options would have helped retirees in the past, and it is unclear how much comfort they would provide to participants going forward.[41]

Guaranteed government-sponsored plans tend to be more substantial. For example, the provident funds in Singapore and Malaysia offer a minimum nominal return of 2.5 percent.[42] Rate of return guarantees are also imbedded in many individual account systems in Latin America.[43] More substantial guarantees are possible in public systems, because citizens acting in concert through the government can

Table 11.1 **Combinations of Contribution Rates and Rates of Return Needed to Generate 20 Percent Replacement Rate at Retirement**

Contribution Rate	Rate of Return
2.0%	7.3%
3.0	5.8
4.0	4.7
5.0	3.8
6.0	3.1
7.0	2.4
8.0	1.8

Source: Author's calculations.

impose arrangements—such as intergenerational risk sharing—not possible by private credit agents acting on their own. Given that governments have tools not available to the private sector, it may be useful to reconsider the advantage of focusing on equity investment in the United States through the Social Security Trust Funds.

Capture Equity Returns in the Social Security System

The link between introducing a new tier of savings, as proposed above, and investing the Social Security Trust Fund in equities, is as follows. The higher the expected return on plan assets, the lower the cost will be of providing a retirement income target. Therefore, to keep costs low, participants in a new tier should invest a substantial portion of their funds in equities. But equity investment involves substantial risk, as we have just seen. Therefore, it may make more sense to take a broader view of the retirement income system and put equities in a component of the system where individuals can be protected through intergenerational risk sharing. Social Security appears to be the component that best satisfies this test. Equity investment would likely reduce the required contributions to Social Security, thereby freeing up funds for the new tier that could be invested relatively conservatively.

Some might argue for skipping the new tier altogether and simply expanding Social Security. But several considerations argue against such an approach: the new tier should be viewed solely as a mechanism for generating replacement income, and not as part of a program with redistributive goals; the funded nature of a new tier will supplement the pay-as-you-go structure of Social Security in a way that provides a more balanced retirement system; and, from a political standpoint, providing additional savings through the private sector is likely to be much more palatable than substantially expanding a government program.

THE THEORY

Theory would say that the ability to spread risk over a number of generations would improve the expected outcome from either a defined benefit or defined contribution plan. Indeed, a recent paper demonstrates that the expected real return could be raised by 100 basis points from such intergenerational risk sharing.[44] The gain comes because a better sharing of risks across generations makes it efficient to invest more in risky assets and thereby gain from the equity premium without increasing the risk at the individual household level. The challenge is that unless the contract is well specified—that is, participants know the exact rules of the game and can be assured that some mechanism will prevent decade after decade of bad experience—they will not be willing to continue to participate. And once rules are imposed—that the insurance fund remains solvent and workers receive a guaranteed minimum return on their contributions—the potential gains from spreading risks over generations, while still positive and substantial, are reduced somewhat.

THE PROPOSAL

The proposal to invest Social Security Trust Fund assets in equities, which emerged from the 1994–1996 Advisory Council on Social Security, would likely have two beneficial effects.[45]

The first potential benefit of this policy is that it would improve intergenerational risk sharing.[46] In general, efficient risk sharing requires individuals to bear more risk when young and less when old.[47] However, the young often hold no risky, high-yielding assets, and their implicit asset—Social Security—is invested in bonds. Introducing equities into the Social Security system has the potential to shift risk from the old to the young and could make all generations better off.[48]

The second argument in favor of equity investment, which is central to the theme of this chapter, is that it could make Social Security less expensive. Assuming that the portfolio restructuring had no effect on the real economy, the burden of paying for Social Security benefits would be met through a reduction in the capital income of investors, who would hold fewer equities and more bonds than they would otherwise, rather through higher payroll taxes.[49] To the extent that the realized return on Social Security assets turned out to be higher, participants would be required to contribute less to the system than they would have otherwise, thereby freeing up contributions that could be used to finance a new tier. (Of course, given that Social Security is facing a long-term deficit, the introduction of equities would mean that less in *additional* contributions would be required to finance scheduled benefits.)

The thorny issue remains of how to treat risk when doing the accounting of the system's finances.[50] Some experts argue that holding equities should reduce the projected contributions because, after all, stocks yield 7 percent after inflation and bonds yield only 3 percent. Others claim that this argument is nonsense. The higher expected return on equities reflects their greater risk, so any serious evaluation must "risk adjust" these returns. After accounting for risk, the amount of contributions needed to fund future pension obligations is the same, regardless of whether the assets are invested in stocks or bonds. Thus, from this perspective, projections using the risk-adjusted rate would produce no savings. However, if the government created an effective risk-sharing mechanism with clearly defined procedures for allocating benefit cuts and tax increases over generations when returns deviated from projections, then a case could be made for recognizing the higher returns from equities in evaluating the system's finances.

FOREIGN EXPERIENCE

Several countries have introduced equities as part of the financing of their national pension systems, and the recent financial meltdown has provided a stress test of this style of financing. In three prominent cases—Canada, the Netherlands, and Sweden—policymakers who designed the systems attempted to specify ahead of time, at least in part, the response to a drop in equity prices, but the outcome in each case is less than perfect. Nevertheless, a brief look at developments in these three countries highlights the nature of the challenge.

Canada

The Canada Pension Plan (CPP) is a defined benefit plan, similar to the U.S. Social Security system, that pays a benefit at age 65 roughly equal to 25 percent of average indexed covered earnings. Intergenerational equity—defined as each generation contributing much the same share of earnings while working and receiving benefits that replace the same share of earnings at retirement—is an explicit goal of the CPP. Given the rapid aging of the population down the road, this goal requires the CPP to build up a large fund to help pay benefits in the future. CPP assets are invested in a diversified actively managed portfolio, with a significant portion in equities.

The value of the assets was severely affected by the financial crisis. If the chief actuary were to report—which he has not done to date—that the minimum contribution necessary to sustain the program is greater than the current rate, the "stewards" of the system could increase contribution rates or reduce benefits to bring the program back into balance. They could also agree to defer the decision to the next triennial review. If the stewards fail to restore the program's finances or agree to defer the decision, automatic stabilizers go into effect that would increase contributions by half of the shortfall, amortized over 75 years, and eliminate the cost-of-living adjustment for retirees until the next triennial review. This automatic adjustment, which will typically fall disproportionately on current retirees, is not really designed to go into effect, but to pressure the stewards to act. Thus, although Canada appears to have automatic rules in place, those rules are designed to produce such an inequitable outcome that they serve as a powerful stimulus for political action.[51]

Sweden

The Swedish pension system also is designed to respond automatically to financial instability.[52] The system consists of two components: (1) a notional defined contribution (NDC, a pay-as-you-go model) plan with a contribution rate of 16 percentage points; and (2) funded individual accounts, the premium pension, with a contribution rate of 2.5 percent.

The financial crisis created a deficit in the NDC plan because the buffer funds, which hold 60 percent of their assets in equities, experienced a large loss and contributions slowed because of the ensuing recession.[53] These developments meant that the "balance ratio"—the ratio of the system's assets (the capitalized value of contributions and the current value of the buffer funds) to liabilities—fell below one.

A balance ratio of less than one triggers an automatic reduction in indexation of earned pension rights and current benefits. The adjustment occurs with a time lag, so the 4.5 percent scheduled *increase* in pension benefits in 2009 was not affected by the financial crisis. But, as a result of the automatic adjustment mechanism, pensions were scheduled to *decrease* by 4.6 percent in 2010 and are scheduled to decrease 1.7 percent in 2011. The cuts are designed to continue until the system regains financial balance.[54] With current projections, the outlook improves only in 2012. Any surpluses that occur after balancing are used to increase indexation until the value of pension credits and benefits are restored.

The proposed cuts generated an immediate response from the five Swedish political parties that stand behind the pension reform: they developed a proposal to smooth out income shocks over the coming years and maintain as stable a benefit as possible under the economic circumstances. They proposed a change in the procedure for valuing buffer fund assets from market value to a three-year average in order to smooth the pattern of +4.5 in 2009 and -4.6 in 2010.[55] The government has decided to go forward with the change. As a result, the impact will be more attenuated and therefore less severe, but it should take longer for the system to return to balance. Overall, the effect of the economic crisis on the NDC scheme is large, and the impact is primarily on a broad group of retirees.[56]

The Netherlands

When the financial crisis struck in 2008, the Dutch in some ways seemed perfectly situated to respond. In the wake of the 2000 so-called "perfect storm" (when falling stock returns and falling interest rates significantly hit pension funds), they had responsively changed the structure and risk-sharing of their quasi-public employer-based supplementary defined benefit plans, which cover 90 percent of workers.[57] Most of the defined benefit plans moved from basing benefits on final earnings to indexed career average earnings.[58] The new indexed career-average plans are much like traditional defined benefit plans, in that accrued pension rights are based on an employee's wages and years of service, and contribution rates can be raised in response to a funding shortfall. But they are also like defined contribution plans in that benefits are not strictly defined, but rather are tied to the fund's financial status—and, therefore, investment returns—via the annual indexation factor, which is applied to both the accrued rights of active workers and the benefits of retired workers. As a result, these hybrid defined benefit/defined contribution plans have two mechanisms—contribution rates and indexation—to respond to the underfunding created by the recent financial and economic crisis.

The Dutch government requires that a funding position below the nominal funding ratio of 105 percent be restored by the end of five years.[59] But in the case of severe underfunding, the government did not specify how a return to solvency should be accomplished. Should the employer make additional contributions? Should retirees absorb nominal cuts in benefits? Should workers accrue less in benefit rights? Or should all parties do nothing and hope the financial markets rebound? Thus, although the pension funds are ideal vehicles for intergenerational risk sharing, the intergenerational contract is incomplete because all possible responses have not been defined for extreme funding situations. This situation has led to inertia as policymakers attempt to figure out how to respond.[60]

LESSONS FROM ABROAD

The experience of countries that have used their social security programs as a vehicle for investing retirement savings in equities is reasonably promising. Government pension funds are ideal vehicles for intergenerational risk sharing, addressing a key concern in using equities in retirement savings programs.

The intergenerational risk-sharing mechanisms in the three systems reviewed—interestingly enough—placed a disproportionate share of the burden on current retirees, who tend to be the most risk-averse portion of the population. Ideally, those who are more risk averse should bear less of the aggregate risk.[61] Unlike retirees, employed workers can adjust their earnings and consumption and how long they might work; and because their remaining life expectancies are longer, they can more easily smooth consumption following an unexpected income shock, by making smaller adjustments over more years. These considerations should be taken into account when designing any intergenerational risk-sharing mechanism for the United States.

The Canadian, Swedish, and Dutch experiences also suggest that countries with such intergenerational risk-sharing mechanisms tend to have incomplete contracts. Property rights have not been defined for extreme funding situations, producing a combination of inertia and ad hoc adjustments as policymakers attempt to figure out how to respond. As Social Security and retirement income programs are extremely long-term arrangements, it is clearly impossible to expect intergenerational risk-sharing mechanisms to address all potential contingencies. But mechanisms designed in the future should be able to respond to the recent market shock.

Conclusion

The recent financial crisis has underscored the vulnerability of individuals in the current U.S. retirement income system. Given the rapid advent of 401(k)s and IRAs and the decline of traditional defined benefit plans among employers, most workers with pension coverage are left to shoulder investment risk on their own. Such exposure has led to a steep drop in the 401(k) account balance of the typical worker nearing retirement. And this exposure to risk is only one of two major shortcomings of the retirement income system. The second is that the whole system is contracting—including, notably, Social Security replacement rates—while retirement income needs are increasing due to rising longevity and health care costs.

In response, a new direction is needed that would tackle both problems—concentrated equity exposure and insufficient retirement income—at the same time. The best bet is to establish a new tier of universal retirement savings that would aim to replace about 20 percent of a worker's pre-retirement income. Individuals would be either strongly encouraged (through defaults) or required to join; the program could be largely managed in the private sector. However, the question of how to handle the investments in such accounts is a vexing one.

One option would be to have the government guarantee a rate of return. For such a guarantee to be consequential, it would need to be above the riskless rate. While an analysis of past market returns suggests that such an approach would have been quite feasible, guarantees for unknown prospective returns would work only if the government were less risk averse than the market as a whole. Theory suggests that the government could shoulder greater risk, but setting up a new system of universal accounts run by private investment managers with a meaningful government guarantee could prove challenging.

Therefore, a second approach would maintain the idea of a new account system, but would take away the challenge of equity risk. The new accounts would instead invest more conservatively, while the Social Security Trust Fund would take on the task of equity investment. This approach would thus use an existing mechanism to share equity risk across generations and, by reducing the cost of funding Social Security, it would free up government resources to help subsidize the new individual accounts. In this new system, 401(k)s would return to their original place as a third tier on top of a strengthened Social Security system and a universal second-tier savings account with low risk exposure.

The final challenge would be designing the Social Security equity investment program to adjust to financial shocks in an equitable way. Other countries with central equity investment have adjustment mechanisms, but the impact of the market crash suggests that these mechanisms are incomplete—they are not well-designed to spread risks optimally among workers, retirees, and future generations. Surmounting this hurdle is important for establishing a system that can stand the test of time.

Acknowledgements

The author would like to thank Josh Hurwitz and Laura Quinby for excellent research assistance. Three colleagues at the Center for Retirement Research—Andy Eschtruth, Richard Kopcke, and Steven Sass—provided more than the usual amount of help. Annika Sunden and Eduard Ponds kindly supplied updates on developments in Sweden and the Netherlands, respectively. Finally, Peter Diamond provided valuable comments throughout.

Notes

1. Steven A. Sass, *The Promise of Private Pensions: The First Hundred Years* (Cambridge, MA: Harvard University Press, 1997), 4–8.
2. Ibid, 10–11.
3. J. Moen, "Essays on the Labor Force and Labor Force Participation Rates: The United States from 1860 through 1950" (PhD diss., University of Chicago, 1987). In addition, the federal government greatly expanded Civil War pensions to include all veterans, not just the sick and disabled, and the availability of these pensions significantly expanded the retirement of Northern native-born men. Dora L. Costa, "Displacing the Family: Union Army Pensions and Elderly Living Arrangements," *Journal of Political Economy* 105 (1997): 1269.
4. The earliest programs were pension plans set up first by railroads and public utilities and then by large manufacturers and service-providing enterprises. Patrick W. Seburn, "Evolution of Employer-Provided Defined Benefit Pensions," *Monthly Labor Review* 114 (1991): 16.
5. Congressional Budget Office, *History of the Employment-Based Retirement System*, prepared by the United States Congressional Budget Office, 2006, http://www.cbo.gov/OnlineTaxGuide/Page_1A.htm.
6. *Social Security Act of 1935*, Public Law 271, 74th Cong., 1st sess. (August 14, 1935), 1 ("An act to provide for the general welfare by establishing a system of Federal old-age benefits, and by enabling the several States to make more adequate provision for aged persons . . . and the administration of their unemployment compensation laws").
7. Alicia Munnell and Steven A. Sass, *Working Longer: The Solution to the Retirement Income Challenge* (Washington, DC: Brookings Institution Press, 2008), 38.
8. These plans, which had become an essential component of corporate personnel systems, grew as corporate big business blossomed. The special tax treatment of employer pensions also became significantly more valuable in the face of mass income taxation. And unions, which had gained powerful collective bargaining rights, made pensions a standard component of labor agreements throughout the unionized sector in the decade that followed.
9. Greenspan Commission, *Report of the National Commission on Social Security Reform*, prepared by the National Commission on Social Security Reform for the President and Congress in accordance with Executive Order No. 12335, 1983, http://www.ssa.gov/history/reports/gspan.html.
10. ING North America Insurance Corporation, *Managing Key Risks to Make Your Retirement Income Last* (Winsor, CT: ING Special Report, 2009), http://www6.ingretirementplans.com/SponsorExtranet/ManagingKeyRisks.pdf.
11. For married couples (and most Americans retire as part of a married couple), Social Security already replaces a significantly smaller share of household earnings than it did as recently as 1990, and will replace even less going forward. Alicia H. Munnell, Geoffrey Sanzenbacher, and Mauricio Soto, "Working Wives Reduce Social Security Replacement Rates," *Issue in Brief* 7–15 (Chestnut Hill, MA: Center for Retirement Research at Boston College, 2007). The reason is the dramatic increase in the labor force participation of married women. As married households have increasingly relied on the earnings of working wives, these earnings have not produced a comparable increase in Social Security benefits due to the program's benefit structure.
12. Alicia H. Munnell and Annika Sunden, *Coming Up Short: The Challenge of 401(k) Plans* (Washington, DC: The Brookings Press, 2004).
13. See, e.g., Jonathan Skinner, "Are You Sure You're Saving Enough for Retirement?" *Journal of Economic Perspectives* 21 (2007): 59; Jack VanDerhei, "Measuring Retirement Income Adequacy: Calculating Realistic Income Replacement Rates," *Issue Brief* 297 (Washington, DC: Employee Benefits Research Institute, 2006); Alicia H. Munnell, Anthony Webb, and Luke Delorme, "A New National Retirement Risk Index." *Issue in Brief* 6–48 (Chestnut Hill, MA: Center for Retirement Research at Boston College, 2006).

14. Alicia H. Munnell, Richard W. Kopcke, Francesca Golub-Sass, and Dan Muldoon, "An Update on 401(k) Plans: Insights from the 2007 Survey of Consumer Finance." *Working Paper 2009–26* (Chestnut Hill, MA: Center for Retirement Research at Boston College, 2009).

15. Bureau of Labor Statistics. *Economic News Release: Table 4. Median Years of Tenure with Current Employer for Employed Wage and Salary Workers 25 Years and Over by Educational Attainment, Sex, and Age, January 2008*, prepared by the Bureau of Labor Statistics, United States Department of Labor, 2008, http://www.bls.gov/news.release/tenure.t04.htm.

16. See, e.g., Richard Thaler and Cass Sunstein, *Nudge: Improving Decisions about Health, Wealth, and Happiness* (New Haven, CT: Yale University Press, 2008).

17. David Laibson, Andrea Repetto, and Jeremy Tobacman, "Self-Control and Saving for Retirement," *Brookings Papers on Economic Activity* 1 (1998): 91.

18. See Richard Thaler and H. M. Shefrin, "An Economic Theory of Self-Control," *Journal of Political Economy* 89 (1981): 392; David Laibson, "Golden Eggs and Hyperbolic Discounting," *Quarterly Journal of Economics* 62 (1997): 443.

19. Luke Delorme, Alicia H. Munnell, and Anthony Webb, "Empirical Regularity Suggests Retirement Risks," *Issue in Brief* 6–41 (Chestnut Hill, MA: Center for Retirement Research at Boston College, 2006).

20. Ruth Helman, Craig Copeland, and Jack VanDerhei, "The 2010 Retirement Confidence Survey: Confidence Stabilizing, but Preparations Continue to Erode," *EBRI Issue Brief* 340 (Washington, DC: Employee Benefit Research Institute, 2010), http://www.ebri.org/pdf/briefspdf/EBRI_IB_03-2010_No340_RCS.pdf.

21. Alicia H. Munnell, Anthony Webb, and Luke Delorme, "A New National Retirement Risk Index," *Issue in Brief* 6–48 (Chestnut Hill, MA: Center for Retirement Research at Boston College, 2006).

22. Author's estimates based on the methodology described in Alicia H. Munnell and Dan Muldoon, "Are Retirement Savings Too Exposed to Market Risk?" *Issue in Brief* 8–16 (Chestnut Hill, MA: Center for Retirement Research at Boston College, 2008).

23. Ibid.

24. The defined benefit story is actually more complicated than the initial impact of the market collapse. If sponsors of private sector defined benefit plans respond to the required increase in contributions by freezing their plans and replacing them with 401(k)s, as they did in the wake of the "perfect storm" in 2000, then participants—primarily those in mid-career—will be hurt. If plan sponsors terminate their plans and turn their assets and liabilities over to the Pension Benefit Guaranty Corporation (PBGC), then those who expected a pension higher than $4,500 per month at 65 or those who retire before 65 and receive actuarially reduced benefits will suffer losses. Public plan participants actually have a higher degree of protection than their private sector counterparts. Many state courts have ruled that the public employer is prohibited from modifying the plan as it affects existing employees. Thus, current employees in most state and local plans will not see any changes in their retirement benefits as a result of the financial crisis. The important point for the following discussion, however, is not possible second-round effects on participants but rather that the immediate burden in defined benefit plans fell to the plan sponsor. Munnell and Muldoon, "Are Retirement Savings Too Exposed to Market Risk?"

25. In fact, a number of states have already increased employee contributions and reduced benefits for new employees primarily by increasing the age for full benefits, and two states—Minnesota and Colorado—have cut back on the cost-of-living adjustments for retirees. Jeanette Neumann, "Pension Cuts Face Test in Colorado, Minnesota," *Wall Street Journal*, June 12, 2010, http://online.wsj.com/article/SB10001424052748704463504575301032631246898.html.

26. The only real option for those approaching retirement who lost substantial sums is to work longer. Indeed, labor force activity of older workers increased in the wake of the market collapse. See Alicia H. Munnell, Dan Muldoon, and Steven A. Sass, "Recessions and Older

Workers," *Issue in Brief* 9–2 (Chestnut Hill, MA: Center for Retirement Research at Boston College, 2009). http://crr.bc.edu/briefs/recessions_and_older_workers_5.html.

27. See Andrew A. Samwick, "Social Security Reform in the United States." *National Tax Journal* 52 (1999): 817.

28. Brigitte C. Madrian and Dennis F. Shea, "The Power of Suggestion: Inertia in 401(k) Participation and Savings Behavior," *Quarterly Journal of Economics* 116 (2001): 1149; James Choi, David Laibson, and Brigitte C. Madrian, "Plan Design and 401(k) Savings Outcomes." *National Tax Journal* 57 (2004): 275.

29. Even before the Pension Protection Act, policymakers had attempted to reduce the cashing out of small balances in 401(k) plans through changes in Department of Labor regulations.

30. One obstacle for employers was state laws that required employers to obtain an employee's permission before making payroll deductions. The PPA amended ERISA to preempt state laws that conflict with automatic-enrollment provisions. To qualify for the safe harbor, the plan sponsor must enroll employees at a deferral rate of at least 3 percent of compensation, increase the employee's deferral percentage by at least 1 percentage point annually up to 6 percent of compensation, and provide matching or non-elective contributions for the non-highly compensated of 100 percent on the first 1 percent of contribution and 50 percent on the next 5 percent, for a total match of 3.5 percent. *Pension Protection Act*, U.S. Code 26 (2008) §§ 402–403.

31. Profit Sharing/401(k) Council of America, *52nd Annual Survey of Profit Sharing and 401(k) plans* (Chicago: Profit Sharing/401(k) Council of America, 2009); Vanguard, *How America Saves 2009: Defined Contribution Plan Data* (Washington, DC: Vanguard Center for Retirement Research, 2009), https://institutional.vanguard.com/iam/pdf/HAS09.pdf; David Owens, "Getting Retirement Savings Back on Track: Employer Views on the 401(k) and Financial Education in the Workplace," *CFO Research Services* (Boston, MA: CFO Research Services and Charles Schwab, 2009), http://www.aboutschwab.com/media/pdf/getting_retirement_back_on_track.pdf; Kathi S. Brown, *Automatic 401(k) Plans: Employer Views on Enrolling New and Existing Employees* (Washington, DC: AARP Research and Strategic Analysis (2010); Towers Watson, "Automatic Enrollment in 401(k) Plans Now Dominates at Large Employers, Towers Watson Survey Finds" (New York: Towers Watson, 2010) cites slightly higher numbers.

32. Firms with fewer than 100 employees can offer a SIMPLE, which can be set up as an IRA for each employee or as a 401(k) plan. The SIMPLE has a number of advantages. Firms can either match the contributions or contribute a fixed percentage of their payroll. Once established, the SIMPLE is administered by the employer's financial institution, and does not even require the employer to file an annual financial report. Furthermore, most employers are eligible for tax credits the first three years after starting the SIMPLE. Employee Benefits Security Administration, *SIMPLE IRA Plans for Small Businesses,* prepared by the Bureau of Labor Statistics, U.S. Department of Labor, 2009, http://www.dol.gov/ebsa/publications/simple.html.

33. This outcome is not surprising in that costs and administrative considerations are not the main reason that small businesses do not offer plans. Much more important are business-related concerns, such as uncertainty of revenue, and employee considerations, such as high turnover or a preference for cash wages. Employee Benefits Research Institute, *The 2003 Small Employer Retirement Survey (SERS) Summary of Findings* (Washington, DC: Economic Benefits Research Institute, 2003), http://www.ebri.org/pdf/surveys/sers/2003/03sersof.pdf.

34. Department of the Treasury, *General Explanations of the Administration's Fiscal Year 2010 Revenue Proposals,* prepared by the United States Department of the Treasury, 2009, https://www.treas.gov/offices/tax-policy/library/.grnbk09.pdf. And although IRAs can hold enormous amounts of money and may thus appear to contain a greater proportion of overall retirement savings, these balances largely reflect rollovers from 401(k) plans.

35. The ERISA Industry Committee, *A New Benefit Platform for Life Security* (Washington, DC: The ERISA Industry Committee, 2007), http://www.eric.org/forms/uploadFiles/ccea00000007.

filename.ERIC_New_Benefit_Platform_FL0614.pdf; Keith P. Ambachtsheer, *Pension Revolution: A Solution to the Pensions Crisis* (Hoboken, NJ: John Wiley & Sons, 2007).

36. See William G. Gale, Jonathan Gruber, and Peter R. Orszag, "Improving Opportunities and Incentives for Saving by Middle- and Low-Income Households," *Hamilton Project Discussion Paper* (Washington, DC: Brookings Institution, 2008), http://www.brookings.edu/comm/events/Gruberpowerpoint.pdf. The 30 percent match would apply for all contributions up to the minimum of either: (a) 10 percent of adjusted gross income; or (b) $20,000 for 401(k) accounts and $5,000 for IRAs. These limits would be indexed for inflation.

37. This assessment assumes that insurers share the market's aversion to risk with a coefficient of relative risk aversion of 2. This figure rests at the low end of the range reported in the literature, which tends to cluster between 2 and 10, depending in part on whether the estimates are derived from portfolio theory, purchases of insurance, economic experiments, or preferences over lotteries (Chetty 2003).

38. Turner and Rajnes (2003) finds that, in several cases, guarantees have been reduced in response to declining market returns.

39. Germany: The supplementary pension system, launched in 2001, requires that plans—in order to receive preferential tax treatment—guarantee the nominal value of contributions at retirement (zero-percent nominal rate of return). See Allianz Global Investors AG (2009b). Japan: The pension system introduced in 2001 requires employers to provide at least three investment options, one of which guarantees the nominal value of contributions at retirement (zero-percent nominal return). See Clark and Mitchell (2002).

From 1990–2004, the Austrian government required private pension funds (*Pensionskasse*) to guarantee a minimum rate of return on all investments. A 2004 reform made this provision optional, allowing pension funds to drop the guarantee upon joint consent from employers and employees. See Allianz Global Investors AG (2009a).

40. Switzerland: Employer-based defined contribution plans are required to guarantee annual returns on mandatory employee and employer contributions. From 1985–2003, the guarantee was 4 percent. In the wake of the bad performance of capital markets, it has been reduced gradually to 2 percent for 2009. See Allianz Global Investors AG (2009c).

41. Ghilarducci (2008) proposes a plan for the United States with a more substantial guaranteed real return of 3 percent and would allow a Board of Trustees to raise the guarantee if the economy performs better than expected.

42. World Bank (2005).

43. Walliser (2003).

44. Christian Gollier. "Intergenerational Risk-Sharing and Risk-Taking of a Pension Fund." *Journal of Public Economics* 92 (2008): 1463–1485. See also Jiajia Cui, Frank de Jong, and Eduard Ponds, "Intergenerational Risk Sharing within Funded Pension Schemes," *Discussion Paper* 2006–016 (2009), which demonstrates that, for more realistic collectively funded pension arrangements than those described by Gollier, well-structured intergenerational risk sharing can be welfare enhancing.

45. For more details on the proposal, see U.S. 1994–1996 Advisory Council on Social Security, *Report of the 1994–1996 Advisory Council on Social Security*, prepared by the Advisory Council on Social Security for the Social Security Administration, 1997, http://www.ssa.gov/history/reports/adcouncil/report/toc.htm; Alicia H. Munnell and Pierluigi Balduzzi, *Investing the Social Security Trust Funds in Equities* (Washington, DC: American Association of Retired Persons Public Policy Institute (AARP PPI), 1998). http://assets.aarp.org/rgcenter/econ/9802_sstrust.pdf. Alicia H. Munnell and Steven A. Sass, *Social Security and the Stock Market: How the Pursuit of Market Magic Shapes the System* (Kalamazoo, MI: W.E. Upjohn Institute for Employment Research, 2006).

46. Henning Bohn, "Social Security Reform and Financial Markets," in *Social Security Reform: Links to Savings, Investment, and Growth*, eds. Steven Sass and Robert Triest (Boston: Federal Reserve Bank of Boston, 1997), 193–227; Peter A. Diamond, "Macroeconomic Aspects of Social Security Reform." *Brookings Papers on Economic Activity* 2 (1997): 1–66.

47. The reason is that it is easier for the young to work more if they suffer a capital loss. They can also average returns over time and take advantage of the fact that declines in stock prices are typically associated with higher returns in the next period. As the old are in the process of liquidating their equity holdings, they cannot take full advantage of this property. It is also reasonable to assume that the young are less risk-averse and more inclined to carry stock market risk.

48. Kenneth J. Arrow and Robert C. Lind, "Uncertainty and the Evaluation of Public Investment Decisions." *American Economic Review* 60 (1970): 364.

49. Questions about the economic impact of investing trust funds assets in equities have been address by Bohn, "Social Security Reform and Financial Markets" (1997), and Peter Diamond and John Geanakoplos, "Social Security Investment in Equities," *American Economic Review* 93 (2003): 1047. Bohn suggests that the effect of portfolio restructuring relative rates of return would be expected to be small. The equity premium would decline to reflect the increased efficiency of risk bearing, as equity risk spreads to the young as well as the old. This decline should be modest, however. Some movement would also be expected in interest rates. Interest rates are largely determined by the supply and demand for physical capital, and while the supply of capital will not change, the demand will be affected by the reduction in the equity premium. Again, the movement would be expected to be small. Diamond and Geanakoplos found that if the population is heterogeneous with respect to saving, production, assets, and taxes, then the portfolio shift will have real effects on the economy. Social Security diversification would weakly increase interest rates, lower the equity premium, decrease safe investment, and increase risky investment. The effects on aggregate investment and long-term capital values depend on assumptions about technology.

50. For a more extensive discussion of this point, see Alicia H. Munnell, Steven A. Sass, and Mauricio Soto. "Yikes! How to Think about Risk?" *Issue in Brief* 5–27 (Chestnut Hill, MA: Center for Retirement Research at Boston College, 2005),

51. Ashby H. B. Monk and Steven A. Sass, "Risk Pooling and the Market Crash: Lessons from Canada's Pension Plan." *Issue in Brief* 9–12 (Chestnut Hill, MA: Center for Retirement Research at Boston College, 2009).

52. Several characteristics contribute to financial stability. Benefits are linked to lifetime contributions; the account balance grows with annual contributions and the rate of return on the account. The rate of return is set equal to per capita real wage growth to link earned pension rights to earnings of the working population. At retirement, the account balance is converted to an annuity by dividing by an annuity divisor so benefits are automatically tied to changes in life expectancy. World Bank, "Notional Defined Contribution Plans as a Pension Reform Strategy," World Bank Pension Reform Primer (Washington, DC: World Bank, 2001), http://siteresources.worldbank.org/INTPENSIONS/Resources/395443–1121194657824/PRPNoteNotionalAccts.pdf.

53. The bulk of the funded individual accounts, the premium pension, was also invested in equities and thus affected by the stock market crash. However, benefit payments from the Premium Pension are still modest, so the effect on current beneficiaries will be small.

54. Balancing affects the NDC benefit. Beneficiaries without income-related benefits or with low NDC benefits can qualify for the minimum guarantee government benefit. Among Sweden's 1.8 million retirees, approximately 800,000 have some guarantee benefit. When the NDC benefit is reduced, guarantee benefits will increase for beneficiaries with both benefits. Thus, the net effect on total benefits will be less for this group.

55. The Social Insurance Agency was asked to analyze the issue and advised against the change.

56. Annika Sundén, "The Swedish Pension System and the Economic Crisis," *Issue in Brief* 9–25 (Chestnut Hill, MA: Center for Retirement Research at Boston College, 2009),

57. Niels Kortleve and Eduard Ponds, "Dutch Pension Funds in Underfunding: Solving Generational Dilemmas." *Working Paper* 2009–29 (Chestnut Hill, MA: Center for Retirement Research at Boston College, 2009), http://crr.bc.edu/images/stories/Working_Papers/wp_2009–29.doc_compatibility_mode.pdf.

58. In an average-wage plan, individuals accrue pension rights annually based on the salary earned in each year of their working life (rather than the final year, as in a final-pay plan). Earnings are usually revalued upward (or indexed) each year to take account of inflation or wage growth. The accrual rate is 2 percent or even higher, because a total pension equal to 80 percent of the average wage generally corresponds to 70 percent of final pay. After retirement, benefits are mostly inflation-indexed or wage-indexed.

59. The nominal funding ratio is the ratio of assets valued at market to accrued liabilities discounted by the nominal yield curve. In other words, the nominal liability is the value of liabilities when no indexation is provided.

60. Kortleve and Ponds explore various policy options and their distributional effects.

61. Nicholas Barr and Peter A. Diamond, *Pension Reform: A Short Guide* (Oxford: Oxford University Press, 2010).

12

Government's Role in Aging and Long-Term Care

ANDREW E. SCHARLACH AND AMANDA J. LEHNING

Introduction

The most notable feature of long-term care (LTC) policy in the United States is the lack of federal policy leadership. By default and design, responsibility for LTC has fallen to local and state governments, and ultimately to the elderly individuals requiring assistance and to their families. Lacking any overall nationwide approach, the United States has a fragmented patchwork of isolated community-based programs which, while sometimes innovative, serve relatively small numbers of disabled seniors. The consequences for those in need of LTC include inadequate care and substantial vulnerability to impoverishment in later life, especially for the most disadvantaged Americans. Further, this system depends on the unpaid contributions of family caregivers, who provide the majority of long-term care in this country, as well as the underpaid services of formal providers.

This chapter begins with a brief discussion of the context of long-term care policy in the United States, including an overview of long-term care settings and financing. We then describe disparities regarding care needs and related costs, followed by an analysis of public reimbursement and regulatory policies that have contributed to these disparities. We conclude with proposed policy solutions that could result in a more equitable distribution of long-term care costs and burdens, and help federal, state, and local governments better meet the needs of long-term care recipients and their families.

Context

Long-term care (LTC) refers to a "variety of ongoing health and social services provided for individuals who need assistance on a continuing basis because of physical or mental disability."[1] Approximately 10 million adults in this country require some type of long-term care assistance, and 60 percent of these individuals are older adults, representing about one out of every six persons age 65 or older.[2] The number of older adults requiring assistance is projected to rise dramatically during the first half of the twenty-first century as a result of three related trends: (1) the aging of the baby boom generation, those 80 million Americans born between 1946 and 1965, who will begin turning 65 in 2011;[3] (2) increased longevity after the age of 65, resulting in a 350 percent increase in the number of persons age 85 and older over the past century;[4] and (3) increased rates of chronic illness and disability among baby boomers, potentially reversing health improvements experienced by current cohorts of elderly persons.[5]

WHERE IS LONG-TERM CARE PROVIDED?

Long-term care services are provided by a wide variety of formal sources (e.g., government agencies, nonprofit organizations, for-profit organizations) and informal sources (e.g., family, friends, neighbors). Informal sources provide the vast majority of long-term care assistance. Of elders who receive in-home care, about two-thirds receive care only from informal sources and only about 4 percent receive no assistance from family members or friends.[6]

Formal long-term care settings include nursing homes, assisted living and other residential facilities, and home- and community-based services. About 20 percent of disabled older adults (equivalent to about 4 percent of all elderly persons) reside in a nursing facility,[7] and this percentage has been dropping steadily even as the population has gotten older. Assisted living facilities (ALFs) cater to a somewhat less disabled population than nursing homes and offer considerably more privacy and autonomy. ALFs have expanded rapidly in recent years and now serve about 10 percent of all disabled older adults, although the lack of consistent definitions makes estimates unreliable. There is significant variability across states and even from one facility to another, with some settings virtually indistinguishable from nursing homes and others offering shared accommodations but minimal actual care.[8] Almost 80 percent of elders who require long-term care do not live in an institution and receive home- and community-based services (HCBS) such as home health care, personal assistance services, household chore services, companionship, or adult day health care.[9]

WHO PAYS FOR LTC?

LTC expenses totaled almost $207 billion in 2005.[10] Nursing home and home health costs nearly quadrupled between 1980 and 2005, and some predict that costs could quadruple again by 2050.[11] These costs are paid for by a combination of public programs, private long-term care insurance (LTCI), and individual consumers' out-of-pocket expenditures. However, much of the money spent on LTC by consumers and their families (e.g., for home health aides who are not employed by an agency) is not monitored by the Centers for Medicare and Medicaid Services (CMS) or state governments because of the lack of adequate tracking systems, and is therefore not reflected in national estimates of long-term care spending. Moreover, LTC can be accompanied by a variety of secondary tangible and intangible costs, such as lost wages incurred by family caregivers, which are not included in national cost calculations.

Many Americans believe that Medicare, the public health insurance program for older adults, provides LTC coverage. Yet Medicare pays for only about a fifth of all official LTC expenditures. While it covers temporary nursing home and home health treatment for an acute illness or injury under Part A (inpatient care), reimbursement is limited to a maximum of 100 days of care in a skilled nursing facility, and only when services can be expected to improve functioning or provide rehabilitation, rather than simply maintaining individuals who have chronic disabilities.[12]

Medicaid, which covers health care costs for individuals with low incomes and minimal assets, accounts for around half of reported LTC expenditures.[13] Because nursing home care is a mandatory entitlement under Medicaid, the vast majority of Medicaid LTC spending is for institutional care ($47 billion for nursing home care versus $17 billion for home- and community-based care in 2007).[14] However, the percentage of Medicaid LTC expenditures for home- and community-based services has been growing steadily, nearly doubling in the past decade as a result of expanded availability of options by which states can use Medicaid funds to pay for home care and community services.

In addition, Older Americans Act funding provides about $1.2 billion annually to states to pay for community-based social and nutrition services of potential benefit for seniors, including: Meals on Wheels, congregate meals, senior center programs, health promotion, transportation, information and referral, and support for family caregivers.[15] Older Americans Act services are available to individuals age 60 or older, but states are required to target services to persons with the "greatest social or economic needs, with particular attention to low-income minority individuals."[16]

Although about 9 percent of individuals age 55 or older have purchased a long-term care insurance policy[17] and more than six million policies are currently in force,[18] private long-term care insurance and health insurance combined made up only 7 percent of long-term care spending in 2005.[19] Direct out-of-pocket spending by individual consumers outpaces that of private insurance, accounting for a little less than one-fifth of long-term care spending.[20]

Conditions and Features of Risk

Three features of the distribution of costs and risk in the LTC field stand out. First, across gender, race/ethnicity, socioeconomic status, and living arrangement, there are dramatic disparities in disability rates and the consequent need for LTC. Nearly 69 percent of older adults needing LTC are women.[21] A significantly higher percentage of older African Americans and Hispanics report limitations in activities of daily living (ADLs) compared to whites.[22] People who never graduated from high school are at twice the risk for physical limitations as high school graduates.[23] Those in the bottom 20 percent of the income distribution experience impaired physical functioning at a rate of three or four times higher than those in the top 20 percent, and lower earners' level of physical functioning deteriorates with age twice as fast as higher earners.[24] Finally, older adults who live alone require greater long-term care expenditures than those who live with family.[25]

Second, U.S. long-term care policy is based on a residual or "safety net" model, in which individuals and their families are required to take full responsibility (but often with insufficient tools) for providing, managing, and paying for LTC until their resources are exhausted. Only after individuals become impoverished does public support become available. In a recent national poll of Americans age 40 and older conducted by the National Academy of Social Insurance, the majority of respondents were greatly concerned about their ability to pay for LTC, and 70 percent believed that the government should do more to help people meet the costs of LTC.[26] For the average 65-year-old, lifetime costs for uncovered long-term care are estimated at $44,000, far exceeding estimated lifetime costs for uncovered medical care ($16,000).[27]

Third, the quality of care—and, ultimately, the quality of life of older adults requiring assistance and their families—is both uneven and neglected. Many older adults who need long-term care remain inadequately served or not served at all by the existing system. For example, many nursing homes provide care that is of poor quality. In 2001, the Institute of Medicine (IOM) Committee on Improving the Quality of Long-Term Care concluded "serious problems concerning quality of care apparently continue to affect residents of this country's nursing homes," including "pain, pressure sores, malnutrition, and urinary incontinence."[28] While the situation in these facilities has improved markedly in the past 10 years as a result of standardized reporting requirements and industry-initiated innovations (e.g., Minimum Data Set, Medicare's online Nursing Home Compare, Eden Alternative model), one out of every six nursing homes continues to experience serious quality problems, with rates varying dramatically, from 6 to 54 percent of homes across the 50 states.[29] There are no federal quality standards and little state or local oversight regarding assisted living.[30] In terms of home- and community-based services, approximately 30 percent of disabled older adults in the United States have unmet needs for basic personal care (compared to only about 1 percent of this population in Sweden).[31]

Moreover, this highly inequitable LTC system is even more burdensome on the most vulnerable populations than it initially may appear, as it is dependent upon the unpaid contributions by family members and the underpaid contributions of formal care providers, who predominantly are women and minorities. Informal caregivers, most of whom are women, have been called a "shadow workforce" in LTC, whose uncompensated contributions are essential to the system's functioning yet are largely invisible in public calculations of costs.[32] Unpaid care by family members and other informal sources is valued at more than $375 billion a year,[33] making informal care the largest source of long-term care in the United States.

Caregiving family members also incur substantial secondary costs, including lifetime economic losses of approximately $650,000 in foregone wages, pension benefits, and Social Security benefits.[34] Family caregivers are at increased vulnerability for poor physical health[35] and experience higher rates of psychological distress.[36] When family caregivers experience high rates of physical or psychological stress, their elderly care recipients have a 150 to 200 percent greater risk of entering a nursing home.[37] The deleterious impacts of caregiving contribute to women's long-term risk for chronic disabling conditions, thereby increasing their eventual likelihood of becoming LTC recipients themselves. The demands on family members have increased as acute care hospitals (encouraged by Medicare's payment policies as well as changes in private payers' behavior) have discharged patients sooner with greater ongoing needs for assistance.

Nursing aides, orderlies, and home health aides comprise the majority of the paid long-term care workforce. Approximately 80 to 90 percent of these direct care workers are women, and half are members of racial and ethnic minority groups.[38] About 25 percent of home care workers and 15 percent of nursing home aides speak a language other than English at home.[39] Low wages and limited benefits mean that many of these direct care workers are also poor. In 2007, average hourly pay for direct care workers was $11.05, while home health aides made $9.88 per hour.[40] Further, approximately 25 percent of nursing home aides and slightly more than 40 percent of home care providers lack employer-based health insurance coverage.[41] This is particularly problematic given these workers' vulnerability to job-related injuries due to the physically and psychologically stressful nature of their work. Nursing home aides and orderlies rank third behind truck drivers and laborers and material movers in terms of work-related injuries and illnesses.[42] Yet where regulations exist, regulatory policy toward LTC is almost entirely concerned with protecting service recipients and pays little attention to providers' needs or concerns.[43]

In sum, America's LTC arrangements are highly inequitable and place an inordinate amount of responsibility and burden for LTC on unpaid family members and underpaid care providers. In addition, many of these same women and ethnic minority families already suffer from disadvantages associated with restricted access to the very services they are providing to others. This results in substantial unmet basic care needs among some of the most disadvantaged members of society, including persons who are disabled, poor, elderly, female, immigrants, or racial or ethnic minorities.

Causes of Increased Risk Burden

The increasing risk and responsibility for long-term care assumed by older adults and their families stems primarily from the absence of a comprehensive federal LTC policy and a financing system that favors expensive nursing home care over other forms of long-term care.

Bias in public reimbursement and regulatory policies continues to privilege nursing home care over other forms of residential care and over home and community care, even though older adults consistently prefer to age at home rather than in care facilities, and there is no evidence that nursing home care produces better health outcomes. As the largest source of funding for LTC in the United States, Medicaid reimbursement policies exert a strong influence over access to various forms of long-term care. Nursing home care is a mandatory entitlement under Medicaid, and consumes about 70 percent of public long-term care expenses.[44] Nursing home care is expensive. In 2008, average national rates for a semi-private room in a nursing home were $191 per day, or $69,715 per year.[45] Based on conservative estimates of the cost of being in a nursing home for two or three years, 73 percent of older adults would need to impoverish themselves to pay for LTC costs, either by relying on Medicaid immediately or by spending down their assets in order to qualify for Medicaid coverage.[46] Nursing home usage is highest among white Americans[47] and individuals who live alone.[48]

In contrast, Medicaid reimbursement for assisted living varies dramatically from state to state[49] and is frequently lacking or inadequate, leaving non-skilled residential care as a primarily out-of-pocket expense. It is a costly expense: in 2008, the average rate for assisted living care was $3,031 per month, or $36,372 per year.[50] Perhaps not surprisingly, given the limited Medicaid reimbursement for assisted living, individuals living in assisted living facilities are more likely to be white, single, and better educated, compared to their counterparts in nursing homes.[51]

Finally, home- and community-based LTC services are paid for through a mix of Medicaid (roughly half of spending), Medicare (roughly a quarter), and private sources.[52] Medicaid spending for home- and community-based care is provided primarily under the Sec. 1915(c) HCBS waiver program,[53] which allows states to use Medicaid dollars to pay for community-based long-term care services for individuals who would otherwise be cared for in institutional settings.[54] However, Medicaid HCBS waivers are governed by eligibility standards that are more restrictive than those for nursing facilities, and services are offered only in select locations and for select populations, often constraining access for some of the most disadvantaged elder. In 2005, states on average spent only $12,627 per person on Medicaid-funded community-based care, as compared with approximately $60,000 per person for nursing home care.[55] Utilization of home- and community-based care is lower for older adults who are female, live alone, and have lower levels of educational attainment.[56]

Private long-term care insurance currently does little to rectify the public reimbursement bias toward expensive nursing home care and to improve access to long-term care. While long-term care insurance could allow older adults and their families to cover LTC expenses without exhausting all of their financial resources, currently LTCI plays a relatively small role. Individual purchases of LTCI are constrained by a number of factors, including: the high cost of premiums; underwriting practices that make policies unavailable to those most likely to need long-term care; benefits that do not keep pace with rising costs or changing care practices; complex product designs that are confusing to purchasers; and, frequent shake-ups in the insurance market that prompt concerns about the long-term viability of the companies offering LTCI products.[57] Disincentives such as these enhance the risk of adverse selection, whereby individuals with a relatively low probability of needing LTC are deterred from purchasing LTCI products, resulting in a high-risk pool of covered individuals, which drives up LTCI premiums and thereby further discourages low-risk individuals from purchasing LTCI products. Purchase and effective utilization of LTCI products is also constrained by the demands on individual purchasers to understand complicated policies, make complex calculations regarding future risk of requiring various types of LTC, and access policy benefits at a time of substantial physical and cognitive frailty.[58] Costly premiums and complex policy information contribute to dramatically lower purchasing rates among individuals who have low or moderate incomes, limited assets, and have not attended college.[59]

Federal and state governments have struggled for years to rein in the high costs of LTC, either by constraining access to nursing homes or by trying to create incentives for less expensive community-based care. However, efforts thus far to reduce costs by keeping people out of nursing homes have proven most successful only when those with severe functional impairments receive most of their care from family members.[60] Further, innovative community-based programs that aim to provide comprehensive long-term care (e.g., Program of All-Inclusive Care for the Elderly, California's Multipurpose Senior Services Program, or Medicaid coverage of assisted living) serve relatively small numbers of seniors compared to the at-need population overall.

Policy Responses to Date

Recent public policy has focused primarily on trying to reduce federal responsibility for LTC by (1) promoting increased responsibility among individuals and their families, and (2) shifting the federal government's fiscal risk to state and local entities.

FEDERAL POLICIES AND PROGRAMS

Clinton Era LTC Initiatives

Although the Clinton administration failed in efforts to pass comprehensive health care legislation, it did push through federal LTC policies directed at supporting family care. The Family and Medical Leave Act, passed in 1993, enables qualified workers to take up to 12 weeks a year of unpaid, job-protected leave to care for an ill parent, spouse, or child; provide care to a new child; or because of personal illness. Restrictions on eligibility limit the act's applicability to only about 30 percent of family caregivers. The National Family Caregiver Support Program, established in 2000 as part of the reauthorization of the Older Americans Act (PL 106–501), provided (a modest) $125 million to enable local area agencies on aging to offer support services to adults caring for elderly family members.

The second major aspect of Clinton's LTC policy was a coordinated effort to promote individual responsibility through the purchase of private LTC insurance. Central to this effort was an information campaign designed to educate consumers about the fact that the government would neither provide care for them in their later years nor protect them against the overwhelming costs they were likely to incur in paying for that care. The federal government hoped to encourage employers to step in and offer LTC insurance as an employee benefit by serving as a "model employer" and offering group long-term care insurance to federal employees and annuitants.[61] The Kennedy-Kassebaum Health Insurance Portability and Accountability Act of 1996 also promoted the purchase of LTC insurance by making LTC insurance premiums and benefits tax-deductible as long as policies met certain basic standards designed to protect consumers.

Bush Era LTC Initiatives

As with the Clinton administration, a major thrust of the George W. Bush administration's LTC policy was to encourage individual responsibility for care and its associated costs. Reflecting the notion of an "ownership society," a centerpiece of Bush's LTC policy was the "Own Your Future" campaign, designed to convince Americans of the importance of planning ahead for their own long-term care needs. Aging and Disability Resource Centers were established in 175 communities as one-stop information points "to make it easier for consumers to learn about and access the existing services and supports that are available in their communities."[62] CMS also launched web sites to assist consumers to make appropriate choices among nursing home and home health care providers. In addition, the Administration on Aging launched an Evidence-Based Prevention Grants Program designed to support a small number of such programs and provide elderly consumers with better information about their effectiveness.

Obama Era LTC Initiatives

In March 2010, President Barack Obama signed into law the Patient Protection and Affordable Care Act (H.R. 3590) (PPACA), which included as Title VIII a "Community Living Assistance Services and Supports Act" (CLASS Act). This voluntary insurance program, to be funded by payroll deductions, will provide a cash benefit to offset some of the cost of LTC services, such as home health care, adult day health care, accessible transportation, and institutional care in an assisted living facility or nursing home.[63] Eligibility will be limited to adults with functional and/ or cognitive impairments who have contributed to the program for at least five years and were employed for at least three of those five years. While the administration has yet to put forth many of the details of this program, and the design will not be finalized until 2012, the Congressional Budget Office estimates that initial average premiums of $123/month will be required to provide benefits of about $75 per day.[64] The CLASS Act is expected to reduce federal spending on long-term care by billions of dollars[65] by reducing the use of Medicaid, especially for institutional care.

Olmstead Decision

One of the most influential federal actions affecting LTC in the past 30 years was not promulgated by the executive or legislative branches, but rather by the judiciary. In 1999, the Supreme Court issued a decision in *Olmstead v. L.C.* that redefined LTC as a civil rights issue, a holding that has had both positive and negative consequences for the provision of LTC.[66] In redefining the issue, the decision helped to shift the focus of LTC from institutional care to community care, thereby simultaneously shifting fiscal and regulatory responsibility from the federal level to the state and local levels, and increasing the responsibility borne by LTC recipients and their families.

In its *Olmstead* decision, the Supreme Court held that people with disabilities have the right to live in "the most integrated setting appropriate for their needs," and that public entities must make "reasonable accommodations" to provide the range and level of services that are necessary to integrate disabled individuals into mainstream society to the fullest extent possible.[67] States also were required to develop comprehensive plans to end unnecessary institutionalization. This requirement, enhanced by the threat of litigation from the Department of Justice, has helped to focus states' attention on LTC, especially ways to reduce nursing home utilization and its associated costs. At the same time, it has provided legal cover for states' efforts to save money by restricting admission to nursing homes and other high-cost care facilities, potentially reducing care options for some high-risk individuals.

STATE AND LOCAL INITIATIVES

Rebalancing

In the wake of the *Olmstead* decision, states initiated efforts to rebalance their LTC expenditures in order to achieve a more equitable distribution between institutional care and home- and community-based services. These efforts were supported by the Bush administration's New Freedom Initiative, which gave states considerably greater flexibility in the use of Medicaid funds. As a result, HCBS waiver program expenditures nearly doubled between 1999 and 2004.[68]

The federal government has tried to support states' rebalancing efforts. In 2005, the federal Deficit Reduction Act gave states the ability to offer Medicaid-funded HCBS without having to obtain a waiver from the Department of Health and Human Services, and allowed states to develop different eligibility criteria for institutional care and community care, making it easier to qualify for HCBS. DRA also authorized a five-year, $1.75 billion "Money Follows the Person" demonstration project that provides enhanced federal funding for home- and community-based services that enable Medicaid-eligible individuals to move from institutional to community settings, with the hope of saving state dollars and potentially improving patient outcomes.[69] The recent Patient Protection and Affordable Care Act of 2010 extends these provisions, while also increasing federal assistance to states that opt to offer additional home- and community-based services to Medicaid recipients with disabilities who are eligible for institutional care.[70]

Rebalancing has proved difficult, however, due to administrative and financing fragmentation as well as the institutional bias of Medicaid eligibility. Nursing homes and community services are typically administered by different state departments and have separate budgets and funding sources.[71] Moreover, local government generally has responsibility for community-based services but not for institutional care, creating disincentives for keeping seriously disabled persons out of nursing homes.[72]

Managed Care Initiatives

Some states have attempted to control LTC costs by creating more integrated and efficient LTC financing and delivery systems. Oregon, Washington, and Vermont, for example, have dramatically reduced nursing home expenditures as a percentage of overall LTC costs by integrating administrative and funding authority for their LTC programs into a single state agency.[73] Other states (e.g., Arizona, Minnesota, and Massachusetts) have implemented managed care delivery systems, whereby all nursing home and community-based services, and many acute care services, are provided at a capitated rate.[74]

Consumer Direction Initiatives

A contrasting strategy for reducing government risk for LTC expenditures is to increase consumer responsibility for and control over the amount and type of assistance they receive. "Consumer direction" models vary from simply allowing consumers to participate in the process of hiring a care worker to enabling them to spend a predetermined amount "in whatever way they feel will best enable them to remain in the community."[75]

For example, the Cash & Counseling demonstration model (available under Medicaid) provides consumers with a monthly allowance, which they can use for virtually any care-related expenses, including household appliances, home modification, hiring workers to perform a wide range of non-care household activities, and deciding how much those workers will be paid.[76] Within an agreed-upon plan, consumers have total control (and responsibility) for hiring and overseeing care providers, which may include hiring family members and in some cases spouses.

Concerns have been raised about the lack of quality control for this program, especially for older persons whose cognitive impairment or other conditions compromise their ability to manage their own care. As some commentators have noted, "most states do relatively little to help clients cope with the management tasks inherent in consumer-direction, leaving clients to find their own way."[77] However, preliminary evaluations of Cash & Counseling and other consumer-directed models generally find that consumers report fewer safety concerns, fewer unmet needs, and greater satisfaction levels than do those receiving traditional agency care, at least in part because independent providers are better able to personalize care and are not constrained by agency guidelines and professional standards that limit work hours and authorized services.[78] It should be noted that some evaluations have found consumer-directed care to be more expensive than traditional agency-directed care,[79] even though workers receive less in the way of health benefits, vacation, and other fringe benefits.[80] There has been little attention paid to the potential increased risk and responsibility experienced by the service providers themselves under this model.

Solutions

FINANCING LTC

The current system of long-term care in the United States rests squarely on the shoulders of a large unpaid or underpaid labor force predominantly comprised of women and immigrants. More than two-thirds of older adults currently lack any protection against LTC costs, resulting in substantial unmitigated personal, family, and societal impacts. While government responses have expanded in recent years, potential enhancements to current government efforts are needed in four areas: public LTC coverage, special public coverage of catastrophic costs, individual LTC accounts, and private LTC insurance.

Comprehensive Public LTC Coverage

The CLASS Act represents a relatively efficient approach to financing LTC, although substantial concerns have been raised about the program's viability as currently proposed. As noted above, the program creates an insurance fund that will collect voluntary payroll deductions and provide a cash benefit to offset the cost of future LTC expenses for workers that paid in. In so doing, it represents the first real effort by the federal government to assist nonimpoverished individuals to reduce the risks associated with long-term care, while potentially reducing the burden on Medicaid.

The voluntary nature of the program, however, raises serious concerns about adverse selection, which could undermine the program's long-term viability. Participation is voluntary for employees and employers alike, and employers do not receive any subsidy to offset the administrative costs of participating. Further, the CLASS Act limits administrative costs to 3 percent of premiums, which will severely constrain the federal government's ability to market the program to employers and consumers who have been reluctant to purchase long-term care insurance in the past.[81] Consequently, it is not unlikely that the program will enroll a relatively small percentage of current workers, with enrollment skewed toward current workers who are nearing retirement age, have a reasonable expectation of needing LTC benefits in the near future, or are already disabled. To the extent that those who do enroll are more costly than average, premiums may need to be increased substantially, making the program even less attractive to those with little immediate need for long-term care services, further exacerbating adverse selection and endangering the program's actuarial soundness.

A second concern is the modest level of cash benefits initially proposed, with the expected benefit of $50 to $75 per day substantially lower than the typical reimbursement of $125 per day offered by private LTCI.[82] Although individuals with the necessary income could purchase supplementary private insurance if they wanted more extensive coverage, it seems likely that LTC will continue to require substantial financial and in-kind inputs from family members, and that individuals with limited incomes and assets will continue to suffer from inferior care, as will the estimated 75 percent of disabled individuals who do not participate in the program.

A more desirable and comprehensive approach would be a mandatory federal social insurance program providing a package of basic LTC services through a combination of dedicated payroll and income tax receipts. This could most easily be done by expanding Medicare to include LTC, and either making participation mandatory or offering sufficient incentives to attract the vast majority of eligible individuals. Medicare Part B, for example, while voluntary, enrolls about 90 percent of eligible older adults. Making this proposed LTC program mandatory would reduce premium costs from about $120 per month to only $40 per month, and would reduce Medicaid expenses by an additional $260 billion over a 25-year period, according to some estimates.[83]

Public Coverage of Catastrophic Costs

A more modest form of social insurance would provide protection against catastrophic long-term costs by liberalizing Medicaid eligibility, but only for individuals who have purchased private LTCI. For example, the long-term care partnership policies currently available in at least 30 states allow purchasers of approved LTCI policies to shelter some of their remaining assets rather than deplete them entirely in order to become eligible for Medicaid coverage.

Individual Long-Term Care Accounts

Tax-based savings accounts for health care expenses[84] could be expanded and liberalized to enable workers to set aside funds that could be used to purchase either long-term care services or long-term care insurance. Funds would grow tax-deferred and, other than regulation of abuse and some amount of forgone taxes, the government role would be modest. Making such savings accounts mandatory (as the federal government does with programs like Social Security), and beginning at younger ages, would spread the risk of long-term care costs dramatically. However, while tax benefits could be structured to be more equitable, tax breaks are inherently more beneficial to higher-income taxpayers, both because of higher marginal tax rates and their greater likelihood of purchasing private LTCI products. Therefore, individual tax-based savings programs could at best be only one component of a comprehensive long-term care financing system, and would need to be complemented by public subsidies for less affluent individuals.

Another approach could involve tax incentives for the 80 percent of older adults who are home owners to use reverse annuity mortgages or home equity conversion mortgages to pay for home modifications and home services designed to enable individuals to remain in their home or apartment and prevent costly institutionalization. Adequate consumer protections would be needed in order to prevent financial exploitation of vulnerable elders.

Private Long-Term Care Insurance

Unless a mandatory federal LTC program is instituted, private LTCI will continue to be necessary for those persons who do not participate in the CLASS program and also as a supplement to the benefits received by those who do. Given popular concerns about the complexity of LTCI products and the future viability of LTCI companies, as noted above, greater government regulation of LTCI would do a great deal to increase consumer confidence and promote sales. The government might, for example, mandate certain basic consumer protection criteria (e.g., noncancellation, lapse protection, inflation protection) or award some kind of "seal of approval" to policies that meet criteria such as these and are underwritten by stable, highly capitalized companies.

Expanding the group LTCI market and making purchase and premium payment more automatic would greatly increase penetration, especially among younger, healthier individuals. This growth could be achieved through tax incentives for employers and other organizations to offer group LTCI plans that can be purchased through payroll deduction with pre-tax dollars, perhaps coupled with enhanced tax deductions or tax credits for the purchasers. Some industry experts estimate that, given sufficient tax incentives, the penetration of private LTCI could grow to cover nearly 30 percent of nursing home costs by 2030.[85] However, tax subsidies could further exacerbate discrepancies in financial vulnerability, as subsidies, unless they are refundable credits, are apt to be of greatest benefit for individuals who already can afford to purchase policies, rather than for those who are unable to do so.

ASSURING QUALITY IN LTC

To date, the private market has failed to assure an adequate supply or quality of LTC services, leading to unacceptably high levels of unmet need among disabled elderly persons. Indeed, LTC might be considered a classic example of "market failure," because consumers have little ability to withdraw their purchasing power from undesirable or inefficient products and avail themselves of better or less costly products. An expanded government quality assurance role is needed to assure that vulnerable elderly persons receive adequate care, have basic needs met, and are not abused or neglected. Standards for home- and community-based services, assisted living facilities, and nursing homes need to balance autonomy with consumer protection. Further, they should be accompanied by adequate monitoring and periodic quality of care inspections, especially for elderly disabled consumers whose physical, psychological, or cognitive limitations make it unrealistic for them to independently oversee the complex care arrangements required by a fragmented LTC system. One promising approach to quality improvement in LTC is the use of quality-adjusted reimbursement systems, whereby providers receive financial incentives for providing high-quality care. CMS has launched a four-state demonstration project in Arizona, Mississippi, New York, and Wisconsin that will provide performance rewards to nursing homes that receive the highest quality scores or show the greatest improvement in quality measures.

The federal government also has an important role to play in protecting vulnerable older adults against abuse, neglect, and exploitation. The recently passed federal Elder Justice Act, part of the 2010 health care bill, for the first time provided dedicated federal funding for local adult protective services and long-term care ombudsman programs, and established an Elder Justice Coordinating Council to improve coordination among local, state, federal, and private agencies in their efforts to address elder abuse.[86] However, adult protective services still does not have the same level of oversight and support as other kinds of protective services (such as child protective services), as there is no agency dedicated to overseeing elder abuse reporting, establishing practice guidelines, or setting standards for service delivery.

In addition to better serving the needs of disabled elders, LTC workers also need protection and support. The quality of LTC, and indeed of the entire LTC system, rests squarely on the backs of a workforce that is underpaid or not paid at all, consisting primarily of low-income, poorly educated racial and ethnic minority women. LTC financing approaches should include wage "pass-through provisions" (additional Medicaid funds for increasing LTC workers' compensation) for improving working conditions of personal care providers, including pay and benefits commensurate with the demands of the work; adequate worker protections consistent with other service professions; and career ladders that enable workers to receive appropriate remuneration for their expertise and experience. Workers also need adequate training, supervision, and support, both to assure the quality of care and to enable workers to progress in their careers. These protections, responsibilities, and supports also need to be extended to family members who are providing care, whether paid or unpaid. At a minimum, an assessment of caregiver training and support needs, well-being, and capacity to meet consumers' care needs should be required under Medicaid HCBS waiver programs, as is already being done in ten states.[87]

REDUCING THE NEED FOR LTC

While most public policy is focused on reducing the cost or improving the quality of existing LTC services, three strategies hold substantial potential for actually reducing the need for LTC and thereby improving quality of life for older adults and their families: (1) health promotion; (2) technological innovations; and (3) community interventions.

Health Promotion

A growing body of research indicates that efforts to increase healthy behaviors, decrease chronic illnesses, and provide greater earlier access to health care reduce disability in later life. Older adults who do not smoke, maintain a healthy body weight, engage in regular physical activity, and consume little alcohol are most likely to avoid physical limitations.[88] Between 2003 and 2007, the Centers for Disease Control and Prevention's Health Aging Program and the U.S. Administration on Aging provided small grants to select states to implement evidence-based health promotion and prevention programs.[89] For example, in 2007, Michigan, Minnesota, and New Mexico received grants to improve state health department preparedness for promoting healthy aging.[90] A comprehensive government-led initiative to promote regular exercise and other lifelong positive health practices can dramatically reduce future disability rates. For example, a city-wide effort to foster improved health and wellness practices in Albert Lea, Minnesota, resulted in projected increases in life expectancy of 3.2 years, average participant weight reductions of three pounds, a 21 percent drop in absenteeism, and a 49 percent decrease in health care costs for city employees.[91]

Technological Innovations

Technological innovations also hold substantial promise for reducing older adults' need for human assistance. Assistive technology (e.g., walkers, grab bars) and environmental interventions (e.g., ramps, removal of trip hazards) can help compensate for functional limitations, resulting in fewer falls and decreased health and LTC costs.[92] Monitoring devices (e.g., fall sensors, motion detection sensors) can identify problematic situations and patterns and notify appropriate helpers. Telemedicine/telehealth innovations can improve access to health care for isolated elders, while electronic communication, such as social networking sites, can help to identify incipient crises and reduce social isolation while improving access to relevant care-related information and services. The federal government could promote these kinds of technological innovations through tax incentives, information dissemination, and standardized protocols to assure usability, protect consumer privacy, and overcome inequities to access. The United States already is far behind the European Union and Japan in investing in such technologies.

Community Interventions

Environmental innovations that alter a community's physical or social infrastructure can enhance older adults' functional independence, delaying or even eliminating the need for costly LTC services. "Aging-friendly" infrastructure improvements, from housing designed for lifelong occupancy to adequate transportation and mobility options to comprehensive health and supportive services and opportunities for community participation, can facilitate personal independence and community engagement. Supportive service programs directed at areas with high densities of older persons can help those older adults to "age in place."[93]

Some existing efforts have been initiated by national foundations, some by local governments, some by community organizations, and some by consumers themselves. Yet other than a small amount of funds for demonstration projects provided in the 2006 OAA reauthorization, most of these community initiatives are financed by local government or nonprofit organizations and receive limited federal government support. Medicaid HCBS waivers should include provisions for supporting community innovations designed to foster aging-in-place in order to reduce LTC risk and costs.

Conclusion

Until recently, the federal government has played a largely (and sometimes deliberately) passive role in long-term care. As the need for LTC has grown, therefore, more and more responsibility has fallen on state and local governments, the private sector, and, ultimately, older adults and their families. The result is that the most disadvantaged Americans are saddled with the highest levels of LTC burden. First, there are dramatic disparities in disability rates and the consequent need for LTC, with higher levels of need for women, African Americans and Hispanics, individuals with low educational attainment and incomes, and older adults who live alone. Second, older adults who require LTC typically must exhaust all of their financial and social resources before they can receive public assistance, which often comes in the form of Medicaid reimbursement for nursing home care. Third, many older adults who need long-term care remain inadequately served or not served at all by the existing system. Finally, the highest levels of burden for providing long-term care fall on family caregivers, who are at risk for significant health and economic costs, and low-wage direct care workers, many of whom are women and racial/ethnic minorities.

Despite public efforts to rebalance the long-term care system toward home-and community-based care, to date these initiatives have primarily created small, innovative programs that serve only a small percentage of the 6 million older adults who require assistance with daily activities. Federal policy that targeted three areas could alleviate existing service disparities. First, in terms of financing, the recently passed CLASS Act represents a first step toward a more comprehensive federal LTC policy designed to allocate more equitably the direct and indirect costs of LTC among government, individuals, and families; to enhance the quality of services provided and ameliorate disparities in the benefits received; and to incentivize innovative new initiatives designed to reduce the need for LTC. Yet the CLASS Act is not sufficient, and in this chapter we have shown how coverage could be broadened though both public and private means. Second, the federal government needs to move beyond its traditional focus on cost control to pay more attention to cost effectiveness and the quality and adequacy of the care that is being provided, so as to promote the best possible quality of life for disabled elderly persons. Third, federal support of health promotion programs, technological innovations, and community interventions holds the promise of improving the health of Americans throughout their lives, thus reducing the need for long-term care. Ultimately, there must be adequate community supports for all older adults, regardless of race, ethnicity, gender, or location of residence. If existing service disparities are to be overcome, greater federal involvement, of the kinds described in this chapter, will likely be required.

Notes

1. Institute of Medicine, *Improving the Quality of Care of Nursing Homes* (Washington, DC: National Academy Press, 1986), 398.
2. Ari Houser, *Long-Term Care—Fact Sheet* (Washington, DC: American Association of Retired Persons Public Policy Institute (AARP PPI), 2007), http://assets.aarp.org/rgcenter/il/fs27r_ltc.pdf.
3. William H. Frey, *Mapping the Growth of Older America: Seniors and Boomers in the Early 21st Century* (Washington, DC: The Brookings Institution, 2007).
4. Administration on Aging, *A Profile of Older Americans: 2008*, prepared by the Administration on Aging, U.S. Department of Health and Human Services, 2008, http://www.aoa.gov/AoA-root/Aging_Statistics/Profile/2008/index.aspx.

5. Beth J. Soldo et al., "Cross-Cohort Difference in Health on the Verge of Retirement," *National Bureau of Economic Research* (2006), http://www.nber.org/papers/w12762.

6. Office of the Assistant Secretary for Planning and Evaluation, *Informal Caregiving: Compassion in Action*, prepared by the U.S. Department of Health and Human Services, 1998, http://aspe.hhs.gov/daltcp/Reports/carebro2.pdf.

7. U.S. Bureau of the Census. *Facts for Features: Older Americans Month: 2009.* prepared by the U.S. Department of Commerce and the U.S. Bureau of the Census, 2009, http://www.census.gov/newsroom/releases/pdf/cb09-ff07.pdf.

8. Catherine Hawes et al., "A National Survey of Assisted Living Facilities," *The Gerontologist* 43 (2003): 875.

9. Agency for Healthcare Research and Quality. "Long-term Care Users Range in Age and Most Do Not Live in Nursing Homes: Research Alert," (Rockville, MD: Author, 2000)

10. Harriet L. Komisar and Lee Shirey Thompson, *National Spending for Long-Term Care* (Washington, DC: Georgetown University Long-Term Care Financing Project, 2007), http://ltc.georgetown.edu/pdfs/natspendfeb07.pdf.

11. Leonard E. Burman and Richard W. Johnson, *A Proposal to Finance Long-Term Care Services Through Medicare with an Income Tax Surcharge* (Washington, DC: The Urban Institute, 2007), http://www.urban.org/UploadedPDF/411484_medicare.pdf.

12. Barbara J. Edlund, Sylvia R. Lufkin, and Barbara Franklin, "Long-Term Care Planning for Baby Boomers: Addressing an Uncertain Future," *Online Journal of Issues in Nursing* 8 (2003): 88; Centers for Medicare & Medicaid Services, *Medicare Coverage of Skilled Nursing Facility Care* (Washington, DC: Centers for Medicare & Medicaid Services, 2007), http://www.medicare.gov/publications/pubs/pdf/10153.pdf.

13. Ibid.

14. Ari Houser, Wendy Fox-Grage, and Mary Jo Gibson, *Across the States in 2009: Profiles of Long-Term Care and Independent Living* (Washington, DC: AARP PPI, 2009), 12, http://assets.aarp.org/rgcenter/il/d19105_2008_ats.pdf.

15. Jean Accius, *The Role of the Older Americans Act in Providing Long-Term Care-Fact Sheet* (Washington, DC: AARP PPI, 2008), http://assets.aarp.org/rgcenter/il/fs12r_oaa_ltc.pdf.

16. *Older Americans Act of 1965*, U.S. Code 42 (1965), § 3001 et seq.

17. Burman and Johnson, *A Proposal to Finance Long-Term Care*, 10.

18. Anne Tumlinson, Christine Aguiar, and Molly O'Malley Watts, *Closing the Long-Term Care Funding Gap: The Challenge of Private Long-Term Care Insurance* (Washington, DC: The Kaiser Commission on Medicaid and the Uninsured, 2009), http://www.ltcforagents.com/docs/2009_Closing_LTC_Funding_Gap_KFF_Report.pdf.

19. Komisar and Thompson, *National Spending for Long-term Care.*

20. Komisar and Thompson, *National Spending for Long-term Care.*

21. Sheila P. Burke, Judith Feder, and Paul N. Van der Water, eds., *Developing a Better Long-Term Care Policy: A Vision and Strategy for America's Future* (Washington, DC: National Academy of Social Insurance, 2005), http://www.nasi.org/usr_doc/Developing_a_Better_Long-Term_Care_Policy.pdf.

22. Dorothy D. Dunlop et al., "Racial/Ethnic Differences in the Development of Disability Among Older Adults," *American Journal of Public Health* 97 (2007): 2209.

23. Vicki A. Freedman and Linda G. Martin, "The Role of Education in Explaining and Forecasting Trends in Functional Limitations among Older Americans," *Demography* 36 (1999): 461.

24. John Mirowsky and Catherine E. Ross, "Socioeconomic Status and Subjective Life Expectancy," *Social Psychology Quarterly* 63 (2000): 133.

25. Richard H. Fortinsky, Juliane R. Fenster, and James O. Judge, "Medicare and Medicaid Home Health and Medicaid Waiver Services for Dually Eligible Older Adults: Risk Factors for Use and Correlates of Expenditures," *The Gerontologist* 44 (2004): 739.

26. Peter D. Hart Research Associates and American Viewpoint, *Long-Term Care: The Public's View* (Washington, DC: National Academy of Social Insurance, 2005), http://www.nasi.org/sites/default/files/research/HIS_Brief_No_8.pdf.

27. James R. Knickman and Emily K. Snell, "The 2030 Problem: Caring for Aging Baby Boomers," *Health Services Research* 37 (2002): 849.

28. Institute of Medicine, *Improving the Quality of Long-term Care* (Washington, DC: Institute of Medicine, 2001), 2, http://www.iom.edu/~/media/Files/Report%20Files/2003/Improving-the-Quality-of-Long-Term-Care/LTC8pagerFINAL.ashx.

29. Government Accountability Office, *Nursing Homes: Despite Increased Oversight, Challenges Remain in Ensuring High-Quality Care and Resident Safety*, prepared by the United States Government Accountability Office, 2005, http://www.gao.gov/new.items/d06117.pdf.

30. United States Senate Special Committee on Aging, *Assisted Living: Quality-of-Care and Consumer Protection Issues: General Accounting Office Testimony*, 106th Cong., 1st sess.

31. Steven H. Zarit et al., *Patterns of Formal and Informal Long Term Care in the United States and Sweden*, AARP Andrus Foundation Final Report (State College: The Pennsylvania State University, 1998).

32. Ann Bookman and Mona Harrington, "Family Caregivers: A Shadow Workforce in the Geriatric Health Care System?" *Journal of Health Politics, Policy and Law* 32 (2007): 1005.

33. Ari Houser and Mary Jo Gibson, *Valuing the Invaluable: The Economic Value of Family Caregiving, 2008 Update* (Washington, DC: AARP PPI, 2008), http://assets.aarp.org/rgcenter/il/i13_caregiving.pdf.

34. MetLife Mature Market Institute, *The Metlife Juggling Act Study: Balancing Caregiving with Work and the Costs Involved* (New York: Metropolitan Life Insurance Company, 1999), http://www.caregiving.org/data/jugglingstudy.pdf.

35. Peter P. Vitaliano, Jianping Zhang, and James M. Scanlan, "Is Caregiving Hazardous to One's Physical Health? A Meta-Analysis," *Psychological Bulletin* 129 (2003): 946.

36. Martin Pinquart and Silvia Sörensen, "Differences Between Caregivers and Noncaregivers in Psychological Health and Physical Health: A Meta-Analysis," *Psychology & Aging* 18 (2003): 250.

37. Joseph E. Gaugler et al., "Caregiving and Institutionalization of Cognitively Impaired Older People: Utilizing Dynamic Predictors of Change," *The Gerontologist* 43 (2003): 219; Alan M. Jette, Sharon Tennstedt, and Sybil Crawford, "How Does Formal and Informal Community Care Affect Nursing Home Use" *Journal of Gerontology: Social Sciences* 50B (1995): S4.

38. Lauren Harris-Kojetin et al., *Recent Findings on Frontline Long-Term Care Workers: A Research Synthesis 1999–2003*, prepared for the U.S. Department of Health and Human Services, Office of Disability, Aging and Long-Term Care Policy, 2004, http://www.ohca.com/workforce_center/docs/Recent_Findings_on_Frontline_LTC_Workers.pdf.

39. Rhonda J. V. Montgomery et al., "A Profile of Home Care Workers from the 2000 Census: How it Changes What We Know," *The Gerontologist* 45 (2005): 593.

40. Figures 22 and 23, Bureau of Labor Statistics, *Chart Book: Occupational Employment and Wages, May 2007*, prepared by the Bureau of Labor Statistics, United States Department of Labor, 2007, http://stats.bls.gov/oes/2007/may/chartbook.htm.

41. Debra Lipson and Carol Regan, *Health Insurance Coverage for Direct Care Workers: Riding Out the Storm (Issue Brief No. 3)* (Washington, DC: Better Jobs Better Care National Program Office, 2004), http://www.bjbc.org/content/docs/BJBCIssueBriefNo3.pdf.

42. Anne B. Hoskins, *Occupational Injuries, Illnesses, and Fatalities among Nursing, Psychiatric, and Home Health Aides, 1995–2004*, prepared by the U.S. Bureau of Labor Statistics, 2006, http://www.bls.gov/opub/cwc/sh20060628ar01p.1.htm

43. Robyn I. Stone, "The Direct Care Worker: The Third Rail of Home Care Policy," *Annual Review of Public Health* 25 (2004): 521.

44. Charlene Harrington et al., *Home and Community-Based Services: Public Policies to Improve Access, Costs and Quality* (San Francisco: UCSF Center for Personal Assistance Services, 2009), http://www.pascenter.org/documents/PASCenter_HCBS_policy_brief.pdf.

45. MetLife Mature Market Institute, The MetLife Market Survey of Nursing Home & Assisted Living Costs (New York: MetLife Mature Market Institute, 2008), http://www.pioneer-network.org/data/documents/mmistudies2008NHALcosts.pdf.

46. Knickman and Snell, "The 2030 Problem," 849.

47. Steven P. Wallace et al., "The Persistence of Race and Ethnicity in the Use of Long-Term Care," *Journal of Gerontology: Social Sciences* 53B (1998): S104.

48. Ibid.
49. Martin Kitchener et al., "Residential Care Provision in Medicaid Home- and Community-Based Waivers: A National Study of Program Trends," *The Gerontologist* 46 (2006): 165; Robyn I. Stone and Susan C. Reinhard, "The Place of Assisted Living in Long-Term Care and Related Service Systems," *The Gerontologist* 47 (2007): 23.
50. MetLife, *The MetLife Market Survey of Nursing Home & Assisted Living Costs*.
51. Celia S. Gabrel and Adrienne Jones, "The National Nursing Home Survey: 1997 Summary," *National Center for Health Statistics, Vital and Health Statistics, Centers for Disease Control and Prevention* 3 (2000): 116; Catherine Hawes et al., "A National Survey of Assisted Living Facilities," *The Gerontologist* 43 (2003): 875; Brenda Spillman, Korbin Liu, and Cary McGilliard, *Trends in Residential Long-Term Care: Use of Nursing Home and Assisted Living and Characteristics of Facilities and Residents*, prepared by the U.S. Department of Health and Human Services, Office of Disability, Aging and Long-Term Care Policy, 2002, http://aspe.hhs.gov/daltcp/reports/2002/rltct.htm.
52. Anne Tumlinson and Scott Woods, *Long-Term Care in America: An Introduction*, prepared for the National Commission for Quality Long-Term Care, 2007, http://www.qualitylongtermcarecommission.org/pdf/ltc_america_introduction.pdf.
53. Laura Summer, *Medicaid and Long-Term Care* (Washington, DC: Georgetown University Long-Term Care Financing Project, 2007), http://ltc.georgetown.edu/pdfs/medicaid2006.pdf.
54. Charlene Harrington et al., "Predicting State Medicaid Home and Community Based Waiver Participants and Expenditures, 1992–1997," *The Gerontologist* 40 (2000): 673; Laura P. Sands et al., "Comparison of Resource Utilization for Medicaid Dementia Patients Using Nursing Homes Versus Home and Community Based Waivers for Long-Term Care," *Medical Care* 46 (2008): 449.
55. Harrington et al., *Home and Community-Based Services*.
56. Steven J. Katz, Mohammed Kabeto, and Kenneth M. Langa, "Gender Disparities in the Receipt of Home Care for Elderly People with Disability in the United States," *Journal of the American Medical Association* 284 (2000): 3022; Theresa Norgard and Willard Rodgers, "Patterns of In-Home Care among Elderly Black and White Americans," *Journals of Gerontology Series B*: 52B (Special Issue) (1997): 93–101.
57. Judith Feder, Harriet L. Komisar, and Marlene Niefeld, "Long-Term Care in the United States: An Overview," *Health Affairs* 19 (2000): 40.
58. A. Scharlach, T. Dal Santo, and K. Mills-Dick, "Assuring the Quality of Long Term Care Insurance Benefits," *Journal of Aging & Social Policy* 17 (2005): 39–59.
59. Lifeplans, Inc., *Who Buys Long-Term Care Insurance? A 15-year Study of Buyers and Non-Buyers, 1990–2005* (Washington, DC: America's Health Insurance Plans, 2007), http://www.ahipresearch.org/PDFs/LTC_Buyers_Guide.pdf.
60. Rosalie A. Kane, "Expanding the Home Care Concept: Blurring Distinctions among Home Care, Institutional Care, and Other Long-Term Care Services," *Milbank Quarterly* 73 (1995): 161.
61. *Long-Term Care Security Act*, U.S. Code 5 (2000), §§ 9001 et seq.
62. Josefina G. Carbonnell, interview by Adam Stone, *Assistant Secretary for Aging Works Toward New Balance in Long-Term Care Spectrum*, Assisted Living Federation of America, June 2007, http://www.alfa.org/alfa/Interview_-_Josefina_G_Carbonell_-_ALE_6_.asp?SnID=2; Administration on Aging, *Choices for Independence: The Older Americans Act Amendments of 2006* (Washington, DC: Administration on Aging, 2006), http://www.aoa.gov/AoARoot/AoA_Programs/OAA/oaa.aspx.
63. Kaiser Family Foundation, *Health Care Reform and the CLASS Act* (Washington, DC: Kaiser Family Foundation, 2010), http://www.kff.org/healthreform/upload/8069.pdf.
64. Biff Jones and Joe Barnett, *The New Long-Term Care Entitlement* (Washington, DC: National Center for Policy Analysis, 2010), http://www.ncpa.org/pub/ba707.
65. Douglas W. Elmendorf, *Letter to Speaker Pelosi*, prepared by the Congressional Budget Office, 2010, http://www.cbo.gov/ftpdocs/113xx/doc11355/hr4872.pdf.
66. *Olmstead v. L.C.*, 527 U.S. 581 (1999).
67. Ibid. at 591.
68. Cynthia Shirk, *Rebalancing Long-Term Care: The Role of the Medicaid HCBS Waiver Program* (Washington, DC: National Health Policy Forum, 2006), http://www.nhpf.org/library/background-papers/BP_HCBS.Waivers_03-03-06.pdf.

69. Shirk, *Rebalancing Long-Term Care.*
70. The White House, "Title II. The Role of Public Programs," The White House, 2010, http://www.whitehouse.gov/health-care-meeting/proposal/titleii/community-first.
71. Shirk, *Rebalancing Long-Term Care.*
72. Anna L. Zendell, "Impact of the Olmstead Decision Five Years Later," *Journal of Gerontological Social Work* 49 (2007): 97.
73. Larry Polivka and Helen Zayac, "The Aging Network and Managed Long-Term Care," *The Gerontologist* 28 (2008): 564.
74. Ibid.
75. Barbara Lepidus Carlson et al., "Effects of Cash and Counseling on Personal Care and Well-Being," *Health Services Research* 42 (2007): 467.
76. Ibid.
77. Jane Tilly and Joshua M.Weiner, "Consumer-Directed Home and Community Services Programs in Eight States: Policy Issues for Older People and Government," *Journal of Aging and Social Policy* 12 (2001): 1.
78. A. E. Benjamin, Ruth Matthias, and Todd M. Franke, "Comparing Consumer-Directed and Agency Models for Providing Supportive Services at Home," *Health Services Research* 35 (2000): 351; Carlson et al., "Effects of Cash and Counseling," 467.
79. David C. Grabowski, "The Cost-Effectiveness of Noninstitutional Long-Term Care Services: Review and Synthesis of the Most Recent Evidence," *Medical Care Research and Review* 63 (2006): 3.
80. Tilly and Weiner, "Consumer-Directed Home and Community Services Programs," 1.
81. Howard Gleckman, "The CLASS Act: Can a Unique Long-Term Care Financing Mechanism Succeed?," (paper presented at The Maxwell School at Syracuse University, Syracuse, New York, June 10–11, 2010).
82. Ibid.
83. Ibid.
84. 26 U.S.C. § 106(b).
85. Mark Merlis, *Financing Long-Term Care in the Twenty-first Century: The Public and Private Roles* (Washington, DC: The Commonwealth Fund's Program on Long-Term Care for Frail Elders, 1999), http://www.commonwealthfund.org/usr_doc/merlis343.pdf.
86. Elder Justice Coalition, "Elder Justice Bills Clear Congress, Obama to Sign into Law," *Elder Justice Coalition*, March 22, 2010, http://www.elderjusticecoalition.com/docs/Elder-Justice-Coalition-March_22_2010.pdf
87. Lynn Friss Feinberg and Sandra L. Newman, "A Study of 10 States since Passage of the National Family Caregiver Support Program: Policies, Perceptions, and Program Development," *The Gerontologist* 44 (2004): 760.
88. Andrea Z. LaCroix et al., "Maintaining Mobility in Late Life. II. Smoking, Alcohol Consumption, Physical Activity, and Body Mass Index," *American Journal of Epidemiology* 137 (1993): 858.
89. U.S. Centers for Disease Control and Prevention, *Healthy Aging: History of Grant Programs*, prepared by the U.S. Centers for Disease Control and Prevention, 2009, http://www.cdc.gov/aging/states/history.htm.
90. Ibid.
91. Blue Zones, "Vitality Project 2009: Albert Lea, MN," Blue Zones, 2010, http://www.bluezones.com/albertlea.
92. William C. Mann et al., "Effectiveness of Assistive Technology and Environmental Interventions in Maintaining Independence and Reducing Home Care Costs for the Frail Elderly," *Archives of Family Medicine* 8 (1999): 210.
93. Barbara A. Ormond et al., *Supportive Services Programs in Naturally Occurring Retirement Communities* (Washington, DC: Office of Disability, Aging and Long Term Care Policy, Office of the Assistant Secretary for Planning and Evaluation, U.S. Department of Health and Human Services, 2004).

Part Five

CONCLUSIONS

13

Seeing, Bearing, and Sharing Risk

Social Policy Challenges for Our Time

MARTHA MINOW

As Ralph Waldo Emerson once said, "As soon as there is life, there is danger."[1] Throughout human history, conditions of risk have accompanied each human life. As the chapters of this book document, however, allocations of responsibilities for dealing with those risks have shifted over time across individuals, families, groups, and governments—though recent shifts within the United States fail to engage public participation or debate. Indeed, the dominant rhetorical framework obscures the real choices and stakes by using crude alternatives of private markets and collective responsibility, with inadequate attention to the details that determine incentives and reallocations. There is thus important intellectual and political work to be done in articulating government and collective roles in preventing risks, in assigning where risks fall, and in nudging private behaviors to prevent and to manage risks. Yet the very omissions and gaps in these areas hint at the deeper problem: securing sufficient political will to address and respond to the social shift of economic risks to individuals requires overcoming the psychological, cognitive, analytic, and ideological barriers to seeing and caring about the risk assignment.

The severity of recent economic crises may help alert and mobilize people to attend to the issues of risk, but the problems are deeper, longer term, and more systemic than the bursting of the housing bubble and the governmental failure to regulate opaque and risky financial instruments. Academics, journalists, and public leaders can increase public conversations about the incidence and distribution of economic risk—and in so doing, can reshape public understandings to cultivate a sense of mutual duty rather than merely self-reliance.

Risk's Recent History

While dangers to human health, welfare, and well-being are natural and inevitable, how risks are exacerbated or mitigated, and how the costs of risks are incurred, are anything but. There have been many shifts in the allocation of responsibilities between governments and markets over time; there is no natural division of labor or costs associated with risks of poverty, illness, or other disasters. Families, clans, neighbors, fraternal organizations, and religious groups have each shared varying degrees of the burdens and challenges from individual and societal risks. Market-based capitalism spread with the aid of property and contract rules—and with market capitalism, business cycles, or economic fluctuations, created disruptive burdens of recessions and depressions. In response, people in the United States and other countries have supported government regulations to moderate or spread these burdens.

In the twentieth century, political solutions tackled the risks of poverty and economic hardship through big and contrasting philosophies. Experiments with communism, regulated capitalism, and social democracy proceeded, but by the end of the twentieth century, the ideal of free markets triumphed—spreading a faith in individual freedom and limited governmentally sponsored redistribution of resources to aid individuals confronting risks.[2] The triumph of free market ideals has carried particular benefits and risks. Extending over more of the globe than ever before, legal and political structures support economic markets. Social programs offered income supports for those dealing with unemployment, disability, and family duties, but the United States, Europe, and former Communist countries spent the end of the twentieth century shrinking safety-net social programs and economic and financial regulations in pursuit of more limited government and less-regulated economic markets.[3] In the United States, more than half a century after the New Deal and decades after Great Society programs, federal and state governments joined with private employers and insurers to shift more and more of the risks of unemployment, illness, disability, and family duties to individuals and families. New financial innovations, taking advantage of the deregulated environment, in turn created new kinds of risks, so that even people with jobs and homes found themselves facing devastating consequences as economic bubbles in the credit and housing industries burst.[4] First a Republican administration and then a Democratic administration authorized huge government programs to bail out and manage failing industries, even as the dominant public discussion treated economic devastation to individuals and families largely as private problems, to be borne by those individuals and families.

Contrary to the dominant rhetoric, even the apparent division between public and private is manufactured and subject to shifts. In this country, for most of the nineteenth and twentieth centuries, public reliance on private actors proceeded largely through indirect means to advance individual and general welfare. Federal and state governments offered subsidies to private actors to encourage enterprises to enhance the general welfare. Public charters and municipal corporations straddled the public-private divide in the eighteenth and nineteenth centuries. Even the private corporations held charters calling for public benefits, rather than imbuing the private sphere with public-mindedness. In many ways, American local, state, and federal policies have supported private

enterprise. Public policies here reduced risks to and facilitated efforts of entrepreneurs and business people.

After the Great Depression, widespread disillusionment with the private
sector led to entrusting public institutions with greater responsibilities. The government grew dramatically—but the American way diverged from European
social welfare and opposed collectivist solutions of communism and socialism. By
the late 1970s, even the governmental role in moderate social provision came
under political assault in the United States. There was renewed enthusiasm for
private markets and competitive practices. Both the Ford and Carter administrations, building on initiatives begun by President Richard Nixon, took significant
steps to deregulate industry and introduce market competition. In the 1980 presidential campaign, Ronald Reagan ran on an explicit agenda of downsizing a
wasteful and bloated public sector. The Clinton administration in the 1990s
sought to "reinvent government" largely by shrinking the federal workforce and
infusing it with private sector methods and metrics. The goal of that administration's National Performance Review was to create a government that "works
better and costs less."[5] It was President Clinton who declared: "[t]he era of big
government is over."[6] President George W. Bush pressed for major tax cuts in a
strategy intended in part to reduce government programs, and proposed (unsuc-
cessfully) to convert Social Security into individual private investment accounts.
The conception of a world divided between government and private markets intensified even as governments and private investors, employers, and individuals
continued to expand complex interconnections of subsidy and regulation. At the
same time, the nation's economy shifted largely from manufacturing to services.
More people came to face periodic and often long-term unemployment. Work
skills in the changing economy now often become obsolete even before an unemployed individual can find a new job.[7] Even inadequate legal protections are often
under-enforced.[8]

After the collapse of a global housing bubble in 2007, financial institutions,
including banks and investment houses, faced such shocking losses that economic
activities froze. Banks restricted credit, consumer purchasing fell, and vast
numbers of enterprises had to reduce or halt hiring and lay off existing employees.
Dramatic actions by the federal government to stabilize the economy would have
seemed unimaginable, given bipartisan pronouncements against government engagement in the economy. In the United States, the Federal Reserve injected $41
billion into the money supply in hopes of easing lending. Then the federal government injected additional funds in an effort to salvage investment house Bear
Stearns and to broker a sale to JP Morgan Chase in order to avoid the bankruptcy
of these major private sector institutions. The federal government placed into
conservatorship the two large private but government-sponsored entities (Freddie Mac and Fannie Mae) that supported the secondary home mortgage markets;
the government took equity stakes with conditions through a $700 billion fund in
order to infuse money into the banking system, and the government loaned

nearly $50 billion to General Motors to save it from economic disaster. All of these steps remade the relationship between government and the private sector, but proceeded in a form meant to maintain at least the appearance of a private market, operating apart from the government. At the same time, economic hardship, especially for those who were already disadvantaged, hit people especially hard. Government programs shrank. The language of private responsibility resurged with moral force.[9] Political slogans of private responsibility failed to acknowledge how legal and financial frameworks made home ownership and consumer credit the routine devices for wealth and consumption. Public policies steered people deliberately into these practices even while bolstering the language of private property and personal responsibility. In these respects, the policy debates today reflect lines laid down during the twentieth century when political and rhetorical pressures elevated private markets and restricted government social provision and regulation—despite the realities of massive government engagement with markets and the new record in numbers of Americans living below the official poverty line.

Why Is It Hard to See Risk and Its Shifts?

The chapters in this book show in multiple ways how the risks of economic dislocation have in recent years shifted from government and businesses to individuals and families. This is not obvious; it requires the kind of analysis offered by the chapters of this book. The chapters also suggest that individuals often have difficulty analyzing risks that they themselves face, and that they fail to see and track the larger patterns in the growth and distribution of economic risks. Scholars have documented how psychological, cognitive, and analytic barriers affect people's recognition of risk and their treatment of related information.[10] Quantitative measures of risk are often difficult to comprehend and even difficult to construct fairly and reliably.[11] As financial institutions and practices grow more complex, their operations diverge from personal experience and the understandings of many people.[12] Greater awareness of these problems can inform policies that actually influence behavior and reduce risks.[13] Yet this kind of awareness is impaired as the rhetoric of private responsibility persists, alongside a stylized conception treating private markets as natural, financial risks as inevitable, and enactment of government policies as counterproductive.

To mitigate individual risk, government policies do not have to reject private markets or substitute collective ownership, pricing, and management. Public policies redressing escalating economic risks need not rely largely on public social provision. Instead, government can provide incentives for private planning and insurance and default rules that guide people's conduct toward prudent behavior.[14] Yet even these kinds of policies are remote if the very recognition of the problem of risk remains elusive—and it will remain elusive if people continue to blame the poor judgment of ordinary individuals for entering into risky investments, ballooning mortgages, or credit card debt with escalating interest rates.

Work to Be Done

The chapters in this book go a considerable distance in naming and tracing the shifting of economic risks to individuals and families. The chapters also help to decode how government policies exacerbate risks to individuals in the terms used to finance their homes and purchases and in the inadequate design and management of retirement benefits and social safety nets. As the authors of each chapter show, particular burdens are experienced by the younger generation—who are having an especially hard time moving into stable employment even as their situations are left unaddressed by most income security programs.

Income support, consumer credit reforms, and other sensible policy suggestions to meet contemporary needs can be devised and debated. Yet any substantial administrative success with such new policies will require overcoming the psychological, cognitive, and analytic barriers at work in the current misunderstandings of risk and in the faulty assumption that markets are private and that government regulation endangers them. The continuing financial crisis since 2007 has alerted people to systemic risks, and may make it easier to mobilize voters for policy changes. But the problems are deeper and more long-term than the current crisis, and require more systematic solutions. The most profound problem concerns how public conversations can be framed to overcome slogans and emotional blame-games, to cut through simplistic divisions between public and private responsibility, and to support rather than erode the development of a sense of mutual duty. For it is the sense of mutual duty, rather than individual self-reliance, that will be crucial to changing our patterns and distribution of risk. Yet contemporary debate circles around blame and individual responsibility, leaving this profound problem intact.

The problem is profound because it lies behind any long-term solution. It is also profound because it exposes a paradox. Devising suitable and workable policies to reduce and deal with rising economic risks requires a sufficiently shared sense of "we" to motivate democratic action—yet democratic action toward these ends cannot emerge without a greater sense of shared risks and responsibility.

The complexity and apparent technicality of the issues is partially to blame. But so is the seeming invisibility of public decisions, enabling and even spurring the shift of risks to individuals and families. Market-style economic analyses help identify the power of competition in generating innovation, spurring individual efforts, and inspiring alternatives to monopoly even where government provides a service. Indeed, scholars of market methods have indicated how incentives and competition around performance standards can help government achieve public ends when the community cannot agree on particular techniques and the task is complex.[15] Yet market theories neglect how power differentials affect private choices, how social structures shape private preferences, and how barriers and disincentives constrain the information crucial to evaluating success and failure. Market theories miss the value and vitality of collective normative debate and struggle, even as they understate their own reliance on public norms. Public norms governing property and contract, for example, shape the preconditions of private markets. But market theories offer no tools for determining what the shape of these entitlements should be or when other norms should rise to the level of preconditions within which market-based competition and incentives should operate. Market measures also render the contributions of public subsidies and incentives invisible, through the rules governing private property, tort, taxation, and the like. When market theories assume that individuals operate out of rational self-interest, the theories have little to say about children, people with mental disabilities, people who are seriously ill, people with little education, and people with substance abuse problems—the primary targets of social provision efforts.

Poor people, children, people who are or become ill, people who lack employment, and other vulnerable populations have always depended on the willingness of others to help. The group with needs expands as foreclosures push middle-class home owners to or beyond the brink and unemployment devastates entire communities. These problems should be matters of collective concern, yet the very notion of collective concern has itself become a polarizing target of partisan politics.

As circular as the problem seems to be, it will change if more people talk differently. If people discuss seemingly invisible public elements and supports of private markets, describe how their own experiences of worry and risk echo experiences of others, and talk about the social and political fabric within which private jeopardy arises, there will be more occasions for people to perceive the shared contexts of privately felt pain and to find common cause. The authors contributing to this volume have started the conversation. It just remains for others to take part.

Notes

1. Madame de Stael, *Germany* (New York: 1813, III), 285, quoted in Ralph Waldo Emerson, *Journals and Miscellaneous Notebooks of Ralph Waldo Emerson, Vol. VI: 1824–1838* (Cambridge: Belknap Press, 1966), 37.
2. Ian Bremmer, *The End of the Free Market: Who Wins the War Between States and Corporations?* (New York: Portfolio, 2010); Gale Stokes, *The Walls Came Tumbling Down: The Collapse of Communism in Eastern Europe* (New York: Oxford University Press, 1993).
3. See Mihály Simai, *The Age of Global Transformations: The Human Dimension* (Budapest: Akadémiai Kiadó, 2001); Nicholas Laham, *The Reagan Presidency and the Politics of Race: In Pursuit of Colorblind Justice and Limited Government* (Santa Barbara: Praeger, 1998); Jeffrey

Sachs, *Poland's Jump to the Market Economy* (Cambridge, MA: MIT Press, 1994). *See also* Liz Alderman, "Why Denmark is Shrinking Its Social Safety Net," *New York Times*, August 16, 2010, http://economix.blogs.nytimes.com/2010/08/16/why-denmark-is-shrinking-its-social-safety-net/.

4. See Simon Johnson and James Kwak, *13 Bankers: The Wall Street Takeover and the Next Financial Meltdown* (New York: Pantheon, 2010); Michael Lewis, *The Big Short: Inside the Doomsday Machine* (New York: W. W. Norton, 2010); Lawrence G. McDonald and Patrick Robinson, *A Colossal Failure of Common Sense: The Inside Story of the Collapse of Lehman Brothers* (New York: Crown Business, 2009); Paul Muolo and Mathew Padilla, *Chain of Blame: How Wall Street Caused the Mortgage and Credit Crisis* (New York: Wiley, 2010); Andrew Ross Sorkin, *Too Big to Fail: The Inside Story of How Wall Street and Washington Fought to Save the Financial System— and Themselves* (New York: Viking Press, 2009).

5. See Al Gore, National Performance Review, *From Red Tape to Results: Creating a Government That Works Better and Costs Less*, special report prepared for the National Partnership for Reinventing Government, September 7, 1993, http://govinfo.library.unt.edu/npr/library/nprrpt/annrpt/redtpe93/index.html.

6. President William Jefferson Clinton, "Address Before a Joint Session of Congress on the State of the Union," January 23, 1996, printed in *Congressional Quarterly Weekly Report*, January 27, 1996, 258–262.

7. See Jacob S. Hacker, "Sharing Risk and Responsibility in a New Economic Era," chapter 1 of this volume.

8. See Katherine Porter, "Misbehavior and Mistake in Bankruptcy Mortgage Claims," *Texas Law Review* 87 (2008): 121.

9. See Andrew E. Scharlach and Amanda J. Lehning, "Government's Role in Aging and Long-Term Care," chapter 12 of this volume.

10. See James R. Bettman, Information Processing Theory of Consumer Choice (Reading, PA: Addison-Wesley Educational Publishers, 1979); Daniel Kahnerman et al., eds., *Judgment under Uncertainty: Heuristics and Biases* (Cambridge: Cambridge University Press, 1982).

11. See Richard M. Cundiff, Jr., "Statistical and Cognitive Barriers to Effective Disclosure of Mutual Fund Risk" (submitted in satisfaction of the written work requirement, Harvard, 1996), *cyber.law.harvard.edu/rfi/papers/cognitiv.PDF*.

12. See Karin Knorr Cetina and Alex Preda, "The Temporalization of Financial Markets: From Network to Flow," *Theory, Culture & Society* 116 (2007): 116.

13. See Cass R. Sunstein and Richard H. Thaler, *Nudge: Improving Decisions about Health, Wealth, and Happiness* (New Haven: Yale University Press, 2008).

14. See id.

15. David Riemer, "Government as Administrator vs. Government as Purchaser: Do Rules or Markets Create Greater Accountability In Serving the Poor?" *Fordham Urban Law Journal* 28 (2001): 1715.

Conclusion

America's Next Social Contract

Lessons from the Past, Prospects for the Future

JACOB S. HACKER AND ANN O'LEARY

The history of American risk-sharing is not a simple linear tale. From the 1930s through the 1970s, public and private protections did indeed expand more or less continuously, gradually shielding more and more Americans from the direst consequences of what President Franklin Roosevelt famously called the "hazards and vicissitudes" of economic life.[1] As this volume has documented, however, the last generation has witnessed a very different trajectory. Instead of shifting upward toward public and private systems of insurance, economic risk has shifted downward from government and employers onto individual American workers and their families. This transformation has occurred across a range of policy areas and aspects of Americans' economic lives, from health care to pensions to job security to personal finances to family strategies for balancing work and caregiving.

And yet, even amid this Great Risk Shift, not all developments have lessened the government's role as risk manager. For instance, a major expansion of Medicaid health coverage for the poor and the Earned Income Tax Credit have provided substantial help for workers most disadvantaged by rising economic inequality and insecurity. And in the last two years, as this volume has documented, large-scale steps have been taken to try to push back against inequality and insecurity, including the upgrading of unemployment insurance in the economic rescue package of 2009, increased consumer protections enacted as part of the financial reform bill, the expansion of direct student lending in the health care reform bill, and of course the health reform bill itself.

The back-and-forth movement of economic risk—over time and across policy areas—should remind us that there is nothing inevitable about either broader social insurance or greater individual risk. Instead, these are political choices. They are political not just because they are shaped by national and state policies, but more fundamentally because they reflect the relative power and competing ideas of actors struggling to define and redefine the role of government, employers, families, and individuals in a new century.

Despite the policy breakthroughs of 2009 and 2010, that grand struggle is very much still with us. As we complete this volume, in January 2011, the Republican-controlled House has just voted to repeal the health care reform law, and two federal courts have struck down as unconstitutional the individual mandate to purchase health insurance. Neither is close to the final word on the future of reform: the Republican repeal legislation died a quick death in the Democratic-controlled Senate (and would have been vetoed by President Obama had it not), and the constitutionality of the mandate will ultimately be decided by the Supreme Court. But each occurrence is a powerful indication of the continuing debate over how risk and responsibility should be balanced and shared.

The overarching argument of this book is that this debate should take place with full awareness of the options before us and the consequences of difference choices. Remembering that the scope of economic security reflects the political decisions that we make as a society does not mean presuming that the challenges we face will be easily met. After all, even if insecurity is not our inevitable economic destiny, the signs that our elected representatives can work across party lines and tackle the hard questions of the day are hardly encouraging. But understanding the political context does call on us to step away from the immediate fights to examine the deeper undercurrents of public opinion, which continue, despite popular perception, to suggest a desire for government action to protect the middle class against economic risks. And this broader inquiry also presses us to take a fresh look at the trends outlined in the first part of this book—trends that suggest the need for a robust role for government in sharing and managing risks that cause or increase the economic insecurity faced by families today. In the end, the prospects for creating a new governing philosophy that emphasizes the economic security of the middle class rest on how the lessons of history and the challenges of the day are understood—and how that understanding informs and drives efforts to forge a new American social contract.

What Americans Really Think about Government and the Economy

As anyone with a TV or Internet access knows, dissatisfaction with government is rife. In a recent public opinion poll conducted by the Pew Research Center, 77 percent of Americans reported that there were frustrated or angry with the government, compared to only 19 percent who reported that they were basically content.[2] Beneath this dissatisfaction, however, lie strong convictions that government can and should solve major economic problems on behalf of the middle class. The paradox of Americans' anger toward government is that it reflects what people *don't* see the government doing at least as much as it reflects what people perceive the government to be doing.

Indeed, the very same Pew poll showing widespread anger toward government also indicated that, for many Americans, frustration with government reflects a sense that political leaders are not doing *enough* to solve the kind of problems we address in this volume. Two-thirds of Americans believe that middle class people get less attention from the federal government than they should, compared to only 54 percent who reported this concern in 1997.[3] Moreover, this sentiment holds true across political lines: 68 percent of Republicans, 67 percent of Democrats, and 65 percent of Independents all pinpoint lack of attention to the problems of the middle class as a serious governing failure.

Still at the same time that large majorities say that government needs to do more for the middle class, there is broad skepticism that government has the ability to fix today's economic woes, or to solve big problems in general. As the economy nose-dived, Americans' belief that the government could fix the economy fell as well—from 68 percent who believed in the government in July 2008 to 56 percent in October of that same year.[4] Americans increasingly report believing that the government is almost always wasteful and inefficient (rising from 47 percent in 2004 to 57 percent in 2008).[5]

This skepticism seems to be more general than specific—that is, centered on a government seen as wasteful and inefficient overall, rather than in reference to specific public responsibilities. In fact, Americans continue to believe that government has an essential role to play in regulating the economy and providing economic security. For example, in the same year that a Gallup Poll was showing that more Americans than at any time in the previous decade were reporting that there is too much government regulation (45 percent),[6] a separate poll from the Pew Research Center was showing that Americans still solidly believed that government regulation was necessary to protect the public interest (50 percent).[7]

Similarly, Americans believe that the government needs to reduce the federal deficit in the abstract. But these same people are extremely skeptical of specific cutbacks in existing programs that provide economic security, and, when asked, say they strongly support raising their own payroll taxes to pay for a continuation of Medicare and Social Security benefits rather than cutting the benefits.[8] Even with the rise of the conservative Tea Party, the largest public social programs remain overwhelmingly popular. Indeed, older Americans are the age group that is simultaneously most supportive of the Tea Party and the fiercest defenders of Social Security and Medicare.

American's feelings about their government are complex. Americans are dissatisfied with government, yes, but in large part because they think government has abandoned the middle class. They worry about whether the government has the capacity to address the nation's economic challenges, but that does not mean they oppose government playing a role in addressing the concerns of the middle class. They see the government as inefficient and wasteful, yet support the social insurance programs that they have come to know and rely upon. And while they believe that the government is regulating too much, they see the value in and importance of regulations as a means to serve the public interest.

For those seeking to act on the recommendations of the prior chapters, the message is that measures to improve economic security must be framed as directed toward and beneficial for the middle class. In addition, they must be seen not as expanding government for the sake of a larger public sector, but rather as providing the means for individuals, families, and employers to better manage and share the economic risks they face. In many cases, this means that financing of these initiatives should be portrayed, as payroll taxes for Medicare and Social Security are, as contributions that are made by these stakeholders to their own future economic security. Finally, advocates must tell a compelling story about how private risk management is not feasible in the specific areas where it has failed—a story to which, the surveys suggest, many Americans will be receptive.

History and Trends in American Risk Management

The public's mixed views of government are not so surprising. The upheavals of the last several years would be enough to challenge any American's faith in the capacity of government to police the private sector and ensure economic security. Add to this the massive changes in government's role in managing economic risks over the last generation, and it is not hard to find the key sources of public concern. The broad majority of Americans that have not shared in the large economic gains experienced at the top of the income distribution have seen their economic lives increasingly buffeted by the winds of economic change.

To many commentators, the economic downturn that began in 2007 was an unexpected storm in an otherwise sunny economic environment. Yet, as the chapters in this volume have shown, the Great Recession followed on the heels of three decades of government and employer withdrawal from the business of risk management that had shifted more and more economic risks onto families, particularly in the areas of health insurance and retirement savings.

Like the public opinion trends just reviewed, the shift of economic risk is multifaceted. It has not occurred in the same way or to the same degree across all areas of American economic life. David Moss reminds us, for example, that the power of the government as the ultimate risk manager has, if anything, expanded in recent years when it comes to the management of systemic economic, national security, and environmental risks, from the meltdown of financial markets to the 9/11 terrorist attacks to the BP Gulf Coast oil spill. As Moss explains, the success of risk management hinges on both sides of the intuitions expressed by Americans in public polls. Risk management works best when government both deploys broader risk protections as well as puts in place mechanisms for monitoring and controlling excessive risk-taking by the insured.

The role of government in managing the most severe risks, whether in national security or economic security, is also a theme of chapter 4 by Mariano-Florentino Cuéllar and Connor Raso in this volume. Cuéllar and Raso effectively demonstrate the deep intertwining of national and economic security—from the fiscal effects of one on the other to the human and social capital impacts—and remind us that "people make enormous sacrifices to protect their nation because of what they think it represents, and its role as a bulwark against economic insecurity is no small measure of what nations promise their citizens."

The American story of risk shifting comes into starker relief when it is contrasted with developments in other advanced industrial nations—few of which have seen trends similar to the United States until now. In chapter 3 of this volume, Neil Gilbert shows that the equilibrium between private and public responsibility for social risk management may be finding a resting place somewhere in the middle, as other OECD countries retract their public programs in favor of more private-sector support and the United States begins to increase the government's role in risk management as the private sector role shrinks. It is this potential trend toward an expanded role for public management of individual and family economic risks that is the focus of the central chapters of this volume.

Forging America's Next Social Contract

No one can doubt the need for rethinking American risk management. From one direction, the problem is public-sector overload. From another, it is the failure of the public role to adapt as employers have moved away from the provision of social benefits and families have faced new economic risks rooted in the transformation of the economy and the structure of families themselves.

The proper balance of risk and responsibility is the concern of many of the authors in this volume, who have developed forceful, innovative, and practical ideas for retooling our existing system of risk management to meet the needs of tomorrow's workers and families. The authors provide specific ideas and solutions to the increasing risks that Americans face in areas ranging from job security to home ownership to wealth-building to retirement savings. But underlying these ideas are at least four unifying themes.

THE NEED FOR NEW PUBLIC-PRIVATE PARTNERSHIPS

Our nation has long had a compact between the government and employers to protect workers against certain risks. Yet it is clear from this volume that this old social compact has broken down and that a new partnership must be created.

Perhaps the most vivid examples come from Alicia's Munnell's informed explanation of how retirement risks—once borne in common within workplaces—have shifted to individuals, who are having grave difficulties saving adequately for retirement or protecting themselves from the risks that attend long-term retirement planning. As she argues in chapter 11, workers are exposed to much greater risks today because our employer-based retirement system has significantly increased risks on workers and the generosity of Social Security benefits has diminished. Unfortunately, these changes to the social compact have occurred just as the retirement income needs of workers are increasing due to improved longevity and increasing health care costs. To address these new risks, Munnell presents an innovative proposal to tackle both the concentration in risk exposure and the problem of insufficient retirement income faced by most workers: a new tier of retirement benefits that would provide a government guarantee of 20 percent of one's pre-retirement income. She suggests that this new tier could be aggressively invested and managed by private sector investors, or that it could be conservatively invested and the Social Security Trust Fund could be more aggressively invested.

Finding the right mix between public and private risk is a theme of all the proposals in this volume. Andy Scharlach and Amanda Lehning demonstrate that the government and the private market have done a dismal job in insuring against the risk of long-term care costs, leaving the burden mostly on unpaid women in the family or on a very low-paid care workforce. They suggest a spectrum of possible roles for the government and the private sector—ranging from mandatory federal insurance for long-term care to incentives to increase the private long-term care market coupled with government mandates to guarantee certain basic consumer protections.

In the area of home ownership, Katie Porter and Tara Twomey also promote an aggressive oversight role for the government in private-sector mortgage products. They look to the Food and Drug Administration for inspiration. Just as society requires that drug companies first test drugs in a limited market before making them widely available, lenders should be required to test their products to ensure that the default rate is not too high before offering the product more broadly.

Heather Boushey suggests that it is not just building new forms of institutional risk-sharing about which we should be concerned. For job creation and job security to flourish, we also need to revisit the agreements that we have on the books to ensure that the government and our employers are living up to their promises. The government should recommit to its goal of full employment and should insist on employer compliance with existing labor laws.

In all of these proposals, the role of the government is not to provide complete protection against economic risks, but to provide a backstop that allows private risk protections to flourish in areas where market failures are chronic, information is often highly imperfect, and individuals are prone to a range of basic planning errors. In this respect, a major theme of the book is the need for fostering a new role for both government and the private sector that recognizes the limits of employer responsibility in an increasingly dynamic economy but does not let key private-sector actors, from insurers to mutual funds to corporations, completely off the hook.

Another theme is that government has a range of tools to provide economic security—from tax incentives to regulations to direct public spending—and that each has strengths and weaknesses in promoting private and public risk-sharing on a relatively equal basis across Americans. It is to this second theme that we now turn.

GREATER FLEXIBILITY IN THE USE
OF SOCIAL INSURANCE AND TAXES

Not only should government reconsider its compact with employers and the private sector more broadly, but it should also reconsider its agreements with workers and families about how they use existing programs and incentives. Both Stephen Sugarman and coauthors Christian Weller and Amy Helburn suggest that the existing boxes or silos embedded in public programs impede families from fully accessing the protections they need against a range of risks.

Weller and Helburn explain that we should allow workers and families to exercise more control over how to save and put their savings to use. While encouraging short-term and long-term savings, they have argued that it would be more efficient and lead to higher rates of savings if the government allowed families to define their own savings goals instead of prioritizing one over the other (e.g., savings for home ownership over education). And they suggest that workers will save more if the government also allowed families to define how to use their savings in the future (e.g., borrowing against one's retirement savings for specified uses).

Stephen Sugarman makes a similar proposal with regard to individuals who need income replacement while out of work for a variety of reasons—be it a temporary disability or the need for a vacation day. Sugarman would end all of today's existing programs—unemployment insurance, worker's compensation, paid vacation, and paid sick days—in favor of a much more flexible short-term paid leave program that would allow workers to accumulate days to be used for any of these reasons. Like Weller and Helburn, Sugarman would require workers to plan for longer-term needs by banking some of these leave days for future use.

Neither of these proposals envisions a major expansion of the tax and spending role of the federal government, but instead imagines a restructuring of existing incentives to better target them, make them more equal (unlike current tax breaks, which generally favor the wealthiest), allow them to be used more flexibly across a range of risks, and ultimately make them more effective. This is a more general theme of nearly all the proposals—fiscal constraints make it imperative to rationalize and restructure, not just expand, government's role.

THINKING ABOUT FISCAL
POLICY IN BROADER TERMS

The rise of fiscal austerity measures is a dominant feature of the political landscape across advanced industrial democracies—not just the United States, and not just in the last few years, but broadly and over the last two decades. As national welfare states have matured and public-sector spending and taxation have bumped up against broad limits created by economic incentives and the willingness of voters to pay higher taxes, a wave of rationalization efforts has swept across the advanced industrial world. These efforts have of course been accelerated in recent years by the economic crises faced by many European countries and a more general political turn toward the Right in most rich democratic nations.

It is important to recognize, however, that the United States is distinctive from many wealthy democracies in two crucial respects. First, prior to the downturn, the U.S. public sector had largely been caught in a holding pattern. As a share of the economy, the federal government has more or less remained stable in size over the last three decades. Second, American taxation levels are at the bottom of the OECD pack. Indeed, high deficits incurred before the downturn were almost entirely due to reduced tax revenues and higher military spending, not increased public spending on social benefits.

That will not be true in the future. If health care costs continue to rise much faster than the growth of the economy—the pattern until now, and not one that is envisioned to change dramatically due to the 2010 health care legislation—public social spending will rise as well. Overwhelmingly, the long-term deficit problem is a health care cost problem; Jacob Hacker in chapter 10 of this volume therefore focuses heavily on the cost controls in the health care bill and how they can be strengthened.

All of the chapters, moreover, have emphasized that federal costs are not the only costs that should be taken into account. Many existing policies impose large costs on individuals or employers (which then pass those costs on to employees in the form of lower wages). Many policies also involve substantial inefficiency. Foreclosure and bankruptcy laws, for example, impose substantial private costs and are often highly inefficient at providing relief, as well as poorly targeted—a major argument of chapter 8 by Porter and Twomey, on the one hand, and chapter 7 by Weller and Helburn, on the other. Similarly, charity health care is an inadequate response to the lack of broad insurance—and poses a cost that is increasingly hard for health care providers to bear.

The challenge of fiscal austerity is therefore about more than minimizing federal costs. Indeed, some risks might better be addressed through direct federal action, financed with up-front contributions, rather than by after-the-fact legal remedies or safety-net measures that are neither efficient nor well targeted. Policies, like personal spending, can be penny-wise and pound-foolish.

STATES AS LABORATORIES

Just as with austerity proposals, the debate over the respective roles of states and the federal government has often been treated as a zero-sum game in which one level is inherently superior and the management of risks by one means the abandonment of responsibility by another. Instead, as Ann O'Leary suggests, states need to be incubators for creativity and innovation in forging the social compact of tomorrow, but this can only occur *in tandem* with innovative federal action. O'Leary begins with the premise that states already have the ability to provide some protection against income volatility for workers who must exit or scale back their income due to work-care clashes. Indeed, she maps out the innovative ways in which some states are using welfare, unemployment insurance, and state-based temporary disability and paid family leave programs to provide income replacement, and she has suggested that states could go much further. The prospect for these efforts to succeed, however, depends on greater flexibility in existing federal policies to allow experimentation without removing minimum floors of protection.

In chapter 10, Hacker takes on the new health reform bill and urges states to creatively experiment with cost containment and greater coverage. One way to do so, he argues, would be for states to create a Medicare-like public option of their own under the new law through the creative use of the state exchanges.

The Future of American Economic Security

It is only through innovations like those suggested in these chapters that the United States will find the right balance of risk sharing. Without examining competing models in practice, debates over these issues tend toward abstraction and ideology. Comparing the real-world results of innovative policies is the key to advancing economic security.

To be sure, these innovative ideas will only come to pass with the support of the public and the development of a political environment that is receptive to new policy departures designed to make Americans more secure. That in turn will likely require political reform. Over the last generation, both our society and our democracy have become more unequal, as both economic and political power have become more concentrated at the top of the economic ladder.[9] Deep-pocketed interests in the financial and insurance industry, the political challenge of the powerful filibuster in the Senate, the confusion and disengagement of voters, the reality that politicians are more swayed by organized interests—all of these factors stand in the way of proposals to respond to the Great Risk Shift.[10]

But there is reason for hope. Americans want greater economic security, and they believe that government has a deep responsibility and a fundamental role to play in bringing it about. In the long sweep of time charted in this book, risk shifting has occurred in both directions—toward individuals who cannot always bear the load and toward institutions of shared fate that help manage and pool those risks so they do not cause individual devastation. To rebuild our faith in the capacity of our democracy will require joining together to tackle the growing economic insecurity that Americans face.

Notes

1. Franklin Delano Roosevelt, *Message to Congress Reviewing the Broad Objective and Accomplishments of the Administration*, June 8, 1934, http://www.ssa.gov/history/fdrstmts.html#message1.
2. *The People and Their Government: Distrust, Discontent, Anger and Partisan Rancor* (Washington, DC: The Pew Research Center for The People & The Press, survey of 2,505 adults conducted March 11–21, 2010, published April 18, 2010), http://people-press.org/reports/pdf/606.pdf.
3. Ibid.
4. *Obama Clearer Than McCain in Addressing Crisis: Public Not Desperate about Economy or Personal Finances* (Washington, DC: The Pew Research Center for The People & The Press, survey of 1,485 adults conducted October 9–12, 2008, published October 15, 2008), http://people-press.org/reports/pdf/458.pdf.
5. Ibid.
6. *Americans More Likely to Say Government Doing Too Much* (Washington, DC: Gallup Poll, survey of 1,026 adults conducted August 31–September 2, 2009, published September 21, 2009), http://www.gallup.com/poll/123101/americans-likely-say-government-doing-too-much.aspx.
7. Pew Research Center, October 15, 2008 poll.
8. *Reducing the Deficit* (Washington, DC: *New York Times*/CBS News Poll, survey of 1,036 adults conducted January 15–19, 2011), http://documents.nytimes.com/new-york-timescbs-news-poll-reducing-the-deficit.
9. Jacob S. Hacker and Paul Pierson, *Winner-Take-All-Politics: How Washington Made the Rich Richer and Turned Its Back on the Middle Class* (New York: Simon & Schuster, 2010).
10. Ibid.

Index